Fractured Identities

In memory of Michael Martindale,
who dedicated his life to the ideal of a better life
for all in the community

Fractured Identities

Changing Patterns of Inequality
Second Edition

Harriet Bradley

polity

The right of Harriet Bradley to be identified as Author of this Work has been asserted in accordance with the UK Copyright, Designs and Patents Act 1988.

First published in 1996 by Polity Press
This edition first published in 2016 by Polity Press

Polity Press
65 Bridge Street
Cambridge CB2 1UR, UK

Polity Press
350 Main Street
Malden, MA 02148, USA

ISBN-13: 978-0-7456-4407-3
ISBN-13: 978-0-7456-4408-0 (pb)

A catalogue record for this book is available from the British Library.

Library of Congress Cataloging-in-Publication Data

Bradley, Harriet.
    Fractured identities / Harriet Bradley. – Second edition.
        pages cm
    Includes bibliographical references and index.
    ISBN 978-0-7456-4407-3 (hardcover : alk. paper) – ISBN 0-7456-4407-4
(hardcover : alk. paper) – ISBN 978-0-7456-4408-0 (pbk. : alk. paper) –
ISBN 0-7456-4408-2 (pbk. : alk. paper)   1. Equality.   2. Social classes.   3. Group
identity.   I. Title.
    HM821.B73 2015
    305–dc23
                        2015012741

Typeset in 10.5 on 12 pt Sabon
by Toppan Best-set Premedia Limited
Printed and bound in the UK by Clays Ltd, St Ives plc

For further information on Polity, visit our website: politybooks.com

Contents

Acknowledgements

This book originally arose out of some work written for the Open University course D203 'Understanding Modern Societies'. I wish to thank David Held of Polity for offering me the chance to expand on my exploration of 'interacting dynamics'. At times it has seemed an act of sheer hubris to write a book dealing with so many aspects of social inequality. I have drawn on the advice of people more expert than myself in specific areas. Jonathan Skerrett has been a patient and forbearing editor. Thanks go to two anonymous reviewers for useful comments on this second edition.

Introduction to Second Edition

Much has changed since the publication of *Fractured Identities* in 1996. In the following year, 1997, a long period of Conservative government in the UK came to an end, with the election of the 'New Labour' government under the leadership of Tony Blair. Thus, what has become known as the 'Thatcher Era' was succeeded by the 'Blair years'. The New Labour method of running the country involved a mix of economic conservatism with progressive social policies, with a strong focus on confronting inequalities, opening up opportunities to people of all classes and backgrounds and bringing an end to child poverty. At the election, Blair proclaimed that 'Education, Education, Education' was the key to producing a fairer and more just society, and a mass of policies have been developed over the past decades targeted at making schools more effective and opening further and higher education to all. Some students using this new edition of my book on inequality and identity may have been the beneficiaries of such policies.

However, while there have been improvements in some areas of disadvantage, the gap between rich and poor has not been closed; on the contrary, the latest figures show that it has become wider than ever in Britain, and the same is true of the United States of America. In later chapters of the book, I shall be addressing the reasons for this, but, very broadly, it can be argued that the attachment of Bush and Blair to neoliberal economic policies impeded any attempt to break down the barriers of class and poverty. In Britain, the widening of the gap has been even more marked since the coming to power of the Coalition government of David Cameron and Nick Clegg in

2010. It will be argued in subsequent chapters that the policies of
austerity espoused by the Conservative – Liberal Democrat Coalition
have benefitted the rich while pushing the poor and unemployed into
severe poverty, opening up the spectre of 'Food Bank Britain', while
bankers' bonuses continue unchecked.

The past eighteen years have also seen some crucial and devastating political events which have had very strong impacts in the field
of ethnic relations. The terrible events of 11 September 2001, when
two planes hijacked by Muslim terrorists plunged into the twin
towers of the World Trade Center in New York, causing the towers
to collapse in front of the eyes of millions of horrified TV watchers
and killing some 3,000 people, was to bring to the fore issues about
the relation between Islam and the rest of the world. America
responded by declaring a 'War on Terror'. In 2003, tensions were
compounded by America's decision to invade Iraq, with the support
of Tony Blair, despite the vocal opposition of thousands of Britons.
Bombs exploded by suicide bombers on the London Underground
and on a bus in Tavistock Square on 7 July 2005 brought the realities
of the 'War on Terror' to London, with important impacts on the
lives of Britain's Muslim populations (Bangladeshis, Pakistanis, North
Africans and Somalis, among others).

Less dramatic, but equally important in its impact on ethnic relations, was the enlargement of the European Union (EU) with the
addition of ten new member states, largely from the old Soviet bloc,
and including Poland, Hungary, Latvia, Slovakia and Cyprus. This
added 100 million people to the Union, and was followed in 2007
by the accession of Bulgaria and Rumania. Since citizens of member
states have rights to work in other EU countries, this opened up new
patterns of immigration, thereby increasing the diversity of the UK's
multiethnic population. Many Eastern European migrant workers,
especially Poles, have come to Britain and Ireland to find better-paid
jobs than those available in their home countries.

These developments have led to extensive debates about nationality, identity and integration within the UK, seen as one of the world's
most ethnically diverse nations. In particular, a controversy has
evolved around the notion of multiculturalism, which will be discussed in chapter 6 of this book. Arguably, all the political events
mentioned above have kept ethnicity and racism to the fore as a
particular focus for sociological research and discussion, with some
of the other aspects of social differentiation, such as gender, receiving
rather less public and academic attention. The combination of
European migration to Britain and public panic about Muslims,
described by sociologists as Islamophobia, has led to much more

overt expressions of racism, contributing to the increased political presence of racist and anti-immigration parties, such as the English Defence League; in 2014, the UK Independence Party, headed by the charismatic if controversial Nigel Farage, made major advances in local and European elections and achieved a 13 per cent share of the vote in the 2015 General Election.

Multiculturalism and migration are often linked to processes of globalization. Globalization, which has economic, cultural and political dimensions, is hardly a new phenomenon, but it can be argued that the last eighteen years have seen global processes increase in intensity and rapidity. These increases have been encouraged by technological developments, such as the spread of cheap air flights, the enhanced power and capacities of 3G mobile phones and the phenomenal expansion of the internet as a medium for the provision of information, for economic transactions, for social networking and for cultural exchange. It can be stated that we have now definitely entered the Digital Age. Globalization and new technologies will be discussed in chapter 3.

All these developments have led to important changes in the lives of the citizens of the twenty-first century. Some of the trends that were discussed in the 1996 edition, such as social fragmentation, increased geographical mobility and the growth of insecure employment, are now more deeply embedded. The latter trend has led to the identification of a new class grouping, known as the 'precariat', which will be discussed in chapter 4. Processes of social identification, as a result, can be seen to be even more complex and fluid than in 1996. It is sometimes difficult to resist the impression that we live in a shifting society, where the old certainties are being constantly eroded. However, within this scenario of change, one thing remains constant. Britain continues to be a deeply divided society, with marked patterns of class, gender, ethnic and age-based segregation. In this new edition, these four dimensions of social difference remain the centre of analysis and, in the chapters dealing with them, I indicate the impact of the changes sketched above on these entrenched patterns of inequality in additional sections.

I originally chose these four types of social division to explore in detail because they have long been the focus of sociological study and debate. However, there are obviously other forms of social division which figure largely in some people's lives, so in this edition I have included an extra chapter which deals briefly with three of these: disability, sexuality and religion.

This is not to say that these are the only forms of difference we could study. For example, in Britain and other countries regional differences are often marked; we talk of the North–South divide. If we are thinking about some of the currently fashionable social policy issues we could argue that our Western obsession with body size and weight is bringing a social division between thin and fat people! There is much talk about a 'social epidemic of obesity' which is overburdening the National Health Service, and this has led to stigmatizing of larger people as lazy, self-indulgent and undisciplined, while the slimmer citizens labour away working out in gyms and controlling their food intake. Randy Newman satirized this tendency for people to formulate reasons for difference and discrimination in his song 'Short People', the prejudiced narrator saying 'I don't want no short people around here', on the grounds of their little hands, feet and tiny teeth!

However, there are good reasons for focusing on these three particular additional aspects of discrimination. In 2010, the Labour government produced a new Equality Bill, designed to consolidate the existing 117 pieces of existing legislation dealing with discrimination and equal rights. This followed the institution in 2007 of a new single equalities body, the Equality and Human Rights Commission (EHRC), which replaced the Equal Opportunities Commission (EOC), the Commission for Racial Equality (CRE) and the Disability Rights Commission (DRC). This exemplifies the prolonged attempt by Labour, mentioned above, to use legislation to counter discrimination and make Britain a fairer society. The brief of the EHRC is to deal in an integrated way with the six forms of inequality already covered by British law: race/ethnicity, gender, age, disability, religion and sexual orientation, plus three other aspects of people's lives which may lead to discriminatory action (marriage and pregnancy, gender reassignment and marriage / civil partnership). These nine aspects are described in the legislation as 'protected characteristics'. Public-sector organizations have a duty to take steps to prevent discriminatory employment practices on any of these grounds and were meant to submit any proposed structural or policy changes to 'equality impact assessments': although this provision was overturned by the Coalition, it is still considered good practice by progressive organizations. It is notable, though, that these protected characteristics do not include class, although the Labour politician Harriet Harman, who was the main architect of the legislation, was greatly concerned with class divisions. Ironically, one month after the Act was passed, Labour was defeated in the General Election and the Coalition took over government.

During the eighteen years that have passed, there have also been some changes within the discipline of sociology itself. In 1996, there was a sharp divide between proponents of a postmodernist or post-structural perspective and the defenders of the older structural approaches, which were linked to modernism and built on concepts from the sociological classics. This theoretical conflict provided the framework for *Fractured Identities*. Reviewing both positions, I argued that a 'both/and' approach, drawing on insights from both post-structural and structural perspectives, should be sought, rather than espousing an 'either/or' stance. To some extent, this seems to have happened. Certainly the heat has gone out of the debate, which is no longer such a central concern, with both sides appearing to tolerate the other's work and theoretical parameters. Currently, both sides appear to be converging in a concern with studying the impacts of the political doctrine of 'neoliberalism', which espouses the primacy of the free market and seeks to remove all barriers to the operation of markets (including equality legislation). This was the position espoused by the Conservative side of the Coalition.

Instead of the structural/post-structural split, it appears to me, there has evolved a kind of theoretical and methodological pluralism which has led to a fragmentation within sociology. It is much less clear which are the key issues and theories that might form the body of a sociology undergraduate programme. Rather, students are presented with a range of options in a pick-and-mix approach. The borders between sociology, social policy, cultural studies and political science seem less clear, with options on topics such as nationalism, multiculturalism, identity, health, music, crime and deviance often breaching disciplinary boundaries. Yet there can be perceived signs of some contrary tendencies. There is still a feeling that social divisions should be a core part of the discipline, and while, as I have already mentioned, ethnicity and racism continue to be 'hot' topics, there has at the same time been a clear re-emergence of interest in class. This rediscovery of class, which is dealt with in chapter 4, does not necessarily mean a return to the classic forms of class analysis. Rather, much of the new work on class draws on Pierre Bourdieu's ideas of *habitus* and different forms of capital. In 1996, the biggest theoretical hero in sociology was Michel Foucault. Although Foucault's influence and ideas remain strong, arguably Bourdieu has taken his place as sociology's preferred leading man. At the same time, as environmental issues become a major sociological and political focus of the current decade, there has been a growth in interest in Ulrich Beck's conceptualizations of risk.

The introductory chapters of the book have been adapted to reflect these sociological trends. Nonetheless, the conclusions I reached in 1996 about the nature of identities in the contemporary world, and about contradictory tendencies to polarization and fragmentation, remain valid today. One of the symptoms of this is an increasing concern with the notion of *intersectionality* – that is, the ways in which different forms of social division interact with each other to create distinct patterns of disadvantage and difference, say, for example, in the lives of Pakistani women, or of young gays and lesbians. This is one response to the fragmentation of the discipline, with an attempt to pull differing areas of analysis together. This notion of intersectionality and consequent fracturing of identities was a key theme of the original version of *Fractured Identities* and is developed further in this edition.

Attempting to do justice to all the dynamics of inequality discussed in this book has been quite a daunting task. Readers should be aware that I cannot do full justice to the wealth of literature in each area. Rather, the focus in the book is on intersections and complexity: with regard to each dimension, I merely seek to pull out the key strands of debate alongside some empirical data, and focus on recent changes.

Sociology as a discipline has always been concerned with both continuities and change. In this new edition, I seek to highlight continuities in patterns of inequality, while at the same time situating them in the context of contemporary change. The notion of context has becoming increasingly common in sociological analysis and is certainly part of the legacy of postmodernism. We are now more sensitive to the dangers of abstraction, and aware that each phenomenon we study must be analysed within its particular context, even if that does somewhat undermine the ability of sociology to make generalized statements about social life. But it seems to me that the exploration of uniformities within differences has always been a key task for the discipline and remains so today. It is a delicate balance, but one we must pursue, if we are to understand the persistence of inequalities within changing and increasingly diverse societies.

1

Introductory: Inequality and Identity

Thinking about Inequality

Inequality has long been a central concern within sociology. Unequal distribution of wealth, privilege and power has been a major focus of analysis and research. Although at times some sociologists have suggested that resources are being distributed more equally as societies develop, data continue to show that this is not the case. Although the total wealth of Western societies has increased, the way that wealth is shared out continues to be deeply skewed. The development of a global capitalist economy has brought even sharper disparities between those at the top and the bottom of the social hierarchy. Even in the wealthiest and most powerful of the world's nations, inequality remains a problem. In the United States of America, almost one in four children lived in poverty in 2012 according to UNICEF (2012). In 2014, we have surpassed that in Britain with 27 per cent of children in poverty: 3.5 million of them (Child Poverty Action Group (CPAG) 2014). Moreover, it is predicted that this will increase in the next five years. Old people, young people, ethnic minority members, the unemployed, the disabled and low-paid women workers are among those who are losing out as a result of current processes of social and economic change in Britain and other European countries, especially the adoption by governments of economic policies of austerity. The losers are increasingly marginalized and excluded from the prosperous lifestyle enjoyed by the elite groups. To give a small – but, to many citizens, significant – example: a ticket to watch a match at Manchester United football club in 2015 costs at least £31, and one has to pay for travel to get to the ground. An unemployed single person on Job Seeker's Allowance (JSA) gets £72.40 per week.

This book is concerned with the different dimensions of equality and the ways in which they have been conceptualized and studied within sociology. We focus on four aspects of inequality which have for many decades been major topics of sociological analysis: class, gender, ethnicity and age. We also take a briefer look at three further types of inequality which have emerged more recently as major causes of sociological concern: disability, sexual orientation and religion. We shall explore how sociologists have theorized these different aspects of social differentiation and in what ways these types of inequalities are generated and continue to persist.

I also wish to explore how these forms of inequality impact on individuals. We shall be exploring this through the concept of social identity, which emerged as a central concern within sociology in the 1980s. The title of this book, *Fractured Identities*, reflects a common argument that, as societies and patterns of interaction within them have become more complex, older forms of identification have become shattered. Do people still identify as members of the working class? What does it mean to be British in the twenty-first century? Do women from different ethnic backgrounds feel they have anything in common with each other? Are we living in a secularized world or is religion still a key influence in people's lives? Such questions continue to preoccupy social scientists, but also have important effects on the social and political conflicts which shape all our lives.

These issues are introduced in more detail in chapter 2. This introductory chapter sets them in context by means of a brief overview of how sociological approaches to social inequalities have changed over the years, and then outlines the key principles that underlie the arguments set out in this book.

Inequalities and Modernity

Study of inequality is still, then, a key sociological task. However, the focus in the study of inequality has shifted as the discipline has evolved and continues to do so. Many of the original ideas about inequality were derived from the work of those who are considered to have produced the classics of early sociological thinking: Karl Marx, Max Weber and Emile Durkheim, whose arguments are reviewed briefly in chapter 2. The notion of class was central to the work of Marx, whose vision of societies divided by class is still influential today. Weber and Durkheim were both critical of his work, but themselves continued to explore the issue of divisions and inequalities, why they existed and what their social consequences were. Many of the sociologists of the early twentieth century, such as Talcott Parsons, Herbert Marcuse and Karl Mannheim, in differing ways continued a dialogue, often very critical, with ideas derived from Marx.

In the immediate period after the Second World War, which saw the expansion and development of the modern university system and its array of disciplines, class analysis lay at the core of the British sociological agenda. There were vigorous debates between followers of Weber – such as Anthony Giddens, John Goldthorpe and Frank Parkin – and neo-Marxists, such as Nicos Poulantzas, Eric Ohlin Wright and Bob Jessup. These debates focused on such issues as the definition and social functions of different classes, the boundaries between them, and their political role, especially in terms of the revolutionary potential of the working class as predicted by Marx. However, by the 1980s, the primacy of class was being challenged. One critic, Peter Calvert, even suggested that the concept of class was so problematic that it should be discarded (1982, p. 216). Andre Gorz, himself a Marxist, nevertheless argued that the working class was shrinking away because of the automation of industrial production (1982). Pakulski and Waters (1996) were among a number of sociologists who wrote about the 'death' of class.

These challenges to class theory came from many quarters, but we can discern three major strands among them:

1 It was argued that, since the post-war period, the class structure had changed so rapidly and radically that the old frameworks for thinking about class were now no longer applicable.
2 A second and more fundamental critique came from theorists of gender and of race and ethnicity who questioned the idea that traditional class theory can be adapted to explain gender and ethnic differences. For example, a leading sociologist of race relations, Paul Gilroy, highlighted the theoretical challenges to class-based analysis posed by 'writers and thinkers from radical traditions struggling against forms of subordination which are not obviously or directly related to class. These may be based on gender, race, ethnicity or age and are often found in political locations removed from the workplace' (1987, p. 18). Although there is still considerable debate about the relationship between class, 'race' and gender, it has emerged as a new orthodoxy that other forms of social inequality are not reducible to those of class. Each needs to be considered in its own right, while an awareness and

understanding of their interaction is retained. Increasingly, there has been concern to explore how that interaction occurs. Currently, the concept of intersectionality is being employed in such explorations. This is the approach espoused in this book.

3 An even more fundamental challenge came from the intellectual movement known as postmodernism, which predominated in the 1980s and 1990s in many areas of social science and humanities. This is a bundle of new approaches (discussed further in chapter 3) that reject traditional forms of general theory, predominantly that of Marx, as invalid. Such 'grand narratives' are seen to embody unacceptable views of historical development in terms of progress to a stated goal – in the case of Marxism, that of a class-free socialist Utopia. Such theories must be replaced with accounts which focus only on specific limited local contexts. This approach is also known as 'relativism'; there are no absolute certainties, truths or rules. Postmodernism has thus focused attention on the diversity of social experience in a way that, at the least, endorses new forms of pluralism through its focus on the specific positions of different groups, and, at its most extreme, can undermine all notions of collectivities, such as classes, and promote a view of society as made up of atomized individuals.

Postmodernist thinking has also been accompanied by an interest in 'deconstructing' linguistic categories such as 'class' or 'women'. For deconstructionists, such collective terms are socially constructed concepts which have no necessarily 'real' basis beyond our use of them. The use of such concepts only serves to put limits on people, who are forced to accept polarized identities, such as those of 'man' or 'woman'. Classes and genders are denied existence outside of the way we choose to apply such labels. This contention is accompanied by an interest in how such terms are used in various verbal and written linguistic and conceptual frameworks or 'discourses'. Such approaches, which draw particularly on the work of French social theorists Jacques Derrida, Michel Foucault and Jacques Lacan, are often described as 'post-structuralist'. Indeed, the postmodern approach within sociology moved away from the analysis of social *structures* to a study of social *meanings* and the way they are embodied in *cultures* and *discourses*. This movement has also been described as 'the cultural turn'.

Such an approach does not necessarily imply an abandonment of the study of class, gender and ethnicity, since at the very least they can be studied as examples of discourses or of social constructs. But postmodern approaches sit uneasily with study of material factors such as inequality and deprivation, and those influenced by the ideas of postmodernism have tended to avoid these topics. Indeed, it is not quite clear whether such study can legitimately be carried out, certainly within existing frameworks, since postmodernism opposes itself to 'foundationalist' accounts of society (that is, accounts that seek to identify the bases or underlying structures upon which society is founded and which generate specific patterns of social behaviour) and to 'totalizing' narratives about society. Marx's analysis, which sees economic relations as the 'base' on which the whole superstructure of society depends, is a classic example of a foundationalist and totalizing theory. Postmodernist theorists would identify the theories of capitalism and of patriarchy as examples of unacceptable foundationalist thinking, and consequently their position seriously undermines classic approaches to class and gender.

In this book, I explore the way the analysis of inequality and identity is now evolving in response to these challenges. Throughout the book, I try to integrate some empirical evidence of inequalities in society with discussion of the range of theories developed to explain them. A key objective is to pull together classical or modernist approaches to understanding inequalities with the newer perspectives which were inspired by postmodernism and post-structuralism, and those which have developed in more recent years.

Rethinking the Problem: New Approaches to Inequality and Difference

Over the past decade, many writers on inequality have grappled with the first two sets of challenges outlined above. Within class theory, there has been a focus on the way old class alignments are breaking up and discussion of new class groupings such as the 'underclass' or more recently the 'precariat'. While the classic framework of Karl Marx had posited the idea of class polarization, newer approaches stress the multiplication of class groupings and the evolution of new types of class cleavages – for instance, those based on different patterns of consumption. Classes are seen as 'fragmenting', rather than polarizing.

In fact, we are currently seeing something of a return to analysing class, but approaching it in new ways. Particularly influential has been the work of French sociologist Pierre Bourdieu, who attempted to integrate analysis of structure, meanings and cultures through the notion of 'habitus'.

This concept is a complex and contested one. Jenkins (1992) describes it as being usefully imprecise, so it can be adapted for use by many theorists. Atkinson defines it as 'the dispositions formed out of practical engagement with the materially shaped environment shared by those close in social space' (2010, p. 11). Put more simply, we can see it as a set of acquired patterns of dispositions – that is, of thoughts, behaviours and tastes – which shapes the way we perform as social actors. Individuals are born into a specific habitus which has a major impact on their future life chances. For example, the habitus into which a working-class child is born may be at odds with the 'institutional habitus' of school, so that the child adapts less well to school demands than a middle-class child whose habitus is more compatible. Bourdieu explores how the habitus shapes our development and determines the resources we have to make our way in society, in terms of different forms of capital (economic, social, cultural and symbolic). This is a way of analysing class which builds on from the cultural turn.

Moreover, the demands from postmodernists and post-structuralists to avoid 'grand narratives' of inequality have led sociologists to explore class, gender and so forth within specific and differentiated *contexts*, rather than to make unqualified generalizations. This, too, has led to an interest in how the various dimensions of inequality interact upon one another to produce distinct specific social positions. The work of Kimberle Crenshaw on 'intersectionality' (1991) has been particularly influential. Crenshaw showed how ethnicity and gender came together in the USA to produce forms of disadvantage for Black women which are different from those of Black men or white women. Thus an intersectional approach explores how different forms of inequality combine to create very specific patterns of difference and disadvantage, which are characteristically intense. This general framework is one in which inequalities are viewed as complex, multiple and interrelated, something I have described as 'multiple positioning' (Bradley 1999a).

Ideas of fragmentation have been employed in other senses. While early approaches to 'race' centred on a major divide between 'Black' and 'white' groupings in Britain and America, recent work has focused on the different social positions of a plurality of racially and ethnically defined groups in Britain – for example, African-Caribbeans, Indians, Pakistanis, Jews, Chinese and Irish. Contemporary patterns of migration have also meant the consolidation of new ethnic groups, such as Somalis, Hungarians and Rumanians. Rather than the single category of 'race', sociology now concerns itself with the interconnecting categories of ethnicity, nationality, culture and religion, and the way these may divide up a country's population.

Analysis of gender, too, has moved away from the view that women as a group are unified by a common experience of male domination, and has started to explore the situations of different groups of women. Such new feminist approaches focus particularly on the diverse experiences of women of different ethnic groups. Theorists of 'race', too, have taken the lead in exploring the way in which different aspects of inequality interrelate. Pioneering studies, such as those of Phizacklea (1990) and Anthias and Yuval-Davis (1993), explicitly set out to examine the way racial inequality is structured by class and gender relations.

The challenge from postmodernism has perhaps been harder to accommodate. It was more or less ignored in books on class written in the 1990s (Saunders 1990; Scase 1992; Edgell 1993). Rosemary Crompton, in a well-liked text, acknowledged that 'class analysis might be viewed as a particular example of a "totalizing discourse" which postmodernist thinking might reject' (1993, p. 178), but failed to explore fully the consequences of such a view. However, the challenge was taken up by many theorists of 'race' and ethnicity and gender, who utilize the techniques of deconstruction in their analysis (for example, Riley 1988; Donald and Rattansi 1992). The postmodern stress on diversity and pluralism sits easily with the interest in fragmentation and the intersection of class, gender and ethnicity which were outlined above. Kobena Mercer states that 'like "identity", difference, diversity and fragmentation are keywords in the postmodern vocabulary' (1990, p. 49). Within feminism, interest in the study of 'discourses' brought a greater involvement in the study of literary and cultural texts and how the categories of gender are displayed within them, with a consequent move away from studying the economic manifestations of gender inequality. Such moves reflected a growing uncertainty as to how material inequalities should be analysed in the face of the anti-foundationalist stance of postmodernism. However, a new generation of feminist writers has returned to more traditional approaches to understanding gender; while they focus particularly on sexual exploitation and media representations, they also deal with pay disparities and the gendered patterning of the labour market (Banyard 2010; Mackay 2011).

Analysing Inequalities: Fluidity and Stability

The 1980s postmodern challenge to the structural theories of class and gender elaborated in the 1960s and 1970s can be seen as the latest manifestation of a divide which has always been present in sociology. Alan Dawe (1970) pointed to the existence of 'the Two

Sociologies': the sociology of action and agency, as exemplified by Weber and Simmel, and the sociology of structure and system as exemplified by Marx and Durkheim. Dawe speculated, like many before and after him, as to how this seeming chasm could be bridged. One influential attempt to integrate the analysis of structures and of actors and meanings was Giddens's theory of 'structuration' (1976, 1984). Giddens discusses what he calls 'the duality of structure': structures are seen both as the *means* through which social practices are enabled and their *outcomes*. In this vision, structures are constituted by the actions of agents (people, institutions), but action itself is organized within the parameters of existing structures.

The difficulty with which generations of sociologists have struggled, and which Giddens's concept of structuration attempts to encapsulate, is that social reality presents two faces. One perception of it emphasizes chaos and confusion, the limitless welter of apparently unrelated events. In this view, society is fluid or 'liquid' (Bauman 2000), so that social behaviour and relationships are inherently unstable, endlessly changing. Each piece of interaction is unique, never to be replicated. Human beings are unique individuals and the diversity of human experience is infinite. The other perception is that, despite the surface confusion of events, society is ordered. Patterned regularities of social behaviour emerge and persist over time, as manifested in statistical rates. Social institutions may change gradually, but also show remarkable stability; there are marked resemblances among institutions of the same kind in any given society, and indeed across different societies and in different historical periods. In given situations, human beings are likely to behave in similar ways, and social action is thus, at least to a degree, predictable.

The paradox is that *both* these apparently contradictory views of society are viable. Societies are chaotic, but also orderly; behaviour is infinitely variable, but also regular and predictable; social relations change, but are also stable and persistent. The problem for sociology is that it has found it remarkably hard to develop a perspective that can encompass both sets of truths. The history of sociology shows regular swings between one perspective and the other as the dominant one.

Those who emphasize fluidity and chaos have often been drawn to the study of interaction between individuals. They explain the apparent orderliness of society as a social construct: order has to be constantly renegotiated through interaction processes. The stress on fluidity is also linked to the study of meaning and the way meanings are embedded in cultural practices or discourses. Language, meaning, social action and culture are the key concepts which reappear in these kinds of approaches. The most radical versions, such as that of ethnomethodology, deny any validity to notions of social structure; ethnomethodologists suggest that sociology should confine itself to the study of actors' accounts of social interaction, a position which is close to the postmodernist stress on language and discourse. Ethnomethodology instructs us to talk about how people talk about inequality, not about inequality itself. Postmodernism can be seen as the latest phase in this sociological strand. It was described by one of its most influential commentators, David Harvey, as displaying 'total acceptance' of 'ephemerality, fragmentation, discontinuity and the chaotic' (1989, p. 44).

By contrast, those who emphasize order have made structure their key concept. They have focused on discernible regularities in social relationships, often using statistical sources as evidence. Such regularities may be considered as structures in themselves or be taken as manifestations of underlying mechanisms or 'deep structures', such as 'the capitalist mode of production', which are seen to regulate society. In structural approaches, societies are frequently conceptualized as systems in which parts work together to provide an integrated whole. Individual behaviour is seen as constrained by social structures. While the concepts of culture, meanings and action may be employed by sociologists who emphasize order, they tend to see them as circumscribed by prevailing structures, or at least enmeshed in a circle of causality with them: 'men make history, but they make it under circumstances not of their own choosing'. At its radical extreme, such a position, as in various forms of Marxist structuralism, may deny the validity of the concept of the individual or the human agent. Postmodernism evolved partly as a challenge to such views.

The framework employed within this book is one that tries to retain the concept of structured inequalities while at the same time accepting some aspects of the postmodern framework. In this way it is acknowledged that societies are both stable and fluid, both variable and orderly. Marshall Berman has argued that, in the twentieth century, sociological theorizing of change became more rigid and inflexible, as compared to the 'classical' approach of the nineteenth-century thinkers who were ready to acknowledge the ambiguous and contradictory nature of society: 'open views of modern life have been supplanted by closed ones, Both/And by Either/Or' (Berman 1983, p. 24). This book espouses a 'both/and' view, which, I believe, has become increasingly prevalent within sociology. While a few continue to work within the framework of traditional class analysis and others continue to espouse a radical post-structural position, there seems to be an increasing mutual tolerance between these two positions. Many people, like myself, who conduct empirical research into social inequalities and divisions, will draw on ideas from both perspectives. We appear to be in a period marked by greater methodological pluralism and flexibility.

On the one hand, class, gender, 'race', age, sexual orientation, disability and religious affiliation can indeed all be viewed as social constructs, categories used to define, explain and justify the various forms of social differentiation. As social categories they are inherently unstable, and indeed contestable. Even where they may have some basis in biological and physical differences (for example, gender or disability), these categories are seen to have substantial social aspects and thus to be socially and historically variable. For example, age as a biological fact refers to the amount of time that has passed since an individual was born and to certain physical signs and developments that accompany the ageing process. But age as a sociological category refers to differential power relations between individuals of differing ages, different access to economic resources and to social privileges, different rules governing behaviour seen as suitable for different age groups. In this sense age is socially defined and culturally variable. Moreover, Donna Haraway's work has alerted us to the fact that even biological facts, such as reproduction, seen to be immutable, are in fact susceptible to social construction through new technologies (1990). The writings of William Gibson and the cyberpunks play with the idea that, with the development of the cyborg, the ageing process may be overcome, by means of technologies involving the replication and replacement of body parts. Recent developments in nanoscience and biogenetics bring such future possibilities edging nearer. 'Blade runner' Oscar Pistorius can run faster on his artificial limbs than most of us could using the legs we were born with.

However, these socially constructed categories derive from lived sets of social relationships which are orderly and persist over time, although subject to longer-term processes of change and shorter-term fluctuations. These sets of relationships *lie outside of the way in which we categorize them*, although the processes of categorization will affect the ways in which the relationships evolve. They are in fact what the sociologists of order have called 'structures'. However, the metaphor 'structure', borrowed from natural and mechanical sciences (as in the structures of an atom, a leaf or a bridge), may be an inappropriate one in over-emphasizing the element of fixity. Rather, in this book, I have chosen to employ the metaphor 'dynamic' to convey the sense that these relationships are constantly evolving. I hope by the use of this term to convey the notion of the two faces of social reality outlined above: continuity within change, order within variability, fixity within fluidity.

These sets of relationships, then, are the structures or dynamics which work together to produce and perpetuate inequalities and social hierarchies. The four main sets of relationships considered in this book – class, 'race' and ethnicity, gender and age – are all seen as having different bases – 'different existential locations', in the phrase of Anthias and Yuval-Davis (1993, p. 17). Mannheim (1952) used the term 'social location' to indicate the common placing of certain individuals within the power structure of a society, citing class and age as two types of social location. These different locations are sketched out in chapter 2.

The remainder of this book explores these two elements: the changing social categories of class, 'race'/ethnicity, gender, age, etc.; and the changing lived relationships which these categories attempt to encompass. I suggest there is no contradiction between seeing social phenomena as social constructs and seeing them as objectively existing lived relationships, as long as the mutual and circular relationship between these two aspects is acknowledged.

Chapter 2 provides an overview of current patterns of inequality and the way sociological approaches to them have been changing in the post-war decades; particular attention is given to the notions of polarization, fragmentation and identity.

In chapter 3, we consider ways in which societies have been categorized; a view of the nature of society as a whole is necessary in order to understand fully the operation of particular social institutions. The notions of industrialism, capitalism, modernity, post-industrialism, postmodernity, globalization and neoliberalism are briefly outlined and discussed.

Chapters 4 to 7 constitute the heart of this study. Each deals with one dynamic of inequality: class, gender, 'race'/ethnicity and age. Each follows approximately the same format, dealing first with classic approaches; newer conceptualizations are then discussed. Each chapter also explores the intersection with other dynamics of inequality and how changes are affecting processes of identification.

These four chapters are designed to be accessible to undergraduate students. Each can be read as a self-contained unit. I have tried to avoid the excessive use of sociological jargon and technical language and to simplify complex ideas to make them comprehensible; it is my experience as a teacher that many students are deterred by the complicated styles in which some texts are couched. More advanced readers may find these chapters somewhat over-simplified; inevitably the attempt to compress such wide fields of analysis into one single chapter means it is impossible to do justice to the complexities and nuances of debates. Each chapter, then, is to be viewed strictly as an

introduction to the area and each concludes with a short list of
further reading designed for students who wish to explore the topic
in more depth.

Chapter 8 provides a brief account of three other forms of inequality which are covered in the Equality Act: disability, sexual orientation and religion. There is not space to cover these in full in the
way utilized in chapters 4 to 7. I merely highlight some of the key
issues and studies concerned with inequality and discrimination in
these areas.

The concluding chapter returns to the theme of fragmentation and
polarization in relation to the debates reviewed in preceding chapters.
Throughout the book, the theme of change, in terms both of social
categories and of the lived relations they seek to represent, is stressed.
While persistent patterns of inequality are identified, it is emphasized
that the structures of stratification are volatile. My hope is that this may
indicate how some of the difficulties associated with classic structural
analyses, which the postmodern critique illuminated, may be resolved
through the development of a 'both/and' approach to social reality.

A 'Both/And' Approach: Materiality and Meaning

It would be nice if the social world were no more than a contestation
of meanings, so that, merely by renaming the world, we could change
it. Thus, for example, Pringle and Watson, working within a post-
structuralist feminist framework, argue that what various diverse
groups of women have in common is the experience of 'discursive
marginality': that is, the fact that prevailing linguistic frameworks are
constructed by men around men and have at their centre the assumption of the male subject as the norm (Pringle and Watson 1992, p.
68). It would follow, then, that if women were able to rewrite these
discourses and relocate themselves at the centre, the balance of power
between the sexes would alter in women's favour. While there is no
doubt that such a discursive transformation would be beneficial to
women, my argument would be that this disregards the multi-dimen-
sionality of gendered power, which has both cultural and material
aspects. Why do some discourses stick and others not? After all, the
wealth of feminist writing which has been carried out both outside
and inside the academic world has certainly contributed to the project
of rewriting history from female points of view; yet it has had little
effect on the exploitation of women by entrepreneurs around the
world, nor does it prevent many male academics from continuing to
work with the assumption of male experience as the norm.

Our everyday engagement with the process of defining the world takes place within relationships of power which involve differential control of and access to a range of resources: material, political, cultural and symbolic, including the utilization of means of force and violence. Power relationships put constraints upon our ability to remake the world, even at the level of our own small personal 'life-worlds' (Luckmann 1970). We may, for example, be firmly committed to the idea of equal sharing within marriage, but find ourselves quite unable to work out equitable arrangements about housework with our partners within our own relationships. The prevailing conditions of employment, by which men are more likely to work full-time and to earn higher pay than women, put constraints upon our ability to 'choose' equality, as do the social norms specifying what work is suitable for women and men, and which emphasize the special link of mother to child as the base of domestic arrangements. Long-hours' cultures typical of many sectors of the economy make it difficult for mothers, responsible for 'school runs', to take full-time jobs and compete equally with men Thus our 'free' choice is in reality 'constrained', structured by our location within the dynamics of gender.

Class, 'race'/ethnicity, gender and age are all aspects of these prevailing power relationships. While symbolic aspects of power, such as those highlighted in discourse theory, are extremely important, they are only one aspect of the power relationships that are embodied in social inequalities. To return to Pringle and Watson's post-structuralist arguments, men are able to dominate women not only by marginalizing them in discourse, but also by controlling the distribution of social wealth (economic power), by confining them to lower-rated positions in the division of labour, subjecting them to male authority and keeping them out of some social functions altogether (positional and political power), and by using violent tactics, such as bullying and harassment, rape and assault, to keep them in place (physical power). Clearly all these forms of power interlock, so that discursive frameworks are part of the social processes which enable men to exclude women economically and politically, and legitimate the use of psychological and physical violence by many men. Pringle and Watson, in fact, seem to me to acknowledge this by adding the comment that 'inequalities at every level' are an accompaniment to the 'discursive marginality' which might unite women (p. 69). It is not, after all, clear whether 'inequalities' can be elided with 'discourse'.

In other words, I am arguing that materiality and meaning ('things' and 'words' in Michèle Barrett's (1992) phrase) are different, but can hardly be separated. Approaches which seek to prioritize one to the exclusion of the other, be it Marxism on the one hand or post-structuralism on the other, are distorting social reality. The need to consider both is a key assumption of this book, as is the fact that both materiality and meaning are aspects of constraining power relations. The remainder of this book can be seen as an exploration both of processes of 'renaming' and of power constraints.

Thinking Points

- Are societies chaotic or ordered?
- How do different dynamics interact in your own life?

2

Inequality, Fragmentation and Identity

A Crisis of Inequality

According to Seumas Milne, Britain in 2007 was facing a 'crisis of inequality':

> We are witnessing the 'return of the robber barons' of the 1920s and a winner-takes-all society. It's not just the billionaire oligarchs and tax-avoiding Lear jet commuters who flaunt their wealth alongside run-down housing estates or the boardroom kleptocrats in gated communities who award themselves eye-watering bonuses at the expense of insecure low paid workers. Almost all the main indicators are moving in the wrong direction as Britain heads back towards Victorian levels of inequality. The gap between the top and bottom has widened remorselessly. Last year the share of the poorest fifth fell as that of the richest fifth grew larger. The highest one per cent of earners' share of national income is up three per cent over the decade...The proportion of wealth held by Britain's richest 10 per cent has increased from 47 per cent to 54 per cent under New Labour, and this year child poverty and both relative and absolute poverty are up again. (Milne 2007)

As Milne's vivid account shows, there are a number of ways in which we conventionally measure inequality: comparing the income of the top fifth and bottom fifth of earners; considering how much wealth (fixed assets, such as shares, housing and land, as opposed to income) is held by the top 1 per cent and 10 per cent; measuring relative poverty (the proportion of people whose household income falls below the society's average) and absolute poverty (the proportion of people falling below a certain level of subsistence judged necessary for existence, often known as the poverty line); comparing the lifestyles of the rich and poor; looking at the degree of residential and geographical segregation of the rich and the poor. On all these measures, inequality has risen since the turn of the new century.

While the income gap increased under New Labour, under the Coalition government formed by the Conservatives and Liberal Democrats things got even worse, as a result of the stringent economic measures adopted in the name of 'austerity' by the government as a response to world economic recession. The welfare state, set up after the Second World War by Beveridge as a 'safety net' against poverty, has been under savage attack. The present government maintains we cannot afford such levels of public spending and has instituted a programme of privatization, inviting private investors to take over schools, universities, and hospital and care services. When this happens, the new owners push down wages and working conditions to increase profits. As a result, many people who used to hold secure, reasonably well-paid jobs – especially women – have lost them and been forced into unemployment or lower-paid work. Meanwhile, those who are out of work have seen benefits disallowed, removed or pegged at levels well below the rising cost of living. This is justified in terms of abuses of the welfare system, with the government arguing that it will act as an incentive for claimants to find work. However, in many areas of the country there are no jobs to be found, while employers are reluctant to employ people with disabilities or long-term sickness, many of whom depend on benefits. In fact, the bulk of the welfare bill consists of pension payments, not benefits. As a result, the poor are getting poorer, with many having to depend on food banks to survive.

In the UK, this period has also seen the emergence of what has been called the 'super-rich', a trend promoted by the prevailing conditions of globalization and economic boom. The income gap spiralled. In 2007, the Gini coefficient, which is used to measure inequality, rose to its highest level since measurement started in 1961 (Brewer et al. 2008). As an example, in 2007 Giles Thorley, CEO of Punch Taverns pub group, was paid £11,276,000, 1,148 times the average annual wage within his company, which was £9,821 (Seager 2007a). In the same year, the combined earnings of the 1,389 directors of Britain's 100 top companies passed £1 billion pounds for the first time: enough to pay for 15 new hospitals or the salaries of 50,000 nurses (Finch and Bowers 2007). As Seager (2007b) notes, the 'super-rich' are not ashamed to indulge in conspicuous consumption: in that same year there was a 29 per cent rise in sales of Bentley cars, with a five-year waiting list for Rolls Royces, while 668 super-yachts were purchased. Because the rich spend their money on these kinds of status goods, their wealth does little to stimulate the basic sectors of the economy.

The wealth of the rich has also been augmented by the long boom in the housing market. Because of this boom, many people invested in property under the 'buy to let' scheme. Especially in London, this has led to scarcity of affordable housing for less afflu-ent people. Spiralling prices have made it exceedingly hard for young people to purchase a property of their own, while unscrupu-lous landlords seeking to maximize their investment have also led rents to rise continually. As a result, many young people – for example, students graduating from university – are forced to return to live in their parents' homes. In 2013, some 3.3 million British adults between the ages of twenty and thirty-four were living with parents: 26 per cent of the age group. The number had increased by a quarter since 1996.

In America, this led to the growth of the 'sub-prime' mortgage market, whereby people with low incomes were lent mortgages when their assets were really insufficient to warrant the loan. The collapse of this market in 2007–8 sent shock waves through the world economy, leading to a recession in the USA, the UK and elsewhere. Recessions hit everybody, but they hit the poor hardest, with loss of jobs and rising prices; holders of sub-prime mortgages in the USA have seen their houses repossessed.

A snapshot of Britain in the summer of 2014 is depressing for anybody who believes in social equality, despite the fact that an eco-nomic recovery was underway. The figures tell a grim story. The Joseph Rowntree Foundation (JRF) sets a minimum income standard based on what are considered to be the basic necessities of life. Current benefit levels for a couple only amounted to 60% of that income level – and for a single person, only half. Poverty had doubled over the last 30 years, so that 33% of households were without basic necessities, and 21% were behind with their bills. The JRF research showed that, since 2008, the cost of a family's basic needs had risen by 46%, while average earnings had only risen by 9%. It was esti-mated that 600,000 children would be living in poverty (JRF 2014). The Citizens' Advice Bureau recorded 27,000 people struggling to pay their council tax, a 7% rise on the previous year. Any savings less wealthy people had were being eroded: it was reported that in 2014 the poorest 20% would spend £1,910 more than they earned, while the richest 20% would add an extra £18,680 to their savings.

In my own city, Bristol, a relatively affluent place, there were seven food banks used every month by around 1,000 people.

These figures point to the polarization that was continuing to occur. The rich continued to thrive and enjoy luxurious lifestyles. The Office of National Statistics figures recorded a rise in the post-tax share of National Income taken by the wealthiest 1%, from 8.2% to 9.8%; according to their calculations, there were 62,000 new entrants to the ranks of the 'super-rich'. Oxfam reported that the 5 richest families held as much wealth as the bottom 20%, while 1.75 million families had seen their income fall. A pay cap of 1 per cent a year was imposed on public-sector workers, despite these rapid rises in the cost of living, so that the TUC calculated that their living standards had fallen by 15–20%. In the *Guardian* newspaper low-paid public-sector workers described the impact on their lives, showing that it is not just the unemployed who are struggling:

'I'm on £8.30 an hour and we haven't had a pay increase for 4 years. I can't afford what I used to do, like go out with friends and go swimming. I only eat meat once a fortnight. Once I had to go to a food bank. It was very embarrassing. I'm in work and I should be able to live a decent life.' (Care worker, Leeds City Council)

'We've gone from shopping at Sainsbury's to shopping at LIDL. I don't buy as much food as I used to or as many clothes. I can't remember the last time we had a holiday abroad. The car's on its last legs and we'll be saving a long time for another.' (Tax officer, Newcastle)

Though the UK is seen as a country particularly marked by class divisions and wealth polarization, many other countries have seen increasing inequalities in the same period, including Japan, Argentina, many East and West European countries and the USA. The *American Human Development Report* of 2008 highlighted some of the effects of this. Although the USA has the second-highest per capita income in the world, it only scores 12th place in terms of the United Nation's Human Development Index (developed by economist Amartya Sen). The report shows that 15 per cent of children live in poverty; 47 million Americans are not covered by medical insurance, in a country where there is no free national health care service; in terms of life expectancy, the USA is only ranked 42nd in the world, and on the measure of child survival to one year, it ranked 34th (Sweden is ranked number 1). The USA is home to 5 per cent of the world's population but to 24 per cent of the world's prison population (Burd-Sharps et al. 2008). Major divisions of ethnicity as well as class underlie these statistics. Meanwhile, in Europe, a crisis of the euro precipitated near-collapse of the Southern Europe economies of Greece, Spain and Portugal – leading to job loss, homelessness and poverty for many citizens. Young people were particularly affected, with unemployment rates reaching 50 per cent; many migrated from their countries to seek work in richer areas, while others returned home to work in the rural economy, still marked by subsistence farming – for example, on the Greek islands.

So, contemporary societies are marked by massive social inequalities, as indeed most past societies have been. Only in small, localized tribal societies do we find that there are few differences in wealth and power and that most members of society share a common lifestyle. In urban industrial societies, with a complex division of labour, sharp gulfs characteristically emerge between the richer and poorer members. Those at the top of the social hierarchy are able to procure for themselves privileges and power and a disproportionate share of the social wealth. Such hierarchies may be based on military conquest, ownership of property, occupation, family background, ethnic origin, religious affiliation, educational qualifications, gender and age. In modern societies, they tend to rest on a complex mixture of many of these factors. While social policies of welfare provision and income redistribution have at times offset these prevailing conditions, the trend in the twenty-first century has been to remove such provision and increase inequality.

Those inequalities that are related to the production, distribution and exchange of wealth we have come to know by the complex and rather controversial shorthand term of 'class'. Karl Marx linked the emergence of class to the notion of a social surplus: that is, the pool of wealth left over once the subsistence needs of society's members have been met. As societies grow richer with a larger surplus, it follows that the potential for social inequalities increases. Despite talk from time to time that class disparities are diminishing or even disappearing, the evidence – such as that presented above – of persistent inequalities of wealth shows that class distinctions persist (Bradley 2014). Indeed, as we will see in chapter 4, there are now claims that class is the most pressing form of inequality and that new social policies are desperately needed to combat it.

However, class is not the only basis of inequality, which is also associated with other forms of cleavage in society, such as gender, ethnicity and age. For example, women make up the bulk of those who live in poverty and, in the UK in 2012, they faced an annual gender pay gap of 19.6 per cent if they worked full-time, and 69.8 per cent if they worked part-time (Perfect 2012). In 2012, male managers received an average bonus of £6,442, compared to £3,029 for women, as well as having 25 per cent greater salaries (Huffington Post, 20 August 2013). Many of Britain's poorest families come from the Bangladeshi and Pakistani communities, who are also most likely to be unemployed. Older and younger people also face discrimination at work; unemployment is highest among younger age groups, while men over fifty who are made redundant face the greatest difficulty in becoming reemployed.

These sorts of inequalities in Western societies can be conceptualized as part of a system of social stratification: that is, the division of society into unequal groups or strata which share a common situation. While in the 1960s and 1970s this system of stratification was analysed mainly in terms of class, from the 1980s there has been a growing recognition of the importance of these other forms of inequality. Mann, discussing what he saw as a 'crisis of stratification theory', indicated a need to explore the interrelations of different social actors, which he called 'stratification nuclei', which for him included classes, genders and nations. He concluded that 'a more complex form of stratification is now emerging' (1986, p. 56).

Does Inequality Matter?

Before we go on to discuss these complexities, it is important to address a set of arguments that is often raised when sociologists introduce the topic of social inequalities, and which is commonly expressed by students new to the discipline. What is so wrong about inequality? Since it has been so prevalent throughout history, should we not see it as inevitable? Is equality achievable? Is equality desirable? Are not differences of income necessary to provide incentives to work? And are not hard-working and successful people entitled to enjoy the fruits of their success?

These are cogent questions and are often posed by those who oppose the use of taxation as a means of redistributing wealth in society. To some extent, the answers given to these questions are likely to be based on moral rather than scientific principles. Many individuals see inequality as contravening principles of social justice, arguing, as did Marx, that the wealth of the society is collectively produced and that all citizens are entitled to a fair share of this wealth. This position is also embedded in many of the world's major religions, notably Christianity, Islam and Sikhism. To take this position is not, of course, to demand total equality, which might indeed be seen as unachievable, if only in terms of the differences between people of physical endowments and capacities, and of desires and tastes; it is to say that it is the task of the collectivity to ensure that every citizen has the resources needed to live a decent life and partake of the society's collective benefits.

Is inequality inevitable? Sceptics may answer that 'human nature' is inevitably greedy and competitive. However, sociologists reject the idea of universal human traits, pointing to the cultural variability of human behaviour. Moreover, by using the evidence of history, we can make a scientific judgement that the degree of inequality in society can be altered by political and social actions and that it is therefore neither natural nor inevitable. For example, in many tribal societies wealth is shared among the tribe's families, with only a few individuals, such as chiefs or priests, having a somewhat larger share. While this is easier to achieve in less differentiated societies, the example of contemporary Scandinavia shows that greater equality can be attained. In Norway, Sweden, Finland and Denmark, the gap between rich and poor is much less great, and very few people live in poverty. This is the result of redistributive tax policies and a well-funded universal benefits system which helps the unemployed and other non-earners maintain a good standard of living. This is backed by a culture which values equality and disapproves of spectacular displays of wealth in the form of expensive clothes, jewellery, cars and houses and other consumer goods. On my first visit to Norway, I was immediately struck by the fact that everybody dressed very similarly and one could not judge people's class from their appearances. People do not like to stand out; 'bling' is disliked. Norway and Sweden also prove that people do not need financial incentives to work hard: in these countries, there is a very strong work ethic, which is deeply embedded in the countries' cultures. The values commonly held by people in these countries are very different from the materialist and individualist values currently fashionable in the UK and USA, proving that 'human nature' is malleable and not a fixity.

While most of us believe that people should be rewarded for their achievements, this can be accomplished by moderate incentives which do not leave others deprived and struggling. Apart from the ethical issues discussed above, there are other considerations which suggest that high levels of inequality are bad for all of us: there are clear correlations between inequality and increases in crime and other forms of social unrest and conflict (we have already noted that the world's most economically powerful country, the USA, has the highest prison population). In a justly famous book, *The Spirit Level* (2010), Kate Pickett and Richard Wilkinson collected a wealth of statistical evidence from around the world. They showed that almost all our serious social and environmental problems – such as physical and mental ill-health, lack of community life, violence, drugs, obesity, long working hours, crime and big prison populations – were more likely to occur in a less equal society. In the current recession in Britain, the use of anti-depressants has increased, as has the suicide rate among men. Drug-taking and resultant petty crime increase insecurity in urban areas. Thus, inequality impacts on the quality of life, even for the rich. In their trenchant critique of the culture of greed in Britain, Toynbee and Walker (2008) argue that inequality creates illness as the deprived suffer from stigma and status-anxiety, generating stress-related diseases such as heart disease. Recent increased demand for NHS services show the social costs to us all.

It is usual in considering equality to distinguish between 'equality of opportunity' (fair access to jobs, education and other social benefits) and 'equality of outcome' (equal distribution of social rewards). We have already indicated that absolute equality of outcome might be illusory, so the current social orthodoxy in the UK focuses on equality of opportunity. The problem, though, is that people do not enter the competition (for example, for university places or professional posts) on equal terms, a problem commonly expressed by the metaphor of the 'level playing field'. Consequently, ensuring that all jobs, for example, are open to people from ethnic minority backgrounds and to women may not be enough. Where people are highly handicapped by their backgrounds or life circumstances (for example, attending poorly resourced schools, having to take time out from their career development to look after children) it may be necessary to give them special treatment, a 'leg up' to compensate for these disadvantages.

This is a contentious and complex issue; however, it is worth noting here the attempt by Trevor Phillips of the EHRC to recast equality as 'fairness', a 'value for the twenty-first century' (EHRC 2008, p. 3):

> We believe that Britons today aspire to live in a society where no-one's destiny should be determined by the circumstances of their birth, – who and what their parents were, what race, gender or sexual orientation they were born with... Increasingly, we expect life-events – growing old, having children, developing an impairment – not to put us automatically at a disadvantage.... With fair treatment for all we can live in a country richer both economically and socially. (EHRC 2008, pp. 1, 3)

This claim is backed by a survey carried out for the EHRC which found that 46 per cent of British people believed they have experienced some type of discrimination. Thus, it seems, perceptions of unfairness are becoming widespread. Ethnicity, disability, religion and age were seen as the major bases for unfair treatment.

In a paper introducing the 2010 Equality Act, Labour politician Harriet Harman stated that 'everyone one has the right to be treated fairly and to have the opportunity to fulfil their potential' (Government Equalities Office 2008, p. 5). Fairness and equality are argued to be necessary not only for the individual as a human right, but for the social cohesion of the nation ('an unequal society can't be at ease with itself') and the success of the economy which needs diversity to be competitive (p. 5).

Aspects of Inequality: Class, Gender, 'Race' and Ethnicity, and Age

This political valuation of diversity reflects the awareness of the multiple nature of inequality discussed earlier in the chapter. Social hierarchies can be formed on a number of bases. Sociologists are now interested in exploring many of these aspects of inequality, such as gender, age, 'race' or ethnicity, nationality, religious affiliation, sexual orientation (heterosexual, gay or lesbian, bisexual, transsexual) and dis/ability, all of which are seen to affect the lifestyle and life chances of individuals and the differential distribution of social rewards and privileges.

This book focuses on class, gender, race/ethnicity and age, partly because they have received the most sustained exploration within sociology: class has long been central to the agenda of sociological research and the other three have now become so. All are currently implicated in important processes of social change, both national and international. As subsequent chapters will show, the spread of a globally based capitalist economy has both built upon and transformed existing hierarchies of class, gender, 'race' and age, promoting new patterns of social and economic inequality.

However, other less-studied aspects of inequality, such as disability or sexual orientation, are important, and increasingly the focus of public attention. The post-structuralist critiques discussed in this book suggest that we could evolve quite new ways of categorizing inequalities, which would allow unacknowledged aspects of differentiation to emerge as objects of study. While class, gender, ethnicity and age continue to attract public and academic attention, they may not do so in the future. In chapter 8, we shall considered three bases of discrimination which are now covered by equality legislation: disability, sexual orientation and religious affiliation.

Class

As has already been suggested, class is the form of social inequality that has received the most attention in sociology. The interest in class goes right back to the roots of sociology, playing a major role in the theories of Marx and Weber. Even Durkheim, who is associated with a more harmonistic vision of industrial societies, believed that a meritocratic society could not be achieved unless inherited privileges were abolished. The strongest assertion of the importance of class came from Marx, who argued that inequalities of wealth and power were increasing as the capitalist system developed: tendencies which he saw as inherent in capitalism would serve to widen the gap between the two major classes, the property-owning bourgeoisie and the working class or 'proletariat': 'The epoch of the bourgeoisie possesses...this distinctive feature: it has simplified the class antagonisms. Society as a whole is more and more splitting into two great hostile camps, into two great classes directly facing each other – bourgeoisie and proletariat' (Marx and Engels 1934, p. 10).

In post-war British sociology, class theorists themselves divided into two 'hostile camps', broadly known as neo-Marxists and neo-Weberians (see chapter 4). During the 1950s and 1960s, class and poverty were perhaps the major topics of sociological research. Gordon Marshall's book *In Praise of Sociology* includes five texts dealing with class and poverty among his chosen 'top ten' influential British sociological studies (1990). However, the study of class fell from favour in the 1980s and 1990s, when Bates and Riseborough noted 'the silence gathering round class' (Bates and Riseborough 1993, p. 1). The authors argue that 'class analysis, for over a century central to progressive social thought and political organization, has come to seem anachronistic' (p. 2). In the 1980s, interest switched to other aspects of inequality. However, in the first decade of the twenty-first century the public silence around class began to be broken and sociologists who had kept faith with the concept (such as Beverly Skeggs, Valerie Walkerdine and Mike Savage) were vindicated. In his introduction to the EHRC report on fairness (2008), mentioned above, Trevor Phillips pointed out that material inequality underpinned all the other disparities.

Gender

However, powerful challenge to class theory came from feminists concerned with the exploration of gender differences and inequalities. The study of gender within sociology has a shorter history than that of class. The 'classical' theorists acknowledged inequalities of gender but did not explore them to any great extent, partly because they shared the view, widespread in the nineteenth century, that gender differences were 'natural', arising ultimately from biology. Sydie (1987) has argued that Marx, Durkheim and Weber could not escape from the prevailing gender ideologies of their time. For example, in his classic study of suicide, first published in 1897, Durkheim argued that widows were less likely to commit suicide than widowers because women were less involved in social life: 'Society is less necessary to her, because she is less impregnated with sociability. She has few needs in this direction and satisfies them easily. With a few devotional practices and some animals to care for, the old unmarried woman's life is full' (1952, p. 215). Following a nineteenth-century trend, Durkheim considered men to be 'almost entirely the product of society', while women 'remained to a far greater extent the product of nature' (p. 385).

Within post-war sociology, gender issues only made their appearance in areas of study such as the family, which reflected prevailing norms about 'women's sphere'. In other areas, such as work, deviance or youth cultures, the existence and experiences of women were largely overlooked. This marginalizing of women's experience was epitomized in class theory. Major research projects on class, such as those carried out at Nuffield College by Goldthorpe, Halsey and others, were based upon surveys of men only. It was argued that women took their class from husbands or fathers, that to include women would make it difficult to compare findings with earlier studies which had also omitted women, or that, since women's social roles were primarily domestic, occupational class was not relevant to women. Feminists claim that, when women appeared not to fit into the models and theories of class (or work, or deviance, or youth subculture), rather than discarding those models and theories as incorrect or inadequate, sociologists simply stated that women were 'abnormal' and continued to leave them out.

The view of gender as a major source of social division developed in the late 1970s with the spread of 'second-wave' feminism as a political movement (see Banks 1981). This stimulated an immense interest in the uncovering of women's lost and hidden experience. Different strands of political feminism – often known as liberal, socialist and radical feminism – inspired different theoretical approaches to the explanation of gender differences, which are explored in chapter 5.

In Britain in the 1970s, Marxism was still a strong influence and many feminists tried to integrate an analysis of gender into existing

theories of capitalism. Others, however, preferred to see gender relations as an autonomous system and developed the key concept of
'patriarchy' to explore the origins and operation of such a system
(see chapter 5). Gradually, feminism has moved away from its links
with Marxism and class theory. Attention has shifted to the relationship of gender with other aspects of social inequality, especially
ethnicity and sexual orientation. Post-structuralism has had a major
input into gender analysis and the work of Judith Butler has been
particularly influential. There has also been a broadening of the
gender agenda away from the initial focus on recovering the missing
experiences of women. There is a flourishing subfield in the study of
masculinities, utilizing both structural and post-structural approaches,
alongside Queer Theory developed to explore the situation of gay,
lesbian, bisexual and transsexual people: this type of theory has produced a view of gendered identities as fluid and malleable.

Initial attempts to combine class and gender analysis proved difficult because gender is a much more diffuse source of inequality and
differentiation than class; while class divisions are conceptualized as
deriving from economic aspects of social relations, gender differentiation is not confined to a single sphere. Gender plays a part in every
aspect of social and cultural life (from sexual relations to politics,
from leisure to art and literature). Ulrich Beck has described this as the
'omni-dimensionality of inequality between men and women' (1992,
p. 103). Indeed, gender is a fundamental way in which we organize
every facet of experience; it is an everyday category by which people
make sense of the natural and social world, which is not true of class.

'Race' and Ethnicity

The study of 'race' in sociology has a longer history than that of
gender. Race relations became an important area of academic research
in America in the 1940s (Stanfield 1993). It was firmly established in
Britain by the early 1960s. Its popularity as a topic for research,
however, was linked to a view that relations between different racial
groups in Britain were becoming a widespread 'social problem' as a
result of post-war immigration from the commonwealth countries.
Similarly in America, the sociological study of 'race' was linked to
the perception of Black Americans as a social problem. The early
research on 'race', therefore, dealt with prejudice, discrimination and
conflict and was focused on groups who were defined in terms of skin
colour: the descendants of the slave populations in America, and in
Britain immigrants from the Caribbean colonies (also descended
from slaves) and from India, Pakistan and East Africa. Research has

documented the persistent discrimination faced by these groups in all areas of social life, especially in employment, education and housing (Smith 1977; Brown 1984; Modood et al. 1997). In America, Wilson has described the Black inhabitants of the urban ghettos as 'the truly disadvantaged' (Wilson 1987).

Sociologists challenged the notion that the concepts of 'race' and racial origin have any real scientific basis. Nineteenth-century scientists developed the idea of distinct racial groups, with a differing genetic inheritance which produced differing patterns of behaviour, personality traits, levels of intelligence and so forth. Such ideas, which we would now categorize as racist, were used to justify white supremacy and the domination of indigenous populations by Western colonial nations. However, modern science suggests that there is little validity in these attempts to root 'race' in biological difference, especially in view of the centuries of migration and miscegenation which have passed since Europeans first made contact with the populations of Africa, Asia, Australasia and the Americas. Sociologists argue that the idea of 'race' is a social construct, used to justify discrimination and exclusionary practices. For that reason, some have suggested that the use of the term should be rejected altogether (Miles 1982). However, others have argued that, since people act *as if* 'race' was a reality, 'race' does have real effects on people's lives and it should be retained as a category of analysis (Cashmore and Troyna 1983). One solution is to apostrophize the term to show that it is a construct of dubious validity, a practice which I have followed in this book.

The idea of 'race' is now linked to the broader category of ethnicity. Ethnicity refers to belonging to a particular collectivity or community, sharing a culture, possibly with a distinct language. The bi-polar approach which saw Britain as divided into Black and white groupings has given way to the appreciation that there is a multiplicity of ethnic groups in Britain, each with its distinctive set of cultural practices and many with their own languages. Increased migration, arising from such diverse causes as global employment practices, civil wars and genocides, the break-up of the Soviet bloc, and European Union enlargement, has ensured that the ethnic make-up of Britain is constantly changing. The older ex-colonial migrants have been joined by substantial groups of Poles, Portuguese, Somalis, Kosovans and others. The marketing of higher education overseas has also attracted students from diverse countries such as China, Africa and Russia, some of whom subsequently find employment in the UK, adding to the rich ethnic mix.

The interest in the idea of ethnicity has also been encouraged by these events, especially the collapse of communism. The emergence of long-suppressed ethnic loyalties and conflicts and the formation of new nations have drawn our attention to the force of national and ethnic identities as a base of social conflict, contributing greatly to the notion that social fragmentation is on the increase. In the UK currently, as in other nations, following the traumatic events of 9/11 and the recent rise of the extreme jihadist group Islamic State, a major axis of concern surrounds the relation between the West and the Muslim world. The resulting fear of Muslims, Islamophobia, has become a central node of social conflict (Modood 2007). Heated debates have arisen about the nature and desirability of multicultural-ism as a policy for ethnic coexistence, which are explored in chapter 6. The growing importance of relations between these varied groups greatly complicates patterns of stratification and challenges the tra-ditional predominance of class analysis.

Age

Only recently has age has been treated as an aspect of inequality, and it has received scant attention within the sociology of stratification (Fennell et al. 1988). This is partly due to the fact that age has been seen in the past as a natural phenomenon, which affects every indi-vidual; all of us must go through each phase of the life cycle and suffer its characteristic effects (Rapoport and Rapoport 1975). However, there is now much more awareness of how the fates of particular age groups are socially determined and altered by social and historical contexts. Moreover, we appreciate that all within a particular age group will *not* in fact share a common situation, because the experience of age is affected by the individual's class, gender and ethnic position.

The social standing of elderly people, for example, has altered considerably over the past two centuries. The changes brought to work and family relationships by industrial production meant that older people no longer contributed to the household enterprise (farm, craft or business) until they became unfit to do so. It became harder for those whose strength was on the wane to hold a job as a wage labourer, while at the same time traditional support networks within the family and community were loosening. Increasing numbers of old people were confined to workhouses and mental asylums. In Britain, during the Edwardian period, something like one-tenth of elderly women ended up in the workhouse (Fennell et al. 1988). But as the twentieth century developed, older people were rescued from this fate by the old-age pension scheme and the further provisions of the welfare state and the National Health Service.

However, it can be argued that, in the last decades, the position of the elderly has again deteriorated, owing to the erosion of the NHS and the Social Security system. The state, alarmed by the phenomenon of the ageing population and the growing burden of the cost of caring for the infirm elderly, has tried to thrust the burden of care back onto the community and the family. The result has been growing poverty and insecurity for many old people, especially women. Around a quarter of single women pensioners live in poverty. Confinement in care homes replaces confinement in the workhouse.

Research has drawn our attention to ageism as a prevalent feature of our society (Hearn and Parkin 1993; Bodily 1994). In a society of rapid social and technological change, older people are increasingly seen as a burden and an irrelevance. However, they are not the only victims of ageism. All of us are affected by ageist attitudes, which lay down rules of behaviour seen as appropriate for people of different ages and encourage different expectations of the capacities of each group.

Chapter 7 will concentrate on two particular groups who bear the brunt of age-related inequality: older people, whose declining situation has just been briefly outlined, and young people, who have been particularly vulnerable to the effects of recession and long-term unemployment in recent decades. Research in Bristol highlighted how young adult workers were concentrated in what could be termed a 'low-wage economy' (Bradley and Devadason 2008). It has been suggested by many that youth unemployment is leading to widespread disaffection among young adults in many Western societies. Drug-taking, criminal behaviour, involvement in extreme right-wing political movements, experimentation with alternative lifestyles such as that of the 'New Age' travellers can all be seen as manifestations of this. For example, in 2008 a social panic developed about gangs and knife crime, related to the deaths of a large number of teenaged males in London. Class, ethnicity and age combine to create a vulnerable cohort who are at risk from the alienated responses of their peers. As will be argued in chapter 7, the middle age groups in our society constitute an age elite whose position is sustained at the expense of the young and the old.

Intersectionality and Interacting Dynamics

The discussion so far has suggested that each dimension of inequality should be studied in its own right. The implication is that each can be analysed as a distinct set of relationships with a logic of its own.

However, it is obvious enough that in real life this is not the case. It has become almost a commonplace to say that classes are gendered and that gender relations are class-specific. Similarly, the other dimensions of 'race'/ethnicity and age impinge on individual class and gender experience, and in any particular specific case it is hard to separate out the different elements. If we add in the effects of disability, sexual orientation and religion, the analysis is even more entangled.

Take, for an example, the position of a twenty-year-old African-Caribbean woman, whose parents were manual workers, bringing up two children on her own in inner-city Birmingham, and having to choose between low-paid work as a cleaner and dependency on benefits. How do we start to explain her fate? Is it because of gender that she is faced with responsibilities for childcare with no help from a man and that she faces a limited range of labour market options? Or is it racism which means the only job she can find is the stereotypical 'servant' role which has historically been assigned to Black women? Or is it class which meant she left school early with limited qualifications? Of course, it is all of these things. And age plays a part too, as many employers have a prejudice against young workers, and prefer to employ older married women whom they see as steadier, having 'settled down'.

In the past, a great deal of effort has been expended on arguing whether 'race', class or gender should be seen as primary in cases such as this. Such effort is fruitless because it is impossible to separate these factors from one another and assign a weight to each. Nonetheless, though these dimensions cannot be separated in their effects within concrete social relationships, it is possible to separate them analytically. Indeed, this is a necessary strategy if we are to develop a coherent sociological account of stratification and inequality. It is argued here that each dimension can be seen as based within a different aspect of social relationships, as having a different 'existential location' (Anthias and Yuval-Davis 1993, p. 17). These locations are sketched out here and elaborated in chapters 4–7.

Class is a social category which refers to lived relationships surrounding social arrangements of production, exchange, distribution and consumption. While these may narrowly be conceived as *economic* relationships, to do with money, wealth and property, in this book it is suggested that class should be seen as referring to a much broader web of *social* relationships, including, for example, lifestyle, educational experiences and patterns of residence. Class, therefore, affects many aspects of our material lives.

Gender is a social category which refers to lived relationships between women and men; gender relations are those by means of which sexual divisions and definitions of masculinity and femininity are constructed, organized and maintained. It can be argued that relationships to do with the organization of sexuality and reproductive processes (pregnancy, childbirth and maternity) are particularly central here, and these have been the focus of radical forms of feminism. However, every aspect of social life is gendered; sexual divisions are constructed, organized and maintained not only within the family and private life but also in work and employment, in education, in politics, in leisure activities and cultural production. In every aspect of experience, whether we are male or female has implications.

'Race' and ethnicity are social categories which derive from and are used to explain a highly complex set of territorial relationships; these involve conquests of some territorial groups by others, the historical development of nation-states, and associated migrations of people around the globe. Particularly influential on racial and ethnic relations has been the colonial process whereby the nations of Western Europe carved up other parts of the globe between them. The institution of slavery has also played an important part in the construction of racial and ethnic categories, especially those distinguishing 'Black' peoples of African descent from the 'white' populations of European descent. Through colonialism and slavery, particular hierarchies of 'races' were consolidated, backed by ideologies of the innate superiority of whites. However, the development of racial and ethnic hierarchies did not end with colonialism and slavery. Complex patterns of racial and ethnic stratification have continued to evolve, linked to changing configurations of international relations and processes of migration. It is argued by some that we are now in a 'post-colonial' phase in which new hybrid patterns of ethnic identity are becoming characteristic (Bhabha 1990a), an idea that will be explored in chapter 6. It is also clear that categories of 'race', ethnicity and nation are very volatile, as ideas about nationality and belonging, for example, are perpetually being constructed and reconstructed. Who exactly, for example, are the British in the twenty-first century? How does the notion of British nationality relate to living in England, Wales, Scotland and Northern Ireland? What will happen if the Scottish independence movement, despite defeat in 2014, eventually succeeds, breaking up the United Kingdom? What does it mean to be Black British or British Muslim? Which people living in Great Britain are not British? And who rooted for 'Team GB' at the Olympic Games?

Age as a dimension of inequality relates to social categories derived from the organization of the life course, and lived relationships between people socially located as being in differing age groups. People at different stages in the life course are subjected to different social rules and expectations, which we call ageism. Most Western societies display marked segregation between the various socially defined age groups, along with disparities of economic resources and power between the groupings, which are shored up by stereotypes of differential age capacities. Although ageist assumptions affect all of us, particular age groups suffer more from social marginalization and economic exclusion.

Class, gender, 'race', ethnicity and age therefore refer to different aspects of lived social relationships, although they interweave together to produce an integrated structure of inequality. Age, gender and 'race' have all been popularly conceived as having some kind of biological referent, although sociologists would deny that they derive directly from biological differences. Here, class appears as the odd one out. The lack of any visible physical manifestation in which people can *see* class relationships as being grounded may be one reason why class identity is rather contentious. More than the other three dimensions of inequality, class belongs purely to the social realm.

These sets of social categories and lived relationships together form what I call the *dynamics* of inequality. I have used this term rather than the more conventional sociological term of structure to convey the fact that these categories and relationships are constantly changing. Yet, as was argued in chapter 1, they also demonstrate considerable stability and constancy over time, so that they constitute an enduring framework of social inequalities in our society. So, for example, the *extent* and *precise nature* of ageist practices will vary over time, but the *general fact* of age discrimination remains a constant. Part of the reason for the fluidity of social relations is that these four dynamics, along with others such as those of religion and dis/ability that are more briefly discussed in this book, are in constant interplay with each other. Although we may separate out each aspect of social difference for the purposes of sociological analysis, in our real lives we are positioned at the intersections of multiple dynamics.

As individuals, each of us occupies a social location within a complicated nexus created by this interplay, a tangled network of social relationships. I visualize these as being rather like a display of sculptures by Anthony Gormley which were exhibited at the Hayward Gallery. From a distance they looked like intricate tangles or honeycombs of wire, but when observed more closely, or from certain angles, the viewer could make out the shape of a body framed within these wire networks. Thus, social relationships may appear chaotic in their complexity, but when carefully studied the patternings and regularities emerge. The realization of the complexity of these intertwinings of the dimensions of inequality, now generally described as intersectionality, has led to preoccupation with the idea of 'fragmentation'.

Polarization and Fragmentation

It is commonly stated that society is becoming more fragmented. This is often linked to the argument that Western societies are now entering a distinct 'post-industrial' or 'postmodern' phase of development, in which old-established social relationships are breaking down and being transformed into a more complex web of interlocking social groups: 'Postmodernity is marked by a view of the human world as irreducibly and irrevocably pluralistic, split into a multitude of sovereign units and sites of authority, with no horizontal or vertical order' (Bauman 1992, p. 35). Other reworkings of the older theoretical framework of capitalism, such as Lash and Urry's account of 'disorganized capitalism', also feature themes of fragmentation and social disintegration: 'All that is solid about organized capitalism, class, industry, cities, collectivity, nation-state, even the world, melts into air' (1987, p. 313). Bauman's recent work (2000) centres on the notion of 'liquid modernity' where everything is fluid and uncertain, with structures and values constantly eroding, leaving people isolated and insecure.

The idea of social fragmentation is not new. It derives in part from the writings of Max Weber on stratification, and has long been used as a riposte to Marx's theory of class polarization. As stated earlier, Marx argued that society would become ever more divided into two polar camps as capitalism developed. The logic of competition would force smaller companies and self-employed people out of business, so they must either expand and join the ranks of major capitalists or be forced down into the proletariat; a similar fate would befall members of other groups, such as the aristocracy or the peasantry, left over from earlier modes of production. Marx also believed that tendencies inherent to capitalism would increase the economic gap between bourgeoisie and wage-earners, as deepening crises of over-production and under-consumption left the latter ever more vulnerable to poverty and unemployment.

In contrast, Weber's theory of class pointed to cleavages within each class, with the propertyless wage earners, for example, being split into different segments on the basis of different assets that they could offer in the labour market. Weber also introduced the notion of another form of fragmentation, when he argued that classes were cross-cut by two other types of social grouping deriving from the unequal distribution of power in society: status groups and political parties. Ralf Dahrendorf used these ideas to mount a powerful critique of Marx in his classic book *Class and Class Conflict in Industrial Society* (1959), in which he argued that the capitalist class, the working class and the middle class had all fragmented or 'decomposed', a process leading to a much more complex pattern of class relationships and antagonisms than the simple polarization envisaged by Marx. The working class was split on the basis of skill divisions; the capitalist class itself had broken up into an owning group (shareholders and investors) and a managing group; while Dahrendorf saw the middle class as a heterogeneous grouping, with high-paid professionals and technicians being linked in interests to management, while low-paid clerical workers, foremen and other service workers had much in common with the manual working class.

In *The Fragmentary Class Structure (1977)*, Roberts and colleagues advanced the argument by showing how people's self-perceptions of class contributed to the fragmentation effect: their research showed that some people working in manual jobs described themselves as 'middle class', while others in apparently middle-class white-collar positions nonetheless identified with the working class. Objective class situations, defined on the basis of occupational groupings, and subjective class identifications jointly produced a plurality of class positionings.

Neo-Marxists responded to these criticisms by incorporating the idea of fragmentation into their own class theories. They used the notion of a class 'fraction' to describe a group within a class whose economic situation differed in some significant way from the rest. For example, the skilled, unskilled and semi-skilled groupings in the working class which Dahrendorf had discerned could be described as class fractions, although they still shared together the common characteristics of wage labour: they were dependent on selling their labour to make a living, and were powerless, exploited and alienated in Marxian terms.

The current wave of stratification theories has taken the idea of fragmentation a stage further. Classes are seen as subject to new processes of decomposition; and class is seen to mesh with other aspects of inequality to produce a society made up of a multiplicity of overlapping groupings. Moreover, it is suggested that individuals move about more easily between these different groups. Society is not only more fragmented but more fluid. Indeed, some envisage a further development which involves the breaking up of all social groupings and a loss of all sense of social belonging. This idea is held by some postmodernists and is taken to an extreme by Beck, who speaks of Western societies undergoing 'a surge of individuation': a process of transformation is under way 'in the course of which people will be set free from the social forms of industrial society – class, stratification, family, gender status' (1992, p. 87).

Identities and Fragmentation

Such ideas about the disintegration of classes and the increasing fluidity of social relationships have triggered increased interest in the notion of identity. Social fragmentation is linked to fragmentation of identity: 'It is no longer so easy to talk of the individual or the self as an autonomous and coherent unity but instead we have come to understand that we are made up from and live our lives as a mass of contradictory fragments' (Moore 1988, p. 170).

As a result of social change, people are said to be losing their sense of social belonging, of being rooted in traditional collectivities, such as class, community or the kinship network. In Robert Bocock's phrase, 'a state of flux has replaced earlier forms of stable group membership' (1993, p. 31). Now people draw their sense of identity from a much broader range of sources, including gender, age, marital status, sexual preference, consumption patterns; as Bocock puts it, there is a greater 'proliferation of identities – of the number of yous on offer' (1992, p. 160). Postmodernists argue that identity has become relatively free-floating, detached from the bases of social structure which used to constrain it; we are now freer to pick and choose which of the various 'yous on offer' we want to be 'me': 'Each of us lives with a variety of potentially contradictory identities which battle within us for allegiance: as men or women, Black or white, straight or gay, able-bodied or disabled, "British" or "European". The list is potentially infinite' (Weeks 1990, p. 88).

If we pursue our example of the young African-Caribbean woman, we can illustrate what the postmodernists are trying to convey. Does she identify herself primarily as a woman? Or perhaps as a single mother, in view of the state's preoccupation with the 'problem' of lone parenthood? Does she consider herself working class because of her parents' manual occupations, or because she has experienced low-paid unskilled work options? If she grew up on a council estate, she may take that as a sign of being working class. But if she now lives in a more mixed area of inner-city housing, surrounded by students, perhaps she has developed loyalties to a more complex sort of community? Her ethnic origin will be very important to her. But does she think of herself as African-Caribbean? As Jamaican? Would she categorize herself as 'Black'? As British? Or will she perhaps trace her origins further back to her African ancestry? We can see that she has a wealth of sources of identification open to her and there are plenty of other possibilities we have not begun to explore, such as religion, sexuality, membership of clubs, cultural interests. Which of all these possible 'selves' is the primary one? Or are they all? Which of them will constitute her identity?

This interest in identity is relatively new in sociology, which seems to have replaced an earlier theoretical interest in 'consciousness'. For Marxists, consciousness was a vital link between structure and action; but the concept was often seen as problematic (see chapter 4). Contemporary sociologists have taken up the notion of identity to explore how people are drawn to various forms of political action. In the past, though, identity has been the preserve of social psychologists and its analysis has been relatively underdeveloped in sociology (Hall 1992b). It is worth trying to define clearly what is meant by the term. Jeffrey Weeks defines identity in the following way: 'Identity is about belonging, about what you have in common with some people and what differentiates you from others. At its most basic it gives you a sense of personal location, the stable core to your individuality. But it is also about your social relationships, your complex involvement with others' (1990, p. 88).

Developing Weeks's ideas, we might first of all make a distinction between 'personal identity', which is primarily studied by psychologists, and 'social identity', which concerns sociologists. Personal identity refers to the construction of the self: our sense of ourselves as unique individuals, how we perceive ourselves and how we think others see us. Personal identity evolves from the whole package of experiences that each individual has gone through, and is highly complex and individualized. Social identity is also a complex issue, but is more limited. It refers to the way that we as individuals locate ourselves within the society in which we live, how others see us, and how we perceive others as locating us. Social identities derive from the various sets of lived relationships in which individuals are engaged, such as the dynamics of inequality outlined in this chapter. An alternative and related term, used widely by postmodernists, is 'cultural identity', which has seemed of particular relevance to ethnic minorities affected by the 'diaspora': the spreading of people across the globe from their original homelands, such as Africa or India. Cultural identity refers to the sense of belonging to a particular culture, past or present. Talking of the complex processes which go to construct a Caribbean identity, Stuart Hall emphasizes the way that cultural identities are not fixed but always evolving:

> Cultural identity...is a matter of 'becoming' as well as 'being'. It belongs to the future as much as to the past...Cultural identities come from somewhere, have histories. But like everything which is historical they undergo constant transformation. Far from being eternally fixed in some essentialized past they are subject to the continuous play of history, culture and power. (1990, p. 225)

As the example of our fictional young woman shows, a multitude of factors influence the development of personal and even social and cultural identity. It is probably beyond the scope of sociologists to predict in any individual case which potential aspects of identity, if any, will predominate. This depends largely on 'contingent' factors: specific personal circumstances, individual biographies, particular historical and political events. All that sociologists can do is to suggest what, in any given time and place, are likely to be the most powerful influences on the formation of social identities. For example, it is suggested that changes in work and the break-up of old urban communities have weakened traditional class identities. Or again, for African-Caribbeans in Britain, 'race' is arguably a more potent source of identification than class, because it is so highly visible (Gilroy 1987). Nonetheless, it is perfectly possible for one African-Caribbean to have a strong ethnic identification while another person may view herself in class terms. A third may reject both class and racial identification, saying that she is just a person! A fourth might have developed the sense of a hybrid identity arising from her multiple positioning in the social nexus. This was beautifully illustrated by the case of Sarika Watkins-Singh, a fourteen-year-old girl with Welsh and Punjabi parents, who was suspended from school for wearing a metal bangle as a symbol of her Sikh faith. When granted reinstatement by a court judgment, she told the press: 'I am proud to be a Welsh, Punjabi, Sikh girl' (*Guardian* 30 July 2008). Her statement of identity embraces nationality, ethnicity, religion and gender. It therefore reflects accurately the inevitably multiple nature of identities. As Steph Lawler expresses it:

> No one has only one identity, in the sense that everyone must, consciously or not, identify with more than one group, one identity. This is about more than combining multiple identities in an 'additive' way...Rather, race, gender and the rest interact...so that to be a white woman is not the same – in terms of meaning or experience – as to be a Black woman. Different forms of identity, then, should be seen as

interactive and mutually constitutive, rather than 'additive'. (Lawler 2008, p. 3)

I suggest that it is helpful to identify three *levels* of social identity: passive, active and politicized. 'Passive identities' are potential (and, as Lawler points out, multiple) identities in the sense that they derive from the sets of lived relationships (class, gender, ethnicity and so forth) in which the individuals are engaged, but they are not acted on. Individuals are not particularly conscious of passive identities and do not normally define themselves by them unless events occur which bring those particular relationships to the fore. Class is a passive identity for many people. The majority of the British population do not appear to think of *themselves* in class terms, although they recognize the existence of class inequalities and talk about class quite a lot (Scase 1992; Bradley 1994, 2014).

'Active identities' are those which individuals are conscious of and which provide a base for their actions. Sarika Watkins-Singh's statement quoted above was indicative of a whole set of active identities that were proclaimed by what she chose to wear. Active identities are positive elements in an individual's self-identification, although we do not necessarily think of ourselves continually in terms of any specific identity. For example, as Riley argues, there are times in most women's lives when they clearly perceive themselves as 'a woman' – being whistled at or pestered in the street, for example, or when menstruation starts unexpectedly (Riley 1988). In such circumstances, the individual is likely to respond as 'a woman' to the circumstances. At other times that identification will lapse and she will think of herself simply as a person, not in gender terms. As this example suggests, active identification often occurs as a defence against the actions of others or when an individual is conscious of being defined in a negative way. Active identities are promoted by the experience of discrimination. Thus, 'race' and ethnicity are currently likely to be sources of active identities. Ethnic identities are asserted where cultures and territorial rights are seen to be under attack, as in the former Yugoslavia. Racial identities are often forced on people because of prejudice relating to skin colour or cultural practices, as in the case of British African-Caribbeans, Jews or Muslims. The increasing tendency of young Muslim women to choose to wear a headscarf is an excellent example of the forceful assertion of an ethno-religious identity in the face of racism and stigmatization.

Where identities provide a more constant base for action and where individuals constantly think of themselves in terms of an identity, we can describe it as a 'politicized identity'. Politicized identities are formed through political action and provide the basis for collective organization of either a defensive or an affirmative nature. As our current use of the term 'identity politics' suggests, politicized identities are common in 21st-century society. A proliferation of political bodies has sprung up to fight for the rights of particular groups. For example, the militant gay and lesbian movement in Britain and America has promoted positive and politicized homosexual identities linked to the process of 'coming out'. The feminist movement has also encouraged many women to adopt a politicized female identity; and, ironically, politicized male identities appear to be evolving as a result of the backlash against feminism in America and Britain, where various groups campaigning for 'Men's Rights' or 'Father's Rights' seek to protect male interests they perceive as threatened. But, once again, the most striking example is probably the rise of 'Political Islam', an international movement which unites Muslims fighting against prejudice, Islamophobia and what they see as the contempt of the West for their societies and communities.

Such examples illustrate the complexity of social identification and give support to the theories of fragmentation. These ideas will be explored in subsequent chapters. But since this book has presented itself as a 'both/and' story rather than an 'either/or' one, fragmentation will be explored alongside arguments that processes of polarization can also be discerned in society. This chapter started with discussion of the growing gulf between the rich and poor in Britain and America, which suggests that Marx's insights are not yet exhausted.

Conclusions

This chapter has offered a brief overview of four dimensions of inequality in contemporary societies: class, gender, 'race'/ethnicity and age. It was argued that each should be seen both as a social construct (a way to categorize social relationships) and as a set of lived relationships. Together, these can be seen as 'dynamics of inequality'. Each of these dynamics of inequality derives from a different aspect of social reality, a different 'existential location'. Recently, stratification theory has begun to explore how these dynamics interact, utilizing the notion of intersectionality to explore the specific positioning of particular groups.

So far, the discussion has looked at the dynamics of inequality in isolation from the societies in which they are embedded. Sociology, however, promotes an understanding of the complex ways in which the parts of a society are related to the whole. Most sociologists would claim that we cannot gain a full understanding of any aspect of social life without some account of its context and the type of society in which it is placed. Thus, the pattern of inequality varies as societies change. In turn, changing dynamics of inequality will affect how societies develop. The two things cannot be separated but are locked in what sociologists call a dialectical relationship: they mutually act upon one another to produce change. It is time, then, to think about how we can categorize the type of society in which we live. If we want a full comprehension of how stratification is changing, we must also consider how societies are changing.

Thinking Points

- Why has inequality increased in the early twenty-first century?
- What leads people to develop active or politicized identities? Has it happened to you?

3

Capitalism, Modernity and Global Change

The Power of Change

> Constant revolutionizing of production, uninterrupted disturbance of all social conditions, everlasting uncertainty and agitation distinguish the bourgeois epoch from all earlier ones. All fixed, fast-frozen relations, with their train of ancient and venerable prejudices and opinions, are swept away, all new-formed ones become antiquated before they can ossify. All that is solid melts into air, all that is holy is profaned.
> (Marx and Engels 1934, pp. 12–13)

In these famous words, Marx and Engels celebrated one of the most important features about the society that confronted them. As Krishan Kumar (1978) has argued, something that struck virtually all nineteenth-century observers of industrialization was the pace and power of change. For example, the railway train symbolized to the Victorians the force and compulsion of technological and industrial development (in much the same way as we might take the jet plane to be an image of the post-war world, and the computer the symbol of current development). Although what we now call the 'Industrial Revolution' was an extremely long-drawn-out process, covering nearly 100 years, nobody around at the time could doubt that momentous changes were taking place.

It is significant that writers discussing the idea that we now inhabit a 'post-industrial' or 'postmodern' era of social development have so often been drawn to quote Marx and Engels: 'all that is solid melts into air' (Lash and Urry 1987, p. 331; Turner 1989, p. 11; Bauman 1992, p. 97; Hall 1992b, p. 277; Tester 1993, p. 40; Lyon 1994,

p. 2). Social theorists have continually grappled with the sense of monumental changes in society. Describing the changes in technology that started to occur at the end of the nineteenth century, with the development of mass-production processes and new consumer goods, Georges Friedmann (1955) spoke of a 'second industrial revolution'. In the twenty-first century, we grapple with ideas of a 'Network Society' or a 'Digital Age', brought about by the power and speed of digitalized information and computer technologies, which are transforming the way we spend our work and leisure time. Ever since industrialization, people living in industrial societies have been apt to feel that they are living through major social upheavals and to fear that those upheavals may swallow them up. In 2014, as I wrote this, the abyss was yawning again. Western nations were struggling to re-equilibrate after the recession of 2008–13, while the USA and UK were on maximum security alerts in the face of renewed threats of possible terrorist acts from extremist Muslim groups such as Al Qaeda and ISIS. Wars were raging in the Ukraine, Gaza and Iraq, with considerable loss of civilian life; a Malaysian airliner with nearly 300 passengers on-board was shot down over the Ukraine; extreme weather events, such as untimely floods, storms and earthquakes, which can be linked to climate change due to environmental pollution, were increasingly disrupting lives and livelihoods. Peace and tranquillity remain elusive for many people.

Industrial capitalist society is notably dynamic. Relationships, institutions, technologies, production processes constantly alter, often quite dramatically. In pre-industrial societies, the pace of change is slower and changes tend to be gradual and incremental. In pre-industrial Europe, people saw little difference between their lifestyle and that of their parents and grandparents, while we not only live in a world very different from that of our parents but expect to see major changes within our own lifetime. Life-changing inventions which were not around when I was a child are numerous: jet engines, colour televisions, high-speed trains, credit cards, hole-in-the-wall cash-machines, weather-forecasting satellites, computers, the internet, mobile phones, tablets, Facebook and Twitter – all things now taken for granted. The complex processes we call globalization have also opened up new patterns of change as the boundaries between nations become more permeable, while political relations between them remain volatile.

Auguste Comte, considered to be a founder of the discipline of sociology, argued that the experience of the more violent changes at the end of the eighteenth century – the French Revolution and the onset of industrialization – allowed people to begin to think in sociological terms (Thompson 1976). Before the eighteenth century, people tended to think of society as a natural and persisting order ordained by God. Since then, the writings of the thinkers of the Enlightenment had fostered broader acceptance of the idea that societies could be changed, and by human agency. The French Revolution brought this message firmly home. If societies could change, then it followed that different types of societies could be distinguished, and also that the way one type of society changed into another could be studied and analysed. Thus, all the major contributors to what is now called classical sociological thinking – Comte, Marx, Weber and Durkheim – were concerned with the construction of social typologies (systems of classifying societies).

This chapter looks at the way sociologists have subsequently categorized industrial societies and their key attributes. As I argued at the end of the last chapter, it is a key feature of a sociological approach that changes in social institutions cannot be viewed in isolation from broader social changes. There are many approaches to understanding the way contemporary societies are evolving, most of which highlight the fragmentation processes described in chapter 1. The present chapter briefly reviews classical accounts of 'industrial' and 'capitalist' society, and those that suggest that capitalism has entered a new and distinct phase. Next, approaches suggesting that more radical types of changes have occurred are discussed. Finally we explore the popular framework of globalization, arguing that global capitalism may be the most useful way to think of current societies, especially in combination with the political doctrine of neoliberalism. It must be stressed that these are complex theories with many variants. No comprehensive survey could be offered in such a short space. Rather, the purpose of this chapter is to consider these perspectives in terms of their implication for the analysis of social divisions and inequality.

Industrialism and Capitalism

One obvious way to categorize societies is in terms of the prevailing form of production and its characteristic techniques. Economic historians, economists and anthropologists, for example, have used the terms 'agrarian' and 'industrial' to describe the types of societies that prevailed before and after the Industrial Revolution. Industrial society' has become a familiar term within popular usage, acting as a shorthand to describe societies where the core of the economy is manufacturing and the factory system.

However, within sociology, the use of this term has been particularly associated with the theories of functionalists and other mainstream American sociologists in the post-war period. A classic text of this era, *Industrialism and Industrial Man*, presented a model of 'the inner logic of industrialism'. The authors argued that the organization of industrial production required the development of a particular set of social institutions, which were common to all industrial societies; these included the factory system; urban development; a highly specialized division of labour; a meritocratic class structure with high levels of social mobility; a mass education system; a bureaucratic model for organizations; a welfare system; and a political system based on parliamentary democracy (Kerr et al. 1962). It is interesting that many of these institutions persist, although the factory system has been in significant decline.

This approach was associated with the framework of modernization, which suggested that the advanced industrial societies of the West set the model for the developing societies of the 'Third World'; all such societies must develop the same institutions if they wished to modernize successfully. Kerr et al. argued that a process of 'convergence' was under way, by which all societies, however diverse their original social structures, were becoming more alike: America, the farthest down the path of development, was the mirror of the future. Something similar was later argued by Francis Fukuyama (1989), who considered that the late twentieth century saw the triumph of capitalism and liberal democracy over all other possible economic and political forms of society (particularly socialism and communism). Contemporary America represented the culmination of social development, the 'end of history', and was the goal to which all other societies must inevitably be drawn. The 'end of history' thesis, however, has been challenged by the resistance of some countries, notably the Muslim world, to accepting the values and democratic structures of the West, as witnessed by the prolonged conflicts in Iraq and Afghanistan.

Although the idea of capitalism is often linked to industrialism, the term has different associations. While theorists of industrial society such as Kerr have distinguished societies in terms of the *techniques of production*, theorists of capitalist societies see the *social relations of production* as central (Scott 1979). Both groups see economic relations as the most sociologically important ones, but they conceptualize economic relationships differently.

The idea of capitalism is most famously associated with Marx and his massive study *Das Kapital*. Marx developed a social typology based on the concept of 'mode of production'. Each type of society has a distinct mode of production, the set of relationships by which people come together to produce goods and services. Marx distinguished between two aspects of the mode of production: the technical aspect relating to the use of particular tools, resources and technologies, which he called the 'forces of production'; and the social aspect, the way the different functions of production are allocated to different social groups, which Marx called 'the relations of production'. For Marx and his followers, the social relationships were more important than the technical ones. Thus, class, as a relation of production, became central to Marxist theory.

Marx distinguished a number of different modes of production, but gave most of his attention to a meticulously detailed account of the capitalist mode. The characteristic relations of production under capitalism were those of private ownership of capital and the exploitation by a class of property-owning capitalists of the mass of propertyless wage-earners, who must sell their labour in the market to survive.

Marx's idea of 'exploitation' referred to the way the social surplus was extracted by the most powerful class from the subordinate class. The form in which surplus was procured under capitalism was through the mechanism of the wage. Marx believed that, in a given period of time, workers produced goods or services which were greater in value than the wage they received. This 'surplus value' was taken by the capitalist in the form of profit, which could subsequently be reinvested to increase the capitalist's wealth.

Part of Marx's hope for a socialist revolution lay in his belief that, when the proletariat realized how they were being exploited, they would combine to fight for a fairer system. But this development was impeded by another distinctive feature of capitalism as Marx described it: alienation. Alienation refers to the divorce of workers from the goods they make and the processes by which they are made. Because workers are powerless they have no control over what is made, how it is made or what becomes of it. As Marx believed that production was central to human existence, he stated that alienation extended to people's relations to one another and to their own social selves: they were alienated from their 'species-being'.

Marx was not alone in developing theories of capitalism. Weber also used the term in his famous study *The Protestant Ethic and the Spirit of Capitalism* (1930). This text is taken to be a criticism of what Weber saw as the 'one-sided materialism' of Marx. Weber wished to improve on this by including within it some account of the ideas and motivations that were influential in promoting processes of social change. For Weber, certain types of Protestantism had a special affinity with capitalist values and provided the impetus for individuals to invest their money and efforts in capitalist enterprise, rather than indulging in conspicuous consumption like the rich in the previous feudal epoch.

In another work, the *General Economic History* (1923), Weber set out an account of the development of capitalism dealing more with the economic aspects considered by Marx. While his account had much in common with that of Marx, in the stress placed on property, ownership and the market, he also emphasized the importance of bureaucracy, as the most appropriate and efficient way in which to pursue capitalist enterprise. Bureaucracy was seen by Weber as the institutional form of what he called rationalization, a process he believed to be inextricably involved in capitalist development. Rationalization implies calculating the most effective way to gain a given end. Weber believed that a variety of rationally based institutions – such as a legal system, a banking infrastructure and rational systems of accounting – were needed to promote capitalist development. Technology and science can also be seen as embodiments of rationality. The development of these rational institutions promoted the growth of middle-class groupings, which were highlighted in Weber's theory of class.

Between them, Marx and Weber pointed to a number of elements central to subsequent theories of capitalism: the dominance of profits over needs; the market; private ownership of capital; wage labour; alienation; the pressures of competition and capital accumulation; bureaucracy; the application of science and technology to production; economic rationalism as the key principle of decision-making, popularly labelled 'the bottom line'. For both Marx and Weber, capitalist societies were societies stratified by class (although they conceived class differently). Class features centrally in all theories of capitalism.

Capitalism and Change: Late, Disorganized or Global?

While many would argue that the key elements of capitalism, as listed above, are still the central characteristics of societies such as Britain and America, there can be no doubt that things have changed greatly since Marx and Weber wrote their texts. It was suggested in chapter 2 that the antagonism between capitalists and waged labourers has diminished as the class structure has become more complex. Other important changes include the greater involvement of the state in controlling and coordinating the economy, and the provision of welfare systems to offset some of the hardships brought about by the operation of the market. In addition, since the latter part of the nine-teenth century, capitalism has been becoming steadily more interna-tionalized in its scope and operations. This has occurred, first, through the development of international product markets under colonialism, then by the expansion of capitalist firms' investment and production systems across the globe, and subsequently by the freeing-up of trade and of systems of financial investment and speculation.

These changes, among others, have led many sociologists to argue that capitalism has now entered a new stage or phase. The develop-ment of joint-stock companies as the prevailing form of capitalist enterprise, followed by the emergence in America at the end of the nineteenth century of giant monopolistic corporations – the multinational companies (MNCs) – were crucial elements of this new phase, often called 'monopoly capitalism' (Scott 1979). Others have described it as 'advanced' (Giddens 1973) or 'late' (Mandel 1975) capitalism. The currently popular term, which will be used in this book, is 'global capitalism'.

Advanced, late or monopoly capitalism is contrasted with the 'classic', 'liberal' or 'entrepreneurial' capitalism of the early nine-teenth century, when the typical capitalist enterprise was owned and managed by an individual entrepreneur or family. The competitive demands for expansion and investment inherent to the capitalist economy led to the concentration of capital and the formation of joint-stock companies. Such companies tended to expand both the size and the range of their productive activities, and gradually the giant monopolies emerged to dominate national economies. They also expanded internationally, taking advantage of past colonial links. State support was offered, as governments sought to help com-panies compete in the international markets. The switch to joint ownership of companies also promoted the development of the stock market and associated financial institutions, such as merchant banks, insurance and investment companies. A key feature of contemporary capitalism has been the dominance of the finance sector over indus-trial companies. From the 1980s, and again in the early 2000s, great booms in the financial markets of the City of London epitomized the triumph of speculative capital over productive manufacturing capital.

In the 1980s, it was suggested that capitalism was entering a third stage, referred to as 'disorganized' capitalism (Offe 1985; Lash and Urry 1987). The monopoly stage appeared 'organized' as it involved high levels of state intervention and co-ordination of the economy, along with a complex bureaucratic system of state welfare provisions. In many countries, including the UK, this was accompanied by cor-poratism. This term refers to an alliance or collaboration between the different parties in the economy (the state, employers, working people) through the collective organizations which represent their interests. Government, employers' organizations and trade unions negotiate together over running the country. Trade unions, for example, agree to restrain wage demands and limit strike activity, in return for consultation over government economic policy-making. Germany and the Scandinavian countries continue as prime examples of corporatist states.

In *The End of Organized Capitalism* (1987), Scott Lash and John Urry described the key features of disorganized capitalism as follows: the globalization of economic structures and the spread of capital into 'Third World' countries; the dominance of MNCs, whose power is now so great that nationally based political elites have diminishing control over their activities; the break-up of corporatism and decline of collectivism; the shrinking of the working class and continued expansion of the middle classes; the dismantling of welfare states; and the rise of a more pluralistic culture, promoting social fragmentation. Subsequently, they also spoke of the 'culturalization of the economy', arguing that, in the UK and other leading-edge economies, the production of culture and cultural artifacts was becoming a key part of commercialized activity.

Their account highlights a number of important developments. Since the 1980s, there has been a prolonged attack on state intervention in the economy and erosion of state-run welfare services, notoriously initiated by the UK and US governments headed by Margaret Thatcher and Ronald Reagan, and now pursued by George Osborne and David Cameron. The 'free market' rather than state control became the dominant organizing principle. Despite this, it is doubtful whether 'disorganization' is the best way to describe the current state of capitalist society. It can be argued that capitalist companies are more tightly organized and integrated than ever before, albeit on a global basis. Processes of decentralization in private and public organizations and in the state have been matched by new processes of centralization. For example, if we look at the education and health services in Britain we can see that, while some financial responsibilities have passed from government bodies to hospital trusts and to head-teachers (decentralization), the powers of management have been expanded and the power and autonomy of professionals lower down the hierarchy have diminished (centralization). Moreover, the organization of some aspects of these services (such as the ground-rules for financial organization in the health service, the establishment of a national curriculum and the implementation of Standard Assessment Tests (SATs) in schools) is more tightly under central government control than ever before. Rather than a decline of organization, it appears that new forms of organization are being developed, ones that further the power of private enterprise. The development of highly efficient computerized systems, which can monitor and control many aspects of our lives, including our spending habits, also contributed to a process which we might call the 'reorganization' of capital.

Central to Lash and Urry's arguments is the notion of the globalization of capitalism. Globalization is central to many other accounts of contemporary social development, such as those of Harvey (1989), Giddens (1990), Stiglitz (2002) and Steger (2003). We can argue that capitalism has always been international in its scope. Wallerstein (1974) has analysed the rise of capitalism in terms of a 'world economy' dominated by the colonial powers. Hobsbawm (1968) describes how Britain's precocious start as the originator of industrialism was based upon the economic benefits of the 'triangular trade' in slaves, raw materials and industrial products between Britain, Africa and the British colonies in the Americas. The development of the monopoly phase of capital in the late nineteenth century was linked to further expansion of international trade. However, the current phase of globalization theory involves an intensification of these international links and a shift in the power of leading capitalist enterprises from a national to a transnational base. New microtechnologies, which make capital more portable, and information technologies which permit the flow of communications around the globe, contribute to globalization. The break-up of the Soviet bloc in 1989 extended the scope of a global market culture, based around commercialism and consumerism, into Eastern Europe and Asia.

> Nowadays, goods, capital, people, knowledge, images, communications, crime, culture, pollutants, fashions and beliefs all readily flow across territorial boundaries. Transnational networks, social movements and relationships are extensive in virtually all areas of human activity from the academic to the sexual. Moreover, the existence of global systems of trade, finance and production binds together in very complicated ways the prosperity and fate of households, communities and nations across the globe. (McGrew 1992, p. 66)

We will return to the notion of a globally reorganized capitalism at the end of this chapter. Here, I just wish to note some implications of the frameworks we have discussed for theorizing inequalities. A common feature of theories of capitalism and industrialism is the focus on economic arrangements as the core of the society. All such approaches, then, imply an emphasis on class. Traditional theories of industrialism and capitalism treated inequalities of other types (for example, gender and ethnicity) as secondary, being incidental, not central, to social development. However, the more recent theories of capitalism (disorganized capital, globalization) have taken on board the criticisms of feminists and others and incorporated other dimensions of stratification into their analysis (Williams et al. 2013).

Often they have done this through the concept of 'new social movements'. Original class structures of capitalism are said to be weakening and fragmenting as a social and political force; and new social movements based on a range of communal issues (feminism, 'race', ecology, gay and lesbian rights, consumption) are coming to the fore in the political arena. Nonetheless, the slant of all theories of capitalism is such that the changing relationship between capital and labour is likely to be foregrounded. An important feature of the next set of theories discussed in this chapter is that they push the capital–labour relationship from the centre, allowing for a more open-ended approach to stratification.

Modernity, Risk and Reflexivity: An Alternative Perspective

Since the 1980s there has been a trend within sociology to use the term 'modernity' rather than either industrialism or capitalism in talking about contemporary social development; the work of Anthony Giddens, for example, displays this switch in terminology. At a common-sense level, we may employ 'modern' simply as a synonym for 'capitalist' or 'industrial' societies. But the term modernity has a more precise set of sociological resonances. In part the use of the term by Giddens (1990, 1991) is a response to the challenging position of *post*modernity, which we will consider in the next section; Giddens explicitly rejects the idea of postmodernity and opposes to it the idea of 'late modernity'.

The idea of modernity also links back to older sociological traditions. It can be connected to the work of Emile Durkheim and his functionalist follower Talcott Parsons. Rather than focusing on economic relationships, in his account of social development Durkheim was concerned to categorize societies in terms of what, to him, was distinctively *social*: the nexus of relationships which binds society's members together. Another link is to the work of Georg Simmel, who also focused on the non-economic aspects of society; Simmel provided an influential analysis of modernity in terms of the distinctive relationships of urban living in the 'metropolis'. Simmel's view of modern life is one that focuses on fluidity, impermanence, social isolation, lack of close emotional ties. This melancholy view was influenced by the cultural writings of the poet Baudelaire, who coined the image of the 'flâneur', the stroller on the streets of modern life. Contemporary life is seen in such approaches as 'transitory, fleeting and contingent' (Frisby 1985). Weber has also been a central influence: the less economistic elements of his work provide key concepts for the idea of modernity. Weber described the cultures of the modern world as dominated by rationality, scientific thinking, secularization and what he called the 'disenchantment of the world': the loss of belief in magic and myth. Finally, running through all these approaches is the notion of 'the shock of the new': the sense that the dynamism of modern life persistently confronts us with novelty, with change.

Drawing on such ideas, theorists of modernity focus on the broader social and cultural relationships of contemporary societies. Giddens, in *The Consequences of Modernity* (1990), offers one version. He conceptualizes modernity in terms of four interlinked sets of institutions and relationships: capitalism, industrialism, administrative power and military power. A classic analysis of economic relationships is supplemented by an account of political structures. This allows Giddens to include the emergence of new social movements as a core feature of modern politics; the framework of modernity potentially provides the basis for a more flexible account of social divisions, which goes beyond seeing class as primary. Importantly, Giddens also highlights the link between social relations and the political context. However, his version of 'modernity' also exposes some of the problems of this perspective. In a multi-dimensional model such as this, what precisely is the relationship between the different elements? Which of them is most important and how do they influence each other? A notable omission from Giddens's model is any account of private life and the family. As in theories of capitalism, gender and ethnicity appear as a marginal aspect of social stratification.

Another influential account of modernity is offered by German sociologist Ulrich Beck. Beck (1992, 1998) goes farther than Giddens in breaking away from classical thinking, in developing his ideas of 'risk society' and 'reflexive modernity'. The notion of risk society is based on the idea that the distribution of risk is a key organizing principle of modern society. In the past, the major risks to humanity were natural, such as earthquakes, famine or plagues. Now added to these are more terrible man-made risks, such as nuclear disasters, chemical weapons, planes being shot out of the sky – like the Malaysian airliner; as these are created by people, there is a need for people to come together to tackle them. In the 2000s, the man-made risks that have come to dominate public debates are climate change and the over-utilization of natural resources such as oil, along with explosive devices planted by terrorists. Beck suggests that these risks affect everybody, not just the poor or subordinate groups; thus, the nature of social inequalities is changing.

Beck, along with Giddens, has also developed the idea of reflexivity as a key aspect of modern social life. This is the notion that we are all much more aware of our actions and the consequences of them, and as a result we continuously modify our behaviour. A symptom of this, for example, is the popularity of manuals and self-help books which tell us how to control every aspect of our lives, from our dietary and exercise regimes to handling our relationships and our working careers. This is a very important and significant idea which is often linked to the idea of 'individualization': the idea that, increasingly, people accept responsibility for their fate and deny the existence of collectivities, such as classes.

Beck and Giddens argue that not only individuals, but society itself, are subject to this process of self-monitoring, which increases the pace and intensity of change within global modernity. I believe we could link this idea of a kind of societal self-consciousness to the idea I put forward earlier of *reorganized capitalism*: 'The reflexivity of modern social life consists in the fact that social practices are constantly examined and reformed in the light of incoming information about those very practices, thus constitutively altering their character' (Giddens 1990, p. 38).

As we have noted, most of the key ideas in the above theories derive from classical social theory of the nineteenth and early twentieth centuries. Sociologists writing in these epochs had little to say about gender, partly because they saw sexual divisions as part of the natural order. The same would be true of age differences. Bauman (1992) also draws our attention to the fact that the spatial framework for classical sociological thinking was the nation-state. When discussing social divisions, those thinking in terms of nation-states were drawn to consider *internal* divisions and inequalities (such as class and occupation) rather than *external* divisions and inequalities such as those of nation, ethnos and racial group. Any approach derived from classical sociology is likely to privilege class as the most significant form of social division. To overcome this problem, many have suggested that we need a totally new kind of framework for considering society.

A New Type of Society? Post-Industrialism and Postmodernity

Two still-influential approaches developed in the 1980s suggested that social life had altered so radically that a new theoretical approach was needed to comprehend the nature of contemporary social reality: the theories of post-industrialism and postmodernity. Bauman, for example, speaks of 'a fully fledged viable social system which has come to replace the "classical" modern, capitalist society and thus needs to be theorized according to its own logic' (Bauman 1988, p. 811).

Post-industrialism is, in fact, not a very new idea. It is associated particularly with Daniel Bell, who wrote *The Coming of Post Industrial Society* in 1973. Bell suggested that technological advance was bringing about a new type of society. Computer-based technologies brought new forms of employment which would disrupt the old class system, as manual work was replaced by white-collar and professional jobs. While Bell identified this quantitative shift from manual to service work as already having occurred in the United States, he was more interested in the working out of the qualitative effects of this change. The new society would mean greater material prosperity for all, a rehumanization of work relations, an increase in the amount of leisure time, all as a result of the immense wealth-generating potential of new technology. The result would be greater social harmony, and an end to alienation and class conflict. Bell's work, indeed, was a deliberate challenge to Marxism. Class, as Marx understood it, was now irrelevant, and class conflict would no longer serve as the 'motor of history'. Bell argued that a new 'axial principle' (driving force) in society had replaced the profit imperative. As society moved beyond capitalism into post-industrialism, knowledge would become the axis: scientific knowledge would dictate how the new technology evolved and was applied. This idea has resurfaced in current thinking about the 'knowledge-based' economy and society, which was strongly espoused at Lisbon in 2000 by Tony Blair and other leaders of the European Union.

Bell's original account can easily be criticized. While it is true that service employment has expanded, and continues to do so, in the economies of the West, this has not brought an end to class or class conflict, as we shall argue in chapter 4. Rather than a leisure society, we are plagued by excessive working hours and workaholism. While scientific knowledge is important, it is still subordinated to the objectives of capital accumulation. Only inventions which lead to increased profit are taken up and produced. Global warming is a good example of this: scientists have explained why it is occurring and what we need to do to stop it, but airline companies keep opening new routes, and automobile companies produce high-powered cars and 'gas guzzlers' because of the strong consumer market for them.

Post-industrial theory fell out of favour for a time, given these criticisms. However, the idea resurfaced in the 1980s – ironically, in a very different context. Bell's optimistic vision of the post-industrial society was a product of post-war affluence. By contrast, the post-industrial theories of the 1980s were formulated as a result of the rise of mass unemployment. André Gorz, in *Farewell to the Working Class* (1982), suggested that the advent of information technology, far from bringing wealth to all, was making a proportion of the labour force redundant. So powerful is computerized production that a society no longer requires all its citizens to be employed to produce the goods and services it needs. Thus, Gorz argued, a new class was created, made up of the unemployed and casualized or under-employed workers, which he named the neo-proletariat. In these circumstances, the traditional proletariat, greatly reduced in size, and fearful of losing jobs or being replaced by neo-proletarians, abandons its opposition to capital.

Gorz used these ideas to suggest that the accounts of capitalism offered by Marx and Weber were now redundant. Weber's notion of the 'Protestant ethic' no longer operated in a society where so many people faced a future without work. Equally, Marx's vision of the proletariat posing a challenge to capitalism must be abandoned. However, in a useful critique of the post-industrial thesis, Clarke and Critcher (1985) suggested that this account of the 'death of the pro-letariat' is overstated. Rather, they suggest that, as capitalist econo-mies are highly dynamic, class relations are always changing. They argued that a new working class, consisting of lower-paid service workers, alongside remaining manual workers, was being formed. In the 2000s, Huws (2003) and Gill (2007) explored the idea of the 'cybertariat' as a new form of the working class, a breed of low-paid workers produced by information and computer technology, such as homeworking data processors and call centre workers. I will argue in the next chapter that the twenty-first century has been marked by the expansion of the 'precariat' of casualized insecure workers

It will be seen that the versions of post-industrialism outlined above are concerned with the issue of class, implying that class relations are being transformed or even that class is vanishing. These theories are critical of existing analyses of capitalism and industrialism, but the focus is still firmly on economic relationships, while gender, ethnicity and so forth tend to enter as side-effects of economic change.

A much broader, culturally based critique of theories of capitalism comes from the package of approaches which have become known as 'postmodernism'. As its own adherents have acknowledged (Lash 1990; Smart 1990), the term is often used quite loosely to signify a number of different trends in social thought. Lyon refers to it as a 'multi-layered concept' (Lyon 1994, p. vii). However, there can be no doubt that it poses a radical challenge to previous forms of sociological theory.

Postmodernism was not, in origin, a theory of society. It emerged as a theory about art and cultural change, alongside a philosophical position which attacked 'foundationalist' accounts of social reality (accounts which postulate an underlying base from which patterns of social relationships arise) and the notion of progress in social development. It also challenges the claims of a 'rational' science to a privileged form of knowledge, based on objective and verifiable processes of observation. In this view, there are multiple viewpoints rather than a single reality. This position, referred to as 'cultural relativism', has led critics to label postmodernism a theory of 'anything goes'.

Postmodern theory is complex and can only be briefly explored here. First, the cultural strand of postmodernism deals with the challenge to the modernist movement in art, literature and, particularly, architecture. While modernism was elitist, abstract, based on a strict aesthetic controlled by intellectuals, postmodern culture is popular, based on the experience of everyday life, and is led by commercialism and the market. Postmodern art forms often mix styles from different periods or schools (fusing opera and rock music, for example, or incorporating features typical of Roman or Greek architecture into a modern housing project or public building). Postmodern culture encourages a multitude of diverse cultural forms and a challenge to traditional 'canons' of art and taste. While this may seem remote from the analysis of social divisions, there are ways in which this cultural theory is of sociological significance. It challenges the traditional hierarchies within society and promotes the idea of cultural diversity and social pluralism. The idea of 'difference' and diversity has become a central feature of theories of postmodernity.

The anti-foundationalist philosophical strand has been most clearly expressed in the influential account of Jean-François Lyotard, *The Postmodern Condition* (1984). Lyotard offers an account of 'the condition of knowledge in the most highly developed societies' (p. xxiii) which involves an attack on what he calls 'metanarratives': historical accounts of social and intellectual development which promote the idea of orderly human progress towards a goal, often that of human 'enlightenment' or emancipation. While such metanarratives present themselves as scientifically validated forms of knowledge, Lyotard considers them to be no more than stories or myths used to justify particular views of how societies ought to be. Many classic social theories can be seen as metanarratives of this type, such as the liberal view of history as the triumph of civilization over barbarianism. But, above all, Lyotard's critique is aimed at Marx's theory of capitalism and its Utopian vision of socialist revolution. Lyotard believes that such theories are now discredited; he defines the 'postmodern condition' as 'incredulity towards metanarratives' (p. xxiii).

The implication of Lyotard's argument is that we should abandon attempts to construct grand theories of history and society, especially those which involve the idea of distinct stages of development. Rather than try to understand societies in their totality, we should concentrate on 'local narratives': accounts of events in very specific and limited contexts. In particular Lyotard advises a focus on language and the 'language games' which people use to promote their own definitions of what knowledge consists of.

The types of sociology which would logically appear compatible with Lyotard's position are the various micro-sociologies of action (ethnomethodology, interactionism, phenomenology), which focus on interaction in specific contexts and on the accounts that actors offer to make sense of the interaction. Yet such procedures, while important and perceptive in themselves, have limitations in explaining aspects of social life, such as inequalities of class and gender, which are diffused across the whole of society. How do we move the analysis beyond what happens in any particular school, street, office or factory?

It can be claimed that postmodern thinking has not as yet provided definitive formulations about the nature of the 'social' as opposed to the cultural: the guidelines are unclear as to how changing social relations are to be analysed. David Lyon suggests that many accounts of postmodernity make assumptions about technological change (computerization, information flows, the spread of mass media) but devote little space to linking these to processes of 'social transformation' (1994, p. 50). Curiously, those who espouse postmodernism are often drawn to utilizing the sociological theories of others to combine with their accounts of knowledge and culture. Lyon points to the frequent implicit use of 'a variety of post-industrial theory' which has 'survived its earlier critical battering to be recycled as postmodernity' (1994, p. 46). For example, Lyotard himself draws substantially on Bell's work, although Bell's version of post-industrialism is clearly a liberal form of a metanarrative of progress.

Others espousing aspects of postmodernism, who are sympathetic to Marxism, have drawn on theories of capitalism to supplement their accounts of postmodern culture (Harvey 1989; Jameson 1991). Jameson describes postmodernism as the 'cultural logic of late capitalism', which he sees as entering its 'third (or multinational) stage' (1991, p. 319). Bauman, although not a Marxist, suggests that a postmodern sociology would involve an account of consumer capitalism and its characteristic social relations (Bauman 1992). His recent work on 'liquid modernity' goes a stage further in suggesting the dissolution of stable institutions and identities because of constant and rapid change, but still draws on ideas of consumerism and choice. He uses the image of the rootless 'nomad' for the modern individual who wanders through life-changing relationships and identities (Bauman 2000). None of these influential figures, though, employs a micro-sociological approach such as ethnomethodology. Moreover, these very different postmodernists all draw on existing economically based typologies, meaning that, once again, class, however conceptualized, reappears as a central feature; paradoxically, the stress on diversity and social pluralism, so central to the idea of postmodern culture, seems to slip away at this point.

We may question whether the strategy used by these theorists (even by Lyotard himself) is a legitimate one, if we follow the logic of Lyotard's theoretical position. Indeed, it is not clear whether, within its own parameters, the postmodern epistemological position would permit any kind of *general* account of society (such as an account of 'postmodernity'). The alternative would be to study aspects of social divisions within specific local contexts. As we shall see in subsequent chapters, feminists and theorists of 'race' and ethnicity have adopted this option and moved away from trying to develop more abstract and explanatory accounts towards descriptive explorations of the specific situations of particular groups, such as Somali women in London, or gay and lesbian young Northerners. An alternative and extremely prevalent approach is to move away from the actual relationships and to study the discourses that surround them, combining Lyotard's stress on language with ideas taken from the work of Michel Foucault regarding power and the ways in which we as human subjects are constructed through discursive frameworks (see chapter 5).

An influential element drawn from theories of postmodernism and liquid modernity is the idea of multiple identities, which we explored in chapter 2. We are located in a nexus of relations which allows us many options for thinking about our position in society. Crook et al. (1992) believe that consumption and exposure to the mass media perform a crucial role in affecting people's social identification. This is a useful approach and the chapters that follow frequently draw upon work of this kind. However, a problem is that it is overly voluntaristic (i.e. people are seen as choosing from a package of identities on offer, according to personal inclination). As O'Neill argues, there is a tendency to present identities as detached and free-floating: 'postmodern atomism dislocates individuals from their institutional contexts' (1995, p. 7). For an account of how these identities might be grounded in 'institutional contexts' – that is, how they are linked to sets of lived relationships and *constrained by them* – postmodernists again tend to fall back on traditional accounts of capitalism, although these may be supplemented with ideas drawn from feminism and from theories of colonialism.

Where are We Now? Postmodernity?
Or Globalized Reorganized Capitalism?

Indeed, critics of postmodernism reject the view that we have moved 'post' the 'institutional contexts' of modernity. Our production system is still a capitalist one, and all the features of modern capitalist industrial societies which have featured in the discussion above (for example bureaucracy, the social dominance of scientific knowledge, rationality) are still central to our society. While many changes are occurring, defenders of modernism suggest they are insufficient to justify an 'ontological break', a complete rupture with the past (Pollert 1988; Thompson 1993). All this may throw doubt on the idea of 'postmodernity' as a distinct social phase and explain why postmodernists have found it hard to offer substantive accounts of the social implications of cultural change.

However, some aspects of the philosophical version of postmodernism and its critique of modernist forms of knowledge provide a useful check to conventional theorizing. We need to take a critical approach to claims about scientific objectivity in social analysis and to be cautious in how we apply social typologies. We should acknowledge that totalizing approaches (such as Marxism or functionalism) may indeed distort the complex nature of social reality. As Weber (1949) long ago suggested, the knowledge generated by sociological analysis can only be seen as partial knowledge, at best.

A stronger version of postmodernism, though, renders problematic the whole sociological endeavour of explaining 'how society works', at least in terms of causally based concepts of structure. Indeed, postmodernist approaches have not yet shown us a way to analyse societal relationships (such as the dynamics of inequality discussed in this book) that definitively replaces existing approaches. As suggested in the analysis above, postmodern approaches often smuggle in some aspects of classic theory. Currently, the most popular is the notion of global capitalism.

As discussed earlier, the notion of globalization refers to the intensification of links between nations, especially in terms of trade and economic production. Although global links are not new, it is the proliferation and pace of global relations which is seen as a marking a distinct new phase of development. Multinational companies are major drivers here, gobbling up smaller businesses around the world and siting elements of production where labour is cheaper and markets easily accessible. Both capital and labour (in the form of international migration) have become more mobile as MNCs manoeuvre to win out in the context of heightened international competition. The notion of a triumphant globalized capitalism overcoming all alternatives (such as the state socialisms of China and Russia) and pulling in all the nations in the world has been the predominant vision of the 1990s and 2000s.

This period has seen the ideology of market dominance accepted even in the social democratic countries of the EU. While nations remain distinct in their cultural, social and political goals, by and large all nations accept the economic parameters of *neoliberalism*, the doctrine that accompanies globalization. As the name implies, neoliberalism could be viewed as a return to the old 'liberal' principles of nineteenth-century capitalism, only now on a global basis. It therefore puts into reverse many of the features of organized capitalism (discussed above), such as welfarism, corporatist decision-making and state ownership of infrastructure (railways, utilities) and sections of the economy (mining, steel). Harvey (2005) defines neoliberalism as the belief that market exchange is in itself a beneficial ethical process which should be allowed to drive all economic action, free from interference or external regulation. These policies were instituted in the 1980s in Britain by Margaret Thatcher's government, but were only slightly modified by New Labour when it came to power. However, the Coalition government of Cameron and Clegg took things much further than Thatcher dared to go, with a determined programme of privatization, backed by denunciation of the public sector and state involvement in the economy. Characteristics of neoliberal economic policy, as practiced in the UK, USA, Australia and elsewhere, include: the removal of barriers which restrict free operation of the market; deregulation of the economy; cutting the cost of the welfare state so it does not place a burden on private

enterprise; privatization (or denationalization) of public services; promoting an ethic of individual responsibility which undermines collective action (linking here with the theory of reflexive individualism).
Thus, Pierre Bourdieu (1998) describes neoliberalism as a programme
for destroying collective structures that may impede the pure market
logic. This would include trade unions, which are seen as enemies of
free choice and individual rights. In 2014, after a series of one-day
strikes by public-sector workers organized by the Trade Union
Congress (TUC) and a number of individual unions, David Cameron
announced his intention to limit the legal right of unions to strike.

Abercrombie and Warde define globalization as 'Processes operating on an emergent global level which over time are compressing the
distances between people and places within different societies and
which increase the sense that we live in a single world' (2000, p. 13).
This illustrates the fact that globalization is not just an economic
phenomenon, but something with social, political and cultural dimensions which affects all of us in our everyday lives. Consider the way
that YouTube and Facebook allow you to enter into discussion, and
share ideas, sounds and images with people in countries around the
globe in a way that would have been unimaginable in your parents'
youth. Similarly the reorganizing of capitalism on a global basis
affects all of us, changing the nature of jobs available within our own
countries, opening up differing opportunities of travel and jobs elsewhere around the world, changing the timing of work as new services
evolve, and the nature of consumerism as we learn more about products from other countries.

Conclusions

This chapter has reviewed a number of theoretical approaches that
can be employed in seeking to understand the nature of contemporary
societies. I have outlined the main features of each position and indicated the implications of each for the analysis of social divisions.

I have argued that, because these positions derive from classical
sociological theories, or were elaborated in opposition to them,
within most of them economic relationships emerge as the most
important source of social division, even where the conceptualization
of class is explicitly challenged. Other forms of social division are
sometimes addressed in terms of the concept of 'new social movements', which are seen to arise to fill the gap as class consciousness
is weakened and collective action based on class becomes less significant. But even here, new social movements are generally seen as a

substitute for class; they do not emerge from the 'logic of the system' as do class divisions – they are contingent, rather than necessary.

Postmodern theory goes furthest in moving away from the old economic frameworks, but I have argued that the postmodern approach does not in itself lead to any clear account of social structures or social divisions. Theorists of postmodernity tend to draw upon other theoretical positions, such as post-industrialism (Lyotard) or capitalism (Jameson and Bauman), for their account of social relationships, as opposed to cultural change. An economic orientation creeps back in by the side door. Accounts employing concepts such as multiple identities and focusing on consumption, mass media and information technologies move beyond economism, but remain at the level of speculation and assertion. Postmodernism offers the promise of a plural account of inequality which it has not yet fulfilled.

It can be argued, therefore, that the labour/capital relationship is still a central feature of modern Western societies. Such societies are therefore still capitalist, although it is clear that class relations have changed since Marx wrote his account of capitalism. I suggest that globalized and reorganized capitalism, along with the changing nature of the international division of labour, has produced new configurations of class in both the West and the developing world, as will be discussed in the next chapter

However, economic relationships, of whatever kind, do not constitute the totality of social relationships. There is a general problem in the use of terms such as 'capital*ism*', 'post-industrial*ism*', 'moder-n*ity*' – even 'postmodern*ity*' – which convey the idea of totality. Behind such terms lurks the recurrent sociological image of societies as self-sufficient social systems, which inevitably involves exclusions. The feminist term 'patriarchy' raises exactly the same problems. To describe Britain as 'a patriarchy' inverts Marxism and elevates gender divisions above class and ethnicity. Any system theory will marginalize many important aspects of social reality.

That is why in this book I have used the idea of 'sets of relationships' as a way to conceptualize social order and structuration. While such an approach lacks the appealing clarity, the hard-edged quality, of the system concept, it avoids the closure and exclusions which systems theory involves. Social reality can be made up of an infinite number of interconnected sets of relations. Nor is there any implication, as with the concept of system, that relationships are fixed or that they need to replicate themselves in an identical form; the fuzzier concept of sets of relations is thus better able than the concept of system to cope with change. To put it in another way, it is compatible with a view of reality as process rather than structure. This approach acknowledges the salience of some of the postmodern criticisms of traditional accounts of social structure, while retaining the idea of societies as orderly. But the order constantly shifts and is then reorganized

The next four chapters look at social divisions in terms of four sets of social relationships: class, gender, 'race'/ethnicity and age. I start with class, following my assertion that the notion of a reorganizing global capitalism is useful to explain aspects of social inequalities. Economic relationships dominate our lives, whether in periods of boom, such as the late 1990s or early 2000s, or in an economic downturn such as the credit crunch and recession of 2007–8. Governments are elected to manage the economy. The success of societies and the wellbeing of their citizens is linked *by us as social members* to the efficiency of the economy and the level of material prosperity. Economic considerations are viewed as predominant in managing processes of change in our social institutions. Market principles have now been firmly introduced into all layers of the education system, for example. Economic change, ever more rapid as new technologies transform processes of production and consumption, produces new social configurations of 'winners and losers'. Paradoxically, while at the individual level people are less clear about their class locations and may even deny them, at the societal level we see the economy as increasingly determining every aspect of our lives.

Thinking Points

• Is capitalism better described as organized, disorganized or reorganized?
• Can we pick and choose our identities?
• Are we becoming rootless nomads?

4

The Death and Rebirth of Class

'Class began and continued as a muddle' (Phillips, 1987, p. 33). Ann Phillips's remark pithily encapsulates both the complex and shifting nature of class as a set of lived relationships and the difficulty sociologists have had in defining class as a social category. Class is everywhere and it is nowhere. Because it has no very definite physical signs or markers, it is hard to observe. Sociologists argue about where class derives from, where the boundaries between classes lie and how class should be measured. Class has long been central to the sociological endeavor – indeed, Edgell refers to it as 'the most widely used concept in sociology' (Edgell 1993, p. viii). Yet sociologists acknowledge that it is an 'essentially contested concept' – that is, one about which there can never be ultimate agreement because different definitions of class rest upon totally different assumptions (Calvert 1982).

The analysis of class as a sociological concept has historically taken the form of a set of debates, arising from the initial positions staked out by Marx and Weber. As well as continuing disagreements between neo-Marxists and neo-Weberians, Rosemary Crompton pointed to another damaging set of 'pseudo-debates', within British class analysis. She suggested (1993) that a schism had developed between people studying class structure and social mobility using highly sophisticated statistical techniques, and those who focus on class formation and consciousness employing historical or ethnographic approaches. Conflicts between and within these two methodologically opposed camps had led to a stalemate, causing other sociologists to lose interest in class analysis, perceived as increasingly technical and arid. As Marshall comments, preoccupations with redefining occupational

classification schemes encouraged 'taxonomical exercises which tend
to lose sight of the reasons that we should be interested in class
analysis in the first place – to understand...processes and consequences of social inequality' (Marshall 1994, p. 48).

Here I offer a broad definition of class: it is a label applied to a
nexus of unequal lived relationships arising from the social organization of production, distribution, exchange and consumption. These
include: the allocation of tasks in the division of labour (occupation,
employment hierarchies); control and ownership relationships within
production; the unequal distribution of surplus (wealth, income, state
benefits); relationships linked to the circulation of money (markets,
shareholding, investment); patterns of consumption (lifestyle, living
arrangements); and distinctive cultures that arise from all these
(behavioural practices, community relations). Class is a much broader
concept, then, than occupational structure, though the latter is often
taken as a measure of it.

This chapter will argue for the persistence and centrality of class
relations through notable periods of change. However, in the 1980s
and 1990s, some sociologists argued that class was of declining relevance in a service-based post-industrial society. A controversial book
by Jan Pakulski and Malcolm Waters was entitled *The Death of Class*
(1996). The authors argued that a wealth of other forms of social
identity, many generated by consumerism and affluence, had brought
an end to any sense of class, while occupational change and social
mobility had broken up traditional communities with their class
loyalties. It was possible to argue this in a period marked by prosperity and what I later labelled 'a climate of equality' (Bradley 1999b)
in which people seemed to assert their rights to be treated as individuals, not on the basis of their social origins or places in the dynamics
of stratification. At that time, there was a tendency to argue that even
the traditionally class-ridden UK was moving towards classlessness,
while in the USA a discourse on class was secondary to anxieties
around racial divisions.

The idea of 'classlessness' was not a new one. Indeed, it seems that
as soon as forms of inequality such as class are 'discovered' by
researchers, people start to proclaim their disappearance! The uncovering by feminists in the 1970s and 1980s of all sorts of inequalities
between the sexes in modern society was rapidly followed by declara-
tions that we live in a 'post-feminist' society in which gender inequality is a thing of the past. The imminent death of class has often been
pronounced. In the Victorian era, this was linked to the now unfashionable idea of 'progress'. The Victorians believed that the advances
of science, technology and knowledge, linked to economic growth,

were leading to a steady improvement in the social condition which would usher in a 'new age' of equality and prosperity. Similarly, in the twentieth century, the period of economic expansion and affluence after the Second World War led some sociologists to develop the notion of 'embourgeoisement': that is, the idea that the working classes were being absorbed into the middle classes and adopting middle-class lifestyles. While there might be a small powerful economic elite at the top and a small disadvantaged group at the bottom, the majority of the British populace, it was argued, could be seen as a homogenized mass living in relative affluence.

Although the embourgeoisement theory fell into disrepute during the 1970s, with the advent of mass unemployment, the idea of classlessness resurfaced in the 1980s. This time the focus was less on equalization of living standards, and more on the idea that economic opportunities were open to all, regardless of birth, background or educational qualifications. John Major's election to Prime Minister was seen to symbolize this trend, as Major came from an unorthodox family background (his father was said once to have been a circus artiste), had attended a state school and had not been to university. Major himself frequently proclaimed his attachment to the notion of a classless society and his government's attempts to promote it. At issue here was not really a society without classes but a meritocracy, a society in which access to social rewards is determined by the talents and achievements of individuals, not their background. Looking back, there is an interesting contrast with our current government, with a cabinet packed with Old Etonians and millionaires, such as David Cameron, George Osborne and Boris Johnson.

While most British sociologists rejected the idea of classlessness, there was certainly what Woodward et al. describe as a 'reorientation of emphasis and a move from class as central to sociological critiques' (2014: 427). Attention to other forms of inequality combined with the postmodern critiques of structural theories to push class from the centre of the stage. Postmodernist thinking challenged traditional Marxist class theory, seen to ignore other dynamics of inequality and reduce the multiplicity of social positionings to its single 'metanarrative' theme of the antagonism between capital and labour: 'the monologic concept of class struggle is inadequate to the plurality of conflicts at work in contemporary society' (Mercer 1990, p. 48). As O'Neill (1995) points out, some postmodernists simply ignored class. Others suggested that, as the postmodern phase developed, class identities would be replaced by 'a mosaic of multiple status identities' (Crook et al. 1992, p. 133).

In response, class theorists pointed to the persistence of class inequalities, as discussed in chapter 2. Although, as we have seen, things have got worse since then, even in the prosperous 1990s there was plenty of evidence of gaps of wealth and income between the classes. The Rowntree Report of 1995 revealed that inequalities in Britain were increasing at a rate faster than in any other industrial country. A report for the Institute of Fiscal Studies found that one-fifth of the British population were living below the Council of Europe's poverty line – over 11 million people – compared with the century's lowest number of 3 million in 1977. Over the thirty-year period from 1961 to 1991, the share of national income of the poorest tenth of the population fell from 4.2 to 3.0 per cent, while the richest tenth increased their share from 22 to 25 per cent (Goodman and Webb 1994). Moreover, the 1980s and 1990s witnessed a series of scandals about the enormous increases in salaries of entrepreneurs and 'chief executives'. For example, a survey of top executives' pay in 1994 revealed an average annual rise of nearly 25 per cent; the top directors of Warburg (the merchant banking firm), Barclays and the Royal Bank of Scotland received rises of around 200 per cent, in a year when many employees in banking and finance had been made redundant (including many staff at Barclays). Men at the top of such successful capitalist enterprises may be earning salaries of over £1 million a year. Such evidence suggested that class inequalities were actually increasingly significant, rather than disappearing.

This chapter surveys the debates on class, particularly in the light of contemporary changes. It starts with a brief account of changing class relations in Britain, reviews classic class theories, before considering the challenges from post-industrialism and postmodernism, and then discusses what has been called the 'new sociology of class', strongly influenced by the work of Pierre Bourdieu.

Classes Old and New

Marx developed his account of capitalist class relationships in the context of industrialization and the upheavals that accompanied it. Many ordinary people feared and resented the destruction of old ways of living and imposition of new forms of work organization. Loss of agricultural jobs and the decay of traditional craft-based systems of production would eventually force most male labourers into the factory system, but at first this change was resisted. The period of industrialization in Britain was a time of social and industrial conflict, marked by strikes, demonstrations, machine-breaking, riots, petitions to parliament, along with political campaigns for votes for working men and for regulation of hours and conditions within the factories. Public attention was drawn to the bitter and conflictual relationship between the labouring classes and their masters. It is not surprising that Marx's theorization of the new class relations of industrial societies rested on these two groups. It also reflected a longstanding perception of the gap between 'the rich' and 'the poor', which persists in popular usage to this day: 'it's the rich that gets the pleasure and the poor that gets the blame!', as the song has it.

Weber and Durkheim were working at a later date, when industrial societies had matured into a more stable state (Giddens 1973). Where relationships between the classes appeared more settled and harmonious, attention was diverted to the various gradations within classes and allied forms of status distinction (Briggs 1974). In such a context, Weber was able to develop his more sophisticated account of a plurality of classes, and Durkheim to suggest that the social division of labour had a positive integrating function. As industrial production became more technically sophisticated and firms became larger, bureaucracy and the employment of specialized staff expanded. Such developments are reflected in Weber's interest in the growing size of the middle classes.

Marx and Weber between them laid the ground for an account of what we might call the 'traditional class structure' that developed with industrialization. Post-war sociologists of class tended to adopt a three-class model of upper (or capitalist) class, middle class (the heterogeneous white-collar groupings) and manual working class (for example, Giddens 1973). Research was especially concerned with the 'traditional' working class, the core of which was manual workers from heavy industries. On the basis of occupations such as mining, shipbuilding, foundry work or textile production, stable working-class communities in specific residential areas had evolved with their own distinctive cultures. A sense of solidarity and class membership was imputed to the traditional working class, manifested, for example, in union membership and voting for the Labour party. Their experience and culture cut them off sharply from the other social groupings; they led 'a life apart' (Meacham, 1977). Although it is suggested that this vision of a solidaristic united working class is romanticized (Marshall et al. 1988), studies testified to the existence of communities displaying some of these characteristics (Dennis et al. 1956; Blackwell and Seabrook 1985). In the post-war period, however, better-off workers in newer industries developed more materialistic lifestyles and privatized values, moving into new suburban housing areas, as described in the *Affluent Worker* studies (Goldthorpe et al. 1969).

Gradually this class model was cast in doubt by the expansion of service employment. The traditional working class and the affluent workers were both said to be in decline. The attention of sociologists shifted towards the middle classes, while new classes were identified as arising from the demise of the traditional working-class; these included an expanding self-employed group, the growing body of people dependent on benefits and often described as the 'underclass', and, in the twenty-first century, a group of people, including benefit claimants but also low-waged and insecure workers, labelled the 'precariat' because of the insecurity and volatility of its economic situation.

As we have seen in previous chapters, there has been considerable change in the nature of British society since the Second World War: the decay of industrial employment; women's changing labour market position; the collapse of established working-class communities; attempts to dismantle the welfare state; the globalization of economic relations; the dominance of neoliberal policies; and the changes brought by digital technologies. Can traditional class theory cope with these changes in the 'lived relationships' of class, or must the old categories be abandoned?

The Classic Inheritance

Three useful texts on class assert, in different ways, the continuing viability of the concepts derived from classic class theories. Richard Scase's study of class (1992) is a defence of Marxism. Scase operates with the traditional Marxian distinction between 'class in itself' (the existence of objective class relations which individuals may or may not be aware of) and 'class for itself' (the development of a common sense of class awareness among class members). For Scase, basic antagonistic capitalist class relations as described by Marx still generate patterns of inequality, although he accepts that many people demonstrate little awareness of class. Stephen Edgell advocates an approach which combines elements from Marx and Weber (property ownership and market divisions). He states that, taken together, the two 'provide the essential conceptual tools for analysing contemporary class structures' (Edgell 1993, p. 15). Finally, Peter Saunders calls for a re-examination of the 'long-neglected' functionalist theory, suggesting that it shows us that class divisions are not necessarily a 'bad thing' (1990, p. 130). The fact that all these writers emphasize the continuing relevance of classic theories more than 100 years after Marx wrote *Das Kapital* shows how powerful the original insights were. It is still impossible to review theories of class without considering the influential classic legacy.

Marx's theory of class has already been touched on in chapter 2. He believed that each 'mode of production' produced characteristic class relationships, involving a dominating and a subordinate class. These two classes were linked together in a relationship of exploitation, in which the subordinate class provided the labour that generated a social surplus and the dominant class then appropriated the surplus. Under the feudal system, which preceded capitalism, surplus was secured by the legal power of the feudal lords over the serfs and peasants who worked on their lands. Legal power could be reinforced by violence and repression if the peasantry resisted handing over the surplus produce. Under capitalism, the extraction of surplus is managed more subtly, through the mechanism of the wage. The wage is only equivalent to some of the value of the work performed by the labourer; the remaining 'surplus value' is taken by the capitalist in the form of profits. What is going on is concealed from the labourers under the idea of 'a fair wage for a fair day's work'. Thus, in a capitalist society, the power and wealth of the dominant class are seen as legitimate, rather than simply backed by coercion as they were in feudal societies.

The typical class relations of a capitalist society involve the private ownership of the 'means of production' (factories, land, machines, tools) by the capitalist class. The labourers own nothing but their labour power (capacity to labour) which they sell in the 'free' market for a wage. Wage labourers are peculiarly powerless and vulnerable, dependent on their employers for subsistence, and with minimum autonomy over their work. Capitalism produces a relationship of mutual dependence between the bourgeoisie and the proletariat (without labourers, capitalists cannot make profit), which is also inherently antagonistic: the interests of the two main classes are opposed. Marx believed that various tendencies in capitalism would promote class conflict. The progressive development of technology would bring deskilling of jobs, creating a more homogenized and potentially united labour force; the relative gap in wealth between the dominant and subordinate classes would steadily increase; and processes of capital accumulation and competition would generate periods of recession and unemployment. Such factors would combine to produce ever more extreme 'crises' of capitalism, generating heightened class conflict and eventually social revolution.

This idea of class polarization, which Marx set out in the *Communist Manifesto*, contributes to the perception that Marx's theory of class is essentially a dichotomous one. However, in his more historical and descriptive writings, Marx referred to many other classes in capitalist society, such as peasants and aristocracy (remnants of feudalism), the petite bourgeoisie (small owners and the self-employed) and the lumpenproletariat, something similar to the 'underclass' or what are contemptuously referred to in popular parlance as 'chavs'.

In the *Communist Manifesto*, Marx and Engels suggested that these middle groupings would be absorbed into the two major classes. However, the *Manifesto* was an early and highly polemical piece. In a later work, *Theories of Surplus Value*, Marx wrote of the growth of what we now call the new middle classes: managers, technicians, professionals and bureaucrats. Marx called them the 'surplus class' as they worked for capitalists but, unlike the working class, they did not produce surplus value. Instead, their salaries were paid out of the surplus. Capitalists were prepared to yield some of their profits for this as the surplus class performed very useful services for them, helping to keep the proletariat in order. Marx labelled them the 'flunkeys, bootlickers and retainers of capitalism' (Nicolaus 1967). However, Marx can be criticized for his failure to perceive the growing social and economic significance of this new middle class. The major focus of Marx's interest was in the overarching relationship between capital and labour; it was this relationship that, for Marx, determined the shape of the class structure as a whole and provided the axis for conflict. This remains a defining feature of Marxist class theory and is rejected by Weberian opponents.

The other most controversial feature of Marx's class theory is the notion of class struggle and the socialist revolution, which Weberians question. Weber believed a socialist revolution was an unlikely outcome, and, if it did occur, it would not improve the lot of ordinary citizens but would lead to heightened bureaucracy and tyranny (as in Soviet Russia). He also felt that economic conflicts did not occur around a single axis, but were complex and as likely to occur within classes as between them. History has vindicated Weber, in the sense that most working-class people have not espoused the socialist ideal or acted as the 'revolutionary actor' envisaged by Marx. Even Scase, a contemporary supporter of Marx, accepts that this part of Marx's theory is untenable; the course of historical events in the twentieth century has been to discredit attempts to construct socialist alternatives: 'To share with Marx his ideas for abolishing class must, towards the end of the twentieth century, be seen as Utopian...It is the rise and fall of state socialism which the twentieth century has witnessed rather than the demise of capitalism. The question is no longer whether or not capitalism but of what variety or type' (Scase 1992, p. 89).

The continuing appeal of Marxian theory lies in the fact that he provided such a systematic account of the origins and basis of class divisions. However, those parts of his theory that deal with class consciousness and class action are seen to be flawed, 'the weakest link in the chain' (Lockwood 1988). Moreover, as discussed in chapter 2, Marx's framework cannot deal adequately with other dimensions of inequality. To conceptualize a society as a 'mode of production' is inevitably to privilege economic relations over other aspects of inequality.

Weber set out a more potentially open-ended framework for studying inequality. His class theory used to be presented as in opposition to Marx; nowadays, we tend to view it as an extension (Edgell 1993). Weber accepted some aspects of Marxian theory, especially the notions of the broad cleavage in society between the owners of the means of production and the 'propertyless classes'. But he also emphasized the divisions within both propertied and propertyless groupings. The propertied were split according to what kind of property they possessed (for example landowners, major entrepreneurs, small family businesses, financial speculators, rentiers), distinctions still useful today. The propertyless were divided in terms of what they had to offer in the market. Some had credentials and qualifications, others had apprenticeships and craft experience, others nothing but sheer physical labour power. Followed through, this could lead to an almost infinite plurality of propertyless groupings, each with its distinct market offering. But most neo-Weberians accept a fundamental distinction between mental labourers (offering credentials like university degrees and professional training) and manual workers. Weber, with his interest in bureaucracy, focused strongly on white-collar groupings, but rather than seeing them as servants of capitalism as Marx had done he emphasized that they too were deprived of ownership, in their case of the means of bureaucratic production; as we so often observe when we deal with bureaucrats such as local government officers, these workers do not create the rules, they just have to apply them – often rather mindlessly!

Weber's concepts are the base for theories of class fragmentation. This is reflected in Weberian thinking about class action, which focuses on a plurality of competitive struggles between and within class groupings. There is no single dynamic of class struggle and so no thrust towards the demise of capitalism. Instead, differing interest groups will continuously compete for a better deal within the system. Often such conflicts take the form of exclusionary practices, by which groups fight to keep lower-qualified or lesser skilled groups from their section of the market (Parkin 1979). Like Marx, Weber saw economic relations as inherently conflictual, but felt such conflicts could be accommodated within a democratic pluralist system.

The other great advance of Weber's class analysis was to consider the interaction of class with other dimensions of stratification. Weber described stratification in general terms as related to 'the distribution of power within a community' (Gerth and Mills 1970, p. 181). As well as economic power (class), Weber drew attention to 'status' (social prestige) and 'party' as two other aspects of power. Party, which refers to political dimensions of power, is the least developed of Weber's three categories. It seems to refer to a variety of groupings, including, but not confined to, those we now refer to as political parties, which mobilize for political power and influence. This notion challenges the Marxian view of political power as ultimately derived from economic power. It is possible for members of the economically subordinate classes to mobilize successfully and procure political resources, either through their own distinct organizations (trade unions and Labour parties) or by participating in political movements of other groupings. For example, working-class people may join a party associated with the dominant political class (such as the Conservative party) and use it to gain resources for themselves.

Weber argued that, in any given society, class, status and party relationships could be found cross-cutting each other. It was a matter of historical context which form of stratification would be dominant, although he suggested that in stable times status came to the fore, while class interests would predominate at times of social upheaval. Thus, Weber moved beyond a position that inevitably privileges economic relationships.

The appeal of Weberian class analysis and his understanding of the politics of capitalism rests in its pluralism and its acknowledgement of the complexity of lived social relationships. Current thinking on social divisions, with its stress on diversity and fragmentation, seems more compatible with a Weberian approach. However, until the recent ascendancy of Pierre Bourdieu's approach to class, debates between followers of Marx and of Weber shaped sociologists' work in this area.

The Legacy of Marx: The Struggle Continues

The broad objective of neo-Marxian class theorists was to adapt the principles of Marxian analysis to produce a model or 'map' of the class structure which better fitted contemporary societies. While recognizing the limitations of Marx's original account, neo-Marxists retained some of its key features: the assumption that class is based in relations of production; the concept of exploitation; the concentration on capital and labour as the two most significant classes; the notion of class conflict and class struggle.

Neo-Marxist class analysis is often quite abstract and has been marked by complex theoretical disagreements, which are well summarized in a number of studies (for example, Parkin 1979; Abercrombie and Urry 1983; Crompton 1993) and are not considered here. Instead, I discuss some strands of neo-Marxist theory which appear currently relevant: the idea of a 'ruling' class; the proletarianization thesis; and the notion of 'contradictory class locations'.

The Ruling Class?

An important distinguishing feature of Marxist class theory is a continuing interest in the capitalist class. By contrast, much Weberian class analysis has been based on survey data, in which the numbers of capitalist owners are too small to merit much discussion. As a result, Weberian theory focuses very much on the next group in the hierarchy, which Goldthorpe calls the 'service class' or 'salariat' (2000). Most Weberians acknowledge that a capitalist elite exists, but it tends to slip out of sight in their writings. For Marxists, however, the continued existence, and indeed increasing power, of the capitalist class is still perhaps the most crucial feature of the contemporary class dynamic.

John Scott, although himself an advocate of a Weberian approach (Scott 2000), has conducted a series of important studies of the dominant economic and social groupings in Britain, defined by ownership and control of corporate wealth (1979, 1982, 1991). This 'inner circle' (Useem 1984) of individuals and families is tightly linked together by common social background, shared educational experience (attendance at public schools and 'Oxbridge' colleges) and intermarriage. It is also linked through complex arrangements of shareholding and through the institution of 'interlocking directorates' whereby powerful entrepreneurs have seats on the boards of a number of companies. Such links maintain the economic and social dominance of the class and help it to secure disproportionate political power. This group is closely allied with the British Conservative party, through both family and business links. Scott concludes: 'Britain is ruled by a capitalist class whose economic dominance is sustained by the operations of the state and whose members are disproportionately represented in the power elite which rules the state apparatus. That is to say, Britain does have a ruling class' (1991, p. 151).

The ruling class may be divided into fractions (finance capital versus industrial capital, big business versus small and medium-sized firms). Despite these internal divisions, the power of the capitalist class is seen as increasing not waning. Coates (1989) described the British ruling class as being of 'immense political sophistication' (p. 43) and as 'one with truly hegemonic power' (p. 20), able to persuade the majority of the people that its interests are legitimate and represent those of the nation as a whole. He concluded that 'in the battle between the classes it has so far taken all the honours' (p. 43). Since Coates was writing, the ruling class has consolidated its power more fully through its global reach, with the 'super rich' discussed in earlier chapters at its core.

A Changing Proletariat?

Bottomore and Brym (1989) link this increased capitalist power to the waning of the working class. In every advanced capitalist society, the growth of service employment has brought a decrease in jobs in manufacturing, diminishing the numbers of the factory-based proletariat. Esping-Andersen summarizes: 'the older cornerstone of class theory, the industrial working class, is in rapid decline' (1993, p. 7). This is the kernel of post-industrial theory.

However, neo-Marxists reject the notion of post-industrialism and argue that the working class is not vanishing but changing in composition. Because capitalist development is so dynamic, we can expect that the main classes will be in a process of constant transformation. It is suggested that we are continually witnessing the 'remaking' of the working class (Blackwell and Seabrook 1985; Clarke and Critcher 1985). Low-paid unskilled service employment can be seen as the basis for this emergent new proletariat. Seabrook (1988) explored a 'new servant class' which is developing to cater for the needs of the capitalists and the 'yuppie' section of the middle classes: an army of nannies, cleaners, caterers, beauticians, leisure specialists, tutors, coaches and so forth. In the latest version of this, Guy Standing (2011) has popularized the idea of the 'precariat', a class of growing global significance: a mass of people employed in insecure, unregulated employment, lacking any employment protection. The precariat derives from employers' search for 'flexibility'; it consists of people on low wages, irregular contracts, who drift in and out of employment, may be employed in the illegal or 'black economy', have spells on benefits and generally face economic instability and precarity. The increased number of people on 'zero hours contracts' that offer no guarantee of fixed hours of work in any week is an example of what Standing is talking about.

These latest developments can be related to the older idea of 'proletarianization', derived originally from Marx's discussion of polarization. In the early twentieth century, Klingender applied it to clerical workers. He argued (1935) that the traditional status and skills associated with office work in the nineteenth century were disappearing; the job conditions and pay of clerks were now little different from those of factory workers. Klingender's ideas were criticized by Weberians, notably by David Lockwood in *The Black-Coated Worker* (1958). Lockwood revealed many continuing differences in the market situation and job conditions of clerks and factory workers: clerks had better chances of promotion, more fringe benefits, more autonomy at work and were more closely linked to managers. Above all, Lockwood suggested that the status gap between office work and 'dirty' factory jobs was noticeable: clerks considered themselves 'a cut above' manual labourers, and factory workers despised clerks as effete and parasitic 'pen-pushers'.

Despite the Weberian critique, the proletarianization thesis has been constantly revived and applied to other groups of workers, such as public-sector employees, whose autonomy and pay have been subject to curbs since the Thatcher years. Its best-known proponent was Harry Braverman (1974), who argued that new technology was being used to degrade the labour process. In his view, computerized office systems had reduced this mental labour to little better than automatic manual work. Braverman anticipated that other white-collar groups would eventually be subject to this downward pull, seeing proletarianization and degradation as inherent tendencies in a capitalist production system. While Weberians have continued to resist this position, many Marxists view lower white-collar groupings as part of the working class. It is also the case that, in the twenty-first century, white-collar workers and even professionals (such as temporary university lecturers) make up part of Standing's precariat (Bradley 2014)

Many of these jobs are filled by women, by migrant workers or by young people. This illustrates the interaction of class with other dynamics of inequality. The original Marxist version of the proletariat often seemed to refer only to male manual workers. We now accept that the working class has two sexes. But this raises questions about the composition of the working class that are not easily answered within the Marxian framework, which links class to production and wage labour. How do we incorporate women working at home in domestic labour into this class 'map'? The retired? The unemployed? We shall return to this issue, but note that this need not invalidate the idea of a 'new working class'.

Between Capital and Labour: Contradictory Class Locations

While lower-grade non-manual workers may be viewed as proletarians, there remains the broader problem of how to fit the heterogeneous groupings of the new middle classes into a model of the class structure. What can connect a lawyer, an airline pilot, an actor, a nurse, a teacher, a business manager and the whole mix of occupations that fall under the umbrella of 'white-collar work'? At what point exactly does the cut-off point between them and the working class occur?

One solution offered by neo-Marxists is the idea of 'structurally ambiguous' or 'contradictory' class locations (Wright 1976; Carchedi 1977; Crompton and Gubbay 1977). The middle classes are half-way between capitalists and proletariat, sharing some aspects of the class situation of each group. Like the proletariat, they need to sell their wage labour, are barred from ultimate procedures of decision-making and contribute to the process of realizing profits for capital. But they have much more autonomy over the day-to-day features of their jobs; as Marx's notion of the surplus class implied, they also help capitalists to secure profits by keeping wage labourers in order. They are, at the same time, exploited wage-labourers and the allies of capital. The higher up the white-collar hierarchy, the more they fall into the latter category.

An influential account of contradictory locations was provided by Eric Ohlin Wright (1976). Wright's original model involved the identification of three main class positions: the capitalists, the working class and the petite bourgeoisie. Between each pair of these lies a set of contradictory locations: small employers between capitalists and petite bourgeoisie; semi-autonomous employees, such as craftsmen or artists, between the working class and petite bourgeoisie; and a range of white-collar employees (managers, technicians and supervisors) between capital and labour. Wright distinguished these groups in terms of how much control they exercised over the production process, with the working class lacking all control, the capitalists all-powerful, and other groups having varying degrees of control.

Wright's ingenious model has been criticized by some neo-Marxists because it neglects the key issue of exploitation and surplus value. However, in a revised version, Wright faced up to this criticism. In this model, class locations are distinguished on the basis of different forms of ownership: of property and, among the propertyless, of organizational assets (positions of power) or of skills and credentials. The 'polar classes' are the bourgeoisie (owning property) and the proletarians (owning nothing). The other groups have varying degrees of organizational assets and skills. For example 'uncredentialled managers' have powerful positions in companies but no qualifications, and 'experts' have qualifications but no organizational assets (Wright 1985). Wright believes this schema restores the notion of exploitation. However, the stress on divisions among the propertyless groups and the importance placed on assets have led Savage et al. (1992) to label Wright 'a closet Weberian'. In fact, Wright's work seems to me an appealing fusion of ideas from Marx and from Weber.

Indeed, as Edgell claims, 'there has always been an overlap between the Marxian and Weberian conceptualizations of class' (Edgell 1993, p. 36). However, this discussion has attempted to highlight the distinctive features of the neo-Marxist approach. First, there is a much stronger stress on the centrality of the capitalist class. Second, the focus is still firmly on the two main classes, as identified by Marx. The position of the middle classes is defined in relation to these 'polar' groups. Third, the goal of neo-Marxist theorists is to provide an account of the structure of class locations, 'empty slots' in Esping-Andersen's phrase (1993, p. 226). They are not very concerned about how individuals are allocated to them, whereas such a concern is central to the neo-Weberian approach.

The Legacy of Weber: Flux and Fragmentation

The more complex, pluralistic vision of neo-Weberianism appears to fit better with contemporary perceptions of change and fragmentation. The title of Erikson and Goldthorpe's book *The Constant Flux* (1992) nicely encapsulates the paradoxical perceptions of the Weberian approach: that class inequalities do persist, but at the same time class relations are fluid and open. This leads to some crucial concerns different from those of Marxism: social mobility; fragmentation; and the role of the middle classes.

Social Mobility: An Open Society?

The Weberian interest in social mobility – that is, the movement of individuals between different classes – might be linked back to Weber's own statement that sociological explanation should be adequate at the level of meaning as well as causally adequate. Consequently, Weberians are interested in studying actors' perceptions as well as structures. What does class mean in people's lives? Weberian class theorists have produced many useful empirical studies, such as the *Affluent Worker* studies (Goldthorpe et al. 1969) or the Nuffield mobility surveys (Halsey et al. 1980), which deal with class consciousness and with mobility.

While Marxists have neglected the study of social mobility, Weberians argue that it has a strong effect on how people view class divisions. If a class structure is open, class will be invested with less hostile meanings and the pattern of stratification will be seen as legitimate. For example, Blau and Duncan, who studied mobility in the United States, suggested that 'the stability of American democracy is undoubtedly related to the superior chances of upward mobility in this country' (1967, p. 439). In the case of Britain, John Goldthorpe (1980) claimed that mobility had significant effects on class development. He described the intermediate groupings as classes 'of low classness', because there is so much movement in and out of them, while the relative infrequency of downward mobility in Britain fostered the development of a 'mature' working class.

There is debate about the extent of mobility in Britain. Glass's early study (1954) suggested that mobility in Britain was mainly short-range (such as from factory work to clerical work) and that the elite was more or less self-recruiting. Goldthorpe's later research found considerable evidence of long-term mobility. However, he argued this could be explained by changes in the occupational structure after the Second World War. Expansion of service-class jobs had necessitated the recruitment of people of lower-class origin – in other words, the whole occupational structure had taken a kind of upward heave. Goldthorpe (1980) referred to this as 'absolute mobility', but argued that the chances of a member of the working classes reaching high-level jobs had not increased relative to those of people from higher classes. His research continues to confirm this and shows that, without upward occupational shifts, mobility is limited.

Nonetheless, many individuals in the post-war decades experienced mobility, especially because of the expansion of higher education. A study of families in Bristol, *Ordinary Lives*, revealed a common pattern of movement from agricultural and factory work into professional or white-collar work over three generations (Atkinson and Bradley 2013). Moreover, even those still in manual work had aspirations for their children to achieve upward mobility through going to university. Ironically, these heightened aspirations have developed at a time when social mobility in Britain has apparently stalled (Milburn 2012).

Fragmentation: The Break-Up of Traditional Classes

The notion of fragmentation arises directly from Weber's pluralistic model. Dahrendorf's account of class fragmentation was outlined in chapter 1. He suggested that, as a result of these processes of class decomposition, the class struggle between the capitalists and the working class had been defused.

Divisions among the working class were also explored by Lockwood (1975), who identified three different groups, each arising from a distinct social 'milieu'. Traditional proletarians were the classic working class described earlier in the chapter. Close working relationships were the basis of a strong sense of class solidarity and a 'them and us' mentality. The second group, traditional deferential workers, were associated with agricultural work, retail and small businesses. They had personal links with their employers and they accepted social inequalities as legitimated by the superior talents of those at the top of the hierarchy. Finally, Lockwood identified a growing group of privatized or affluent workers, found in the newer consumer industries. Affluent workers were family-orientated, materialistic and individualistic in their attitudes to work. They measured social success in terms of money and access to consumer goods.

Savage et al. have explored fragmentation among the middle class, distinguishing groups on the basis of the different types of asset they possess (property, cultural and organizational). Managerial groups have organizational assets derived from their place in the employment hierarchy. Professional groups have cultural capital (especially credentials) and some property in the form of housing. The self-employed possess capital. Savage et al. suggested that a new political schism had appeared among the middle classes, 'between a public sector, professional, increasingly female middle class ... opposed to an entrepreneurial, private sector, propertied middle class' (1992, p. 218).

Two influential accounts have been sketched out here, but there are many different ways in which class groupings can be seen as fragmented. Classes are split by region, public- or private-sector membership, gender or ethnic origin, among other things. But Weberians have been most concerned with occupational differences, as is reflected in their interest in the middle classes.

The Middle Classes: Service and Intermediate

Unlike the neo-Marxists, Weberians see the divide between manual and non-manual work as being still significant, while conceding the heterogeneity of white-collar occupations. A particularly influential account of the middle groupings is offered by John Goldthorpe, whose various classificatory systems continue to be the basis for much empirical research. A widely used schema devised by him is an eleven-class model (Goldthorpe and Heath 1992). He suggested, however, that the eleven classes can be aggregated into three: the service class, the intermediate groupings and the working class.

The service class includes managers, administrators and professionals (the wage-earning elite) and also 'large proprietors'. By combining these, Goldthorpe seems to be glossing over the original distinction between the propertied and the propertyless made by Weber. This move negates the importance and distinctiveness of capitalists as the socially dominant group. However, if proprietors are left aside, most would accept that the service groups identified by Goldthorpe are in a position of economic privilege.

Below them is the less coherent group of intermediate workers, in which Goldthorpe includes small owners, farmers, foremen, routine non-manual workers or service workers. Many of these groups are seen by Marxists as proletarianized. While Goldthorpe maintains that the intermediate groupings have distinct work and market positions, he acknowledges the amorphous nature of this group and the fact that individuals are frequently moving in and out of these occupational sectors. Evidence from the USA and Canada shows that lower-grade service jobs are characteristically filled by young people and students at the start of their careers, who may eventually end up in the service class (Myles et al. 1993; Jacobs 1993), while in some European societies it is older workers who take these jobs (Esping-Andersen 1993). The intermediate occupations and the individuals who fill them are a kind of social mish-mash; this can be seen as an important source of fragmentation.

The focus on fragmentation enables the neo-Weberian approach to grapple more successfully than Marxism with the complexities of current employment change. However, Weberians share with Marxism a concentration on employment. Both base their analyses of the class structure on an analysis of occupations, whether these are defined in terms of relations of production or the market. This is an important limitation of traditional class theory, which is also a feature of the functionalist approach.

The Functionalist Alternative: A Meritocratic Structure of Inequality?

Functionalist class theory has been more influential in America than in Britain. Its vision of an inherently orderly and harmonious society is out of line with the British perception of marked social inequalities.

The best-known functionalist account of stratification is that of Kingsley Davis and Wilbert Moore (1945). They viewed classes as inevitable and important for society. Espousing the functionalist premise that if social institutions exist they must have some useful function, they argued that economic inequalities serve to make sure that the best-qualified people get the most important jobs. Pay is related to talent and the amount of investment that individuals devote to gaining qualifications and skills. Davis and Moore posited a consensus as to which jobs are the most socially valuable, which means that inequalities are accepted as legitimate. The class system, then, helps societies function efficiently and does not promote antagonism.

The Davis and Moore thesis was much criticized by British sociologists, who argued that it under-played the importance of class conflict. Class relations were still antagonistic, often leading to industrial and political unrest, so that class could not really be viewed as functional for society. Though the functionalist position has had little academic support in Britain, Peter Saunders has defended it, maintaining that British society is essentially meritocratic. He argues (1994) that the existence of long-range upward mobility from the working class, and of downward mobility from the service class, indicates that people get the jobs they deserve. He believes patterns of inequality are not caused by class privilege but by differential distribution of talents to individuals, as measured by IQ testing: 'not everybody is born equal...In a society which is probably much more meritocratic than is generally believed by sociologists, unequal talents do get reflected in unequal rewards' (1994, p. 109).

Saunders's position is close to that described by Edgell as 'multi-class classlessness' which involves 'the equal opportunity to be unequal' (1993, p. 120). This is the kind of 'classlessness' that John Major aspired to for Britain, and that justifies the claim of many Americans that class is not a marked feature of their society. Meritocratic arguments are currently being used to justify the increasing discrepancies of wealth and income in Britain. Many people from elite and middle-class families adhere to the idea of natural abilities which they believe entitle them to educational and economic success, imputing working-class poverty to lack of abilities and laziness. These kinds of popular attitudes are chillingly exposed by Owen Jones in his influential book *Chavs: The Demonization of the Working Class* (2011).

Education is vital to the arguments of both Davis and Moore and Saunders, as they believe that the education system sorts out which people are equipped for particular jobs. Yet research into education has consistently revealed that members of the privileged classes are able to pass on to their children both material and cultural advantages which give them a headstart in life. Middle-class parents can buy into the expensive private education system, which offers smaller classes, better resources and a more firmly academic atmosphere, while working-class children are often handicapped from the start by their parents' lack of resources for educationally useful expenditure and lack of knowledge of the system (Bradley et al. 2014). Recent research has revealed that, motivated by fears of downward mobility, middle-class parents in Britain and America are investing increasing amounts of time and energy into their children's educational progress (coaching and teaching) and out of-school activities (sports, drama, music and so forth) to ensure that they will progress to the best universities (Devine 2004; Vincent and Ball 2006). The ideal of meritocracy is undermined by these inequalities of condition which give advantage to those from richer backgrounds. Indeed, Durkheim, whose theoretical ideas provided the basis for the functionalist perspective, himself argued that a meritocratic division of labour could never be achieved while inequalities of inheritance existed: inequalities in 'the external conditions of competition compromise meritocracy' (1964, p. 379).

All three theoretical camps have one thing in common: the link of class to occupation. While, for the purposes of empirical surveys, it may be useful to take occupation as an indicator of class, there are dangers in reducing class to employment. For one thing, the problems of assigning particular occupations to different classes mean that many findings about 'class' are no more than artifacts of the particular occupational-class schema employed; for example, if clerical workers are assigned to the working class instead of the intermediate class, it will drastically alter findings about the extent of mobility (which will appear much lower) and the proportion of the populace in the working class (which will be much higher). But, more fundamentally, although employment is clearly an important aspect of class experience, it is not co-terminous with it; making class synonymous with occupation presents great problems in classifying individuals who are marginal to production but are still affected by class dynamics. For example, a young school-leaver from a council estate who has never found employment, a widowed pensioner living in a run-down inner-city area and our previously mentioned young single-parent on benefits are all suffering class fates just as much as a male factory worker. This suggests that class is linked to families and communities as well as individual employment; and that broader processes of economic differentiation, involving the creation, exchange and distribution of wealth, must be considered as well as occupation.

Such an approach would be better able to cope with those groups marginalized by the classic models of class (women, especially house-wives; the unemployed; retired people; children; the sick and dis-abled). Are newer approaches to class more able to handle these deficiencies of classic theory?

Newer Directions: Post-Industrial Classes and Postmodern Questioning

Other approaches to class are inspired by the post-industrial and postmodern frameworks. Post-industrial theory was developed as an explicit criticism of Marxist class theory. Daniel Bell (1973) suggested that technological change would bring an upgrading of the occupa-tional structure and a shift to professional work and white-collar work. A new technical and professional elite would emerge, replacing the propertied capitalist class, while most of the population would be in the middle groupings. In addition, the general prosperity that Bell believed would accompany post-industrial change would lead to the remaining manual workers experiencing better working condi-tions, an increased standard of living and enhanced leisure time. In this way, Bell countered Marx's theory of proletarianization and revolution. However, his position seemed invalidated by the spread of mass unemployment in the late 1970s. But, as discussed in chapter 3, a version of Bell's thesis is incorporated into some postmodern visions that assume the growth of highly skilled and professional forms of work resulting from the spread of information technology.

André Gorz provided a bleaker view of the post-industrial future. In *Farewell to the Working Class* (1982), he suggested that, because of the power of new technologies, there was no longer need for all of a society's population to be employed in order to produce the requisite amount of services and goods, a development often referred to as 'jobless growth'. Gorz linked this to the evolution of a new social grouping, the neo-proletariat, made up of unemployed or partly employed people, while the traditional proletariat would dwindle to a small privileged group of full-time workers. Gorz believed these changes had deprived the working class of its tradi-tional role as 'historic actor' in opposition to capital.

What is novel in Gorz's position is the idea of the neo-proletariat. This is an attempt to bring non-employed people into a class model and move beyond the occupational framework of stratifica-tion. Confusingly, Gorz calls the 'neo-proletariat' a 'non-class'; this is because he is using class in the orthodox Marxian sense of relationship to production, and the neo-proletariat has only a minimal one. We could take the logic one step further and suggest that it could be seen as a class if class is defined in terms of distribution, exchange and consumption, as well as production.

The concept of the neo-proletariat bears some resemblances to another concept of class much discussed in the 1980s, that of the 'underclass'. This term, in the sense of a socially marginalized group outside of the traditional class structure, was initially applied the position of Black people in the ghettos of America. However, the idea of some such outsider or outcast group, seen as posing a threat to the social order, is hardly new (Bagguley and Mann 1992; Morris 1994). The Victorians referred to such a group as the 'residuum', and Marx used the term 'lumpenproletariat' in reference to 'the social scum, that passively rotting mass thrown off by the lowest layers of the old society' (quoted Morris 1994, p. 15).

Glasgow (1981) defined the underclass as a group at the bottom of the class hierarchy, permanently trapped and unable to move upwards because it faces multiple disadvantages. Glasgow was referring to the position of African Americans, but the term was controversially applied by Charles Murray to people dependent on benefits for their income. Murray argued that such an underclass existed in the USA and was emerging in 1980s Britain. He linked it to three social phenomena: young single mothers who chose to bring up children on state benefits; young working-class men who rejected work; and the development of a culture of crime among such young men in neighbourhoods where many people depended on benefits (Murray 1984, 1990). He stated that the underclass develops a set of cultural values which differ sharply from those of the rest of society. It is this culture that marks it out: 'Britain has a growing population of working-aged, healthy people, who live in a different world from other Britons, who are raising their children to live in it, and whose values are now contaminating the life of entire neighbourhoods' (1990, p. 4).

Murray's culturally defined version of the underclass has been widely criticized by British sociologists. Some, such as Field (1989) and Dahrendorf (1987), accept the notion of an underclass, but argue that its genesis is structural, the result of government policies leading to long-term unemployment along with poverty for marginalized groups, such as elderly pensioners and sick and disabled people. Others, such as Pilkington (1992) and Dean (1991) reject the notion altogether, calling it a rhetorical device used to blame the disadvantaged for their own plight and distract attention from those really responsible, the government and the capitalist class. Marxists argue that the unemployed are in fact an integral part of the working class. They constitute a 'surplus population' or 'reserve army', a pool of spare labour available to capital. They point out that in times of full employment this pool is absorbed back into the working population

Though both are linked to the growth of long-term unemployment, there are crucial differences between the notion of the underclass and Gorz's account of the neo-proletariat. Rather than being an additional grouping to the working class, the neo-proletariat is seen as gradually replacing it. It is defined structurally (by its exclusion from full-time employment), rather than culturally. There is no association with deviant patterns of behaviour such as scrounging or crime; neo-proletarians are just like everybody else except they are out of a job. Indeed, Gorz at times envisages a potentially positive social role for the neo-proletariat in challenging the materialistic values of a work-based society and promoting new forms of social critique, though he also acknowledges their lack of power and of an organizational base.

Another account of post-industrial change, which steers between extremes of optimism (Bell) and pessimism (Gorz), was offered by Gøsta Esping-Andersen and colleagues (1993). They studied patterns of employment and mobility in six countries, looking for common trends, concluding that 'a distinctive post-industrial class structure may be emerging' (p. 239).

Esping-Andersen drew on Weber and Marx, but suggested that neither Wright nor Goldthorpe went far enough in 'breaking with theoretical orthodoxy' (p. 226). While Marxists and Weberians see classes as deriving directly from market or production relations, he argued that the class dynamic was also determined by a set of crucial social institutions, notably the welfare state, mass education and institutions of collective bargaining. In particular, the state had a key role in shaping class development. In this way, Esping-Andersen acknowledged that economic differences are structured by forces other than production. Another advance was the stress given to gender relations. Esping-Andersen suggested that the traditional sexual division of labour was breaking down and that the post-industrial economy had a 'female bias'. Service jobs were being feminized, and women were crucial to the new occupational hierarchy.

Esping-Anderson et al. posited a new five-tiered post-industrial hierarchy. At the top was a professional elite. At the base a new service proletariat was emerging, such as that identified by Gorz and Seabrook. The case studies showed considerable mobility in and out of unskilled service jobs. In between was a tier of technicians and members of the semi-professions, and a tier of skilled service workers. But, somewhat prophetically perhaps, Esping-Andersen suggested that a future polarization might emerge based on education, with the elite becoming more closed and self-recruiting and the service proletariat becoming trapped in low-paid work, as described in the Milburn Report (2012) on higher education in Britain. Outside the four occupational classes, he, too, identified an unemployed grouping which he called an 'outsider' or surplus population group (his version of the underclass or neo-proletariat).

Esping-Andersen's theoretical position promised to avoid reducing class to occupation, paying more attention to gender, race and age. However, his five-tier model is still built on occupations. Since post-industrial theory is descended from industrial theory, it replicates many of its assumptions and preoccupations. Above all, post-industrial theory is still concerned with the logic of production

Gorz and Esping-Andersen move class analysis on by incorporating an unemployed group into their model, acknowledging the significance of unemployment in contemporary capitalist economies. Pahl has suggested that the cleavage between the work-rich and the work-poor is now the most important form of social division (Pahl 1984; Wallace and Pahl 1986). In this way, post-industrial theorists have acknowledged some important aspects of change, but it could be argued that their rethinking of class is still insufficient. Can postmodernism offer more radical reformulations?

As suggested in chapter 2, class was not a central concern within original postmodern theory, with its interest in cultural change. However, sociologists concerned to develop a 'sociology of postmodernism' started to explore the issue of social divisions. As we have seen, postmodernism is a broad church with divergent strands. We can distinguish three tendencies, however:

1 some theorists sought to combine a postmodern account of culture with Marxist class theory;
2 others believed that postmodern culture was bringing an end to class inequalities;
3 a third group argued class was still relevant but should be conceptualized in terms of consumption rather than production.

Jameson (1991) was one of the former, as was Harvey (1989). Both linked postmodern cultural developments with analysis of a globalizing capitalism. For Jameson, the significant features of the new phase of capitalist development were the power of transnational corporations and the development of a co-ordinated world market. Harvey and Jameson were interested in the changing nature of the capitalist ruling class and lent support to the arguments of Bottomore and Brym (1989) that capitalist power had been greatly strengthened by globalization. However, neither said much about other class groupings. Jameson justified his vagueness by the idea that the world was in a 'trough' between two capitalist epochs: 'The postmodern may well...be little more than a transitional period between two stages of capitalism, in which the earlier forms of the economic are in the process of being restructured on a global scale...That a new international proletariat (taking forms we cannot yet imagine) will re-emerge from this convulsive upheaval it needs no prophet to predict' (1991, p. 417). While this may be true, it is of little help in developing an account of the contemporary class dynamic.

At the opposite extreme, Beck (1992) and Crook et al. (1992) both suggested that postmodern change was inexorably bringing an end to class and other sorts of inequality. Beck argued that old class communities were breaking down and class ties weakening as a result of what he called 'a social surge of individualization' (1992, p. 87). He envisaged the future as an 'individualized society of employees' (p. 99). It should be noted that Beck's account was derived from his study of European societies, primarily West Germany, a society in which working-class affluence was a well-established fact up to the period of German reunification. Beck actually made an exception of Britain, noting that: 'Class membership is very apparent in everyday life and remains the object of consciousness and identification. It is evident in speech...in the sharp class divisions between residential areas...in types of education, in clothing and in everything that can be included under the concept of "lifestyle" ' (p. 102).

Crook et al. (1992) offered a similar account to Beck, drawing on the Australasian context; they predicted a decline in the social significance of class, gender and ethnicity as society became more individualized and the media played more part in influencing people to identify with particular 'symbolically simulated communities' (p. 111), such as various consumer groups. In stark contrast to Jameson, they suggested that the service class had replaced the capitalist class as the elite; but they saw membership of the service class as so fluid 'that the very existence of a class system will have to be called in question' (p. 118). The future for all forms of stratification, they see as 'fluid and apparently chaotic' (p. 124).

While Beck and Crook et al. presented these arguments as a general theory of change (a position at odds with some postmodernists' insistence on local narratives), we could alternatively read these as accounts of particular societies where fragmentation and individualization have progressed further than in Britain. But their claims ignore the continuing evidence, both quantitative and qualitative, of substantial economic inequalities within most capitalist societies (Edgell 1993), and the lack of substantial proof that collective identification is waning. The postmodern version of classlessness seems to be only a vision of a possible future.

These forms of postmodernism offer two scenarios: one in which nothing very much has changed and one in which everything is changing. An intermediate position affirms the reality of capitalist inequality but offers a new reading of its nature. In this view, consumption rather than production becomes the key aspect of class formation. Lyon states 'if postmodernity means anything, it means the consumer society' (1994, p. 68), and speaks of the new world of 'rock videos, theme parks and shopping malls' (p. 50). Some postmodernists see class dissolving in the face of consumerized lifestyles. Others suggest that consumption-based cleavages – based, for example, on housing tenure – are replacing classes (Saunders 1984). However, whether one owns a house (mansion or maisonette), rents a flat, or occupies a council house would be taken by many sociologists as an indicator of one's class.

Zygmunt Bauman, in a powerful account of a 'postmodern society', argues that its key feature is that capital has freed itself to a considerable extent from a dependency on labour. The core relation between capital and the other social classes has changed: capital now engages labour in the role of consumers rather than producers (Bauman 1992, p. 111). As a result of these developments, a key new social group has come into being, which Bauman calls the 'new poor' (another version of the underclass, etc.). This group, characterized by unemployment, dependency and poverty, is not to be seen as part of the labour reserve but as *permanently displaced*. Because of people's increasing dependency on the market, the social unrest which one might expect in such circumstances does not develop; seduced by the glamour of the new consumerism, most people conform. Capital has made use of the 'pleasure principle' to win the class battle, thereby reinforcing its position of social dominance. However, he argues that the state may be forced to take repressive measures to keep the losers, 'the new poor', in order through increased policing and surveillance, the loss of citizen rights. Seduction and repression become the twin axes of class domination. In 2014, with many arguing that Britain has become a 'surveillance society', such ideas are credible and rather persuasive.

Bauman's account clearly owes much to Marxism in its stress on an all-powerful capitalist class and a manipulated working class.

Others have used the consumption scenario in a less pessimistic way. Turner (1989) suggested that the expansion of mass culture and consumerism, accompanied by the interweaving of 'high' and 'popular' cultural styles that typifies postmodern culture, may erode traditional status hierarchies, bringing a cultural democratization, even if economic inequalities endure. Most influential, though, has been the work of French sociologist Pierre Bourdieu, whose classic text *Distinction* (1986) explored how consumption patterns serve to reproduce class differences. Savage et al. (1992) use this framework to distinguish a number of different consumer groupings within the 'new middle classes'. Managers and bureaucrats share an old-fashioned, middle-of-the-road pattern of consumption, which can be distinguished from that of public-sector professionals, who favour more intellectual pursuits, and a high-minded health-conscious lifestyle, such as that often satirized by reference to '*Guardian* readers'. (The former group, we can assume, would choose *The Times* or *Telegraph*.) The trend-setting group, however, are the upwardly mobile 'yuppie' young private-sector professionals who exemplify the postmodern spirit with its mix of high and low culture (opera *and* rap music, visits to the theatre *and* to theme parks) and its pursuit of expensive pleasures of all kinds.

Consumption patterns, then, can be seen as either equalizing or divisive; but whichever view is held, it is suggested that consumption is becoming more important in people's self-identification. Such consumption groups can be seen as recent manifestations of status, as described by Weber. Turner (1989) argues that in contemporary capitalist societies status is more politically and socially crucial than class, while stressing that it is necessary to analyse contemporary societies in terms of both status *and* class.

The stress on consumption as an aspect of class is to be welcomed in line with my argument that versions of class limited to occupation are too narrow. But there is a danger of going too far in the other direction and ignoring production altogether. There is as yet little empirical *proof* of the assertion that consumption and consumer identities are more important to people than employment and work identities.

Moving On: The New Sociology of Class

As discussed in earlier chapters, the 'postmodern' moment has also been described as 'a turn to culture'. This turn can be observed in what has been referred to as the 'new sociology of class' which, as mentioned above, is strongly influenced by the work of Pierre Bourdieu. Sociologists such as Mike Savage, Diane Reay, Beverley Skeggs and Fiona Devine carried on researching class empirically during the period when the concept was neglected within sociology; they have since led a revival in class theory, sparking interest among a new generation of scholars. Moreover, the recession that commenced in 2007–8 and its aftermath, marked by the imposition of austerity policies, the erosion of welfare provision and the weakening of employment rights, have drawn both popular and academic attention to the growth of inequalities in society, shoring up this rebirth of a view of class as a central social division.

Bourdieu and his colleague, Louis Wacquant, developed their conceptual framework over many years. Although starting out as an anthropologist influenced by structural Marxism, Bourdieu ploughed his own furrow, formulating a set of concepts for understanding how people are differentially located in what he calls 'social space'. His theories are complex and sophisticated, and cannot be fully explored here, but perhaps the three key concepts are habitus, field and capital; Bourdieu referred to these as his key 'thinking tools' (Bourdieu and Wacquant 1989: 50). The notion of *habitus* is a way of explaining why people behave in predictable but differentiated ways without consciously following rules; it can be described as a set of dispositions which inform how we act, think and feel, which are acquired through the unthinking practices of everyday life: it is Bourdieu's way of conceiving agency. The second notion, *field*, refers to the social arena where the habitus is engaged, for example the fields of employment, education or politics. This can be seen as Bourdieu's version of structure. If an individual's habitus is out of kilter with the habitus generally deployed within a given field, she or he can feel 'like a fish out of water'. For example, studies of students from working-class backgrounds who attend elite universities have shown how they find it difficult to fit in with the culture of their tutors and of their middle-class peers (Reay et al. 2009, 2010; Bradley et al. 2014).

Within each field, individuals' fortunes are shaped by the forms of *capital* they possess. This is how Bourdieu approaches the topic of class. He differentiates between economic capital (wealth, income and property), social capital (networks and contacts: who you know) and cultural capital (knowledge of differing kinds, consumption practices: what you know). Middle-class people are seen to have more of all of these, and to deploy them to maintain their class advantage. While working-class people have their own forms of networks and cultural practices, these do not have the legitimacy of middle-class capitals, and serve to keep them separate, blocking their chances of upward mobility (Bourdieu 1986). These practices do not constitute what Bourdieu termed 'symbolic capital'. Lareau (2003), Devine (2004) and Vincent and Ball (2006) have all shown how middle-class parents in Britain and America work to ensure their children get middle-class jobs by close monitoring of and intervention in their schooling, and by putting them through punishing regimes of out-of school activities. Such 'concerted cultivation' of social and cultural capital helps to replicate their middle-class belonging.

In this way, Bourdieu and those influenced by him seek to integrate cultural aspects of class experience into the earlier economistic frameworks reviewed in this chapter. Class is not reduced to occupation, and lifestyle features are built into the model. The most striking example of this is the attempt by Savage et al. (2013) to build a new class map for Britain based on data gathered from what was called the Great British Class Survey. This was organized by the BBC, inviting the public to take part, and gathered information on cultural practices and social links as well as wealth and income. On the basis of this, they discerned seven classes: the elite, established middle class, technical middle class, new affluent workers, traditional working class, emergent service sector and the precariat.

Although Savage et al. claimed to have brought cultural and social factors into their model, it is interesting that the classes they distinguished are not very dissimilar from some of the class schemes reviewed earlier in the chapter. In fact, one could invert their reasoning and say that, rather than redefining class according to cultural and social activities, they have showed that the class groupings based on economic positions tend to share similar cultural activities and socialize together!

I have criticized Savage et al.'s model for various reasons, but particularly because they do not specify the relations between the classes and what binds them together (Bradley 2014). I proposed an alternative which looks more like Esping-Andersen's and draws on the Marxist and Weberian models: the elite, the middle class and the working class. Divisions within these broad groupings can be seen as 'fractions'. These classes are defined by their differential relation to the economy: the elite is distinguished by its ownership of wealth (companies, land, property). Among the elite is a super-rich fraction, which is powerfully linked internationally and has strong political clout. Stephen Ackroyd has researched this fabulously wealthy group and estimates them as 0.01 per cent of the global population (2012). They truly appear as a 'ruling class'. Danny Dorling (2014) demonstrates how, in the UK, this dominant class (he calls it the 1 per cent) is sucking up the social surplus and impoverishing the rest of us.

Next are the middle class, who are primarily linked to the economy by dependence on income, although they may convert some of that into individual wealth (houses and shares). They are increasingly defined by qualifications, as it is more difficult to achieve upward mobility. Fractions of the middle class include the managerial elite, traditional professions and the lower middle classes, who are typically qualified but at lower levels and earn rather less (nurses, technicians, book-keepers, etc.). They continue to hold a 'contradictory class position', being employed by the elite, but often identifying with them.

Finally, the working class are defined by having only their labour to sell, and lack qualifications (they may, of course, have savings and own houses, having paid off their mortgages or purchased their council houses during the sell-off by the Thatcher government). Contrary to Goldthorpe's earlier studies, this class is also fragmented: there is a dwindling group of affluent and aspirant workers, mainly skilled males, augmented by the rapidly growing group of former employees who were made redundant and set up small businesses, the noticeable army of 'white van men'. There is a female-dominated group of low-paid workers in retail, care, leisure and other services; and those who have nothing to sell but their labour but cannot sell it: the unemployed. Finally, there is the precariat, which might be seen as another working-class fraction, defined by moving in and out of employment; but its class position is complicated by the presence in it at the moment of highly educated but casualized people – for example, temporary and hourly paid university lecturers, who in the past would have been seen as middle class. Whether this is a temporary effect of the recession or a longer-term tendency remains to be seen.

This is an example of how change affects the class dynamic, making analysis ever more difficult. A further complication is the growth of self-employment. Self-employment in Britain doubled between 1981 and 1991, and by 1994 3.3 million people were classified as self-employed, amounting to 12.9 per cent of the labour force (*Social Trends*, 1995). The figure has now risen to 4.2 million, with a particular increase since 2011. There has long been debate about the class position of the self-employed. While they could be seen as part of a re-generated 'petite bourgeoisie' as described by Marx, Dale has argued that in some cases self-employment is no more than a disguised form of casualized wage-labour, often marked by dependency on capitalist employers through some kind of sub-contracting system (1986). The Office of National Statistics (ONS) reported that self-employed people tended to be older than employees and were more likely to be male. The four most common occupations for self-employment were taxi or cab drivers, 'other' construction trades, carpenters and joiners, and farmers (ONS 2013). The first three groups are likely to be redeployed manual workers, as I outlined above. Self-employment can be precarious, with the potential for self-exploitation or the exploitation of family members, and the economic rewards may be limited (Curran et al. 1986; Macdonald and Coffield 1991). Self-employed people work longer hours than employees (ONS 2013)

But whether they are seen as part of an expanding petite bourgeoisie, a special segment of the new middle classes, or a distinctive group within the working class, it is clear that this expanding group adds another element to the complexity of contemporary class relations.

Class, Identity and Action

One criticism of the theories of Bourdieu that could be raised is that they throw little light on processes of class identification. A lot of the arguments about the death of class depend on the idea that people no longer think of themselves in class terms. Is this true? Certainly the idea of identification has long been a thorny issue for class theorists; it was originally addressed by the controversial idea of class consciousness.

Marx argued that consciousness rises directly from social being: that is, that material experiences, such as that of exploitation, are the basis of class identification. But Marx also claimed that those who control the means of production also control the production of ideas in society. From this derives the notion of the dominant ideology, whereby the capitalists legitimate their own social domination and which produces a 'false consciousness' in the proletariat that blocks an awareness of their true class situation.

Weberians reject the idea of false consciousness, and point out that consciousness can be influenced by a whole range of factors, not just one's economic situation. But it is notoriously difficult to study class awareness and attitudes. Twenty years after Goldthorpe et al. (1969) had surveyed workers in Luton and concluded that their attitudes to work were instrumental, individualistic and economistic, Devine revisited the affluent workers' community and found that a more ethnographic approach revealed a more complex mix of attitudes (1992). This is supported by Marshall et al. (1988) who argued that working-class culture displays both collectivist and individualistic behaviours, instrumental and solidaristic values, and has always done so. Their national survey of class in Britain in the 1980s, like others subsequently, suggested that people show a clear awareness of class inequalities and of their own class positions. However, sometimes these findings are influenced by the questions that are asked – for example, if people are presented with a list of fixed choices of class positions to select from. Scase argues that sociologists often have to work very hard to get their informants to state a class identification, only achieved with 'considerable assistance' (Scase 1992, p. 79). Where a more open-ended approach is employed, the results are likely to be more ambiguous and complex. Lash (1984) interviewed working people in America and found that they came up with a bewildering variety of images of class. When I myself have interviewed people about class, I have found that they tend to describe themselves as 'ordinary working people' or 'just normal folk' and Savage found the same thing in his Manchester study (Bradley 1999b; Savage 2000).

I suggested in chapter 1 that class is now a passive rather than an active identity. We could go further and say that class identities are now submerged identities, pushed out of sight by others that jostle more urgently for public attention, such as ethnicity, gender and religion. Indeed, people are often reluctant to talk in class terms in a society in which classlessness – though not attained – is the desired ideal. Class becomes a stigmatized or spoiled identity, rather than one acknowledged with pride (Bradley 1994).

For a passive stigmatized identity to be transformed into an active positive one, some form of political activity is usually needed. Class has been the loser in the identity politics of the last decades. While institutions like the Labour party or the unions were originally formed to promote working-class interests, they have been under attack for the narrowness of their constituencies (white, working-class, skilled male workers); subsequently they have attempted to broaden their appeal by shedding their class associations. Class, thus, lost its political voice. However, since the recession of the 2000s, trade unions have begun more explicitly to represent working-class interests in various demonstrations over the impacts of austerity.

In addition, elements of working-class identification still emerge within communities or through industrial struggles. One example is the Miners' Wives Support Groups, which evolved during the coal dispute of 1984–5. Suspicious of feminism, which they saw as a middle-class movement, the miners' wives nevertheless built a campaign on a specific identification of class and gender interests, reflected in their campaign anthem:

United by the struggle, united by the past,
Here we go, here we go, we're the women of the working class!

Class meanings are not yet extinct; and they are more easily judged to be so by people in comfortable positions. Mark Hudson describes tellingly the shock of a middle-class encounter with a traditional working-class community:

> If you had wondered if terms like 'middle class' and 'working class' still had any meaning, or if such a thing as 'working-class culture' could still be said to exist, you were immediately disabused of your illusions. The moment you arrived in East Durham, you were *in it* – up to your neck. In East Durham, it often seemed that there *was* nothing else. (Hudson 1994, p. 73)

Class identification, then, is, as Phillips says, a bit of a muddle. But as John Scott perceptively points out, to focus too much on this issue is misleading since the objective facts of class remain: 'Everybody does not have to believe in the existence of class, nor constantly think of themselves in terms of class identity, for class to be a social division. The system of class situations is not dependent on people's awareness of it' (Scott 2000, p. 53).

Intersecting Dynamics: Class, Gender, Ethnicity and Age

The miners' wives referred to above were fighting in support of their menfolk against pit closures, in order to maintain traditional sources of employment for their husbands and sons; but they also realized that, as women in the mining communities, they had in the past been excluded from politics and confined to domestic roles. The women experienced 'divided loyalties', in Anne Phillips's phrase (1987), demonstrating how class must be viewed as in interaction with other dynamics of inequality. This section of the chapter sets out some thoughts on class in the framework of intersectionality.

Gender

Gender has historically served to divide the working class. In the nineteenth century, capitalist employers set women and men in competition for jobs. Trade unions attempted to keep women out of jobs seen as 'men's work'. This was backed by the campaign for a 'family wage', which would enable a man to maintain a non-employed wife and children at home. Although the family wage remained more an ideal than a reality, it led to the stereotyping of women as housewives and their marginalization in class-based politics.

Classes are not only divided by gender: they are 'gendered' in the sense that gender is integral to processes of class formation, action and identification. While the stereotypical image of the working class is of male workers, women have had a crucial role to play in the reproduction of working-class cultures through their position in the family and community. They have borne the brunt of working-class poverty, constituting the bulk of workhouse inhabitants and of welfare claimants. In times of long-term unemployment, women have to prop up their unemployed menfolk and keep the family going through tight household management, along with their own subsistence activities (Atkinson 2012). Women's efforts serve to forge the working class into a set of distinct communities, rather than an aggregate of wage-earning individuals. While so many secure and well-paid working-class jobs in Europe and America have disappeared in the last decades, on a worldwide basis the globalization of capital has depended crucially on manipulation of low-paid women as new sources of labour. A major constituent of the global precariat are female assembly workers, garment-makers and others who work in sweated conditions, especially in the Global South countries of Latin America, South East Asia and the Indian subcontinent (Williams et al., 2013). In all countries, women are especially vulnerable to poverty; even in the Global North they are forced into dependency on benefits as single mothers, as impoverished pensioners, as low-paid workers and as wives of unemployed men (Morris 1994; McKenzie 2015).

At the top of the class hierarchy, women appear more marginalized, still being under-represented in company boardrooms. But women have a crucial social role in the 'inner circle' in cementing social networks and maintaining elite cohesion through intermarriage with other members of the entrepreneurial class, as well as passing on dominant values to their families. It is, however, in the new middle classes that gender is most clearly an issue, witnessed in the numerical dominance of women in lower-grade non-manual work and in the public sector as education and health professionals. Braverman (1974) pointed out that the typical American working-class couple consisted of a male factory worker and a female clerk. This gendering of white-collar work adds to the general confusion surrounding the middle-class groupings and contributes to the weakness of their sense of class identification. This analysis is taken a stage further in Esping-Andersen's account of the feminized nature of the emerging post-industrial service classes. Overall, we can see that gender is significantly involved in the way that capitalist economies are developing, at both national and global levels.

'Race' and Ethnicity

'Race' and ethnicity also act as a source of division within classes, where, for example, Black and white workers are in competition for jobs. A prime example is America. The relative political and industrial weakness of the American working class can be linked to the presence of a large minority population. Black African Americans and Latinos are at the bottom of the employment hierarchy, therefore allowing white working people to see themselves as in a position of relative privilege. Race struggles and antagonisms have persistently preoccupied Americans and diverted working people from issues of class.

But, like gender, race contributes to processes of class formation in a more integral way. The exploitation of colonial plunder and the labour of colonial slave populations was vital to the emergence of capitalist industrial production. Since then, there has been extensive shifting of both labour and production around the globe to help capitalists increase their profits, develop new markets and appease indigenous working classes. Processes of international migration have been crucial to the ongoing development of neoliberal capitalist economies. Globalization has seen these processes intensify (see chapter 6).

Migrants often find themselves in a very weak position when they arrive in a new country. Thus, minority groups are generally over-represented in the working class in European societies. For example, Asian refugees to Britain from Kenya and Uganda, who had held good professional or entrepreneurial jobs in Africa, had difficulty finding employment in line with their qualifications and former status: many were forced into unskilled jobs. In the 2010s, refugees from trouble spots in the Middle East and Africa, if they manage to gain entry to European countries, are likely to find themselves in the precariat or unemployed; people with a background of middle-class affluence may join displaced peasants as recruits to the 'new poor', struggling to build a fresh life on welfare payments.

Although, in time of recession, ethnic minority members experience a greater threat of unemployment, they are often used to supplement the indigenous working class when labour is short. Characteristically, they fill the worst, low-status 'dirty' jobs rejected by the native populace. The successful post-war West German economy depended greatly on the employment of 'guest-workers' from Turkey, southern Italy and elsewhere. In Britain, Polish migrants have filled shortages of skilled craftsmen, while new migrants from Eastern Europe take lowly regarded jobs in hotels and as fruit-pickers, often in terrible conditions (Lewycka 2012). Better-paid jobs remain the preserve of white workers. Labour, therefore, is not an ethnically neutral category. The working class is characteristically composed of ethnically distinct layers, shaped by the particular patterns of migration in each country.

It is very hard for minority members, especially those of colour, to join the capitalist elite. However, self-employment is an option for those who face racism in the labour market, and is a way out of the working class for Asian men in Britain. By contrast, African-Caribbeans are more prone to join the ranks of the surplus class. Indeed, in America, the 'underclass' is specifically associated with the African American populace, along with increasing numbers of young males of Latin American origin. In France, North Africans from France's former colonies of Algeria, Morocco and Tunisia have suffered a similar fate

While no minority group in Britain has become become marginalized to such an extent as in America and France, McKenzie's studies of the St Ann's estate in Nottingham, notorious for its poverty, show how many young Black males slide into the outsider group and become trapped in unemployment and illegality (McKenzie 2012, 2015). Minority women have suffered in the recession, while increasing experience of racism impels minority members to look for sheltered employment within their own communities. The working class are likely to be fragmented further on ethnic lines.

Age

Age has also been fundamental to capitalist development. Young people are particularly vulnerable to the worst forms of capitalist exploitation. Many of the workers in the early British factories were children, especially vulnerable pauper apprentices. In industrializing America and Japan, young girls from rural areas were a favoured source of labour for the cotton mills. Some were literally kidnapped by labour contractors or sold by their parents into near-slavery, locked into sleeping quarters at night, a practice which continues today in the Global South – for example, in Foxconn's factories in China (Williams et al. 2013).

As capitalism matured and children gained some protection through state legislation and compulsory education, the cheapness of young people's labour continued to be exploited through the apprenticeship system. In periods of recession, young workers often found themselves laid off as soon as they had 'served their time' and become eligible for the adult wage. Globalizing capital continues to make use of the labour of children and of young rural women in many developing countries; such young people are a core component of the precariat.

The best and most secure jobs at all levels of the class structure are occupied by middle-aged people, while old people whose skills are considered redundant are pushed out to join young people in the labour surplus class and risk dependency on the state. Both face ageist prejudices on the part of employers and the vested interests of the middle-aged who have worked themselves into stable and power-holding positions. This trend looks set to continue as global competition pushes employers to cut labour costs: older people are seen as expensive, inflexible and resistant to changing conditions at work.

Young people are currently victims of the changing class dynamic (Howker and Malik 2013). The cultural changes discerned by post-modernists manifest themselves among young people rather than the older age groups. Young people are especially responsive to media and fashion changes and have often formed distinctive subcultures which signify their distance from both wider society and their own parents. For this reason, their awareness of class is often less developed. Lash (1990) argued that the traditional working class, as it became affluent, provided its young people with the means to become consumers; the adolescent youth cultures that developed subsequently undermined traditional working-class values. The growth of youth unemployment contributed to this process of class dissolution. Willis et al. (1990) argued that unemployment meant that young working-class people were no longer socialized by their workmates and through trade union membership into working-class values and practices. For all these reasons, the decline of class awareness is likely to affect young people most fully. But studies show that young people are especially likely to be members of the new social movements (Crook et al. 1992); for example, young 'New Age' travellers in Britain have spearheaded the environmental direct action movement.

Yet, ironically, young people are far from free of class constraints. Many are doomed to poverty and unemployment. Tahlin argues that in Sweden 'age is the most important determinant of overall class transitions' (Tahlin 1993, p. 95). Young people in Greece, Spain and Italy have struggled to find jobs at home since the advent of austerity, and many have used their migration rights to drift around Europe, joining the precarious work-force. Despite their involvement with postmodern cultural change, many young people in global capitalist societies are losing out.

Conclusions

This chapter has surveyed the long and checkered history of class theory. There is still considerable support for classic class theories. The Marxist tradition remains useful for its insistence on the need to study the evolving capitalist class and its relationship with working people, especially in terms of the globalization of capitalist production. Marxists, however, pay insufficient attention to other social groupings. The insights of the Weberian tradition, with its stress on social mobility and social fragmentation within broad class groupings, are needed here. These lead to an appreciation of the fluidity of the class dynamic, although the functionalist view of capitalist industrial societies as open and meritocratic must be questioned.

However, classic approaches have two important limitations. First, their view of class in terms of production or occupation is too narrow. Groups who are not in employment are thus marginalized, although they are still subject to the forces of economic differentiation. Second, despite acknowledgement that class coexists with other forms of inequality such as gender, classic theory still tends to marginalize them.

Post-industrial and postmodern theory go some way to confronting these deficits. Post-industrial theories highlight the existence of the non-employed group and make moves to identifying it as a separate class, with its own unique economic situation, rather than as a segment within the working class. While the term 'underclass' is most popularly used for this group, the moral stigmatization associated with it makes its usage problematic; alternatives, such as Esping-Andersen's 'outsider population', might be preferred.

Post-industrial theory, however, bears the traces of the frameworks of industrialism and capitalism from which it evolved. Postmodernism promised a more flexible approach, which could move the analysis of class to a broader framework and deal with its relation to other aspects of inequality, although some of the assumptions made by postmodern theorists, for example, concerning the decline of class awareness, lack empirical backing. The currently dominant approach in Britain to class, based on the theoretical framework of Bourdieu, seems to combine elements of traditional class theory and the postmodern stress on culture in a promising way. The framework of intersectionality can be used to show how class formation and recomposition are affected by gender, ethnicity and age.

The final message of this chapter is that neither class, as a set of lived economic relationships, nor class analysis, as a set of social categories, is dead. But there must be recognition of how class relations are shaped by other forms of inequality. As Jonathan Rutherford argues: 'Class is still a conceptual necessity for understanding the dynamics of society, but the restructuring of its processes and the decline of old class identities and cultures has coincided with a proliferation and dispersal of other political and social antagonisms' (1990, p. 12).

Further Reading

Probably the most comprehensive introductory texts on class at the time of writing are Rosemary Crompton, *Class and Stratification* (Polity, 3rd edition 2008), and Kenneth Roberts, *Class in Contemporary Britain* (Palgrave, 2011). Also useful are Richard Scase, *Class* (Open University Press, 1992), and Stephen Edgell, *Class* (Routledge, 1993). An interesting collection of papers illustrating the Bourdieusian approach is *Class Inequality in Austerity Britain*, edited by Will Atkinson, Steve Roberts and Mike Savage (Palgrave, 2012). Lisa McKenzie, *Getting By* (The Policy Press, 2015), and Owen Jones, *Chavs* (Verso, 2011), are highly readable accounts of the stigmatization of sections of the working class. Danny Dorling, *Inequality and the 1%* (Verso, 2014), reveals the impact of the super-rich.

Thinking Points

- Why do people find it so difficult to talk about class?
- What has been the impact of the growth of the 'super-rich'?
- Are young people less likely to be aware of class than their elders?

5

Gender: Rethinking Patriarchy

Among the Hamar people of Ethiopia, a girl child is referred to as a 'guest', while a boy child is considered to be a 'person'. This is because the girl will eventually leave the parental home and become the property of her husband, while the male may establish his own household; the girl is considered on loan to her parents until she goes to the home of the man to whom she really belongs. This conceptualization inverts the English folk-saying:

> A daughter's a daughter for all of her life,
> A son's a son till he gets him a wife.

But both show the strength of ideas of gender difference and demonstrate that, historically, women have been seen as other people's property. Gender divisions have a long history.

If class went through a period of sociological neglect (Barrett 1992, p. 216), the opposite is true of gender. From the 1980s, gender has been a topic of burning interest both popular and sociological. The rise of second-wave feminism in the late 1970s forced the issue of inequalities between women and men into the arenas of world politics. Feminism was warmly embraced by women within the academic world who felt that gender issues were ignored or marginalized within their own disciplines. The study of gender has since become an important part of the curriculum in most disciplines within the arts and social sciences. During the 1980s, particularly in North America, the study of gender became the basis of the new disciplinary frameworks of Women's Studies and Gender Studies. A flood of publications on every aspect of gendered experience subsequently poured from the academy. Books from the activist strand of the feminist movement, such as Betty Friedan's *The Feminine Mystique* (1965) and Germaine Greer's *The Female Eunuch* (1971), became best-sellers and led many non-academic women to begin questioning their own lives and relationships. Such explorations of femininity and gender roles also led men to question their masculinity, and Men's Studies was born. More recently texts by younger feminist activists, such as Naomi Wolf's *The Beauty Myth* (1990), Natasha Walter's *Living Dolls* (2010) and Laura Bates's *Everyday Sexism* (2014) have fired up a new generation of feminist activists, while websites and blogs like The F Word, UK Feminista and Vagenda reach out to new audiences.

Throughout this period, the lived relationships of gender have been in a state of flux. Changes under way since the Second World War seemed to take off in a vertiginous fashion in the 1980s. Transformations in the economy hastened the advance of women into the labour market, to such an extent that many spoke of the 'feminization of the labour force' (Jenson et al. 1988; Esping-Andersen 1993), while manufacturing decline brought increased male unemployment. Divorce rates increased and the number of single-headed families grew, along with the numbers of people living alone; in Britain, between 1971 and 2012, the proportion of families with children headed by a lone parent rose from 8 to 26 per cent (ONS 2012); and 16 per cent of people now live in single-person households, compared to 9 per cent in 1973. Cohabitation became steadily more common: opposite-sex cohabiting couple families increased from 1.5 million in 1996 to 2.9 million in 2012. Continued innovations in the field of contraception, the freer availability of abortion and new reproductive technologies made it easier for women (and men) to plan their reproductive life more securely and to explore more liberated patterns of sexuality. The vigorous gay and lesbian movement asserted the rights of people to develop different forms of sexuality and sexual practices and to display their sexuality openly without fear of retribution (although such rights have not yet been fully achieved and vicious persecution of homosexuals is common in many countries, as discussed in chapter 8). Such changes challenged the conventional arrangements between women and men.

The advances made by women during these decades led to assertions (notably in popular journalism) that sexual equality had been gained and that the industrial world was now in a 'post-feminist' state. Young women, in particular, were purported to hold this view. The singer Madonna was taken as an emblem of the new generation, offering a public representation of female power and wealth along-side free and polymorphous sexuality. At the same time, a male 'backlash' (Faludi 1992; Walby 1993) developed, asserting that 'it had all gone too far'; disgruntled men started banding together in groups to call for 'men's lib' or 'father's rights' or to explore ways of 'getting back in touch' with masculine identity, some through follow-ing the back-to-nature prescriptions of Robert Bly, going drumming in the forests. The backlash was supported by conservatives, both male and female, calling for a reassertion of 'traditional' family values and the return of women to maternal responsibility. There were attacks on liberal policies on contraception and abortion, strength-ened by strands of fundamentalism in world religious movements. The swings between advances towards gender equality and conserva-tive backlashes, combined with outbreaks of misogynism (hatred of women), have continued to manifest themselves, in America, Britain and elsewhere (Walter 2010; Campbell 2014).

Indeed, despite the post-feminist claims, gender issues and conflicts remain firmly on the agenda in the early twenty-first century. Around the world, women are subject to rape, sexual abuse and domestic violence. Trafficking of women, prostitution and pornography are on the increase, encouraged by the new migration patterns and new technologies associated with globalization (Williams et al. 2013). In Britain, moral panics over single motherhood; the worries about parenting, teenage traumas and the sexualization of children; the spate in the 2010s of high-profile cases involving sexual harassment, paedophilia and child abuse ; the legal wrangles over rape; the con-cerns about older and post-menopausal women using new fertiliza-tion techniques – these very different issues show that battles over gender are as fierce as ever

I speak of gender in this chapter in reference to lived relationships between men and women, through which sexual differences and ideas about sexual differences are constructed. Some of these differences, which relate to the sexual division of labour both in and outside the home, are economic: women have lesser access to shares of social wealth than men. But gender differences are not only rooted in the economy; in this, they differ from the class relations discussed in the previous chapter. Gender relations are pervasive and operate at every level of social life. For example, girls and boys have different patterns of play, and women's and men's leisure activities are differentiated (men play and watch football, women do yoga and pilates); women are under-represented, or relegated to specific roles defined as suitable for them, within most areas of the public sphere; sexual practices and orientations take different meanings for women and for men; and women and men figure differently in cultural representations of various kinds, from classical paintings to advertisements, from television dramas to the lyrics of rap songs. Every aspect of our individual histories is subtly affected by the fact of being male or female.

There is a longstanding dilemma relating to the non-economic aspects of gender differentiation, regarding whether such differences actually constitute inequalities. Are women and men, perhaps, different but equal? Do not women *choose* different leisure activities, different ways of constructing themselves as sexual beings? Against this position, feminists argue that such differences *do* constitute inequalities, because they occur in the context of discrepancies in power between the sexes. Male social dominance means that men are able to impose their definitions and evaluations upon the social world. Thus, men tell women how they should be; and, as Ortner (1974) has argued, what men do is more highly valued than what women do. Male power is also manifested in the social division of labour, with men assuming positions of authority and using them to control women's labour. Differences in economic power also affect the more cultural aspects of gender difference. For example, women's lower earning-power helps to explain differences in leisure activities: women are less able to afford expensive leisure and are less likely to have a car for transport to venues, thus their leisure tends to be more home-based (knitting, reading, watching soaps), while men go to pubs and sports grounds.

It was conventional in 1970s versions of feminism to make a distinction between *gender*, as relating to the socially constructed aspects of sexual difference outlined above, and *sex*, relating to the biological identity as male or female with which (most) individuals are born. Biological reproductive differences constituted a kind of fixed substratum on which variable social constructs of gender developed. Nowadays, however, this clear distinction is considered less tenable (Butler 1990). Bodily differences are bound up with social identities of gender to such an extent that we can hardly separate them; and biological physical differences are themselves regarded as partly socially constructed and historically variable. Reproductive experiences, for example, are quite different for women in Britain today from those of women in pre-industrial societies. Moreover, the new developments in embryo technology and fertilization throw into question all our longstanding assumptions about 'natural' biological phenomena such as kinship and parenthood (Strathern, 1993). Sex is not fixed. I use *gender* broadly, then, to cover both these aspects of male/female relationships. Growing numbers of people are openly transsexual, changing their gender identity from that assigned to them at birth (see chapter 8), while others display and act upon elements of both sexes, like the famous 'ladyboys' of Bangkok.

This chapter explores how differences of gender have been conceptualized, beginning with the classic contributions deriving from the feminist movements of the nineteenth and twentieth centuries, before moving on to newer approaches influenced by postmodernist and post-structuralist ideas, and thence to the latest preoccupations of a new generation of feminists.

Classic Feminist Standpoints

While I am linking the theorization of gender to the feminist movement which formed in the mid nineteenth century, that does not mean that people ignored gender differences up to that time. People have written about differences between women and men throughout recorded history. In literature, relations between the sexes were often portrayed as conflictual, from Chaucer's wife of Bath seeing off her five husbands, to the playful sparring of the heroes and heroines of Shakespeare's comedies, to the stylized sexual predation portrayed in Jacobean tragedy or, very differently, in Restoration comedy. A prevailing attitude, however, within the history of Western culture was that gender differences were god-given ('male and female created he them') and thus 'natural'. As societies secularized and backing for this view waned, science took over; nineteenth-century biological, medical and psychological sciences again proclaimed that gender differences were innate. The sexual division of labour was said to reflect differences in aptitudes derived ultimately from reproductive function. Michel Foucault describes the processes of 'hysterization' of Victorian women, a 'thorough medicalization of their bodies and their sex' (Foucault 1978–84, vol. II, p. 146), whereby the womb was symbolically extended to encompass the whole female being. Women were seen as vulnerable, neurotic and inherently frail, because of their subjection to the reproductive phases of puberty, menstruation, pregnancy, childbirth and menopause. These weaknesses were believed to make them unfit for non-domestic work and for public life; where they stepped out of their prescribed social roles, their biological functions might be jeopardized. Some American doctors seriously believed that the education of young women would cause their breasts to shrink and wombs to atrophy (Ehrenreich and English 1979). These feminine weaknesses were also thought to make women more vulnerable than men to insanity (Showalter 1987).

Religion and science provided backing for the 'traditional' conservative view, that gender differences are natural and innate, and consequently inequality is justifiable. But, throughout history, individual women and men have contested that view and argued for justice for women. For example, there were impassioned pamphlets written by women in the seventeenth century protesting against their treatment by men and pointing out the contributions made by women to the social good (Kimmel 1987). However, it was the Enlightenment which provided the spur to sustained exploration of gender relations.

Postmodern feminists have criticized the grand narratives of Enlightenment liberalism for their gender-blindness (Scott 1988; Phillips 1992). Yet, as Randall (1982) points out, the liberal framework was crucial to the evolution of the feminist critique in its assertion of individual freedom and civic rights. Feminists utilized the claims about the 'rights of man' to call for the rights of women – for example, Mary Wollstonecraft in *A Vindication of the Rights of Woman*. The classic liberal feminists – Wollstonecraft, John Stuart Mill and Harriet Taylor – were able to use the idea of the rational human agent to attack the view that differentiated gender behaviour was natural. Wollstonecraft, for example, argued that the seemingly 'natural' frivolous, emotional and childish personalities typical among women of her class were a product of the characteristic upbringing of young women. If girls' education was reformed, they could become rational and useful citizens like their brothers. Liberalism, then, allowed feminists to develop ideas about the social construction of gender, with which to counter the biological essentialist position.

Barbara Taylor's study *Eve and the New Jerusalem* (1983) has shown how influential feminist ideas were in the early socialist movements of the nineteenth century. But it was not until the 1850s that feminism really took off as an autonomous movement, first in America, then in Britain and other European countries. Victorian feminism was primarily a campaigning movement, but, like its twentieth-century successor, it also stimulated research into many aspects of women's lives. Although the movement lost part of its impetus with the gaining of the vote and the general social upheaval surrounding the First World War, individual women continued to study gender issues and some influential work was produced, such as Alice Clark's *Working Life of Women in the Seventeenth Century* (1919), Olive Schreiner's *Women and Labour* (1911) or, more latterly, de Beauvoir's *The Second Sex* (1949). Apart from de Beauvoir's great text, the study of gender fell into a slump in the post-war period: because of the welfare state and universal suffrage it was considered that sex equality had been achieved and that remaining gender differences were the result of 'natural' endowments. The 'master' sociological approaches of the 1950s and 1960s were largely gender-blind, as discussed in the previous chapter.

Parsons did give attention to gender differences, distinguishing between instrumental male social roles (based on rationality and competition in the capitalist marketplace) and expressive female ones (based on caring and domesticity). But he considered these functional for society, linking them rather unquestioningly to a stereotypical nuclear family form seen to be 'normal' in society, and rooting them ultimately in reproductive functions. It was left to the second-wave feminist movement, emerging on the heels of the student protest movement and the radical social critiques of the late 1960s and early 1970s, to reformulate those social roles in terms of gendered power and inequality.

It has become conventional to distinguish three main strands or 'perspectives' in feminist thinking which predominated in the 1970s (Charvet 1982; Tong 1989). These are liberal, or equal rights, feminism; socialist or Marxist feminism; and radical feminism. Subcategories, such as materialist feminism, may be distinguished within them, and psychoanalytic feminism added as an additional strand. Later feminists became critical of this approach, suggesting that it tends to 'essentialize' feminist thinking and pigeonhole thinkers into boxes where they may not exactly fit (Barrett and Phillips 1992; Stacey 1993). Indeed, many feminist writers draw on ideas from all three 'perspectives', and their position shifts as their thinking develops. Moreover, these categories do not exhaust the range of feminist positions. The 1980s and 1990 saw a proliferation of newer approaches, such as Black feminism and deconstructionist feminism. Stacey, arguing that the old categorization tends to encourage stereotyping ('all radical feminists are lesbians and separatists') suggests that it 'obscures more than it reveals' (1993, p. 52).

While these criticisms are valid, I believe it is helpful to retain these terms as labels for earlier forms of feminist thinking, as long as it is realized that they do not refer to theoretical perspectives in the more formal sociological sense – that is, they never constituted themselves as self-contained and competing sets of explanatory premises (in the way that, for example, functionalism and classic Marxism did). The image used by Banks (1981), 'faces' of feminism, captures the way in which the strands were interlinked: three facets of a single movement. Alternatively, we may view them as differing 'standpoints', in the sense that Hartsock (1987) has used that term. The notion of a 'feminist standpoint' has been elaborated as part of a critique of mainstream science. This attacks the view that science, or any form of knowledge, can be absolutely detached and objective; all knowledge is 'situated', derived from a specific context which affords a particular angle on reality. I suggest that liberal, Marxist and radical feminism constituted three differing standpoints from which to procure feminist knowledge.

Liberal Feminism

Liberal feminism grew out of the broader liberal movement and shared many of its assumptions, notably the ideals of equality of opportunity, and individual rights. Liberal feminism asserted that women as well as men should attain these goals. Gender differences were linked to blockages to achieving equal rights, such as prejudice, or legal and institutional arrangements set up in less enlightened times. The way forward was through education and legal reform. Liberal feminism was the bedrock of the nineteenth-century movement. It focused on gains for women in the public sphere: the vote, equal opportunities at work, legal rights equivalent to those of men (over property and marriage, for example) and proper representation within democratic institutions.

Liberal feminism has been criticized as insufficiently radical in its explanation of gender inequality. This relates to its acceptance of the broader liberal assumption that capitalist development will inexorably bring with it advantages of freedom and democracy and is part of a long-term movement towards 'the best of all possible worlds', which is signified in Fukuyama's vision of the 'end of history': the global triumph of benevolent capitalist democracy (Fukuyama 1989). Like its (male) parent, liberal feminism has sought reform within the system rather than transformation of the system. Liberal feminist political objectives have been criticized as individualistic, as helping individual women (usually middle-class and white) to gain access to male preserves and achieve equality with male compeers. Indeed, it can be argued that the impetus of liberal feminism is to make women more like men. It does little to question the gendered cultural assumptions that underlie prevailing social arrangements (for example, that it is more socially valuable to go out to work than to stay at home and look after children, or that some types of work, like management and finance, should be more highly rewarded than others, like caring and cleaning). While liberal feminism has arguably been the most effective standpoint from which to develop successful political action, its social critique is limited.

Marxist Feminism

The liberal standpoint has been highly developed in America and Australia, where feminists have been particularly involved in working for women's rights within state agencies (Gelb and Palley 1982; Curthoys 1993). In Britain, where feminists are more wary of the state, the predominant standpoint was Marxist feminism, with its view of the state as an instrument of capitalist (and subsequently patriarchal) oppression. Many British second-wave feminists within academia had been involved in the radical student movement and were influenced by Marxism. Barrett's influential text *Women's Oppression Today: Problems in Marxist Feminist Analysis* (1980) epitomizes British feminist thinking of the period, with its focus on labour exploitation, ideology and the state.

Socialist standpoints within European feminism had developed in the nineteenth century (see Banks 1981; Lovenduski 1986). Politically, socialist or Marxist feminism locates the fight for gender equality alongside the class struggle within the movement to build socialism. Theoretically, Marxist feminists attempt to take the key concepts of Marxism and apply them to gender relations. While critical of traditional Marxism's neglect of gender issues, the Marxist feminist standpoint still viewed gender within the framework of capitalist production relationships. Characteristically, the focus was on economic aspects of gender: women as a cheap form of wage labour, the exploitation of women as a labour reserve, the contribution of domestic labour to capitalist accumulation, the role of the state in promoting the traditional family.

A feature of the Marxist feminist standpoint which is now seen as problematic was its view of society as a unified system. At first, Marxist feminist sociologists tried simply to subsume an analysis of gender within the broad idea of a mode of production. Women's subjection was explained in terms of the needs of capitalism as a system. The political corollary of this was that the struggle for women's rights was only an aspect of the broader class struggle and gender inequality would disappear once socialism was achieved. Indeed, many socialist activists, both male and female, have been critical of feminism, viewing it as a distraction from the class struggle, and sometimes stigmatizing it as a movement of privileged middle-class women (Phillips 1987).

This highlights the problem of the relationship between class and gender as forms of inequality. The Marxist analysis tended to handle the issue of gender inequality by seeing women either as members of the exploited working class (which clearly not all are) or as housewives contributing either directly or indirectly to capitalist profits (which again not all are). Moreover, gender divisions were shown by comparative and historical study to be characteristic of all societies, not just capitalist ones, and to be marked in the Soviet bloc where capitalism had been rejected. It became apparent that it was impossible to conceptualize gender adequately within the single framework of the capitalist mode of production.

The solution taken by Marxist feminists was to combine an account of capitalism with an analysis of a parallel system of patriarchy. Sometimes this took the form of what was known as unified systems theory, discerning a single complex structure of capitalist patriarchy or patriarchal capitalism (Young 1981). Miriam Glucksmann (1990) produced an ingenious version, extending the notion of relations of production to include reproduction and the social division of labour in the household, as well as paid work, which she referred to as the 'total social organization of labour' (TSOL). However, there was still a tendency for gender issues to slide out of sight and imperatives of class to come to the fore. For this reason, most feminists preferred the 'dual systems' option, which conceives patriarchy and capitalism as two equivalent and analytically separable systems, which, however, are always found in interaction in any concrete social context. Feminists such as Hartmann (1981) and Walby (1986) developed an account of patriarchy as a system and explored its historical interaction with capitalism.

Radical Feminism

Dual systems theory could be seen as a way of fusing radical and Marxist standpoints within feminism, for the concept of patriarchy was associated with the radical stance. The term 'patriarchy', literally meaning 'rule of the father', was not new: it had previously been used to denote specific types of family or household structure and forms of inheritance based on the authority of a male head of household over younger male and all female family members. Weber used the term 'patriarchalism' (1964, p. 346) to describe types of society or social institutions where forms of power were analogous to this family model. However, radical feminists broadened the use of the term to refer to a general structure of male domination in society, as defined by Kate Millett in *Sexual Politics*: 'Our society, like all other historical civilizations, is a patriarchy... The military, industry, technology, universities, science, political office, finances – in short, every avenue of power within the society, including the coercive force of the police, is entirely in male hands' (1971, p. 25).

Radical feminism was the newest strand in feminism. It was stronger in America and Northern Europe than in Britain, and acted as a counterpart to the more moderate liberal mainstream. It achieved notoriety for its political strategies, including direct action tactics such as disruptions of beauty queen contests. Especially controversial was the separatist tendency within the radical wing, which ranged from supporting women-only meetings (designed to prevent men dominating the agenda and to allow women to build confidence in a less combative environment) to the espousal of lesbianism as a political strategy. This arose from the key theoretical premise of radical feminism that gender inequality was the primary source of social division, from which all others evolved. The implication, that all men as a category oppress all women as a category, was explored, for example, in Shulamith Firestone's *The Dialectic of Sex* (1971), which inverted Marxist thinking through the idea of 'sex classes'.

Firestone's concern with sexuality and reproduction reflected the radical slogan 'The personal is political.' Where the Marxist feminist standpoint focused primarily on labour, radical feminists prioritized intimate personal relationships of love, marriage and desire. They were interested in the link between sexuality and male violence; rape and pornography were seen as crucial aspects of male social domination, which was ultimately backed up by the threat of force (Brownmiller 1976; Dworkin 1981; Griffin 1981). These analyses moved the feminist critique firmly beyond the public sphere, the focus of the liberal standpoint, and into the private. Indeed, Firestone claimed that 'love, perhaps even more than childbearing, is the pivot of women's oppression today' (1971, p. 142). She believed that gender inequalities fundamentally expressed themselves around men's control of reproduction. Her provocative solution was that women should free themselves from male domination through new reproductive technologies which might remove the need to bear children within their bodies.

Radical feminist politics and theory were considered by many, men and women, to be disturbing. They were meant to be! This was the form of feminist practice which was caricatured and demonized in the popular press (man-hating women in dungarees and bovver boots!). Theoretically, radical feminism can be criticized for its essentialist tendencies. In highlighting reproductive and sexual differences and citing them as the basis of women's oppression, it veered towards replicating the conservative view that biology was destiny (although, unlike conservatives, it saw reproduction as the base of a socially constructed hierarchy of power and inequality). It tended to ignore differences among women rising from class and ethnicity, and to assume a commonality of interests in terms of 'sisterhood'. Men were angered by the way it presented the whole male sex as oppressors, and pointed to complex subtleties of power between the sexes.

While these criticisms point to serious weaknesses in the radical standpoint, its contribution to feminist thinking should not be underestimated. Its great achievement was to highlight the different view of the world that rose from a specifically female way of seeing. While liberal feminism was based on an assertion of asexual *personhood*, portraying the subject of feminism as a free individual fighting for equality, and while Marxism subsumed gender as one position among many in the general struggle against social hierarchies, radical feminism insisted on the distinct nature of female experience and the feminine subject. However crude some aspects of the theorizing may have been, radical feminism laid the ground for the current feminist interest in culture, sexuality and subjectivity. The idea of a specific woman's culture inspired a wealth of autonomous women's organizations, from rape crisis centres and homes for battered women to women's bookshops and theatre groups. These political achievements can be considered to have been as crucial as the liberal feminist campaigns in opening up new horizons for women in the latter part of the twentieth century and the early twenty-first century.

Psychoanalysis and Feminism

In comparison to radical feminism, Marxism was weak on the more personal aspects of gendered experience. This led Juliet Mitchell (1975) to combine a Marxist account of the economic aspects of gender inequality with a Freudian analysis to theorize psychic structures of oppression. She suggested that a theory of the unconscious would explain why, despite the campaigns of feminists, female subordination was so hard to eradicate. Through the interrelations of psychosexual development within the family as described by Freud, acceptance of male superiority and female inferiority became embedded in the individual's unconscious mental processes.

There has been a longstanding, if wary, flirtation between feminism and various forms of psychoanalytic theory. The wariness arises from the fact that psychoanalysis presents accounts of universal patterns of psychic development, based in relations between parents and children, while a key principle of feminism has always been that gender relationships are socially constructed and culturally variable. An appreciation of the wide variety of forms of relations between men and women in families and kinship groups, or of constructs of the

ideal male or female personality, was fostered by study of anthropo-
logical evidence (for example, Rosaldo and Lamphere 1974; Rohrlich-
Leavitt 1975). Nevertheless, the desire to understand the place of
sexuality within gendered inequalities has often induced feminists to
turn to psychoanalysis.

Many feminists have found Freud's version of psychoanalysis hard
to take, despite Mitchell's attempt to show that his theories might be
appropriated and revised for feminist analysis. The prominence given
by Freud to the phallus and genital difference lays his work open to
charges of biological determinism and sexism. The theories of the
Oedipus complex (including the male child's terror of castration) and
of female penis envy portray women as inferior versions of men, with
adult femininity evolving as an incomplete form of masculinity.
Lacking the phallus, could women ever hope to achieve equality
with men? Freud's presentation of his findings as a set of universal
dilemmas that must be solved by everyone if they are to achieve
psychic health and stability as adult sexual beings overlooks the historical specificity of family relations and sexual practices; his theories,
based on white bourgeois families in nineteenth-century Vienna, need
severe modification to fit with today's world of single parents and
flexible family forms.

For this reason, many feminists have found a more acceptable
version of psychoanalysis in Nancy Chodorow's account (1978) of
childhood and gender development, derived from the 'object relations' school of Winnicott. This improves on Freud in focusing on
the social rather than biological aspects of parent/child relationships.
Chodorow bases her analysis on the strong identification babies and
young children have with their mother. To achieve male identity, boys
have to rupture that identification and establish themselves as separate entities. The pain and isolation inherent in this process mean
that adolescence is more problematic for boys than girls and that
masculine identity is more fragile than femininity. To achieve secure
masculinity, the boy may react by vehemently rejecting all aspects of
his own experience and personality that could be seen as female;
from this follows the depreciation of women by adult men. By contrast, the girl's childhood is more secure as she is able to retain
the identification with her mother to a much later date. However,
her individuality is less marked and she has trouble in achieving
the self-confidence and autonomy of the male. Through these childhood processes, the psychic structures of typical masculinity and
femininity continue to reproduce themselves and will only be changed,
Chodorow suggests, if parenting is transformed, with fathers becoming equally involved.

Chodorow's theory indicates why prevailing definitions of femininity and masculinity are so enduring. Indeed, without its psychoanalytic trappings the account makes sociological sense; it is highly compatible with the work done by sociologists on gender socialization in the family, which also suggests that young children internalize gender norms transmitted from generation to generation (Sharpe 1976; Oakley 1981). But Chodorow's approach can be seen as too deterministic. Feminine and masculine identities and sexualities are not fixed; they *do* change.

All versions of psychoanalysis tend towards determinism. They imply that the relations of early childhood are crucial for the development of adult identities, whereas current approaches to gender assert that feminine and masculine identities are perpetually being created and recreated through processes of social interaction. This is a life-long process. All this poses problems in reconciling psychoanalytic thinking with a sociological approach to gender.

The Contribution of Classic Feminist Thinking

Since the mid-1980s, classic feminist thinking has been subjected to a series of intensive critiques commencing with Black feminists attacking its ethnocentric bias. The Black feminist critique opened up the subsequent debate on the diversity of women's experience. Criticisms of a more theoretical nature came from feminists influenced by post-structural and postmodernist ideas. They argued that the classic theories were 'essentialist': that is, based on the assumption that a particular social category is marked by unchanging qualities, a common 'essence' shared by all members of the category. An essentialist approach to gender implies that all women (or all men) are united by common characteristics or interests.

Postmodern thinking also challenged notions of structure and system inherent in Marxist and radical feminist theories. It was argued that these theories were tainted by the rationalist and teleological tendencies of the modernist grand narratives from which they had emerged. In the early 1990s, the volume of criticism appeared to reach a kind of critical mass, to the extent that Barrett and Phillips, in an influential text, spoke of 'a "paradigm shift", in which assumptions rather than conclusions are radically overturned' (1992, p. 2). They discerned a gulf, possibly not bridgeable, between 1970s and 1990s feminism.

I suggest that there is a danger of writing off the classic legacy and undervaluing its achievements. Whatever the theoretical limitations of 1970s feminism, its standpoints acted as stimuli for indispensable research into all aspects of gender relations. The liberal feminist standpoint promoted research into education and the state; socialist feminists explored the inequalities of gender in waged and domestic work; and radical thinking opened up analysis of sexualities and the spectrum of male violence, which is very influential in 'third-wave' feminism. Without this rich basis of empirical evidence, contemporary feminism would not have been able to develop its understanding of the complexities of gendered power and its interrelation with other forms of oppression.

I want to highlight three of the key concepts of classic feminism: patriarchy, the sexual division of labour and compulsory heterosexuality. Insights gained from debates over these concepts have been vital to the development of a sociological account of gender.

Theorizing Patriarchy

As has been implied, the analysis of patriarchy was in many ways the core contribution of 1970s feminism, although the concept has always been the target of critical attack. It was developed to explain systemic arrangements that maintained male social dominance. The project of many feminist theorists, both Marxist and radical, was to develop a model of patriarchy analogous to the Marxian idea of mode of production. There were various attempts to distinguish the 'base' of patriarchy. For example, Hartmann (1981) argued that it lay in male control of female labour power, while Firestone (1971) considered that patriarchy arose from men's control of reproductive arrangements. Delphy (1977), taking domestic labour as central, suggested the alternative conception of two coexisting modes of production: the capitalist mode, in which capital exploits the labour of the working class, and the domestic mode of production, in which men exploit the unpaid labour of women. The influence of Marxism is clear in all these versions. Sylvia Walby (1990) moved further away from the strict attempt to replicate the base/superstructure model of Marxism with her conceptualization of patriarchy, which she defined as 'a system of social structures and practices in which men dominate, oppress and exploit women' (p. 20). She isolated six types of structure: paid work, domestic labour, sexuality, the state, violence and culture.

However, many feminists were unhappy with the concept, arguing that it tended to imply that *all* societies in *all* historical periods were characterized by male domination. Rowbotham's well-known critique (1981) is typical. She argued that the concept was too universalistic and ahistorical; it could not encompass variations in the balance of power between the sexes in different societies, nor the different ways that power was exercised. The framework of patriarchy rules out the possibility of types of society where women and men are equal, or even where women are dominant (a matriarchy).

One response was to explore historically exactly how and to what extent male power was exercised in various social contexts. Barrett suggested that the adjective 'patriarchal' should only be used to describe concrete historical instances in which 'male domination is expressed through the power of the father over women and over younger men' (Barrett 1980, p. 250). Walby, in a series of publications (1990, 1992, 1993), has developed an account of a move from 'private patriarchy' (that is, the control of women by individual men within the household) to 'public patriarchy', where women are subordinated in the public sphere (especially at work and within the state) by structures of segregation:

> In public patriarchy, women are not confined to the household and the mode of expropriation is more collective than individual, for instance, by most women being paid less than men. In private patriarchy the main patriarchal strategy is exclusionary, and women are not allowed into certain social arenas, such as Parliament, while in public patriarchy women are allowed in, but segregated and subordinated there. (Walby 1993, pp. 87–8)

While such accounts emphasize the variability of power relations, other problems with the concept are less easily solved, and were highlighted by postmodernist critiques of classic feminism. Postmodernists saw patriarchy as an inadequate way to conceptualize gendered power. It is a zero-sum concept: that is, it suggests that all the power rests with men, none with women. Contemporary feminists reject the portrayal of women as passive victims of male power. They emphasize the complexity of power relations between women and men, pointing out that some women are in positions of power over other women, and indeed, over men (for example, women of the dominant classes who employ servants of both sexes, or female employers and managers).

Despite these criticisms, feminists have been reluctant to abandon the term altogether. In part, this is because of its important place in the history of second-wave feminist political campaigning: it has become a symbolic marker of a feminist position. It is a theoretical tool which feminist theorists have claimed and developed themselves, by contrast to, for example, the ideas of postmodern feminism, which are borrowed extensively from male writers such as Foucault and

Derrida. For these reasons, many feminists continue to use the term. One strategy is to use it adjectivally ('patriarchal ideologies', 'patriarchal practices'), rather than as a noun which implies a system approach. The use of system theories has already been criticized in this book (chapter 2) for the way it inevitably carries exclusions. But I see it as legitimate to speak of 'patriarchal relations' in reference to the gender differences which are the topic of this chapter. The term is also gaining popularity among contemporary young feminist writers.

The Sexual Division of Labour

Those chary of the term 'patriarchy' have preferred to use the alternative term 'sexual division of labour'. This term has proved acceptable to all feminist standpoints and is commonly used in social research.

Initial explorations of the sexual division of labour in paid work drew on ideas from existing sociological theories. For example, Marxists took up the idea that women were part of the reserve army of labour, drawn in and out of the labour force according to capitalist needs, although study of trends in unemployment suggested that, while possibly true in some historical periods, this did not fit women's labour market experience in the post-war decades: men have lost jobs, rather than women, in some recessions. Alternatively, Humphries (1983) suggested that women, because they are used as cheap labour, constituted an 'ideal proletariat', a position that was criticized because of the history of collusions between employers and organized male workers to keep women out of 'men's jobs' (Hartmann 1976; Bradley 1989). Humphries's arguments about 'female proletarianization', however, merit reconsideration in the 2010s with neoliberal austerity policies hitting women hard, pushing them from secure work in the public sector to low-paid work in retail and hospitality. Beechey (1977) drew on the Marxian theory of value to suggest *why* female labour was cheaper, arguing that, because women were habitually dependent on fathers and husbands, the cost of the reproduction of their labour power was literally less: they could be paid a wage below what was considered necessary for male subsistence. Another strategy was to employ the Weberian framework of dual or segmented labour markets. This states that the labour market is split into segments, between which it is difficult for workers to move, because of employers' requirements for different types of labour. Women characteristically occupy secondary segments in the market, characterized by low pay, tight control, poor conditions and lack of opportunities. Secondary workers are hired and fired to serve employers' need for flexibility, while for stability they rely on the commitment of a core of privileged primary workers, usually male and white.

While these approaches offer insights on employers' deployment of women, all slot women into pre-existing analyses of class, ignoring the gender dynamics which make such discriminatory practices possible. None of the theories is adequately able to explain why and how the sexes were segregated at work, or account for the persistence of segregated structures. The notion of gender segregation, both horizontal (the clustering of women and men in different sex-typed jobs and occupations) and vertical (the concentration of men in top grades in each occupation), became a key explanatory tool. Various factors were seen to contribute to the formation and maintenance of segregated structures: employers' motivations and attitudes; patriarchal and paternalist controls which treated women employees differently from men; the exclusionary policies and practices of trade unions and professional associations; ideologies or discourses of masculinity and femininity; work cultures which promoted preferences for same-sex workmates; sexual harassment which served to police the boundaries between men's and women's jobs (see, for example, Spencer and Podmore 1987; Bradley 1989, 1999b; Witz 1992). Cynthia Cockburn's studies (1983, 1985, 1991) demonstrated the subtle processes through which jobs and workplaces become gendered. She highlighted the role of technology: the association of men with technical competence served to maintain gender hierarchies. Her research also documents the resistance of men to the breakdown of segregation.

The domestic division of labour has also received much attention, starting with the pioneering studies of 'housework' by Oakley and others (Oakley 1974; Hunt 1980). Despite claims that marriages are becoming more symmetrical and domestic tasks being shared more equally, surveys persistently reveal that women still take on the major share of housework and childcare even where both partners work (Berthoud and Gershuny 2000; Sullivan 2000). Where the labour is displaced onto paid helpers, such cleaners, childminders and nannies are inevitably female. In this way, the idea of women's responsibility for domestic labour persists, and with it the view of women as 'naturally' orientated towards domestic life and motherhood (Crowley 1992). There is some evidence, especially where male unemployment is rife, that couples are beginning to renegotiate the domestic division of labour, with men taking more part (Morris 1990; Wheelock 1990; Brannen and Moss 1991). But men remain selective in the tasks they undertake, and the ultimate responsibility remains with mothers. Campbell (2014) shows how the relative amounts of time put into childcare and housework by men and women have altered since the

1970s; women's average housework contribution has diminished from 197 minutes daily to 146, while men's contribution has increased from 20 to 53 minutes (still not a lot); and while men have put more time into childcare (up from 10 to 17 minutes), women's input has increased more: from 26 to 42 minutes. Child-rearing responsibilities are still perhaps *the* major reason for women's restricted labour market opportunities.

The many studies of the sexual division of labour reveal the extent and strength of gender segregation in contemporary societies. While feminist research has recently shifted towards the exploration of cultural aspects of gender, these studies remain the basis of our understanding of gender as a form of inequality.

Compulsory Heterosexuality

While *all* classic feminist thinking encouraged a critical approach to longstanding notions of the public and the private spheres, seeking to bridge the analytical gap between them, the radical standpoint in particular was the base for delving into personal relationships. The traditional view of the family, marriage and romance was that these were areas of freedom and individual fulfilment, set apart from the constraints of economic and public life (Zaretsky 1976; Lasch 1977). Feminists challenged this view, suggesting that marriage was an unequal contract in which women were trapped. Bernard (1976) suggested that men, rather than women, benefited from marriage, while wives suffered from the frustrations and isolation associated with the housewife role. The espousal of romantic ideals by young unmarried women was shown to draw them into same trap as their mothers (McRobbie 1978; Westwood 1984). In this way, marriage and love were portrayed as social, not natural, institutions, which shored up patriarchal dominance.

From this standpoint, feminists were able to attack the view of emotions and sexual orientations as natural and given. In a famous essay, 'Compulsory heterosexuality and lesbian existence', Adrienne Rich (1980) argued against the view that individuals were endowed with a fixed sexual identity. Rather, she claimed, heterosexual and homosexual desires and practices should be seen as points on a continuum of potential sexual behaviours.

Feminism divorces sexual behaviour from biological dimorphism, and suggests that individuals are potentially bisexual and androgynous; heterosexuality is so prevalent merely because it is socially constructed and learned as the norm of sexual behaviour. Those who reject the rules of 'compulsory sexuality' are liable to be stigmatized as abnormal, 'queer' and sick. However, those who accept the conventional version of sexuality also suffer, since their potential for exploring and expressing their individual sexuality in a variety of ways is suppressed. Rich laments the loss through such processes of the wealth of possibilities for warmer, more intimate bonds between women.

Also, since the prevailing or 'hegemonic' version of male heterosexuality (Connell 1987) encourages predatory, aggressive and sometimes violent sexual behavior – the ideal of the male stud 'putting it about' – compulsory heterosexuality contributes to the maintenance of male dominance. The report by the National Union of Students (NUS) on 'lad culture' on university campuses, *That's What She Said*, revealed frightening levels of sexual aggression among young men one might expect to know better: a previous survey had found that one in seven female students had experienced a serious physical or sexual assault while at university, while 70 per cent reported verbal and non-verbal harassment (NUS 2013). It is also important to stress that such norms of heterosexual masculinity put terrible pressures on men to live up to them: men are commonly the victims of male aggression, and male rape is a problem in prison communities.

Recent approaches to sexuality have emphasized the variety of straight, gay, lesbian and transsexual identities on offer, speaking in terms of 'heterosexualities' and 'homosexualities' rather than one prevailing sexual code (see chapter 8). Moreover, postmodern feminism is concerned to emphasize the pleasures and desires that can be enjoyed within sexuality even by women who accept the heterosexual norm unquestioningly. Nonetheless, the work of Rich and others speaking from the radical standpoint opened up exploration of how sexualities are socially constructed. The notion of 'compulsory heterosexuality' is still a very important insight into how we view sexual behaviour and why some forms of sexual behaviour are accepted and others condemned. In such ways, classic feminist analysis laid the foundations for an understanding of gendered subjectivity.

A Paradigm Shift? The Postmodern Critique

In the mid-1980s, the feminist approach to gender took a 'cultural turn' and a 'linguistic turn'. Study of gendered representations and discourses dominated in the 1990s, pushing the old concerns about inequalities of gender to the margins. Above all, an overriding interest in the differing ways in which women experience gender developed, which remains central and is currently stressed through the notion of intersectionality. However, in the twenty-first century, the issue of inequalities has re-emerged, because of the impact of neoliberal austerity policies on women's lives. Interestingly, though, among the emergent generation of young feminist scholars and activists, cultural issues such as pornography and sexuality are of particular concern.

The Black Critique

The initial impetus for rethinking the assumptions of classic feminism came from minority ethnic women who were developing their own standpoint, that of 'Black feminist thought' (Collins 1990). Black feminists argued that the feminist analysis of gender was biased and ethnocentric, taking the experience of white middle-class women as the norm and then claiming to speak on behalf of 'all' women. By contrast, Black critics highlighted the specificity of minority women's experience and how gender relationships impacted on them in quite distinct ways (see, for example, hooks 1982; Anthias and Yuval-Davis 1983; Brah 1992). For instance, while white feminists tended to view the family as an agent of patriarchal domination, Black women argued that for them the family was a source of solidarity and support against the racism and subordination they experienced in white-dominated society. Moreover, Black family forms often differed from white ones, yet the middle-class nuclear family was discussed as if it was common to all social groups. Or again, reproductive controls acted differently on Black women: while white women campaigned for the rights to contraception and abortion as a way to assert their control over their own bodies, Black women were often subjected to pressure to employ contraceptive techniques (sometimes of dangerous kinds) or to undergo abortions because of white fears about Black fertility and their desire to limit it (Amos and Parmar 1984; Collins 1990; Knowles and Mercer 1992).

The notion of 'sisterhood' among women was thus exposed as a myth. Indeed, some claimed that, in its assumption of common experience, white feminism could itself be seen as racist. Amos and Parmar (1984) argued that the gains of feminist politics were often at the expense of Black and working-class women. The freedom gained by white middle-class women to pursue careers or achieve economic equality with men depended on the exploitation of low-paid Black or working-class women acting as servants or childminders. The feminist movement minimized the contributions of Black women and failed to study or prioritize their needs. Moreover, the very theories developed to analyse gender were contributing to making Black women invisible. 'Dual systems' theory, for example, looked at the intersection of class and gender inequalities but overlooked racial hierarchies. The theory of patriarchy elevated gendered power over forms of racial oppression that Black women saw as central to their lives.

While these criticisms were warranted and opened up new areas of research and debate, it can be argued that they were also divisive, at a moment when feminism as a political movement was in some disarray. Looking back on these debates, Parmar (1990) regretted the tendency to construct a 'hierarchy of oppression', with various groups of women asserting their own situation as most demanding of attention. Such arguments could be exclusionary and lead to suppression of genuine debate, as women feared to speak from a position of privilege. It seems more positive to seek unity across divisions. Understanding the diversity of women's situations can promote a more democratic movement based on coalition, or at the least provides opportunity for dialogue and exchange of experiences (Tang Nain 1991; Yuval-Davis 1993).

Theoretically, the Black critique had a crucial effect on the analysis of gender. It was evident that it was no longer possible to employ the category 'women' and assume a common oppression. The category of 'women' needed to be deconstructed (Riley 1988) and the history of different groups of women explored. There was a need to consider how gender linked with other dynamics of inequality, age and class as well as ethnicity.

In this way the Black critique not only highlighted the issues of difference and diversity, but led to an interest in studying identities and subjectivities. Moreover, the criticism of patriarchy as a unidimensional theory added to the growing interest in reconceptualizing power. In these ways, the concerns of Black feminism were similar to those of feminists influenced by postmodern theory and deconstructionism.

Postmodern, Post-Structural and Deconstructionist Feminism

Postmodernism and post-structuralism were the new orthodoxies among feminist theorists of the 1990s. In some ways this was strange, as key postmodern and post-structuralist thinkers, such as Lyotard and Foucault, paid little attention to gender (see chapter 3). There is also unease with the pluralistic and individualistic vision of society which often emerges from such approaches, and which can be seen an potentially undermining the feminist contention that women as a category are oppressed. Is it possible to have a version of feminism without some notion of gender inequalities as structured or built into societal organization? However, what has particularly drawn feminists to postmodernism is its critical stance towards science, with its claims to objectivity and neutrality. This accords with feminism's own longstanding critique of science and of 'malestream' social theories for their gender-blindness, their assumption that male experience is the norm (the 'universal male subject'), along with their rejection of radical work which is considered to arise from subjective and therefore 'biased' political attachments. Such approaches, it is argued, present a partial male vision of the world as absolute and universal truth. The postmodern position allows feminists to pursue their claims that all knowledge is partial and relative to the standpoint of the knower; that, rather than a single objective truth, there are multiple voices and multiple truths; and that emotions and intuitions are as valid a base for the pursuit of knowledge as 'reason' and 'objectivity', so long seen as attributes possessed by men and counterposed to feminine 'irrationality' and 'subjectivity' (Harding 1986; Fraser and Nicholson 1988; Nicholson 1990).

Postmodernism has other attractions for feminists. Postmodernist sociology's interest in multiple sources of identity connected with the Black critique. Postmodernism encourages discussion of sexuality, desires, popular cultural expressions, and the fluidity of subjectivity. The postmodern stress on culture rather than structure allows feminists to discuss how women, as active agents, are involved in the construction of their own worlds, rather than presenting them as victims and puppets of structures beyond their determination. The pleasures women derive from femininity and feminine pursuits can be explored within this framework.

More controversial is the critique offered by postmodernism of the modernist metanarratives of social development, since, as Phillips (1992) and Marshall (1994) point out, feminism itself evolved as part of the modernist quest for equality and emancipation. In an early postmodernist account, Jean Bethke Elshtain (1987) criticized liberal, Marxist and radical feminist approaches as teleological: that is, assuming a progressive development towards a given, possibly Utopian, end-state. Liberal and Marxist accounts she considered to be predicated on a 'sex neutrality' narrative (in Marxism linked to the equivalent idea of a classless society), while the radical narrative of 'sex polarity' suggested that intrinsic differences in male and female experiences would inevitably lead to separation of the sexes, although in an Utopian future such a separation could be based on women's assertion of the value of their own culture.

Whether or not one accepts Elshtain's contention that the feminist narratives rested inevitably on essentialist concepts of gender and on an acceptance of linear progress in society (which could certainly be challenged), it is true that classic feminism was based on views of society as systematic and structured. The analysis of structured inequalities of society was used as evidence for the need for social reform. If the idea of social structures leading to a common oppression of women is abandoned, it can be questioned whether feminism can mount a case for the need to transform gender relations. If all truths are partial and relative, and all versions of the world have equal validity, there is no logical reason why patriarchal and conservative accounts of gender should not be as 'valid' as those of their feminist critics. As McNay expresses it:

> It is not desirable, or ultimately even possible, for feminism to take on the postmodern rejection of metanarratives. Whilst feminism has to guard against the dangers of generalization, it nevertheless rests on the fundamental assumption that the inequality between the sexes is indefensible and unjust. Such an assumption informs feminist analyses of the position of women in society, it underlies their call for a global abolition of gender-related inequalities. (1992, pp. 196–7)

Despite these political difficulties, many feminist theorists were drawn to the post-structural approach elaborated by critics of Marxism and of structural theories of language, such as Derrida, Foucault and Lacan. Derrida's work inspired an investigation of the categories used to understand social reality and the way they themselves become constitutive of it. Foucault developed this into the idea of 'discursive' frameworks, sets of interlinked statements and practices through which we make sense of the world and which are implicated in the reproduction of relationships of power (Foucault 1972; McNay 1992). Lacan offered a linguistic version of psychoanalytic theory, transposing Freud's theory of the phallus to a symbolic level. Individuals develop gendered subjectivity and sexual identity only through entry into language, but language itself is phallocentric, transmitting the patriarchal law of the father. Thus both sexes will come to speak (and think) of masculinity as superior; indeed, the phallocentric nature of language means that women lack a voice of their own and can only speak in masculine terms (Tong 1989). Although the problems of psychoanalysis discussed earlier in this chapter reappear in the Lacanian framework, it has been strongly influential within feminism. Cixous and Irigaray called on women to create their own versions of femininity based on new linguistic forms reflecting the specific female experience of the gendered body and female sexuality (Duchen 1987; Tong 1989).

Post-structuralist influences led feminists to explore dominant discursive frameworks that are used to marginalize women and to promote certain constructs of femininity at the expense of others (for example, Steedman et al. 1985; Scott 1988; Pringle 1989). Pringle and Watson argue that this idea of 'discursive marginality' can be the basis for a new unity among women to replace the old (essentialist) vision of common interests arising from common experience (1992, p. 68).

New Themes

Such new moves in feminism have foregrounded new themes. A number of connected issues are briefly considered here: deconstruction, difference and diversity; plural masculinities; discursive frameworks and power.

Deconstructing Women: Difference and Diversity

The structural view of language sees it as a system of signs which is linked in some intrinsic way to the reality (the material world) it represents. The post-structuralist view treats language as a set of arbitrary and floating signs. Rather than reflecting reality, language is seen as constitutive of it. Put crudely, what we say determines what we see, rather than the other way round. These ideas lie behind the 'linguistic turn' in feminism and the interest in deconstruction and discourse.

Derrida's work has promoted a critique of the categories, especially those based on binary oppositions such as 'man/woman' or 'Black/white', which are used to describe the world. Such categories do violence to the variety of potential experience by forcing it to cohere to one of the polar options. The 'submerged middle' of the range of positions in-between is suppressed. As Donna Haraway (1990) argues, the very act of naming something or somebody (even oneself) brings exclusions. Categories also construct one (essentialized) set of people as 'the other' ('woman' or 'Black'), whose experience is defined against that of the dominant group and often seen as 'deviant' or inferior. These oppressive categories need deconstructing, if a different 'reality' is to be built, allowing individuals to think in different and freer ways

Denise Riley's influential work (1988) set about deconstructing the notion of 'women'. She posed the question of what it means to 'be a woman' and pointed out how this has varied according to historical epoch: '"Women" is historically, discursively constructed and always relatively to other categories which themselves change' (pp. 2–3). Not only is the category of women as an identifiable collectivity with a common political interest unstable, but our individual self-consciousness of ourselves as 'women' (or 'men') is fluid. Most of the time we think of ourselves as 'a person'. To accept being 'a woman' is to accept being part of a category discursively presented as inferior. Discourses of gender induce us to act in certain ways because we are socially defined as being 'a man' or 'a woman'. Preoccupation with the idea of women as a category, which was the analytic slant of radical feminism, conceals the fact that people could also be constructed as, or realign themselves as, members of other categories, such as class or 'race'.

The deconstruction of women as a category signals the need to consider the diversity of women's situations. The initial Black critique opened up an opposition between white and Black women's experience. However, Anthias and Yuval-Davis (1983) pointed out that using the term 'Black' women to represent racial difference covers up the divergent experiences of other minority groups (Jewish, Cypriot, Irish or Polish women, for example). Subsequent research has considered how specific ethnic groups in our societies are located in the gender dynamic; and also explored how differences *within* each ethnic group may be created, in terms of position in the life cycle (age, marital status), class and occupation, sexual orientation, dis/ability, religious affiliation and so forth (Afshar and Maynard 1994; Bradley et al. 2007).

Although the exploration of difference and diversity is now a key theme in gender analysis, the dangers of overstressing difference at the expense of unity have been pointed out (Stacey 1993; Maynard 1994). As the list above indicates, there is the risk of a remorseless fragmentation as each new specific group is distinguished, the more so as Yuval-Davis warns against the tendency towards 'essentializing' each group in turn (Anthias and Yuval-Davis, 1993). Moreover, persistent stress on difference may lead to marginalizing those who do not fit into any of these often dichotomized categories – for example, people of mixed 'race' (Allen 1994). Stress on difference may entail the setting up of uncrossable boundaries between 'them' and 'us'. The other danger is of a spiral into individualism, in which we lose all sight of the commonality of gendered experience. A balance is needed between notions of unity and difference.

Walby (1992) suggests we can achieve this by retaining the broader modernist frameworks for explaining social structure, while remaining sensitive to the need to explore differences, and being careful not to allow slippage back into a unidimensional theorization such as traditional Marxism (p. 33). Her approach entails showing how the various structures (gender, class, ethnicity, age, etc.) interrelate, a task which she suggests has not yet been adequately accomplished. Broadly, that is the approach advocated in this book. An alternative more in line with postmodernist prescriptions is to explore the 'local narratives' of particular groups in particular contexts – for example, young Black women in schools (Mirza 1992), Muslim women in the labour market (Brah 1994), lesbians within academia (Wilton 1993) – and show how they are positioned within the various discourses of gender.

Plural Masculinities

While the concept of difference/diversity has been applied mainly to women, the more postmodern approaches to studying men also emphasized that men did not share any common essence. Rather than discussing 'masculinity,' it was necessary to consider the multiple nature of masculinities.

Connell's highly influential concept of 'hegemonic masculinity' (1987), mentioned above, had anyway been located in an account of gender and power in which hegemonic males remained dominant not only over women but over 'subjugated masculinities', which included gays, colonial men and feminist men. However, answering criticisms that the concept might be too static, in his later work Connell elaborated that hegemonic masculinity should not be seen as fixed or universal, but should be viewed as the form of masculinity that 'occupies the hegemonic position in a given pattern of gender relations, a position always contestable' (2005, p. 76). Thus, recent research has considered the changing nature of plural forms of masculinity, including alternative forms of working-class male identifications – for example, Riches's study of heavy metal fans in Canada who bond through physical activity in the moshpit, or Ward's study of 'Emo' boys in the Welsh valleys (Riches 2014; Ward 2014). An earlier study of 'messages men hear' explored a range of discourses of gender in America, informing various subject masculine positions, such as 'family man', 'Don Juan', 'civic leader' or 'superman' (Harris 1995).

More recently, Anderson and McCormack have argued that young men in Britain are rejecting the homophobic and hyper-masculine forms of masculinity typical of their fathers, embracing softer, more tolerant styles, in what they label 'inclusive masculinity' (Anderson 2009; Anderson and McCormack 2014). They describe current British young males as 'better dressed digital hippies' (2014, p. 126), not afraid to display intimacy, to cuddle and kiss. While this may indeed be a trend in some sectors of society, it is clear that more traditional forms of hegemonic or hyper-masculinity still dominate, seen variously among male politicians in televised debates from the House of Commons, young male football supporters, CEOs (think Sir Alan Sugar in the Boardroom) or drunken youths in town centres on Saturday nights. Such practices may be hard for young men to resist in certain contexts (Ward 2014), especially in tight working-class communities where what have been termed 'obstinate identities' (Pilkington and Johnson 2003) linger on in the face of unforgiving neoliberal modernity.

Discourse

Stuart Hall defines a discourse as 'a group of statements which provide a language for talking about – i.e. a way of representing – a particular type of knowledge about a topic' (1992b, p. 291). These interlinked sets of statements, working together to provide a 'discursive formation', construct the topic under consideration (such as gender) in a particular way, in line with particular objectives or institutional and political strategies. Foucault (1972) used the notion of discourse to challenge prevailing ideas about scientific knowledge and its privileged claim to reveal absolute, objective truth. Science (and, of course, social science) was to Foucault no more than one of many discursive formations laying claim to particular versions of what truth is. Powerful discourses may become part of what Foucault called a 'regime of truth' in any given society or context. Regimes of truth establish what may be known and how it is known.

The idea of discourse became very influential in feminism. Women were shown to occupy subject positions within discourses, where they often appear as 'the Other'. Through their own engagement with such dominant discourses, particularly with popular versions of thinking on gender, women and men are actively engaged in reconstituting gender relations in ways that allow power disparities to be perpetuated.

For example, Davies (1989) has shown that the exposure of very young children to discourses on gender in stories disposes them to accept prevailing views of appropriate male and female behaviour; this is an important way in which children begin to make sense of the world and locate themselves within it. Similarly, Pringle's research into secretaries (1989) revealed how their involvement with prevailing discourses on femininity and masculinity helped to reproduce power relations within the office; the secretaries associated certain types of behaviour (such as bitching about other women, or favouritism and bossiness displayed by women in positions of power) with being female, and so accepted the view that men were more fitted to hold superior positions. The research of Wetherell et al. (1987) into students' attitudes to gender and equality revealed how exposure to competing discourses about gender produces confused and contradictory attitudes. The young people believed in an equal division of labour within marriage yet still felt that women should be ultimately responsible for childcare. Such discourses act to constitute and recreate patterns of gender inequality.

A problem with the concept of discourse is that it may be used quite vaguely. Some people employ it merely to indicate linguistic practices, while others, such as Pringle and Watson (1992) claim that it also includes 'material practices'. The relationship between linguistic practices and material aspects of inequality, between 'words' and 'things' as Barrett puts it, is ambiguously presented in these accounts. Barrett (1992, p. 201) points out that Foucault proclaimed his desire to 'dispense with things'. Others are not so sure. Moreover, since we are given to understand that people are active in constituting new meanings, it is not clear why some discourses stick and others do not. For example, Davies shows that young children reject alternative discourses on gender when presented in feminist rewritings of fairytales. To solve this problem, some theory of power is needed.

Power

Foucault linked truth regimes and knowledge to power, and many feminists drew on his ideas to replace the much-criticized notion of patriarchy with a more subtle account of gendered power (McNay 1992). Rather than presenting power as exercised hierarchically from the top down (men holding power over women, the bourgeoisie over the proletariat), Foucault sees power as embedded in everyday relationships at every level of society, and as commonly operating through various regimes of discipline and surveillance. Moreover, for Foucault, power is not just linked to repression; it is also used 'to incite, exhort and create' (Still 1994, p. 152). The experience of power can be pleasurable to its objects. For example, Foucault shows how regimes of control and surveillance designed to discipline and normalize the body (for example, sport, exercise and health programmes) are experienced pleasurably by those who undergo them. 'Going to the gym' is now an important aspect of enjoyable recreation for both women and men, while everybody from myself to George Osborne has adopted the 5-2 diet with its two days of fasting!

Foucault's framework allows for analysis of the subtleties of power in everyday interactions between women and men. A problem for feminists, however, is that this theory of power lacks a subject. Foucault, as a post-structuralist, will not link power to any account of structured inequalities. He shows us *how* power is exercised, but not *why*. However, some feminists have combined a Foucauldian analysis with an account of patriarchy. Bartky, for example, considers women's preoccupation with their bodies, beauty and slimming as a case of a disciplinary regime. She suggests (1990) that, in a patriarchal society, women have internalized men's definitions of ideal female bodies and continually subject themselves to an imaginary male gaze, a kind of psychic panopticon.

An alternative approach to power used by some feminists is offered by Anthony Giddens (Davis et al. 1991). Giddens conceptualizes power in terms of access to and control of various social resources. Such a framework offers a multi-dimensional view of power which can allow for complexities and variations, while also incorporating a view of agency and interests. For example, men may control more resources than women and so be dominant, but women may control certain types of resources, such as domestic skills, and use them to challenge and control men; social changes may open up greater access to certain resources to women – for example, their greater chances of acquiring professional jobs.

Although Giddens himself does not apply his theory to gender, I suggest that his ideas hold potential for a more satisfactory theory of gendered power. It is possible to identify a number of dimensions of power in terms of access to and control of different resources, and investigate how these are deployed in specific settings. For example, we might distinguish economic resources (property, wealth and money); positional resources (access to various positions of authority in both the public and private spheres); symbolic resources (including language, the various media of communication); domestic resources (control over family needs in the household); sexual resources (the giving and withholding of sexual pleasures); and personal resources (use of individual character and qualities to exercise control). Although, historically, men have appropriated more of the first three of these, women's control of sexual, domestic and personal resources has often allowed them to exercise power especially in personal relationships or in the home.

'New Waves' of Feminism in the Twenty-First Century: The Re-Emergence of Patriarchy?

One of the key features of feminism, as both a social movement and an academic discipline, is its dynamism, so it should be no surprise that various proclaimed 'new waves' of feminism have appeared over recent decades. A group of young activists in the USA coined the term 'third wave' in their manifestos, and set up the Third Wave Foundation. Drawing on the postmodern critiques of the 'second wave', they emphasized the importance of extending feminist analyses to young women of diverse backgrounds, foregrounding in particular the experiences of ethnic minority women and transsexuals. More controversially, they advocated a positive stance to pornography and the sex industry, issues which have always caused splits and arguments among feminists. I suggest this is a type of feminism which embraces the individualism and consumerism of American culture, in a way reminiscent of celebrity advocates of 'girl power', Madonna and the Spice Girls (Bradley 2012). For this reason, many of the young feminist activists in Britain reject the label of 'third wave' (Mackay 2011), seeing themselves rather as inheritors and developers of second-wave principles.

This is primarily an activist movement, which organizes conferences, workshops and summer camps, and campaigns on specific local issues. A particular concern of its activities has been the spread of 'lad culture' and a pervasive hyper-sexualization of society, seen as degrading and constraining to women. This has been documented in the works of its spokeswomen such as Walter (2010), Banyard (2010) and Bates (2014). The apparently unstoppable spread of the pornography and sex industries – greatly facilitated by availability on the internet and social media – the greater public acceptance of lap dancing and strip clubs, the springing-up of pole-dancing clubs and beauty contests on university campuses are seen to promote a view of women that reduces them to sex objects and body parts. Women are induced to parade themselves for men's delight, mistakenly reading these practices as a form of 'empowerment'; as Walter cogently sums up: 'When we talked about empowerment in the past, it was not a young woman in a thong gyrating around a pole that would spring to mind, but the attempts by women to gain real political and economic equality' (Walter 2010, p. 7).

The bleak picture of resurgent sexism and misogynism that emerges from the critical writings of these younger feminists is echoed in two powerful books from long-term contributors to thinking on gender. Angela McRobbie argues in *The Aftermath of Feminism* (2008) that young women have been caught up by a culture of hedonistic consumption, which is effectively undermining the gains of feminism. She attributes this to the domination of neoliberal ideas which promote the illusions of 'market freedom' and 'choice' while actually trapping women into subordination to men and denying them true equality. She describes a complex 'double entanglement' (a term drawn from Butler's work) of political ideologies typical of modern societies: on the one hand, neoliberalism promotes an 'aggressive individualism' (2010, p. 7), whereby people become their own brand and indulge in endless self-promotion; yet this is curiously combined with a moral conservatism, which preaches the value of the traditional family and conventional sex roles, and deplores those (single mothers, lesbians, people on benefits) who depart from those norms. I have noted this confusion among female students: they are encouraged to present themselves like showgirls (T-shirts with slogans such as 'porn star' are popular) but at the same time to prepare themselves for responsible professional careers and motherhood.

McRobbie notes that this cult of individualism and consumption is combined with what she calls a 'swaggering resurgent patriarchalism' (2010, p. 7), whereby men reassert their right to hold superior positions in the public sphere, and view women's bodies as theirs to command. This idea is echoed in Beatrix Campbell's *End of Equality* (2014), which talks of a 'neoliberal neopatriarchy'. Campbell argues that commitment to sexual (and other types of) equality, which was fostered by 1970s and 1980s feminism and held sway in the last quarter of the twentieth century (in my own research (Bradley 1999b) I referred to this as a 'climate of equality'), has since been overturned by neoliberalism. Increasing economic inequality is justified by the political elites in terms of meritocracy and the belief that the existence of a class of (deserving) wealthy people is beneficial for society as a whole: prosperity will 'trickle down'. Campbell concentrates on two aspects of this 'neo-patriarchy': the gap between women and men's economic prospects and the widespread violence against women on a global scale. Discussing her 'manifesto for the twenty-first century' on the Our Kingdom website, Campbell sums up pithily:

> In no society in the world does the criminal justice system take the side of women. In no society or system are women paid the same as men for a day, a week, or a lifetime's work. In no society do men share equally the work of care with women. Sexism finds new cultures and contexts; violence and sexual aggression attract impunity.... And in a world dominated by neoliberal neo-patriarchy there is little indication that this will change in favour of women – without a gender revolution. (Campbell, 2013)

Gendered Identities

Barrett suggested that part of the appeal of post-structuralism for feminists was its focus on 'the issues of sexuality, subjectivity and textuality that feminists have put at the top of the agenda' (1992, p. 215). Such new concerns brought the issue of identity to the fore.

Unlike class, gender is more commonly an active and politicized aspect of identity. The feminist movement, with its stress on 'consciousness-raising', promoted the notion of being a woman as a crucial aspect of individual subjectivity. Involvement in feminist activities of various kinds made gender central to many women's identities. Even women who reject or actively oppose feminism may demonstrate an active gender identity because of the high level of awareness about gender issues raised by, among other things, equal opportunities programmes and media coverage of women's issues. Men's groups, both traditional and radical, also promote identification with different types of masculinity.

But there are many ways of being a woman or a man. Gender may for feminists be a source of politicized identity which leads them to work for equality and women's causes. For other women, awareness of gender may involve traditional ways of displaying femininity, through domestic or caring roles, motherhood or assertion of sexuality. Given that gender experience is so differently felt by women of different ethnic groups, ages, religions, nationalities or sexual orientations, it is evident that there are multiple versions of womanhood. The experience of the gendered body is also important here. For a post-pubescent young woman exploring the pleasures (and problems) of her newly sexualized body in relation to young men, the experience of womanhood is quite different from that of an ageing post-menopausal woman, struggling to adjust to bodily changes in a culture that puts high valuation on youth and fertility.

Early feminist research borrowed the concept of consciousness from stratification theory to explore this issue. Research was directed to the debate as to whether class or gender consciousness was more significant to working-class women (Pollert 1981; Porter 1983). These studies suggested that women did have a specific consciousness, a 'woman's consciousness' rather than a 'feminist consciousness'; this was linked more to home lives than their work experience (Cavendish 1982; Westwood 1984). By contrast, work has commonly been linked to masculinity, especially in relation to men's breadwinner role (Cockburn 1983). Men have historically dominated in class-based organizations such as trade unions or the Labour party. But the long history of women's involvement in industrial struggles shows that class, too, can be a politicized identity for women in specific contexts, such as the miners' strike discussed in chapter 4 (Phillips 1987; Briskin and McDermott 1993). These findings show us the error of conceiving the problem in terms of whether class or gender is the dominant source of identity. Rather, the interplay of gender and class dynamics (along with others) is displayed in shifting processes of identification. Under the influence of postmodernism, the concept of identity has displaced the analysis of consciousness and more easily allows for the understanding of the multiple elements constituting an individual identity.

The assumption is that gender is more central to identity than class in contemporary societies; the weight of research certainly indicates that gender matters to women, especially through the medium of the female body. Increasingly, women are pressurized to conform to certain social ideals of bodily presentation. McDowell's classic study of women in the City of London showed the dilemmas over what to wear faced by women in this arena, where women's bodies appear as intrusive 'Others'; they have to avoid being too pretty (flowery skirts), but also should not ape masculinity by wearing trousers (McDowell 1996). Current requirements about acceptable feminine bodies include slenderness, a groomed appearance (make-up, nail polish, coiffeured hair) and removal of body hair. This need for acceptable feminine appearance keeps awareness of gender at a high level in everyday life.

By contrast, masculinity, at least until recently, could be seen as a more passive element in identity. Kitzinger and Wilkinson use the term 'default identity' to describe those which 'constitute the "normal, natural way to be"', such as white, able-bodied or male. They argue (1993, p. 32) that default identities are always 'less articulated, less self-conscious, than are oppositional or oppressed identities: lack of reflectiveness is the privilege of power'. However, at certain historical moments when a 'crisis of masculinity' occurs (Kimmel 1987), men may become much more reflexive about their gender. Such a crisis has been identified in many contemporary societies, as men faced the feminist challenge to conventional gender relations and experienced the erosion of the breadwinner role. The emergence of men's consciousness-raising groups and the men's rights campaigns of the 'backlash' are different ways in which masculinity may be displayed in more active or politicized forms of identity.

Riley's work (1988) alerts us to the fact that our gender is not to the forefront of our awareness all the time. She suggests that the awareness of being a woman is likely to emerge when gender becomes a source of adverse attention from others (discriminatory behaviour, harassment in the street), or indeed of positive attention. Similarly, the awareness of being a man may be heightened where masculinity is under threat (a challenge from a wife to her husband's authority, derogatory comments from other men) or strongly affirmed (in activities featuring 'male bonding', such as sport or drinking). In these circumstances, men may demonstrate their sense of manhood through displays of expected masculine behaviour, such as violence, fighting, physical feats, sexual assertiveness or sexist banter. But, as with women, there are many ways to be a man. Many men resist hegemonic forms of masculinity (Connell 1987, 2005): masculine identities are cross-cut with different expectations linked to ethnicity, age and sexual orientation.

For example, it is suggested that African American and African-Caribbean British men adopt an exaggerated form of machismo, often manifested through the assertion of control of physical spaces seen as 'their' territories. This streetwise masculinity is their response to racism and denigration by white society, and offsets their sense of being considered inferior to white men (Wallace 1990; Westwood 1990).

Sexuality is also an important aspect of gendered identity. The gay and lesbian movement has promoted homosexual identification of a highly active and politicized kind (see chapter 8). By contrast, Kitzinger and Wilkinson (1993), commenting on a collection of writings by heterosexual feminists, suggest that heterosexuality is another taken-for-granted default identity. In fact, within the feminist movement, heterosexuality has been seen as problematic and may even be stigmatized, counterposed to the assertion of woman-centred values and the espousal of lesbianism as a political strategy. But for non-feminist women, heterosexuality may be an important source of self-affirmation. This illustrates the way identities are highly informed by political contexts. It also points again to the multiple nature of gendered identities which must be viewed within the logic of interacting dynamics.

Intersecting Dynamics: Gender, Ethnicity, Class and Age

Ethnicity

While all women experience some aspects of gender inequalities (responsibility for domestic work, gender segregation at work, the threat of male violence), the specific nature of gender inequalities varies for different ethnic groups, classes and age groups.

For example, in Britain, women of colour face specific restrictions in the labour market because of their long-term exposure to processes of individual and institutional racism. In schools, ethnic minority youths face racial harassment from white pupils and stereotyping from teachers which may affect their educational progress (Fleming 1991; Mirza 1992). Women of colour enter a racialized as well as gendered labour market (Bradley and Healy 2007). Skilled minority ethnic women are twice as likely to be unemployed as white women; they face difficulties in gaining access to some parts of the female labour market, such as clerical work. African-Caribbean women have been concentrated in lower-grade caring work and public-sector jobs; Pakistani and Bengali women have low participation rates: if they have jobs, they tend to be in factories, or they may work at home or in family businesses (Brown 1984; Allen and Wolkowitz 1987; Bruegel 1989; Bradley et al. 2007). African-Caribbean women are more likely than white women to work full-time, since Black males suffer greater risks of unemployment and typical family relationships have promoted an important breadwinner role for mothers.

The Black feminist critique promoted research interest in uncovering the ways in which women of different ethnic groups experience gender. Such research is still under way and we know relatively little about the situation of women in some ethnic groups (for example, Chinese and Turkish women in Britain). It is clear that the position of each group is in many ways unique, a point that can be illustrated by referring to one example, that of Muslim women in Britain. The role of religion means that in some ways this can be seen as an exceptional case (it is certainly controversial), but it illustrates admirably the intersection of gender divisions, ethnic identity and racial discrimination.

Haleh Afshar's study of Muslim women in Yorkshire (1994) reveals the difficult situation of women, especially unmarried young women, 'who have to tread a tightrope of double identities, double values and double standards' (p. 141). The international revival of Islam has opened up a positive identity and source of solidarity and pride for Muslim women, as opposed to the experience of being the stigmatized 'Other' in the playground. Thus, many women willingly embrace Islamic dress styles, such as wearing a headscarf or veil. Abu Odeh's (1993) work shows that such women welcome the protection the veil offers them against male intrusion in the form of sexist abuse and sexual harassment. But fundamentalist versions of Islam – just like Christian, Jewish or any other form of fundamentalist religion – involve 'reinvigoration of patriarchy and the control of women' (Brah 1993, p. 20). Patriarchal rules, which set restrictions on women's participation in various aspects of public life, may create difficulties for women who must participate in the British labour market, which displays different rules on gender. Afshar points out the double standard whereby males may share aspects of Western lifestyle (drinking, smoking, flirtations, wearing Western fashions) while women must bear the burden of displaying proper Islamic behaviour and maintaining family 'izzat' (honour). Women's limited labour market chances may be further restricted by employers' prejudices around the adoption of Islamic dress. Afshar's finding that the women she studied were more preoccupied with the issues of marriage and motherhood than with education and employment illustrates the variability of the experience of gender for women of different ethnic groups.

Class

Afshar suggests that middle-class Muslim families are more likely to have 'integrated' into the British way of life; middle-class Muslim women use qualifications and economic privilege to negotiate their way through gendered and racialized barriers. White middle-class women, too, can buy out of some of the effects of gendered inequalities.

Anne Phillips (1987) has traced out the way the feminist movement has faced disunity because of the 'divided loyalties' of class and gender. The experience of gender is class-specific. It can be argued that, in the nineteenth century, upper- and middle-class women suffered greater restrictions from gender differentiation as they were more subject to the doctrines of domesticity and 'separate spheres' which justified their exclusion from paid work. The frustrations of life in the 'gilded cage' gave impetus to the Victorian feminist movement, which eventually helped to open up educational and career opportunities for middle-class women. Meanwhile, the realities of working-class life meant that for many families the breadwinner/housewife family remained an unachievable ideal. Working-class women faced exceptionally hard lives as they struggled with both paid work and having to maintain often large families, but at least the experience of wage labour gave them a modicum of independence and authority in the family.

In the contemporary world, the situation is reversed. Women from the service and capitalist classes are able to use the 'qualifications lever' to pursue managerial and professional careers, thereby achieving financial independence and near-equality with men (Crompton and Sanderson 1990; Witz 1992). They can use their wealth to buy out of the 'double shift' of paid labour and housework through employing cleaners and childminders. By contrast, working-class women are encumbered by increasing workloads in the home and in employment; their labour market opportunities are often restricted to low-paid service work. It is more difficult for them to gain full financial independence, which leaves them more vulnerable to violence in the home.

Recent decades have seen increasing economic polarization between a middle-class professional elite and working-class women. That effect is heightened if we consider the position of women in the labour surplus class fraction (see chapter 4). Such women face poverty and are often responsible for holding the family together. Many women on benefits are lone parents, often stigmatized for their status. Some receive little support or financial aid from their children's fathers, and are pressured by the state to take up jobs, although the demands of current work and parenting regimes make it hard for them to do so. Benefit caps imposed by David Cameron's government threaten such women with homelessness and the inability to feed their children. Despite the growing numbers of women who shoulder the task of bringing up children alone, the state is reluctant to abandon the gender norms which decree that a family must have two parents, or to accept that the support of children should be a public as opposed to a purely private function. At the bottom of the class hierarchy, the weight of gendered inequality is disproportionately felt (Glendinning and Millar 1992).

Age

The effect of age on gender is an under-researched topic, especially with regard to older women (Arber and Ginn 1991a). Indeed, it could be argued that feminism has replicated the ageism of society as so much of its analysis deals with the experience of women of child-bearing age. We know, though, that older women face particular economic problems. Growing up in a climate which encouraged women into the housewife role and offered them limited educational and employment opportunities brought many to face poverty in old age. As Groves argues, 'women's greater share of unpaid domestic work and their labour market position, including low pay, have inhibited their ability to generate an adequate income for old age' (1992, p. 206). Because of women's greater longevity, many older women live alone, and fear of violence acts to circumscribe their movements. The cult of youth and the high valuation placed on appearance for women means that they are held in less esteem; older women, as discussed in chapter 7, often experience themselves as socially 'invisible'. However, the positive side of this invisibility may be freedom from the bodily surveillance and self-policing surrounding younger women. As the popular poem has it, older women can act 'disgracefully' and 'wear a purple hat'!

We have more information on younger women and men. It is suggested that young women are often unsympathetic to feminism or consider it of little relevance to their lives (Stuart 1990; Lees 1993). Until they enter the labour market or get married, their personal experience of gender inequality may be limited; although gender biases operate at school, they are less visible than the evident inequalities of class and race. Adolescence is a time marked by considerable segregation of the sexes in leisure and growing awareness of sexuality, experienced differently; but these differences are often experienced by young women as pleasurable and exciting rather than as a form of disadvantage. Yet younger women are particularly vulnerable to the pressures of compulsory heterosexuality. It may lead some to unwanted pregnancies, while most must learn to handle sexual pestering and sexist abuse from boys (Wood 1984; Halson 1991). Young people who do not conform to heterosexual conventions, either because they are lesbian or gay, or because they cannot or will not join in with the adolescent culture of dating and courtship, are marginalized and made to feel misfits.

In fact, childhood and adolescence are crucial periods for gender relations, as times when young women and men have to make many choices which are vital to their later lives. Yet these are made in the context of differentiated gender expectations, and of discourses of masculinity and femininity that promote male dominance.

Nayak and Kehily (2008) argue that, in the current context, while 'young women emerge as the ideal neo-liberal subjects for post-industrial times', young men are characteristically viewed through 'the lens of crisis' (p. 52), as the disappearance of manufacturing jobs and the increased educational attainments of young women threaten them with unemployment and loss of masculine status. As McDowell (2000) expresses it, rather than 'learning to labour', this generation of young working-class men have to 'learn to serve'. As this suggests, it is not all young men but particular groups of young men who may be facing a crisis. Indeed, the whole idea of the crisis of masculinity is problematized by Roberts (2014), who rightly suggests that this is more of crisis of employment, affecting young women as well as young men – an issue that will be discussed in chapter 7 – and by Nayak and Kehily (2008), who assert that working-class youths they interviewed did not see themselves as afflicted by doubt.

Conclusions

This chapter has explored the analysis of gender inequality largely through an account of feminism. This is because gender was neglected in mainstream sociology until second-wave feminists forced it onto the agenda. Since then, it has become a major research topic within social science.

Classic feminist standpoints provided valuable insights into gender inequality, stimulated a wealth of important research and provided key concepts for thinking about gender. However, the classic theories came under attack for their oversimplified view of gender relations, and because they reproduce the analytical strategies of modernist theories rejected by postmodernists as essentialist and unidirectional. In particular, the classic approaches failed to recognize the diversity of experiences among women; and the theory of patriarchy was considered to rest on a crude and one-dimensional account of power.

What Barrett and Phillips called '1990s feminism' was influenced by postmodernism, post-structuralism and deconstructionism. It was concerned to avoid essentialism by exploring difference and deconstructing the key categories with which we think about gender. It also promoted the exploration of gender as an aspect of social identity. Gender is an important element within the 'fragmented identities' characteristic of post-industrial society, and it has been argued here that gender identities are themselves multiple; there are many ways of being a woman, a man, a sexed subject. It is perhaps not surprising that the concept of intersectionality, now a fashionable tool for exploring inequalities, derived from the study of gender.

While postmodernism rightly pointed to differences in the experiences of working-class and minority ethnic women, there was an irony here. The preoccupation with 'sexuality, subjectivity and textuality' does not resonate with the struggles of working-class women faced with poverty and unrewarding work. The current revival of feminism among young women is heartening and exciting, but its focus on sexual politics, violence and embodiment perhaps needs to broaden out to the more traditional material aspects of gendered inequality.

The interest in gender has also generated a lively literature on masculinities, which has only been touched on briefly here for reasons of space. Connell and others have highlighted the multiplicity of masculinities and the problems caused for men themselves by macho forms of masculinity. Men, like women, have seen their social roles challenged by neoliberal capitalism, leading to increased male unemployment and precarity for many younger and older men. Nonetheless, as a sex, they have retained their dominant roles at the top of the public sphere.

The lived relations of gender are complex and volatile, operating at all levels of society. Classic feminism attempted to link the different aspects of gender together through the concept of patriarchy, as exemplified by the work of Walby. However, in line with the theoretical framework espoused in this book, I suggest it may be preferable to adopt a looser approach, conceiving gender as interconnected and evolving sets of relations, both material and discursive, which create and recreate gender and sexual difference; some of these can be described as patriarchal. There is still a need to develop a more adequate and multi-dimensional theory of gendered power, which may be used to integrate the discussion of the diverse aspects of gendered reality.

Further Reading

Useful introductory books are Sara Delamont, *Changing Women, Unchanged Men* (Open University Press, 2001); Raewyn Connell, *Gender* (Polity, 2009); Amy Wharton, *The Sociology of Gender* (Wiley-Blackwell, 2011); and Harriet Bradley, *Gender* (Polity, 2012). Sylvia Walby, *Theorizing Patriarchy* (Blackwell, 1990), remains a classic, and Rosemary Tong, *Feminist Thought* (Unwin Hyman, 1989), is a clear and comprehensive introduction to feminist theory. Engaging books by the new generation of feminists are Kat Banyard, *The Equality Illusion* (Routledge, 2011), and Natasha Walter, *Living Dolls* (Virago, 2010). *Men and Masculinities* by Stephen Whitehead (Polity, 2002) is a great overview of the field.

Thinking Points

- How can the idea of postfeminism be challenged?
- What are the major sources of difference among women?
- Is masculinity in crisis? What about femininity?

6

'Race' and Ethnicity: 'Travelling in the West'

In *The Happy Isles of Oceania*, Paul Theroux describes his travels in Australasia and the South Pacific and presents us with a devastating picture of the ways in which European colonialism has adversely affected the lives of indigenous populations. In Australia and New Zealand the aboriginal people, dispossessed of their lands, their culture despised by many whites, live on the margins of society. Many are confined to reservations or eke out a basic existence on welfare payments. Australian aborigines did not receive the right of citizenship until 1967. In the Pacific islands, colonialism has impinged at varying levels. Some islanders have abandoned their traditional cultures and ways of living at the instigation of what Theroux calls 'the unholy trinity of the missionary, the trader and the planter' (1992, p. 291). In common with other populations around the world, they are adopting aspects of Western lifestyles, particularly Americanized popular culture with its videos, slogan-bearing T shirts, discotheques and fast foods. Various Christian sects, including Methodists, Seventh-Day Adventists and Mormons, are militantly active in islands such as Tonga, Fiji and Samoa and have ousted traditional religions and beliefs, as have cargo cults. In the Solomon Isles, Theroux found that the native people still lived under the shadow of the Second World War, when the quarrels of other nations were fought out in their waters; they listened in trepidation to radio coverage of the build-up to the Gulf War, believing that if fighting broke out they would once again be sucked into it. The French have used their colonial holdings in Polynesia to carry out nuclear tests. In a few islands, such as the Trobriands and New Hebrides, the peoples have managed to cling on to their lands, and many of their customary beliefs and lifestyles, but the uneasy balance of their lives now faces a new threat from Western and Japanese tourism and business interests. Global warming and rising sea levels also threaten the precarious environments on some of the smaller islands.

In such ways, the European colonialist drive which commenced in the late fifteenth century has indelibly marked itself upon the globe. The indigenous peoples of the Americas, Africa and Asia were subject to conquest, enslavement and genocide at the worst; at the least, to the disruption and transformation of their own economies and cultures. The damage done ranged all the way from the total extermination of tribal groups in the Caribbean, South America and Tasmania, to the subtler psychic damage which still affects the inhabitants of many ex-colonial societies, as movingly described by Amitav Ghosh in his book *In an Antique Land*.

Ghosh, an Indian anthropologist from London, relates his encounters with the Egyptian *fellaheen* (peasants) among whom he was conducting fieldwork. Despite the very different cultural traditions from which they came (Islamic and Hindu), he describes both himself and the Egyptians as entrapped within the framework of Western ideas: as he evocatively puts it, 'travelling in the West'. When debating their different religious beliefs, they were forced to assess cultures in the discourse of Western economic development, 'the language that had usurped all the others in which people once discussed their differences':

> They had constructed a certain ladder of 'Development' in their minds, and because all their images of material life were of those who stood in the rungs above, the circumstances of those below had become more or less unimaginable. I had an inkling then of the real and desperate seriousness of their engagement with modernism, because I realized that the fellaheen saw the material circumstances of their lives in exactly the same way that a university economist would: as a situation that was shamefully anachronistic, a warp upon time; I understood that their relationship with the objects of their everyday lives was never innocent of the knowledge that there were other places, other countries, which did not have mud-walled houses and cattle-drawn ploughs. (1994, p. 200)

Cultural exchanges around the world are overshadowed by the technological, scientific and military dominance of the West, its 'science and guns and tanks and bombs' (p. 237).

The relationships of colonialism and its legacy are one important aspect of the great web of racial and ethnic relations which binds the populations of the contemporary world together. 'Race' and ethnicity are two of the social categories which we have evolved to explain lived relationships which emanate from territorial arrangements and from the migration of people from different territorially based groups around the world. In Anthias and Yuval-Davis's phrase, ethnicity is a construct denoting 'collectivity and belongingness' (1993, p. 2). They see 'race' as an aspect of what they call 'ethnic phenomena' (p. 2), processes by which people are divided up into different communities with clear boundaries between them. In recent history, ideas about ethnicity have tended to converge with the related territorial notions of 'nation' and 'nationality'. Benedict Anderson, in a highly influential account, has offered a definition of nation as an 'imagined community': imagined in the sense that 'the members of even the smallest nation will never know most of their fellow-members, meet them, or even hear of them, yet in the minds of each lives the image of their communion' (1991, p. 6). 'Race' and ethnicity, too, can be seen as forms of imagined community – which, however, are linked to lived relations surrounding territoriality and migration.

Migration, Ethnicity and Hierarchy

While people have defined themselves – and been defined by others – as belonging to different groups or communities as long as there has been historical record, the ordering of such communities into a hierarchy of superior and inferior groups, which is a crucial feature of contemporary racial and ethnic relations, has been particularly influenced by migration. Anderson argues (1994) that it was 'exile', the experience of being apart from one's community, which promoted the nationalist fervour of the nineteenth century. Migration of people around the globe, whether undertaken freely in search of new lands or better prospects, or forced on people because of war, conquest or economic disaster, has involved the mixing of groups of people from different territorially based communities and is currently manifested in the 'multiculturalism' or 'social pluralism' of societies such as America and Britain where a multitude of ethnic groups coexist. London is now perhaps *the* classic example of a multicultural, multi-ethnic global city

Migration has historically been bound up with conquest and warfare. It was encouraged by the establishment of the great empires of antiquity, such as those of Greece and Rome, and later by the Islamic conquest of the Mediterranean areas in the medieval period. European colonialism was the successor to these and can be seen as particularly crucial in promoting substantial inter-continental migration. This laid the grounds for the particular racial and ethnic hierarchies which still characterize the post-colonial world. Conquering groups not only travelled around their conquered territories themselves, but moved subject groups around their empires to provide various types of labour and services, a process which was particularly marked under European colonial expansion since it coincided with the development of the system of capitalist production. The movement of enslaved labourers from Africa to work in the plantations of the Americas and the Caribbean, cultivating crops such as cotton, sugar and coffee, was particularly significant for later race relations and was crucial to the successful development of capitalism (Hobsbawm 1968; Bryan et al. 1985). In the post-slavery period, white European settlers continued to rely on indentured labour, sometimes from the local populace, sometimes brought in from the Indian subcontinent, China, Africa and elsewhere, to carry on agricultural production or to develop industrial enterprises. This trend continues today as, for example, farmers in East Anglia rely on cheap migrant labour from poorer parts of the European Union to work in gangs, living in sheds and caravans, to harvest fruit and vegetables (jobs of the type often rejected by the 'native' population as being too unpleasant and too badly paid).

Conquest and colonialism marked some ethnic communities out as dominant, others as subjected and subordinate. Linked to such power disparities between different ethnic, racial and national groups has been the formation of ideas in which dominant groups identify themselves as different from the subordinate. Robert Miles, in a useful survey, traces out the history of such thinking in terms of 'representations of the Other' (1989, p. 11). For example, the Greeks and Romans thought of those outside the ambit of their imperial civilization as 'the barbarians', and both Muslims and Christians in the medieval period stigmatized those of the other faith as 'infidels'. The language of 'barbarians', 'infidels' and 'savages' unfortunately is still used in inter-ethnic relations in trouble spots such as the Middle East and Palestine. As Hall (1992a) argues, with the development of colonialism, the prevailing version of this 'Othering' became that of 'the West and the rest'. White European societies were presented as the model for the future development of humankind, as Ghosh's account illustrates. Europeans drew on pre-existing ideas about 'the savage' and 'the oriental' to legitimate their colonial rule (Miles 1989). They represented themselves as shouldering the 'white man's burden', the task of 'civilizing' backward peoples and leading them towards enlightenment, abandonment of superstition, modernization and economic development. Native populations were portrayed both as childlike and simple and as cruel and unruly, 'half-devil and half-child' in the phrase from Rudyard Kipling's poem *The White Man's Burden*. Africans in particular were stereotyped as 'less than human', to justify their enslavement. Such views continued to be expressed by colonial administrators and settlers throughout the imperial period, as exemplified by this quotation from the 1920s: 'The typical African of this race-type is a happy, thriftless, excitable person, lacking in self-control, discipline and foresight, naturally courageous, and naturally courteous and polite, full of personal vanity, with little sense of veracity, fond of music, and "loving weapons as an oriental loves jewelry"' (Lord Lugard; quoted in Miles 1989, p. 103).

Colonialism and slavery are viewed as central to the formation of racial and ethnic hierarchies and of racist ideologies. However, the lived relations of 'race' and ethnicity continually change as patterns of migration shift, national boundaries are contested and reshaped, and ideas about ethnicity are challenged and reformulated. Since the ending of colonial rule, patterns of migration have been complex. There has been movement at times between colonies and ex-colonizers. One example was the post-war immigration of commonwealth citizens (especially from India, Pakistan and the West Indies) into Britain as a response to labour shortages caused by the war and post-war economic regeneration; another is the continued migration, sometimes permanent, sometimes temporary, between France and her former North African colonies, Algeria, Tunisia and Morocco.

Globalization has also promoted migration, as it encourages both capital and labour to be mobile in order to seek advantageous market conditions. It has fostered the development of a cadre of highly skilled and professional employees, for example in banking, finance and information technology, who are moved around the globe by trans-national companies (Devadason 2012; Williams et al. 2013). In Europe, membership of the European Community brings to citizens of member states the right to live and work anywhere within it. In particular, the collapse of the Soviet Russian empire and subsequent enlargement of the EU, when ex-Soviet-bloc nations joined it, led to new waves of migration, with East Europeans such as Poles and Rumanians moving in large numbers to countries like Britain and the Republic of Ireland, to find opportunities lacking in their own countries.

More recently, the financial crisis of the Eurozone in the 2000s has led many young Greeks, Italians, Spaniards and Portuguese to seek their fortunes in the less afflicted parts of the EU. A crucial additional element has arisen from the recent internationalization of the increasingly market-oriented university system, with thousands of students from all over the world seeking to study abroad. For example, numerous students from China and the Indian subcontinent have joined Britain's student population, adding to the UK's rich ethnic mix. In sum, it can be argued that populations have become substantially more mobile. These trends are reflected in the immigration figures for Britain in 2014 issued by ONS. Despite the attempts of the Home Secretary, Teresa May, to hold immigrant numbers below 100,000, net migration (the difference between incoming migrants and outgoing emigrants) rose by 68,000 over the year to reach 243,000. Of the 560,000 who entered Britain between April 2013 and April 2014, 177,000 were students, 23,479 were asylum seekers, but the majority were EU nationals coming to Britain to work. While 16,000 of these came from Bulgaria and Rumania, newly admitted to the EU, the bulk came from the Southern European countries worst affected by austerity policies and unemployment, as mentioned above.

Political concerns about the impact of migration have been persistent, as manifested in the rise of UKIP and its campaign for Britain to withdraw from the EU. Definition of 'race relations' and immigration as 'social problems' has led many European societies (and the United States) to adopt policies of immigration control. Control of immigration into Britain since the 1960s has been strict. As Gilroy (1987) and Miles (1989) argue, past state policy has been based implicitly on racist principles that have defined 'coloured' or 'new' commonwealth immigrants as unwanted citizens, as opposed to applicants from the 'old' commonwealth countries of Canada, New Zealand and Australia. British immigration legislation is complex and constantly changing. In particular, 21st-century government policy has sought to stem the flow of unskilled employees into the UK, while leaving the door open for wealthy professionals and investors. While British universities rely on overseas students to balance their budgets, governments have been concerned that this allows 'fake' students to gain entry to the country illegally, and they have thus forced universities to monitor their overseas student bodies persistently.

Panics over immigration have been heightened periodically by warfare and ethnic conflicts in various parts of the world, which precipitate movement of refugees and asylum seekers into Europe and North America. British governments allowed the Asian communities expelled from East Africa in the 1970s to take up residence in Britain as citizens of the British commonwealth. Recent civil wars in Africa and in the Middle East have produced large refugee populations, for example Somalis, Kurds, Congolese and Rwandans. Refugees are often treated harshly, penned up in assessment centres for months

while their pleas for asylum are heard; a survey of female asylum
seekers by the organization Women for Refugee Women found that
one in five women held in detention in the UK had attempted suicide
(Girma et al. 2014). Refugees commonly form the bottom economic
stratum of the countries that allow them residence, along with illegal
migrants who continue to risk their lives, both fleeing oppressive
regimes and seeking improved economic situations.

In today's multiethnic societies, the processes of interaction between
different ethnic groups are volatile and have sometimes taken a conflictual form. In Britain and America since the 1960s, there have been
sporadic outbreaks of rioting involving issues of 'race'. In Britain, the
Notting Hill and Nottingham 'race riots' of 1958 fed in to popular
unease about race relations. Such panics were fuelled through the
1960s by the acts and campaigns of politicians. Enoch Powell's infamous 1968 speech about the 'swamping' of British cultures by alien
elements, with its vision of the rivers of Britain flowing with blood,
gained considerable public support. This was the context of the 1962,
1965 and 1971 Immigration Acts, which limited the intake of 'coloured' immigrants only. But these events also prompted calls for
legislation against racial discrimination and the development of what
has become known as 'the race relations industry'. It also heightened
interest in race relations as a topic for study within sociology.

Racialization and Discrimination

The focus of study was those groups seen to be *racialized*: that is,
defined as different (and inferior) in terms of ascribed racial characteristics, especially skin colour (Mason 2003). Research concentrated
on Caribbean and Asian groups and showed the disparities between
'Black and White Britain' (Brown 1984). Various surveys, along with
what government statistical material was available, have revealed
persistent patterns of disadvantage among these groups in the areas
of employment, unemployment, housing, health and education (see
Daniel 1968; Smith 1977; Brown 1984; Modood et al. 1997).

For example, Black Caribbeans and Asians are more likely to live
in run-down inner-city areas where services are overstretched; in
some cases, such areas may approximate to the 'ghetto' areas of
North American cities. In London, ethnic minority members, especially the young, are four times as likely to be homeless as whites. A
survey by the Runnymede Trust in 2011 found that visible minorities
were reporting discrimination in the private housing sector: while
only 1 per cent of white British reported discrimination, the figures

for African-Caribbeans, Africans and Pakistanis were 29, 28 and 27 per cent respectively. In the area of health, African-Caribbeans are more likely to be diagnosed as schizophrenic than white people. Black British are over-represented in the prison population, and young Black and Asian men are routinely stopped and searched on the street.

Members of racialized minorities are highly vulnerable to unemployment, especially younger people. Labour Force Survey data for 2010 revealed a shocking rise in unemployment for young people aged 18–24 from ethnic minority backgrounds, from 20 per cent in 2007 to 31 per cent in 2010. In contrast, the unemployment rate for white youth was 16 per cent. While there were more Black young men out of work than Black women – at the end of 2010 there were almost 63,000 young males without jobs compared to around 53,000 young women – the rate of increase in unemployment over the three years since 2007 was a worrying 68 per cent for young Black women, with a 24 per cent increase for men. This can be linked to austerity policies and cuts in the public sector, where around 640,000 Black and Asian people were employed in 2010. The TUC estimated that future public sector cuts of around 20 per cent would put around another 127,000 Black workers on the dole, leading the then TUC General Secretary, Brendan Barber, to state that Black workers were bearing the brunt of Britain's recession. This is reflected in the fact that 50 per cent of African-Caribbean and African children live in poverty, and over 70 per cent of Bangladeshi children.

While part of this disadvantage arises from the concentration of African-Caribbean and Asian British in the lower class groupings, studies have persistently revealed the importance of racism and discrimination in perpetuating disadvantage (for example, Smith 1977; Jenkins 1986). Employers attribute characteristics to Caribbean and Asian applicants which are used to exclude them from better jobs (Wrench and Lee 1978; Iganski and Mason 2002). Teachers tend to stereotype Black Caribbean boys as lazy, troublesome and non-academic, Asian boys and girls as hard-working but over-ambitious (Brah 1986; Mirza 1992; Gillborn and Youdell 2000). Reports on specific institutions and localities have highlighted the way racism operates in many areas of social life. For example, the 1989 Gifford Inquiry into racial discrimination in Liverpool found that Black people were confined to certain parts of the city and were targets of hostility and abuse if they moved outside them. Few of Liverpool's 30,000 Black inhabitants held jobs in visible 'white' areas, such as city centre shops. Most shocking of all, while the city council claimed to be an 'equal opportunities employer', only 490 out of a total

30,410 council employees were Black. Nationwide, Asians in particular have been the target of increasing harassment and attacks. Beatrix Campbell in *Goliath* (1993) paints a chilling picture of the everyday harassment experienced by people living in Newcastle's West End: 57 per cent of Black people in Newcastle had experienced racial abuse, 45 per cent attacks on property; schoolchildren described being regularly submitted to racist insults, sworn at and spat at, bullied, taunted and beaten up at school. Victimization only increases if police or teachers are informed of the harassment.

Qualitative and quantitative studies provide ample evidence of racism and the disadvantages suffered by racialized groups in Britain. Recently, however, the trend has been to move beyond the dichotomized model of 'Black and White British' (Mason 2003). Postmodern influences have led to an interest in exploring the position of the many diverse minority groups in Britain (the Chinese, Turkish and East European populations, for example, have been less studied). Statistical evidence indicates the different positions of specific ethnic groups, as in the unemployment figures quoted earlier.

The emphasis in study, then, has switched from a concern with 'race' and colour to a broader concern with culture and ethnicity (Modood 1992; Mason 2003; Pilkington 2003). In such an approach, the investigation of white ethnicities also becomes a task of sociological interest. Being 'British' and white can mean being English, Scots, Welsh or Irish – and also Jewish, Polish, Australian and so on. In the multiethnic world, ethnic identities are multi-layered, 'hybrid' or 'hyphenated' (Bhabha 1990a; Modood 1992, 2007). Moreover, intermarriage between ethnic groups is increasingly common, leading to the presence of large numbers of 'mixed-race' or 'dual heritage' children in our schools.

Previous chapters have emphasized the importance of difference and contextual specificity for the understanding of social inequality. This is even more pronounced when considering ethnicity than in the cases of gender and class. Each society has experienced specific patterns of past migration which inform current racial and ethnic hierarchies. For that reason, it is dangerous to make generalizations about race relations from the experience of one society. Subsequent discussion in this chapter looks mainly at Britain.

The remainder of this chapter outlines earlier approaches which were concerned with racial inequality between Black and white groups, before considering the newer positions, which emphasize the plurality of ethnic divisions. First, however, it is necessary to confront some terminological problems involved in the study of racial and ethnic differences.

Defining Terms: 'Race', Ethnicity and Nationality

Discussion of racial inequality has often become bogged down in debates about the appropriate usage of the key concepts of 'race' and 'ethnicity' and related terms such as racism, racialism and racialization. Disputes also relate to what terms should be used to describe various ethnic groups. Terms like 'coloured' (now thoroughly discredited) or 'Black' can be attacked as being themselves racist, or alternatively as being essentialist and covering up real differences among groups so categorized. By and large, sociologists have tried to use the terms which are preferred by members of the various groups themselves. In Britain, the term 'Black' was adopted by Black Caribbean and Asian activists as a chosen political identity. The term 'of colour' was used in the same way in America. But it can be claimed that such umbrella terms conceal the distinct situations of the different groups involved (Modood 1992); Modood has argued that the specific experience of British Asian groups has been subsumed into 'Black' writings that chiefly express the viewpoint of those of African origin. In this book, I have used 'Black' and 'of colour' where it seemed appropriate to refer to political alliances across ethnic minorities or because these terms are used by authors whose work is under discussion. Otherwise, I specify which particular ethnic groups are concerned.

These debates have been amply explored elsewhere (for example, Miles 1989; Mason 1992). Here I merely indicate how the terms are used in this book. I have drawn particularly on the usages proposed by Floya Anthias and Nira Yuval-Davis, whose approach seems to me analytically coherent and useful.

'Race'

'Race' as a common-sense usage refers to the idea that human beings can be divided into sub-groups which have different origins and are distinguished by biological differences. Such differences can be seen as 'phenotypical' (relating to physical appearances such as skin colour or hair type) or 'genotypical' (relating to underlying genetic differences). These ideas were given backing in the nineteenth century by scientists who extended the systems of classification developed for the study of plants and animals to distinguish different sub-species of *Homo sapiens*: a popular taxonomy distinguished Caucasian, Negroid and Mongoloid races. Modern genetic science tends to reject the concept of race as invalid (although this is still disputed). Even if originally distinct racial types could be distinguished, centuries of migration and interbreeding make the idea that each individual has a specific racial make-up extremely problematic.

Within sociology, 'race' is considered a non-scientific category, and for that reason Miles has consistently argued (1982, 1989) that we should reject the concept altogether. He states that it is an ideological construct: its use only serves to give respectability to discredited racist ideas. But other sociologists have pointed out that *all* forms of social category (such as class and gender) are constructs. Since such constructs inform the way people think and act in relation to others, the effects of 'race' are very real (Cashmore and Troyna 1983; Gilroy 1987). 'Race' can be viewed as *a form of social relationship to which racial meanings are attached by the participants* (Mason 1992).

Cashmore and Troyna suggest that 'race' should be seen as a stigmatized identity forced on other people (as opposed to ethnicity, which is freely adopted and proclaimed). Similarly, Modood proposes that 'race' relates to 'mode of oppression' (how a group is categorized and subordinated), while ethnicity refers to 'mode of being' (how it views its own identity, culture, values). But, while the process of racialization often involves imposition and stigma, this is not always the case. Members of dominant groups may assert a racial identity seen as a positive asset and a cause of their own superiority, as happened in Nazi Germany or among British neo-fascist groups with their belief in the 'master race'. Moreover, a stigmatized identity may be appropriated and subverted as a basis for resistance to dominant meanings, and for positive identification, as in the case of Black Power and similar movements: 'Say it loud, I'm Black and I'm proud!'

The distinctive feature of 'race' as a form of relationship, as opposed to ethnicity or nation, is the imputation of inborn (usually biological) difference (Rattansi 1992). 'Race' is a way of constructing differences 'on the basis of an immutable biological or physiognomic difference which may or may not be seen to be expressed mainly in culture and lifestyle but is always grounded on the separation of human populations by some notion of stock or collective heredity of traits' (Anthias and Yuval-Davis 1993, p. 2). Anthias and Yuval-Davis also believe that 'race' should be seen as a special case of the broader category of 'ethnic phenomena'.

Ethnicity

'Ethnos' and 'ethnicity' are terms with a rather different history. Less common in popular usage (at least until recently), the terms were employed in social anthropology to describe social groups with a shared culture; they could refer to a whole society, but were more commonly used to describe a collectivity within a larger society, as reflected in our usage of the term 'ethnic minority'. Ethnic groups may be defined (or define themselves) on the basis of language, religion or nationality, but the idea of shared culture is perhaps the crucial issue. Also very important (indeed Anthias and Yuval-Davis make this central to their definition) is the idea of a common origin. This origin may be mythical or real, based on a religious text, on historical events or the idea of a (sometimes lost) homeland, or a mix of all of these. The crucial point is that it binds the members of the group together in a sense of belonging and constructs boundaries between them and the rest of the world.

The idea of ethnicity was formerly treated with suspicion by some radical theorists of race relations, on the grounds that it gave too much prominence to culture, rather than racism (Richardson and Lambert 1985), and so could be used to blame the victims of discrimination. 'Ethnic ties' and attachments to culture among immigrant groups could be seen as the reason for failure to achieve educational and occupational success. This could easily lead to the view of ethnic minority cultures as deficient or even 'pathological', for example in the argument that the 'weak' structures of Caribbean families and the prevalence of woman-headed families were causes of school failure and delinquency. Mac an Ghaill (1988) strongly attacks cultural theories of this kind, which are used to explain the apparent 'under-achievement' of Black pupils in school in terms of 'cultural deprivation' or difficulties of communication arising from language difference. He states that differential achievements between Black and white pupils can largely be accounted for in terms of material differences, chiefly the concentration of Caribbean families in lower class groupings, while racism and stereotyping in schools also affect performance.

Recently, postmodern thinking has encouraged a greater appreciation of culture and its impact on social relationships. In addition, the notion of ethnicity allows for consideration of conflicts and hierarchies among groups which are not distinguished only on racial grounds but by culture, language or religion (as, for example, between Protestants and Catholics in Northern Ireland, Sikhs and Hindus in India, or Serbs, Croats and Bosnian Muslims in the former Yugoslavia). This has promoted a widespread adoption of the category of ethnicity, which is currently used more or less interchangeably with 'race'. I share Anthias and Yuval-Davis's view that it is useful to see 'race' as a special case of ethnic division, but also agree with Mason that it is important to employ the term 'race' to distinguish those situations where racial definitions are the crucial feature. Racially defined groups are most likely to suffer exclusion, marginalization and subordination within the social hierarchy. In this text I have followed Mason's usage of 'race', while I use 'ethnicity' more generally to refer to the sense of belonging to a community, which may not necessarily be defined in racial terms.

'Race' and ethnicity are social categories used in reference to divisions within a particular society. A final aspect of the lived relations arising from territorial allocations and migration is the global hierarchy between different nations.

Nationality

The concept of a 'nation' (although often linked to ethnicity) implies a distinct politically defined territory. Anthropologists have viewed nations as extensions of kinship or clan groupings (as in the usage 'Sioux nation'). But nowadays we more familiarly associate it with the 'nation-state' which evolved in Europe from the eighteenth century as the prevailing type of polity. The emergence of nation-states is associated both with the rise of democratic political forms and with the overthrow of absolutist monarchies that preceded them. It has been historically connected with nationalist movements, especially where the formation of a nation-state involved the overthrowing of an occupying power or the ousting of colonial rulers. Indeed, Ernest Gellner argues (1983) that nations cannot emerge until a nationalist spirit is present.

Benedict Anderson defines the nation as 'an imagined political community' (1991, p. 6), a view close to that of Gellner, who suggests that nations come into being when people develop the will to be united with 'all those, and only those, who share their culture' (1983, p. 55). Both Gellner and Anderson link the emergence of nations and nationalism to modernity and the development of industrial capitalism. For Gellner, strongly influenced by Durkheim's account of industrial society, the emergence of complex but integrated modern industry demands that all citizens share a sense of belonging and a common culture. In reality, this involves 'the general imposition of a high culture' (Gellner, 1983, p. 57) on all groups of society and the consolidation of impersonal bureaucratic rule; so, for Gellner, nations and nationalism are essentially illusions by which divided people develop a sense of false unity. By contrast, Benedict Anderson suggests that all types of communities are essentially 'imagined' or invented, and emphasizes the positive features of national identification – in terms, for example, of cultural productions or of the self-sacrifices made by people in nationalist causes. As opposed to a sense of common origin, what unites the nation is a sense of common destiny. Anderson argues that capitalism, together with the development of the technology of printing, created the conditions for the emergence of nations, and allowed the communication of ideas that could inspire a 'national imagination' to the mass of people. This is particularly interesting in relation to the issue of Scottish independence, a hot topic when I was writing this in the summer of 2014. First Minister Alex Salmond, leading the campaign for a 'Yes' vote to the referendum on independence, presented it as a chance for those living in Scotland to shape their destiny in the way they wanted it, rather than focusing on common Celtic origins (given that many English people live in Scotland and many Scots live in England!). Salmond told viewers of a television programme: 'We are a rich nation, a resourceful people. This is our time, it's our moment. Let's do it now.'

Despite Anderson's stress on the positive features of national development, many radical thinkers, especially Marxists, have taken a negative view of nationalism. For example, Perry Anderson has emphasized how in nineteenth-century England nationalist ideology and jingoism were used by the ruling bloc to consolidate their social hegemony and pacify the working classes (Anderson 1964). Gilroy (1987) stresses the way in which British nationalism has been built upon racist definitions of who 'the British' are.

In the past, nationalist movements served to unite groups who had formerly been separated on the basis of class, ethnicity, regional affiliation, religion and so forth. Thus nationalism could be seen as counterposed to fragmentation. In the postmodern cultural world, however, a different form of nationalism has taken hold, one exemplified by events in the former Yugoslavia and the terrible procedures described as 'ethnic cleansing'. The new nationalism is based on the idea that national boundaries should coincide with ethnos: all those, and only those, who share ethnicity (to paraphrase Gellner) should share a common territory. These beliefs, although based on suspect and essentialist premises that it is possible to assign a specific ethnicity to each individual, have inspired many of the recent conflicts in the former Soviet territories and in Africa, and contributed to the rise of racist neo-fascist groups in Europe (Solomos 2003). It is the ideology of the British far right parties such as the English Defence League and the British National Party.

While this book is concerned primarily with stratification within societies, the concept of nation is relevant to our discussion for three reasons. First, the new nationalisms described above inflame racial and ethnic relations on a global scale and exacerbate tensions already existing within nations (Solomos 2003). Second, the term 'nation' can be appropriated by racialized groups as a way of building alliances to challenge the prevailing hierarchies (as in the idea of a 'reggae nation'). Finally, nations are arranged in a 'pecking order', with the advanced capitalist societies of the G7 group at the top of the pyramid and the 'Third World' countries, especially those of Africa, at the base. Such hierarchical ordering of nations reinforces discourses giving sanction to racial and ethnic hierarchies within a society, such as that of the 'West and the rest'. This is the context in which discussion of racial inequalities must be located.

Explaining Racial Divisions in Sociological Theory

The classical sociological theorists, in their preoccupation with industrial development, tended to marginalize ethnicity along with gender. Although showing awareness of existing ethnic divisions and conflicts, they assumed these were forces of the past, which would fade away with the advance of industrialism and capitalism. This assumption was shared by the functionalist mainstream of the twentieth century and enshrined in the theory of modernization, which suggested that all nations must follow the Western trajectory if they wished to develop. Ethnicity was seen as a characteristic of traditional societies which was becoming increasingly irrelevant in modern rationalized societies. 'Race' then, only became a significant issue in sociology when it entered public speech as a 'social problem'.

We can distinguish three main perspectives in the sociology of racial and ethnic divisions as it evolved in Britain in the 1960s. Both Marxists and Weberians turned to the study of 'race', attempting to extend their theories of stratification to include it. The relationship of race to class was their main theoretical preoccupation. A third position was described as a 'race relations' standpoint. This was a less theoretical stance, which was orientated towards policy issues and drew upon concepts from a range of perspectives.

Marxism

Neo-Marxists were drawn to the study of 'race', perhaps because the conflictual nature of race relations confirmed Marxian assertions that relations between dominant and subordinate groups inevitably promoted social conflict. In a similar way to how they approached gender, Marxists sought to explain race relations by incorporating 'race' as an element into the analysis of the capitalist mode of production. Prevailing strategies were to view 'race' as a special case of labour/capital relations or to show the ways in which racial divisions served to further the interests of capital.

American sociologist Oliver Cox (1970) took the latter line in an early contribution that exemplifies traditional Marxism. Cox's arguments reflected the view of class as the primary form of social division. He argued that apparent racial inequalities were in fact manifestations of class relations between bourgeois and proletariat. Capitalists exploited racial divisions to manipulate and divide the working class. In this view, racism is seen as a product of capitalism and serves to shore up capitalist power. In Britain, Sivanandan (1982) developed similar ideas. A theoretical stance which carries this one stage further suggests that race and racism are merely ideological constructions, in the Marxian sense. That is, they are ideas which function to mystify and conceal real material formations and to legitimize and perpetuate prevailing relationships of exploitation and domination (Gabriel and Ben Tovim 1979).

Such approaches minimize the distinctiveness of racial oppression and imply that racial divisions arise as a by-product of class exploitation. But, as has been suggested, the forms of lived relations of territory and migration are heterogeneous and can be found in all types of historical epoch. A more satisfactory type of Marxist approach, which gives more weight to the specific nature of racial disadvantage, treats racialized groups as distinct types of labour. The work of Robert Miles typifies this approach. He suggests that the majority of Caribbean and Asian workers in Britain can be viewed as a 'racialized fraction' of the working class (Phizacklea and Miles 1980; Miles 1982). Miles, as we have seen, does not believe that 'race' has any 'real' existence; but he believes that the stigmatizing of ethnic groups by imputing racial differences to them allows them to be discriminated against and used to fill the kind of jobs that are rejected by the white majority. Black workers occupy distinct labour market positions, are more disadvantaged than their white fellows, and form a distinctive sub-group within the working class. However, they are still part of the proletariat, and Phizacklea and Miles argued that the consciousness of class as well as racial disadvantage had led many Black working people to be active within the labour movement.

Another concept, also utilized by Miles, is the notion of 'migrant labour'. This links the experience of settled immigrant populations (such as Caribbeans in Britain) to the broader processes of international migration within colonialism and capitalist development. It is argued that colonial powers and capitalist employers both used migrant labour as a source of cheap, highly exploitable labour. Castles and Kosack (1973) employed this concept to analyse the situation of ethnic minority workers in Europe, epitomized by the Turkish and North African 'guest-workers' in Germany. Migrant labourers are used as an international reserve labour force to supplement the indigenous proletariat, especially in the 'dirty' jobs which are hard to fill. Because of their migrant status such workers can be expelled to their home countries when their labour is no longer needed, without any cost to the state (it does not have to pay them unemployment benefit, for example). Miles wishes to apply this label to African-Caribbean and Asian workers in Britain, even when they are permanently settled in Britain and have citizen status (unlike the guest-workers). This is because their former immigrant status and their experience of different conditions in their countries of origin make them particularly vulnerable to exploitation. Miles also emphasized how frequently the workers he studied held to the 'myth of return' to the Caribbean or India, which helped to give meaning to the circumstances of their lives in Britain. The rather similar notion of 'internal colonialism' has been employed to explain the position of African Americans; they form a pool of workers who are differentially viewed and utilized by employers because of the past history of slavery and colonialism (Blauner 1969). Unlike other immigrant groups, their labour-market situation has always been circumscribed by compulsion and coercion rather than free choice.

The advantage of the concept of migrant labour is that it extends the analysis from contemporary capitalism, connecting it firmly to the past history of international relations and colonialism. It draws closer to the framework of territorial relations and migration that I have suggested is the context of racial and ethnic divisions. However, it still restricts the concept of 'race' to situations involving 'labour'.

An attempt to move beyond this economistic framework was made by Stuart Hall and his colleagues at the Centre for Contemporary Cultural Studies (for example, Hall et al. 1978; Centre for Contemporary Cultural Studies 1982). Their brand of cultural Marxism was strongly influenced by the work of Gramsci. They considered the way racism and imperialist dogmas had been used to strengthen the cultural hegemony of the ruling bloc in British society. For example, the state's highlighting of 'problems' brought by immigration, such as the social panic over mugging which focused especially on young Caribbean men, served to divert attention from the real causes of Britain's social and economic problems (which they attributed to capitalist development). They viewed racism as deeply entrenched in British society. It not only served to legitimate class domination but also informed the meanings working people attached to their experiences and to their own class position. In Hall's words, 'race is thus...the modality in which class is "lived"...the form in which it is appropriated and "fought through"' (1980, p. 341).

The Marxist approach to race is undoubtedly useful in illuminating the specific ways in which colonialists and capitalists have exploited the labour of racialized groups, and in showing how racist policies have been promoted by the state. But it shares the limitations of the Marxist analysis of gender. Other forms of division are seen as ultimately less important than class relations, and as determined by them (if not reducible to them). Moreover, there is a tendency to talk of racialized groups as analogous to 'labour' as though they were all part of the proletariat. While it is true that minority ethnic groups (especially those of colour) are disproportionately concentrated in lower occupational groupings, past decades have seen the development of an extensive Asian petite bourgeoisie in Britain and of a 'Black bourgeoisie' in the United States. In Britain, some Asians and Caribbeans can be found at all levels in the class structure (for example among the professions). This suggests that, rather than viewing racialized minorities as a distinct class, or class fraction (or even a separate class fraction within each broader class, as suggested by Miles), it is better to think in terms of race and class dynamics intersecting to produce a racialized labour market.

Within Marxism, racial divisions, like gender divisions, are viewed primarily from the standpoint of their contribution to the maintenance of capitalism. Because of this, the importance of racist attitudes and practices among the white population as a whole tends to be underplayed. More fundamentally, as I have argued, racial and ethnic relations have a different existential location from class relations. They cannot be reduced to economic factors. Therefore, Marxist approaches offer only a partial view on racial divisions.

Weberianism

The same criticism can be made of neo-Weberian approaches. Indeed, it is plausibly argued by Sarre (1989) and Anthias and Yuval-Davis (1993) that there is considerable overlap between Weberian and Marxist thinking on 'race'. Both perspectives see racial inequality in primarily economic terms and analyse 'race' in terms of its link to class.

Weber's own framework allows for a more flexible approach to race, in terms of his view of stratification as deriving from the distribution of power in society. This could be used to distinguish different kinds of groups within any particular society. There is no need to reduce everything to class. Indeed, Weber's concept of status provides one way of conceptualizing racial and ethnic divisions. Parkin (1979) suggested that ethnic groups could be seen as negatively privileged status groups. Processes of 'social closure', involving exclusion and demarcation, are used to mark out the social boundaries between groups and maintain the hierarchical ordering of the society. In this way, ethnic minority groups might be kept out of jobs seen as reserved for whites, confined to lower ranks in the occupational hierarchy or excluded from certain areas of social life. This applies well to societies which are highly racially segregated, such as South Africa before the ending of the apartheid system or the Southern states of the USA prior to the successful campaigns of the Civil Rights movement. It can be objected, though, that this is merely descriptive and does not explain why such status differences come about. Castles (1984), shifting from a former Marxist position, tries to do this by combining Marxian and Weberian concepts. He explains the position of minority ethnic workers in Britain in terms of a mixture of class position, capitalist needs and minority status, arising from the colonial past.

The major neo-Weberian contributor, however, was John Rex, who put more weight on the economic as opposed to the status position of ethnic minorities. Rex firmly linked 'race' disadvantage to class, although employing the latter term in the broader Weberian sense which embraces lifestyle differences. For example, he pointed to the different consumption patterns of minority groups, particularly in housing. Research carried out with Moore in the Sparkbrook area of Birmingham was used to formulate the idea of distinct 'housing classes'. The study found that Black immigrant groups were confined to certain types of housing (decayed inner-city properties, rented accommodation and lodging houses); access to housing was bringing the different ethnic groups into conflict with each other as an aspect of 'class struggle' (Rex and Moore 1967, p. 273). In another study, with Tomlinson, of Asians and Black Caribbeans in Birmingham, Rex suggested that Black minorities might form a distinct underclass because of disadvantage in the key areas of employment, education and housing (Rex and Tomlinson 1979). White racism (among the white working class as well as employers) helped to marginalize minority groups, confining them to a distinct class location. Rex and Tomlinson also employed the Weberian concept of the dual labour market (see chapter 5) in their analysis of the employment situation of African-Caribbeans; their research indicated that whites and Blacks were segregated into jobs with different characteristics.

In his many writings Rex appeared to vacillate between the broader Weberian approach, as advocated by Parkin, and a position with many similarities to Marxism. He offered a well-known definition of

a 'race relations situation' as one in which different unequal groups
are in conflict with one another, and where the membership of the
groups is fixed and ascribed (as opposed to achieved) on the basis of
deterministic belief systems – involving, for example, a biologistic
view of race (1970). Such a definition provides a foundation for
analysing 'race' as an aspect of stratification quite distinct from class.
However, as demonstrated above, in his research studies Rex drew
on concepts from class theory to explain the specific position of Black
minority groups. In his later work, he proposed that class theory
should be central to the explanation of ethnic and racial differences:
'class theory is useful – perhaps it is the most centrally useful theory
– in approaching major problems of race and ethnic relations' (1986a,
p. 83).

Like Miles, Rex appeared to view 'race' as an unreal category. For
this reason, it cannot be a basis for action in the way that class is:
therefore, the formation of racialized groups must be linked to
broader economic processes:

> Since what are called racial and ethnic groups are groups (or quasi-
> groups) to whom common behavioural characteristics are imputed,
> rather than groups which have such characteristics, it is clear that the
> creation of such groups may depend upon the non-racial non-ethnic
> context and the motivations to which it gives rise. The study of race
> relations is therefore inextricably tied up with the study of group for-
> mations generally and with the study of social class and status. (Rex
> 1986b, p. 17)

The Weberian approach allows for a multi-dimensional theory of
stratification in terms of interaction between different types of group
competing for power and resources. But, perhaps because Weber
himself did not make it entirely clear how race and ethnicity might
be accommodated in his model (as status groups – as economic
groups?), neo-Weberian sociologists of 'race' have tended to draw on
class concepts. While Rex and Parkin move beyond the view of racial
divisions as a product of capital needs, by giving far more weight to
white racism, the status of 'race' as a separate aspect of inequality is
still imprecise. As Anthias and Yuval-Davis argue, there is consequently remarkable similarity in the explanations offered by Rex and
by Marxists such as Miles. Class still plays too prominent a role in
this analysis.

The Race Relations Approach

This criticism is not so relevant to the 'race relations' group, which
grounds itself on the distinctiveness of 'race' as a sociological topic.

As stated earlier, this approach is not a distinct theoretical position so much as a standpoint from which to think about 'race'. It is particularly associated with the work of Michael Banton, but many other sociologists worked broadly in this tradition.

The race relations approach was based on the proposition that race should be an autonomous and distinct topic for sociological enquiry. Adherents advocated the use of a broad range of applicable concepts from different areas of economics, sociology and elsewhere (Richardson and Lambert 1985). Social anthropology was perhaps the prime influence. Such borrowings might include concepts derived from Marx or Weber. From this standpoint, the broader topics of ethnicity and culture were seen to be of interest, in contrast to the tendency of Marxists and Weberians to concentrate on the dichotomous relations of 'Black' and 'white' groups. Studies looked at the way distinct cultures were evolving among the various ethnic minority groups in Britain; these might be viewed in relation to debates about assimilation, integration or ethnic pluralism and multi-culturalism as possible outcomes of processes of immigration. However, the position of Black minorities in Britain was still central to the race relations endeavour, especially as the orientation of this tradition was strongly towards social policy.

This policy orientation led to concern with the role of the state. Research dealt with topics such as the history of migration to Britain and elsewhere; immigration laws; the history of racist ideas; race relations legislation and equal opportunities; the ways in which minority groups in Britain experienced disadvantage and discrimination. Much of this research was descriptive and empirical rather than theoretical; but it provided a rich pool of information which could aid in the construction of theories.

Despite its lack of specific theoretical allegiance, we could see the 'race relations' standpoint as an example of classic mainstream liberalism. Indeed, it shares many features with the liberal feminist standpoint: the theoretical eclecticism; a reformist political stance, advocating change within the existing system; and a particular concern with legislation, legal reform and education. For Marxist critics, this approach appeared insufficiently radical; there was a tendency to focus on individual racist attitudes and prejudice, rather than on how racial divisions are linked to broader social processes of capitalist and colonial or post-colonial development. However, the eclecticism of the race relations standpoint was useful for opening up wide areas of research. Indeed, its eclecticism is more compatible than the stricter frameworks of Marxism and Weberianism with the newer approaches which have evolved in the study of racial and ethnic divisions.

Postmodernism and Post-colonialism: The 'New Sociology of Ethnicities'

Since Black feminists had taken the lead in challenging the premises of classic feminism, it is not surprising that the study of 'race' and ethnicity was influenced by similar ideas. Postmodern and post-structuralist ideas informed the direction of studies of ethnicity, which became more concerned with issues of culture, identity and diversity (for example, Mercer 1990; Donald and Rattansi 1992; Gilroy 1993). Within literary and historical studies a parallel new perspective, that of 'post-colonialism', developed as a corrective to what are seen as ethnocentric and distorted Western views of culture and history.

Postmodernism, Post-structuralism and Ethnicity

Like feminists, theorists of 'race' and ethnicity have been attracted to the postmodern perspective because of its critique of one-dimensional modernist theories. While theories derived from class analysis tended to portray 'race' and ethnicity as secondary aspects of stratification ultimately determined by capitalist relations, a postmodern approach allows for the development of multi-dimensional accounts of inequality, *in which each dimension can be accorded equal weight.* 'Race' and ethnicity are considered crucial aspects of social differentiation in their own right.

New writing on 'race' and ethnicity has drawn upon many of the features of postmodern and post-structural approaches utilized in the analysis of gender. These include the following:

1 The stress on difference and diversity (Brah 1992)   Each ethnic group experiences different patterns of disadvantage and has developed distinctive responses within its own culture and community. Tariq Modood (1992) has been critical of the way previous studies featuring the experience of 'Black' Britons concealed the specific concerns of the diverse Asian groups and sub-groups, such as Pakistanis, Bangladeshis, Asians from East Africa, Gujaratis, Punjabis, Muslims, Sikhs and Hindus. Modood also argues that too much attention has been paid to skin colour as the basis of racism, whereas racism directed against Asians features themes of cultural and religious difference. The stress on diversity gives more weight to the concepts of ethnicity and culture as opposed to 'race'. The image of Britain and other societies now is that of a patchwork of heterogeneous ethnic groups (Anthias and Yuval-Davis 1993; Afshar and Maynard 1994).

2   *The attack on essentialism (Donald and Rattansi 1992)*   Traditional approaches, even radical ones, are criticized for essentialist views of ethnicity. The older broad categories of 'Black' and 'white' were deconstructed, revealing the divergent experiences of people of various ethnic heritages. Such broad categories were considered social constructs which covered as much as they revealed. For example, the category of 'Asian' obscured differences between Indians, who were faring pretty well in terms of access to professional employment and higher education, and Pakistanis and Bangladeshis, who are among the most disadvantaged ethnic groups. Even the uncovering of the specificity of ethnic experience runs the risk of new forms of essentialism, as Yuval-Davis (1993) warns: it may be implied that 'all Pakistanis' (or Irish, or Cypriots) think or feel in certain ways, or share experiences. This is a particularly dangerous tendency, for example, when considering the rise of Islamic fundamentalism, when 'all Muslims' can be seen as potential terrorists because a minority are. Gilroy (1987, 1993) has termed this 'ethnic absolutism' and campaigns against its manifestations, which, he points out, can lead to such atrocities as have occurred in Bosnia, Rwanda and elsewhere. Closer to home, it promotes the kind of thinking, portrayed tragically in Spike Lee's film *Jungle Fever*, that it is a betrayal of one's 'brothers and sisters' to form a relationship with someone from a different ethnic community. By contrast, postmodernists see ethnicity as fluid and complex. Ethnic purity and the search for 'roots' are delusions – to some extent, we are all mongrels.

3   *Rejection of the presentation of racialized minorities as victims (Gilroy 1987)*   Black groups are not passive recipients of racism and discrimination, but have a longstanding history of political and cultural resistance. Even in the appalling conditions of slavery, African exiles managed to develop their culture (songs, music, dance, rituals, diaries, literature) as a counterpoint to imposed Western values and a basis for opposition and critique. In recent history, oppressed and racialized minorities have been active in opposition to their own subordination, not only through the more obvious forms of anti-racist and civil rights political activity, but also through the elaboration of counter-cultural forms, such as popular music (reggae, rap, bhangra).

4   *The analysis of discourse (Bhabha 1990b; Hall 1992a)*   Various forms of discourse which perpetuate racist ideas and Western images of the 'Other' have become a topic of investigation. Studies of academic, literary and popular texts show how deeply embedded images

of white superiority and non-white 'difference' have been within Western culture. In line with post-structuralist thinking, it is argued that such discourses not only reflect but help to constitute hierarchies between nations and ethnic groups. For example, Edward Said's famous account of *Orientalism* (1985) demonstrates how cultural representations of the relationships between Europe and Asia and the Middle East portray the 'Oriental Other' as exotic, seductive, but wily and untrustworthy. Discourses of this type are not just representations; they have vital effects in terms of how different nations relate in a diplomatic and military context. Indeed, they become deeply embedded into the everyday relations between people of different ethnicities, as demonstrated in the wry description offered by Indian writer Amit Chaudhuri of the Indian restaurants in the Cowley Road area of Oxford:

> The furniture, selected with some tender and innocent idea of opulence in mind, was cheap and striking. Honest Englishmen sat being served among fluted armrests and large mendacious pictures of palm trees and winding rivers, helplessly surrendering to an inexhaustible trickle of eastern courtesy. Everything... from the silvery letters of the sign on the outside, to the decor within was a version of that style called 'the oriental'. (1994, p. 37)

Paul Gilroy's admirable work offers a good example of these newer approaches, which we might call the 'new sociology of ethnicities'. *There Ain't no Black in the Union Jack* (1987) was written as these ideas took hold. In it he still used the concepts of class and class formation, displaying the influence of the cultural Marxism of Hall. Indeed, unlike the postmodern feminists, writers concerned with the 'new ethnicities' (Hall 1992c) did not abandon the concept of class, which, they argue, must be understood as part of the process of social differentiation. But Gilroy criticizes existing accounts of the relationship between class and 'race', either for reducing it to economic issues or for portraying 'race' as merely an ideological effect. He attempts to give more weight to 'race' as a separate factor by focusing on 'racial meanings, solidarity, and identities' (1987, p. 27), suggesting that 'race' should be viewed as a political category (p. 38), and different racial groups as 'political collectivities' (p. 149). In empirical chapters, he traces out a discourse of Black criminality which has developed in Britain over the post-war decades; and he studies various forms of autonomous political and cultural forms through which Black minorities in Britain and America have resisted racial oppression. He argues that Black 'expressive cultures', such as the popular music forms of reggae, hip-hop and rap, can be read as an indictment and critique of capitalism. These chapters display the interest in language and culture which we have noted as typical of postmodern feminism and which is extended in Gilroy's later work (1993).

Anthias and Yuval-Davis (1993) criticize Gilroy for never providing a very clear account of the precise relationship of class and 'race' (is class, too, a political category?) and for the ambiguity of his view of how 'race' is to be grounded. Nonetheless, his work is a very important (if not totally successful) attempt to combine a structural approach (to class formation) with the postmodern interest in meaning, culture, discourse and the social construction of identities. Anthias and Yuval-Davis's own theoretical position is an extension from this. They view ethnicity, gender and class as different aspects of the social processes by which boundaries between collectivities are drawn and social differences are constructed. Each has its own separate 'existential location', but, they argue, they should not be seen as separate since all intersect with one another in any specific context. This resembles the framework presented in this book.

It is noticeable that many of those involved in the new sociology of ethnicities are sociologists of colour. With some exceptions (such as Hall, Sivanandan and Cox), most of the previously prominent figures in the sociology of race relations were white. This may reflect the desire of Black intellectuals to develop their own ways of thinking rather than to rely on adapting concepts from the dominant metanarratives shaped by Western preoccupations and assumptions. There is an attempt to move out of the framework of Western thought and its ethnocentric values, to escape from 'travelling in the West'. This is the thinking that informs the notion of 'post-colonialism'.

Post-colonialism

The label 'post-colonial' implies a link with postmodernism, poststructuralism and so forth; and, indeed, like postmodernism, the term originated within cultural studies rather than sociology. It refers to the attempt to develop a critique of Western culture and thought, led by academics from 'Third World' societies and from minority groups within the West. We now tend to use the terms Global North and Global South rather than 'the West and the rest' but it can be argued that the criticisms still hold true in the twenty first century; Connell (2007), for example, has developed a critique of 'Northern theory'. Post-colonialists and Southern theorists, then, attempt to approach the analysis of classic literary texts, or to reconsider the history of a particular country, from a post-colonial or Southern standpoint, that of the subjugated or marginalized populations and cultures, challenging existing narratives.

Dirlik (1994), in an article critical of the concept of post-colonialism, suggests that the term is ambiguous, but distinguishes three key usages:

1 To describe current conditions in former colonial societies;
2 To characterize the global situation in an era after colonialism has ended;
3 As a critical form of discourse, informed by the experience of post-colonial living, with which to approach the study of post-colonial societies and cultures.

The former two more sociological usages would refer to study of relationships between societies and between different ethnic groups within societies which would take account of the colonial past. In that sense, most of the theoretical positions set out in this chapter could be labelled 'post-colonial'. However, the more common usage of the term is the third. Post-colonialism, in this usage, refers to a standpoint from which to carry out sociological, historical and cultural analysis, similar to a feminist standpoint.

The post-colonialist approach has largely been developed within the study of literature (Bhabha 1990b; Said 1985). It can be seen as another instance of the postmodern 'cultural turn'. For example, Gilroy in his later writing has turned to more extended study of aspects of Black culture, such as writing and music. He analyses this through the concept of the Black 'diaspora' (using a term more commonly applied to the situation of the Jews): that is, the scattering of people of African descent throughout many countries of the globe. He describes a cultural formation that has arisen from the diaspora, which he names the 'Black Atlantic', to convey the idea that it is a hybrid, a mix of elements from Western culture (both American and British), from the Caribbean and from the homelands of the African slaves. Just as capitalism was founded on the trade between these locations, so is the culture shaped by journeys (actual, spiritual and symbolic) between the areas. Gilroy (1993) uses the idea to attack the ideal of the recovery of a 'lost' or 'original' African culture (an aspect of his critique of 'ethnic absolutism').

The sociological issue that arises from this is the notion of 'hybridity', which has been developed by Homi Bhabha to describe contemporary ethnic identities (1990a). For example, Indian people settled in Britain are affected by aspects of both, or all, the cultures to which they are exposed. They are not simply Indian, or simply British, but Indian-British, having what Modood (1992) calls a 'hyphenated' identity which is different from that of an Indian who has never left India. When they return to visit India, British-based Indians often feel a lack of fit, experiencing a double displacement, not completely at home in either culture. However, Bhabha points out that in the global society in which we live *all* cultures and societies are hybrid. There is no such thing as a 'pure' culture, since all have been inevitably affected by processes of migration, travel and tourism, cultural exchange and communication. As stated in chapter 3, theorists of globalization assert that developments in mass media and computer technology are speeding up this international interchange. Bhabha views hybridity positively, arguing that it provides a 'third space', a freedom from total submission to either set of cultural values, from which a critical stance or an opposition to hierarchy can develop.

Bhabha's analysis suggests ways in which the post-colonial framework is useful in analysing racial and ethnic differentiation. The notion of hybridity helps us to explore the complexity of the ethnic dynamic in post-industrial societies (in a post-colonial world) and adds another dimension to theories of fragmentation. It can also serve as a critical commentary on discourses and ideologies which feature the notion of 'races' as absolutely distinct and incompatible entities. The post-colonial framework brings to the fore the notion of racist discourses, which is another very important element within the 'new sociology of ethnicities'.

Racisms

The analysis of racism has been a strand in all the theoretical perspectives discussed here. The classic Marxist approach views it as an ideology: that is, as a set of ideas which is slanted by the interest of particular groups in society. Dominant forms of ideology are used to justify the status quo and legitimate the power of socially dominant groups. Miles (1989), for example, views racism as a set of ideas which helps to obscure the reality of class relations. This usage follows one of the key principles of Marxian analysis, which is to make a sharp distinction between material reality and ideas.

Writers such as Anthias and Yuval-Davis (1993) use racism in a wider sense, not just to refer to ideas or ideologies but also to behaviour and practices. This is in line with the post-structuralist position, which refuses such a sharp distinction between 'words' and 'things'. We saw in chapter 5 that there is ambiguity as to whether the term 'discourse' refers simply to ideas and 'talk' or whether it also covers practices and material relationships. Miles, however, describes this broader usage of racism as 'conceptual inflation' (1989, p. 41). He contends that this usage of the term becomes so comprehensive as to lose its analytic utility and clarity. Almost anything can be described as 'racism'. Perhaps one way to get round this difficulty is simply to specify in each case whether racist ideas, attitudes or practices are under consideration.

Another debate concerns historical change in the operation of racism. Martin Barker (1981) offered an influential account which suggested that older forms of scientific racism were being replaced by what he termed 'the new racism'. Scientific racism is the view, discussed earlier, that distinct races can be isolated on the basis of biological and genetic differences. However, since the scientific backing for this has been questioned, a subsequent brand of racism has emerged which does not focus on innate differences but on the notion of cultural incompatibility. This view, which Barker claims was developed by the New Right and has been employed by the Conservative party and by ultra-right nationalist groups, suggests that it is natural for people to wish to live only among their 'own kind': 'birds of a feather flock together'.

Though these ideas are certainly politically current around Europe at present, it can be questioned whether such a transformation has occurred. David Mason (1992) claims that the notion of cultural incompatibility was always an aspect of the biological view of 'race', and Brah (1993) notes its common use in colonial thinking – in India, for example. Moreover, as Mason points out, ideas of biological determinism linger on. For example, American social scientist Charles Murray, well known for his arguments about the rise of the underclass, revived the idea that intelligence is genetically transmitted and that African Americans are innately less intelligent than whites (Herrnstein and Murray 1994). Such views are still commonly voiced in popular thinking. Rather than talking of a shift from one type of racism to another, we need to grasp that many forms of racism coexist: we should be speaking of racisms, rather than racism.

For example, Philip Cohen (1988) suggests that different classes use different 'codes' embodying different strands of racist thinking. Among the upper class there is a stress on 'breeding' and purity, which reflects historical concerns over inheritance and lineage. Working-class racism hinges round notions of territoriality: what Cohen terms the 'nationalism of the neighbourhood'; racialized groups are seen as 'invading our space', 'dating our girls' and 'taking our jobs and houses'. Finally, the 'bourgeois' code emphasizes inherited intelligence and aptitude, drawing from the tenets of scientific racism. Specific and quite localized situations will produce different types of racist discourse. Brah (1993) discussed the rise of multiple racisms in Europe in the 1990s, with, for example, the revival of anti-Semitism in many countries, a revival manifested in the desecration of Jewish cemeteries; the neo-Nazi dogmas of young German skinheads; and attacks in various countries on specific ethnic groups, such as Turks in Germany, North Africans in France and South Asian Muslims in Britain. Brah concluded, 'What is new about the 1990s is *not* that there is a single neo-racism in Europe but that a variety of racisms (some of which had become less salient) are being reconstituted into new configurations' (1993, p. 20). Brah's analysis fits well with events in the 2010s, such as attacks on Jewish targets in Paris and London. The inexorable rise of Islamophobia following the attacks on the Twin Towers in 2001 is a prime example, dealt with fully in chapter 8.

And we might add that this variability itself is not new. Racism has always been multi-dimensional and specific to different contexts. In an era of increased migration and mobility, racism finds new ways of operating. New forms of racism and complex hierarchies of race arise in today's multiethnic global cities.

Newer Themes: Multiculturalism and Mixing

Current work on racial and ethnic divisions builds very much on the 'new ethnicities' and post-colonial approaches, focusing on difference, complexity and multiple identities. Less attention is now given to exploring economic divisions, perhaps because the situations of the many minority ethnic groups in Britain are so diverse that commonalities are lacking and generalizations are more difficult to sustain than in the study of class and gender (Solomos 2003). It has been suggested that Black British citizens have suffered in the recession, but detailed studies are as yet rather lacking. Theorists of ethnicity at present focus more on inter-ethnic conflicts, cultural differences and the difficulties of communities living together.

Multiculturalism

This leads us to the concept of multiculturalism, which has been the focus of heated academic and political debate in past decades. The vision of numerous ethnic groups living in proximity to one another and maintaining their own cultural practices, while respecting those of people of other ethnic origins, is a powerful and persuasive one, embraced by radical sociologists and activists (Modood 2007). Yet such coexistence may provoke real tensions where cultural values appear conflictual. For example, the Muslim view that women should cover up when in public spaces conflicts with English assertion of the rights of women to wear skimpy clothing and expose flesh as part of female sexual liberation. Both sides may be condemnatory and judgemental about the other's clothing conventions. For this reason, many critics, especially those on the political right in the UK and the USA, have argued that multiculturalism has failed or is at least 'on the retreat' (Joppke 2004).

Many countries of the Global North (as we now tend to name the countries Hall, Ghosh and others termed 'the West') have adopted multiculturalism as an official state policy, with Canada and Australia taking the lead. Such countries saw cultural diversity as an asset, not a threat. This contrasted with earlier ideals of 'assimilation' which argued that migrants should adapt the values and cultural practices of the host country. Britain over the course of the twentieth century switched its official policies from assimilation to multiculturalism. An example of multicultural policy in action in Britain is successive governments' backing for religious minority groups, such as Muslims and Jews, having the right to set up their own schools, which follow their own customs and ethical principles. This can be contrasted with the more assimilationist approach in France, where schools are compelled to be secular and there have been persistent struggles over the rights of young schoolgirls to wear headscarves.

The advocates of multiculturalism, such as Will Kymlicka (1995), Tariq Modood (2007) and Bihkhu Parekh (2002) see it as an issue of human rights that citizens of various ethnic origins should be allowed to retain their distinctive cultural heritage and practices; they argue that cultural diversity enriches the life of all citizens. This does not just imply tolerance of difference but may involve what Kymlicka (1995) calls 'differentiated rights'; for example, allowing people the right not to work on days they consider holy, or to wear turbans and headscarves instead of helmets or caps. Modood (2007) argues against the critics that we need more, not less, multiculturalism, based on values of respect for difference, which he sees as the only possible means of integration in the context of globalization and multiethnic urban life.

However, others argue that cultural incompatibilities lead to conflicts and distrust between different communities, and can even trigger social disorder and crime. American social scientist Robert Putnam (2007) argues that, far from promoting tolerance and respect, multiculturalism leads people in multiethnic communities to 'hunker down', isolating themselves and mixing only with people of their own ethnicity, possibly even coming to distrust everyone. British Prime Minister David Cameron is on record as saying that he believes state multiculturalism in Britain has failed. The scandal of child abuse in Rotherham, which will be discussed in the final chapter of this book, led a *Daily Telegraph* journalist to splutter about the 'toxic legacy of multiculturalism' (*Telegraph* 29 August 2014).

I side with Modood in believing we need more, not less, tolerance of cultural diversity. However, there is a genuine danger of 'ethnic ghettos' developing in our cities, and of the social isolationism described by Putnam being the result, if we do not make conscious efforts to communicate across cultural difference and to educate people about different cultures. Here notions of *interculturalism* are crucial. For example, in the Netherlands, people are encouraged to visit the homes of people from different ethnic backgrounds, eat with them and learn about their ways of living. This exchange breaks down barriers of misunderstanding. Thus Parekh argues that multi-culturalism should involve setting proper terms for the relationships between different cultural communities, which cannot be done by any one culture imposing its principles on others, but by setting up 'an open and equal dialogue between them' (Parekh 2002, p. 13). Interculturalism is the way to promote understanding and avoid the development of stigmatized identities, such as the 'Bearded Muslim' or the 'Veiled Woman'.

Mixing and Miscegenation

Another key issue here is the growing number of children of 'mixed' or 'dual' heritage resulting from the growing trend of intermarriage between people of different ethnic backgrounds, especially – but not at all exclusively – between people of African descent and white Britons. This is, of course, not a new phenomenon, as people of different backgrounds have often married or produced children together, especially in colonial situations where access to women of the colonizers' own ethnicity was limited. These relationships led to the coining of terms such as 'mulatto' or 'mestizo' in countries in the Americas (Meer 2014). A less pleasant term current when I was a child was 'half-caste', which was indicative, as Meer observes, of the stigmatization attached to mixed-'race' individuals in the first half of the twentieth century. But in multicultural contexts, for example European cities like London and Paris, such 'mixed heritage' is now more commonly seen as an asset, something to be celebrated, though it can cause difficulties and uncertainties for the individuals concerned.

Some while ago, the term 'melting pot' was coined in America to express the view that racial distinctions would be overcome by the mixing of populations and the intermarriage of individuals. We are certainly a long way from such a Utopia of racial and ethnic harmony, but probably nearer now than we were then. This increased tolerance of mixing must be in part down to the challenges brought by sociologists and race relations professionals to notions of racial essentialism and their highlighting of ethnically hybrid identities. Migration and mobility also play their part as young workers and students move around the globe, coming into contact with potential partners from an array of backgrounds. Perhaps love does, indeed, conquer all!

Ethnicity and Identity

So, in multicultural societies we confront a real plurality of ethnic identities. 'Race' and ethnicity are generally seen as more powerful forces than class in promoting identification in present-day societies. They are more likely to engender active or politicized identities. This is partly because of the visibility of 'race' where skin colour is an issue. But since some white ethnicities are also strongly felt (as in Serbia, Croatia and Bosnia), this is clearly not the whole story. One factor is the experience of discrimination. As Modood points out, 'the present ferment amongst Asian Muslims illustrates how the sense of being humiliated and marginalized enhances traditional forms of solidarity' (1992, p. 43). In a powerful speech on the *Daily Show* TV programme in America, host Jon Stewart pointed out to white citizens how the daily experience of being Black in American cities means facing 'an indignity, ridiculous, grotesque and on occasion fatal' every few hours, adding 'imagine you cannot get a cab even though you are a neurosurgeon, because you are Black' (*Daily Show* 29 August 2014). This experience of what Bradley et al. call 'everyday racism' (2007) clearly makes people aware of their ethnicity, in the same way Riley described in relation to gender (see chapter 5). In response, 'race' and ethnicity have become bases of political activity over past decades, heightening awareness of ethnic affiliation even where it was lacking in the past.

The emphasis within the new sociology of ethnicities is on the complex and fluid nature of ethnic identity. Allen (1994) stresses that awareness of ethnicity is not constant through an individual's life; it emerges only in specific contexts in which, for reasons such as those given above, it assumes significance as an aspect of individual experience. Hall (1990), espousing a postmodern position, emphasizes the role of discourses about 'race' and ethnicity in creating identities. As Hall puts it, over the course of our lifetimes the 'imagined communities' with which we identify change. He warns against seeing ethnic identities as fixed (sometimes hidden) entities, waiting for us to discover them and our 'roots' and 'our true selves' in the process. Rather, identities change as discourses about ethnic relations change: 'Instead of thinking of identity as an already accomplished fact, which the new cultural practices then represent, we should think, instead, of identity as a "production" which is never complete, always in process, and always constituted within, not outside, representation' (1990, p. 222).

The example of racialized minorities in Britain and America shows the volatility of politicized racial and ethnic identities. The Black Power movement of the 1960s led many of African descent, and Asians, to adopt the identity 'Black' as a statement of a political affiliation, uniting the diverse racialized ethnicities in a struggle against the white oppressors. Then, in the 1970s, an interest in the history of slavery and the African past led those of African origin to locate themselves more specifically in relation to that past. West Indian became Afro-Caribbean then Black or African-Caribbean; Black American became African American. In the 1980s the move towards ethnic particularism led people to identify more narrowly – say, with a specific Caribbean island or region in the Indian subcontinent (Mason 2003). In recent decades, political thinking which emphasizes the idea of 'post-colonial subjectivities' or hybridity has encouraged people to adopt 'hyphenated' identities: Mexican-American, British-Indian and so forth.

Modood's work also alerts us to the important contribution culture and religion may make to identification, citing the case of the Islamic revival and its effects on Asian Muslims resident in Britain. This caused a major reorientation of identity. British Muslims stopped seeing themselves, and being seen, in terms of 'Black', 'Pakistani' or other racialized and stigmatized identities. The attacks on Islam in the wake of the turmoil surrounding Salman Rushdie's *The Satanic Verses*, and other controversies concerning Islamic observance in Britain, promoted a more confident assertion of identity in terms of being a Muslim. As Modood says, 'any oppressed group feels its oppression most according to those dimensions of its being which it (not the oppressor) values the most' (1992, p. 54). Religion became the focus for racism, but also a source of pride and self-assertiveness for supporters of Islam, even as they were becoming the latest in a line of 'demons' denounced by the West. This example also illustrates the need to take into account events that occur outside any given society (here the strengthening of traditional Islam which was initiated outside Britain). Internal relations in migrant ethnic communities are often influenced by changes in class, gender and ethnic power relations in countries of origin.

The interplay of all these factors means that the identity of the 'post-colonial subject' can be confused, especially for those who move between countries of origin and Western societies. This is illustrated in the subtle accounts provided by post-colonialist writers Amit Chaudhuri and V. S. Naipaul, of their own attempts to locate themselves in different contexts. Naipaul describes the strangeness of his return from Britain to Trinidad:

> All the people on the streets were darker than I remembered: Africans, Indians, whites, Portuguese, mixed Chinese. In their houses, though, people didn't look so dark. I suppose that was because on the streets I was more of a looker, half a tourist, and when I went to a house it was to be with people I had known years before. So I saw them more easily. (1994, p. 1)

Chaudhuri describes how in England he studied his compatriots as if through white eyes: 'Only a little way away from me sat the Indian bus driver in his uniform, but for some reason I thought of him as "Asian" and he became for me mysterious and unclassifiable' (1994, p. 35).

Chaudhuri's ironic account illustrates how the white viewpoint becomes the 'natural' one. As we saw in chapter 5, majority status invokes 'default' identities. Since they are seen as 'normal', the 'natural' way to be, people give little thought to them. However, in Britain, minority white ethnicity (Scots, Welsh, Irish) may be the source of a strong politicized identity, as in the case of the various nationalist movements associated with these ethnic groups. The postwar period has witnessed intermittent attempts by Welsh and Scottish people to revive their cultural traditions and their own languages and to demand relative or complete autonomy from the British state, culminating in the referendum for Scottish independence. However, white ethnic identification as English, or as American, is evoked only in the international context (as against German, French, Russian, etc.). That is, English and American identity takes a nationalist, not an ethnic, form.

Frankenberg, however, produced some interesting pioneer work while studying white ethnic identity in America and trying to dig out the meaning of 'growing up white'. She argued that 'whiteness' has three dimensions: structural advantage; a particular way of looking at the world; and an assumption that cultural practices employed by the white majority are 'normal' and universal. Other forms of cultural behaviour are defined as odd, deviant or exotic. Whiteness becomes, in the words of one of her interviewees, 'a privilege enjoyed but not acknowledged, a reality lived in but unknown' (Frankenberg 1993, p. 51).

This discussion reveals the multiplicity of identities relating to territoriality and migration. If we return to the imagined African-Caribbean young woman of earlier chapters, she has available to her identities as British, Caribbean or 'Black'. She may think of herself in terms of the particular island her family came from, such as Jamaica or Barbados, or hark back to the distant past in Africa. She may also see herself in local terms, belonging to Birmingham, or to a particular area, Sparkbrook or Handsworth, within it. Her identity may involve any – or all – of these. And that is without considering the way other stratification dynamics impinge upon her consciousness.

Intersecting Dynamics: Ethnicity, Class, Gender and Age

Class

Incomer migrants enter the labour market on disadvantaged terms, reflecting their relative powerlessness. Moreover, many come from working-class or rural peasant backgrounds in their countries of origin, and are driven by poverty and the hope of achieving economic success abroad. Those who do possess qualifications and training for higher occupational positions often find these devalued or disregarded in their new country, as was the case with many Asians from East Africa. But as migrant populations become settled, new generations can compete for upward mobility through the education systems of the West, and some achieve it.

Racialized minority members in Britain and America are likely to be disproportionately concentrated in working class locations. In Britain, this is especially true of African-Caribbeans, Pakistanis and Bangladeshis; in America, of African Americans and Latinos. Modood (1992) gave an account demonstrating the complexity of class and ethnic stratification among British Indians. He distinguished four strata. At the bottom of the socioeconomic scale were Muslim Gujaratis from rural areas, mainly filling unskilled jobs (as do Pakistanis and Bangladeshis). Punjabis, mainly Sikhs, are the longest-settled group, and Modood suggested that their class profile was equivalent to that of the white population, as was that of Hindu Gujaratis. The East African refugees, who came predominantly from urban middle-class occupations, were regaining their lost class position, after the original setback. Finally, there was a small group of successful urban professionals from a variety of ethnic backgrounds who often act as leaders in their own ethnic communities. Latest figures from the ONS show how the Indians have continued to consolidate their improved class position. Their profile is closest to that of the white population and they have the highest proportion of men in employment. The five top occupations in which Indian men were employed in 2001 were sales assistants, doctors, shopkeepers, software professionals and retail managers; this contrasts with, for example, African-Caribbean men (sales assistants, storage, security guards, postmen and van drivers) or Pakistani men (taxi drivers, sales assistants, shopkeepers, retail managers and packers) (Blackwell and Guinea-Martin 2005).

In America, a 'Black bourgeoisie' is now well established, holding top posts in the professions, the media, the business and financial world, and especially in government agencies and the law. Their social prominence and the power they gain through involvement in the political process can be seen as an important advance for racialized minorities and a challenge to negative stereotyping of Black groups. The triumph of the Black bourgeoisie is symbolized by the election of Barack Obama as the first Black president, along with other prominent figures such as General Colin Powell or the Reverend Jesse Jackson. However, it has been argued that the Black bourgeoisie has turned its back on the rest of the Black population, fearing to be dragged down by association with them. This is well portrayed in Spike Lee's *Jungle Fever*, in which the film's 'yuppie' architect hero shrinks from contact with his 'no-good' crack-addicted brother. There is growing polarization between the Black elite and the demoralized ghetto population.

The idea of the 'Black underclass' has been put forward in both Britain and America. Generally, in Britain, where racialized minority members are distributed more broadly through the class structure, this idea has been rejected (Pilkington 1984). But in America the idea of the ghetto underclass has gained considerable acceptance. William Julius Wilson described its development in the northern cities, drawing on data from Chicago and elsewhere (Wilson 1987, 1993). He uses the term in a specific way in relation to a combination of economic deprivation and social isolation which characterizes the situation in inner cities. The key issue was unemployment among African Americans (and also Hispanics), rising from de-industrialization; working-class Black males were heavily concentrated in blue-collar employment, which was in decline. The plight of the unemployed was worsened by the movement of whites, middle-class Blacks and even employed working-class Blacks out of the inner cities, leaving the ghetto communities deprived of leadership and of positive role-models for the young. The resulting demoralization precipitated a drift into crime, violence, drug-taking and other anti-social behaviours. Wilson suggests that young Black males, unable to present themselves as breadwinners, affirm their masculinity through sexual conquest and fathering children, which in turn pushes young Black women into dependence on welfare. In contrast to Murray's account of the underclass, Wilson emphasizes that these symptoms spring from forced (not voluntary) joblessness, rather than from an autonomous culture of poverty. Whether defined as a ghetto underclass or as part of the precariat (see chapter 4), it is clear that African Americans and Latinos from working-class backgrounds who lack educational qualifications are at risk of economic deprivation.

The notion of the 'Black bourgeoisie' has been less popular in the UK, though some Asian and Caribbean people achieve professional and media jobs (although there is ample evidence of discrimination in areas like law) and there is a small group of very wealthy and successful Asian businessmen, such as Shami Ahmed, the multi-millionaire owner of the Legendary Joe Bloggs clothing company. But more numerous are the self-employed people who can be seen as constituting an Asian petite bourgeoisie. While some interpret this as the result of Asian values of hard work, self-sufficiency and enterprise, others suggest that the rise of Asian enterprise is linked to racism and exclusion (Cashmore and Troyna 1983; Jones and McEvoy 1986). Success depends greatly on the use of family resources (capital from savings and loans, goodwill and, crucially, family labour) and on degrees of self-exploitation (working very long hours in poor conditions). The businesses are orientated to community needs (restaurants, sari shops, travel agencies dealing with the Far East) and many are dependent on the community for custom, although most of us have benefited from the long opening hours of the Asian corner shop.

Asian entrepreneurs have attained a class and status position above others in their ethnic groups. Will such differences of class start to split hitherto integrated ethnic communities and weaken ethnic loyalties? Anthias and Yuval-Davis believe not, because of the strength of ties that rise from shared experience of discrimination: 'In the currency of a racist society, ethnic solidarity is likely to be retained at the expense of class consciousness in differentiating within racialized populations' (1993, p. 88).

Gender

The writings of Black feminists also emphasize the commitment of women of colour towards their ethnic groups. Ethnic solidarity is seen to transcend gender as well as class consciousness. That does not mean that there are no gender inequalities in ethnic communities. However, it is important to avoid stereotyping ethnic minorities as patriarchal and backward in gender terms, in contrast to a more egalitarian white majority. This was one aspect of the Black critique of the white feminist portrayal of issues such as arranged marriages (Carby 1982; Amos and Parmar 1984). Rather, we should explore how gendered power operates differently in different ethnic groups.

The example of British Muslim communities was discussed in chapter 5. A rather different situation is that of African-Caribbean women. Within Caribbean families and communities, women have traditionally been seen to occupy an influential role. They usually work full-time, often assuming responsibility as breadwinners in what is seen as a typically Caribbean family form, the matrifocal or woman-headed family. (Many British Caribbean families, of course, are of the conventional nuclear kind.) Young women are strongly encouraged by their families to work hard at school and develop careers, and appear more committed to educational achievement than their white peers or their Black brothers (Mirza 1992). From this arises what Wallace (1990) termed the myth of the Black 'super-woman': powerful, strong-minded and nurturant. However, this ignores the way family responsibilities act as a particularly heavy burden on African-Caribbean and African American women, who are expected to hold down a full-time job, do the housework and keep the extended family together. Men exercise their male power by refusing domestic labour, expecting their wives to carry the major responsibility for family subsistence. As Fuller argues, 'matrifocality may allow women to develop with a definition of femininity that includes strength, competence and so which enables them to challenge patriarchal relations of sexual domination, but it does not thereby do away with patriarchy' (1982, p. 98).

Black women also face racism in the labour market. Racialized minority women in Britain suffer a triple disadvantage of 'race', sex and class. A classic study by Phizacklea (1990) showed how these three dynamics combined, in the context of the Midlands textile industry, to produce a low-paid female work-force, often labouring in sweatshop conditions. Subject to discrimination in the labour market and dependent on males of their own community because of immigration rules, women – stereotyped as 'naturally' suited for garment work because of their 'nimble fingers' – were at the end of a chain of subcontracting, developed through the operation of transnational companies within global markets.

There has been disagreement as to the relative effects of 'race' and gender. Data analysed by Brown (1984) and Smith (1977) appeared to show that the gap between white and Black men was greater than that between white and Black women. Thus, the poor situation of racialized minority women in Britain was ascribed more to class and gender than to race. However, Bruegel (1989), re-analysing employment data, refuted this. She argues that aggregate data conceal the differences between white and Black women's employment situations. For example, Black women's apparently high average wages relate to the fact that they work longer hours and that their employment is concentrated in London, where all workers are more highly paid. We can conclude that it is futile to attempt to disentangle the effects of the three dynamics. All act together to confine racialized minority women to the least-privileged sections of the employment structure, often working as cleaners, domestics or care workers.

Age

On the face of it, one might assume that older migrants, such as those who arrived in Britain in the immediate post-war years, had faced greater handicaps and hardships. They will have experienced discrimination in the labour market and more overt forms of racism, for example in housing. Their position was made more difficult by lack of British qualifications and, for some, by lack of expertise in the English language. The second generation, growing up in England and participating in the British education system, was expected to have better economic prospects. There is certainly evidence of considerable poverty among some older people who were first-generation immigrants. But Ken Blakemore and Margaret Boneham (1994) pointed out that the specific situation of emigration meant that people expected to undergo hardships and were pleased with any kind of improvement in their standard of living.

In contrast, second- and third-generation immigrants have higher expectations, while bearing the impact of recent recessions. Many of these young people have reacted more aggressively against discrimination than their parents. The feeling that special difficulties were faced by young Asians and, especially, young African-Caribbeans was mirrored in the title of Cashmore and Troyna's book *Black Youth in Crisis* (1982). Concern continues to surround the numbers of alienated minority youth who reject school and its values, immersing themselves in a street culture of gangs, drugs and petty crime. Gillborn (1998), however, imputes this to racist stereotyping by teachers. Although Asian teenagers are often stereotyped as conformist and hard-working, Martin Mac an Ghaill's ethnographic study (1988) revealed that Asian boys, too, were developing anti-school cultures. The latest manifestation of this crisis is the growing number of British Muslim young men, often highly educated, who have decided to turn their back on 'Western' values and join jihadist groups in countries such as Iraq, Afghanistan and Syria, as a result of their experience of racism and discrimination.

We should not overstate this problem. Many young people from ethnic minorities in Britain are conformist, successful and committed to education. Indeed, they are more likely than their white compeers to go on into further or higher education (HE). In 2011, the highest participation rates in HE (over 60 per cent) were among female Black and male Asian groups, compared with 56 per cent of all minority ethnic groups and 38 per cent for the white group, though it is important to bear in mind that the white group is much larger and more diverse in composition (Tackey, Barnes and Khambhaita 2011). As O'Donnell pointed out, most young Blacks share with their white peers respect for the law and a desire for a 'good life'; the difference is that they face more obstacles in achieving this (O'Donnell, 1985, p. 79).

However, there is anxiety that if young people of colour continue to face discrimination and exclusion, the situation may deteriorate and the problems experienced in some cities in the United States, such as New York, Los Angeles and Chicago, could be replicated in Britain. Young African Americans and Latinos in their early teens and younger are dropping out and being sucked into a world of gangs, crime and violence, drugs and guns. Although the reporting of the ghetto culture may sometimes be exaggerated and sensationalized, it appears that young people of colour in America are the victim of an extreme trend towards racial polarization. Unfortunately, with widespread unemployment attendant on global restructuring of capital, the position is set to get worse. In 2014 the anger of young Black people burst out in severe riots in the American city of Ferguson after the killing of unarmed Black teenager Michael Brown, by a white policeman.

Conclusions

Interest in the study of 'race' and ethnicity in Britain expanded rapidly over the course of the twentieth century, and into the early twenty-first. This has been influenced by definitions of race relations as a social problem and source of social conflict. More recently, it has also been promoted by the rise of nationalist and ethnic politics and a worldwide assertion of ethnic identity.

Early approaches to the study of 'race' and ethnicity centred on the division between 'white' and 'Black' groups and drew largely upon concepts from class analysis to explain those divisions. These approaches shed light on the use of migrant labour and treatment of racialized minorities within colonialism and capitalism. But because of the one-dimensional nature of classic theories, both Marxian and liberal, these approaches often treated racial divisions as subsidiary to class.

What I have called 'the new sociology of ethnicities' has supplemented these initial accounts with a broader perspective on ethnicity. Influenced by postmodernist and post-structuralist thinking, writers such as Hall and Gilroy focused on the 'post-colonial subject' and were particularly concerned with identities, cultural practices and racist discourses. However, they have not turned away from the study of racism and power disparities; they do not celebrate diversity at the expense of ignoring inequality. Writers such as Gilroy, Phizacklea and Anthias and Yuval-Davis have led the way in exploring the intersection of ethnicity, class and gender. Although there is sometimes an apparent tension between structural analysis of class, and constructionist and discursive accounts of 'race' (as in Gilroy 1987), the new sociologists of ethnicity appear to have negotiated the crossing of the structuralist/post-structuralist divide.

Our world is currently characterized by increasing ethnic and nationalist tension on a global scale, and by polarization of racial inequalities often exacerbated by the whipping-up of race hatreds within nations. Unfortunately, the troubled situation in many parts of the Middle East and Asia has led to increased inter-ethnic tensions in Europe and America, which are discussed further in chapter 8. Globalization has promoted new patterns of migration, furthering the development of complex racial and ethnic hierarchies in most major cities of the world. Sometimes the experience of multiethnic living may produce positive results, developing cosmopolitan attitudes and intercultural exchanges. It is significant that in the UK the support for UKIP with its anti-immigration stance has been strongest in rural areas where there are fewer migrants: UKIP has made little headway in London. But racism and negative stereotyping remain widespread and, while the international dominance of the advanced capitalist nations continues to shape race relations, the whole world is still 'travelling in the West'.

Further Reading

Among a number of useful books dealing with general perspectives on 'race' are Robert Miles, *Racism* (Open University Press, 1989); Andrew Pilkington, *Racial Disadvantage and Ethnic Diversity in Britain* (Palgrave, 2003); and John Solomos, *Race and Racism in Britain* (Palgrave, 2003). David Mason (ed.), *Explaining Ethnic Differences* (The Policy Press, 2003), is a good collection of essays. Tariq Modood, *Multiculturalism* (Polity, 2007), is a thorough survey of debates on this issue. Annie Phizacklea's *Unpacking the Fashion Industry* (Routledge, 1990), is a classic early account of the intersections of 'race', class and gender in a particular context. Steve Fenton's *Ethnicity* (Polity, 2010) is a comprehensive introduction to the concepts discussed here, with an excellent discussion of patterns of migration.

Thinking Points

- Why is racism so persistent?
- Why do the economic situations of different ethnic groups vary so greatly?

7

Age: Generations and Gaps

No one could fail to notice Joseph's standing in the community. Dealings with him (as with the elderly in many societies) are marked by a jocular respect, a celebration of an old man's importance and authority. To tease the elderly is to show that you are on terms of happy intimacy with your own heritage...And from time to time the young men call on his authority: Is this as far as the fence rails should extend?...Do you ever find lynx on such and such a hillside?...He had not only the expertise but also the authority of his eighty-some years.

(Brodie 1986, pp. 2, 4)

Joseph is an elder of the Beaver tribe of British Columbia in the north-west of Canada. As in many tribal and clan-based societies, elders are treated as an important social resource because of their fund of knowledge and long experience of living; often they act as repositories for myths, folk-wisdom, songs and stories of the society's past. In contrast, it is argued that in industrialized societies, where wealth and power are linked to participation in capitalist production, the social standing of older people has declined (Cowgill and Holmes 1972). Ironically, the institution of retirement, though promoted as a way to ease the lot of older working people, has contributed to a view of them as redundant to society's needs or even a burden upon society. The feeling of 'being on the scrap heap' is reflected in this comment from an elderly man born in Jamaica, speaking of his desire to return to the Caribbean: 'I want to go by 1985 or I'll end up in a mental home   I feel that the elderly black person should try to go home, you have no use as an elderly person' (quoted in Fenton 1987, p. 25).

On the other hand, historians and sociologists of old age have warned against rosy views of the status of older people in non-industrial societies (Fennell et al. 1988). They argue that in many societies negative attitudes have surrounded elderly people. Featherstone and Hepworth (1990) note the long history of distaste for ageing bodies. Younger people have commonly distanced themselves from elderly relatives, considering them a burden rather than willingly taking on the duty of caring for them. Thomas (1976) and Laslett (1977) provide evidence that this was the case in pre-industrial Britain. Age does not *on its own* automatically bring high status, which is often only accorded to those who when younger were powerful or wealthy or community leaders (Featherstone and Hepworth 1990; Blakemore and Boneham 1994). But Brodie's account (1986) of Joseph illustrates how in *some* contemporary communities and societies, such as among native Canadians or in African tribes, *some* older people still occupy a vital and special place.

This contrasts with Janet Ford and Ruth Sinclair's study of older women in Britain today, and the ageist attitudes which serve to render them almost invisible in our society: 'From 60 onwards we shall in all probability be referred to as "elderly", "retired" and "OAPs" by the rest of society. In the west these terms form part of the stereotype about older people, who are seen as unproductive, dependent, restricted in their lives and therefore not very interesting. We have successfully deprived age of authority and of interest' (1987, p. 1). Although their research revealed variety in the ways people adapt to age and cope with its physical restrictions, most of their respondents were aware of the negative images of elderly people held by younger age groups.

Such a contrast reveals that meanings attached to specific age groups differ between societies. While we tend to think of age in common-sense terms as a biological fact relating to the number of years an individual has lived since birth, chronological age has in itself limited intrinsic significance; it gains meaning from the behavioural characteristics imputed to it, so that the idea of a person 'being elderly' or 'being adolescent' triggers off expectations about how that person will act, feel and think.

Age, then, as studied here, is a sociological rather than a chronological phenomenon. It relates to social categories, such as childhood, youth, adolescence, adulthood, middle age and old age, which have been developed to describe lived relationships between individuals and groups as they move through the life course. The term 'life course' as opposed to 'life cycle' is used here, because in biology the latter term is often used as an equivalent to the 'reproductive cycle', which terminates when an individual of a natural species has achieved successful procreation (Harris 1987). The term has also been used by biologists and psychologists to denote rigidly defined life stages through which each individual must pass when they reach a certain chronological age. An example of this is seen in the many books which tell parents what to expect each month as their baby grows. Sociologists prefer the term 'life course', viewing such life stages as socially defined and constructed; they can be distinguished by different social roles associated with them. For example, 'adolescence' or 'youth' in many societies is deemed to end when a young person 'settles down', indicated by securing a permanent job, getting married, establishing a home or starting a family; although the chronological age at which these events occur is variable, they are taken to be social activities associated with the status of 'young adulthood'. Each stage in the life course is differentiated by the social meanings, and imputed activities, associated with it. Social rules suggest what forms of behaviour are suitable for each age group; for example, it is not considered appropriate in our society for children to have a full-time job or be involved in sexual relationships, or for elderly women to bear children or to have relationships with teenaged boys. Many activities are quite strictly segregated by age: we would get a shock if we saw a sixty-year-old sitting at a school desk; nor would we expect to see a twenty-year-old at a boardroom table or on the benches of the House of Lords. However, we must stress that such rules are historically variable. Indeed, postmodernists contend that the boundaries between life-cycle phases are becoming increasingly blurred (Hunt 2005). Many people over sixty take part in activities that were formerly seen as reserved for youth (camping in the mud at the Glastonbury Festival, taking part in extreme sports like bungee-jumping), while children are said to be growing up much more quickly, with pre-teenaged girls wearing make-up and high-heeled shoes.

Age is viewed here as a dimension of inequality because, like class, gender and ethnicity, it involves the construction of social differences which in turn brings differential access to social resources, such as wealth, power and status. In our society, there is an 'age elite' of middle age groups, with the young and the old being relatively powerless. A distinctive feature of age relations in contemporary capitalist societies is that the old and the young are often forced into social dependency on the middle groupings. However, all age groups are affected adversely by ageism. Ageism refers to systematic stereotyping of people and discrimination against them on the basis of characteristics and limitations which are imputed to them simply because of their age (Bodily 1994). Thus, *all* older people are seen as less suitable for employment on the grounds that they are physically slow, lack dynamism and are not very adaptable to change; *all* younger people are suspected of being unreliable, reckless, undisciplined and prone to drug-taking and promiscuity.

While this kind of stereotyping acts particularly against the young and the old, middle groupings too may suffer from aspects of it. For example, middle-aged women applying for jobs as secretaries or receptionists may be told they are 'too old for the job'. Where youth and glamour are associated with particular forms of employment, the middle-aged can be faced with ageist exclusion. In 1994, surveys carried out by the Institute of Personnel Management and the Metropolitan Authorities' Recruitment Agency revealed that in many workplaces age discrimination begins for men at forty and for women at thirty-five; 30 per cent of employers explicitly specified upper age limits, and 40 per cent of employers believed that age was a crucial factor in recruitment (Richards 1994). Although, under the 2010 Equality Act, age discrimination is unlawful, ageism at work continues to be reported by both young and older people. According to *Social Trends* (2008), 12 per cent of employees reported discrimination by age, as compared to 4 per cent reporting discrimination on grounds of ethnicity or religion, and 5 per cent on grounds of gender.

As stated, specific categories of age vary from society to society, and there is considerable debate as to how to categorize age relationships in contemporary societies. Generally, sociologists tend to distinguish five broad groupings: childhood; youth (sometimes more narrowly defined as adolescence); young adulthood; mid-life; and old age. Sub-groups can be delineated in these broad groupings. For example, it is now common to distinguish between the 'young old' (sixty or sixty-five to seventy-four) and the 'old old', those aged seventy-five and over (Arber and Ginn 1991b). Problems of poverty, isolation and physical deterioration are particularly severe among the latter (Gilbert et al. 1989).

It has already been stressed that age has been a neglected topic within sociology. Arber and Ginn (1991a) argue that, although lip-service is frequently paid to age as one of a number of bases of stratification, there are few studies of older people. With a few notable exceptions (Mannheim 1952; Eisenstadt,1956), age has not been treated as a general category or framework for analysis. Rather, research has focused on the experience of specific age groups, such as children, youths or older people. The study of these groups has developed as distinct academic specialisms, such as the social history of childhood, the sociology of youth cultures, and gerontology (the interdisciplinary study of old age). While providing important insights into the inequalities associated with youth and age, they are rarely incorporated into a general theory of age and inequality.

The neglect of age, as with gender and ethnicity, goes back to classical sociological theory. This may be because age was viewed as a natural phenomenon. Since it was assumed that all individuals would pass through all the stages of the life course, it was not seen as a crucial source of *social* disadvantage. Moreover, the preoccupation of the classic theorists with work and the public sphere meant that social groups who were less likely to be involved in production or in political activities (children, older people) received less attention. However, age was treated as a crucial factor in the discipline of social anthropology. Anthropologists writing about non-industrial pre-class societies observed that age and gender were the basis of the social division of labour. But within classical sociological theories, the assumption was often made that occupation- or class-based stratification systems had replaced those based on 'ascribed' characteristics like age and gender.

As in the case of 'race', age emerged as a topic of sociological interest through its definition as a 'social problem'. Three particular developments were involved here. The first was the increasing attention given to the demographic phenomenon of an 'ageing population'. This refers to the growing proportion of the population who are in the older age groups. In 2011, there were 10.3 million people aged 65 and over in the UK, an 80 per cent increase over six decades, from 1951. By 2014, the figure had reached 11 million. The government predict that by 2050 this will rise to 19 million. According to Hunt (2005), in 1951 there were only 271 people aged over 100 in the UK, while by 2001 there were 4,400 and in 2012 13,350 (Age UK 2014). UK government statistics show that in 1971 there were 1.3 million people aged over 80. By 2001, this had nearly doubled to 2.5 million; it is predicted that by 2031 this may reach 5 million.

The ageing population is linked to industrialization, because of the decline in infant mortality which accompanies industrial development, along with general improvements in health care enabling people to live longer. Falling fertility rates in the post-war period have also been a major factor. Ageing of the population is a characteristic of all advanced capitalist societies, not only Britain. In addition, the growing proportion of retired people has been interpreted as a social problem because it increases the 'burden of dependency' on the working population, and creates a growing demand on the welfare state, in terms of both pensions and the cost of health and personal care. In 2005, there were 61 dependent people for every 100 people of working age, even though the burden of dependency has been eased at the other end by falling birth rates and declining family size. In 2013, the Department of Work and Pensions stated that 65 per cent of their spending went to those over working age – amounting to around one-seventh of public expenditure. One response in many European countries has been to raise the age at which people become eligible for pensions (now ranging between sixty-one and sixty-eight in the UK, varying according to sex and birth year); the UK also abolished the age of normal mandatory retirement, formerly sixty-five, to enable people to go on working indefinitely, if they wanted and if their employers allowed it.

At the other end of the life course, two issues have contributed to the view of youth as a 'problem period'. The first has been the development since the Second World War of a series of spectacular and highly publicized youth cultures: teddy boys, mods and rockers, skinheads, hippies, punks, goths, ravers, rastas, New Age travellers and so forth. Often youth cultures are associated by the public with drug-taking, violence, sexual permissiveness and other kinds of behaviour seen as unacceptable or threatening. Sociologists have charted the long history of the 'moral panics' about young people. Fostered by the media, these portray the stability of society threatened by waves of delinquent behaviour among teenagers (Cohen 1972; Pearson 1983).

A linked phenomenon was the student protest movement which arose in the 1960s in America, Britain, France and Germany and other countries, involving many young people from middle-class backgrounds. As well as occupation of university buildings, mass demonstrations against the Vietnam war and other forms of political radicalism, student protest was manifested in a link with the hippie 'counter-culture' of 'dropping out', drug use and sexual experimentation, particularly in America. To anxious parents, it seemed that a whole generation was rejecting their elders' values and lifestyle. Although the student movement turned out to be relatively short-lived, the moral panic surrounding it was a spur to the sociological study of generational conflict, especially in America (Feuer 1969). In Britain, the sociological preoccupation with class was at its height in the late 1960s, and the events of the student protest were interpreted in the light of Marxist theory. Youth protest was seen as largely an aspect of class relations (Hall and Jefferson 1976; Brake 1980, 1985). However, because of the recessions of the 1980s and 1990s, employment and unemployment replaced subculture and protest as key themes in youth studies.

Despite the prosperity of the early years of the twenty-first century, the recession of 2008 reintroduced the spectre of mass and prolonged youth unemployment. Commentators spoke of a 'lost' generation of young people suffering the effects of the credit crunch and business retrenchment. In June 2009 one in six British young people aged 18–24 were recorded as 'NEET' (not in employment, education or training), an increase of around 100,000 from the previous year (Shepherd 2009). Interestingly, this period also saw the rebirth of 'student protest' when thousands of young people, including school-children, took to the streets to protest at the increases in fees for universities, and groups of students occupied their student union buildings in protest at the marketization of higher education.

The remainder of this chapter looks at these themes in more detail. It is constructed differently from previous chapters, because of the relative lack of general theories of age as a form of inequality. The theories that do exist are surveyed in the next section. I have chosen to concentrate on two of the five age groups listed above, youth and old age. This is partly because these groups are most disadvantaged and also because they have received most attention within sociology, (although there is a gradually increasing body of research on children, known as the 'new sociology of childhood', which explores children's rights, needs and values, seeing them as active members of society rather than as the property of their parents).

Sociological Frameworks for Considering Age

Since classical theory provided few clues about the analysis of age, sociologists turned to the ideas of anthropologists when they began thinking about age differences in contemporary societies (Eisenstadt 1956; Abrams 1970; Foner 1975). From anthropology, they drew the concepts of 'age grades', 'age sets' and 'age spans' which have provided the basis for theorizing age stratification.

Age Stratification Theory

An age grade was defined by the functionalist anthropologist Radcliffe Brown as 'The recognized division of the life of an individual as he passes from infancy to old age. Thus each person passes successively into one grade after another, and, if he (*sic*) lives long enough, through the whole series – infant, boy, youth, young married man, elder' (quoted in Davis 1990, p. 25). Anthropologists distinguished a number of such phases, tending – as the quotation demonstrates – to focus on male age groups. Specific expectations and social functions were associated with each age grade; this was believed to stabilize society and integrate the different grades into the whole. Since each individual would pass through each grade, there was no reason for young people to rebel against the power of the elders. In this way, age stratification differs from the dynamics of stratification of gender and ethnicity, where movement between differentiated groups is virtually impossible – or even class, where movement, though possible, is constrained. This fluidity works against potential conflicts of interests between age groups. As Philip Abrams puts it: 'This allows the ruling class, adults, to persuade most of the oppressed class, the young, to accept their lot cheerfully. By agreeing to be a good child one can hope to become a successful adult' (1970, p. 182).

The movement from one age grade to another was often marked by *rites de passage*. Such rituals bound together all those in a particular age grade into a collectivity. Anthropologists also used the term 'age set' to distinguish a group of young people who went through initiation ceremonies (marking the passage to adulthood, or perhaps to warrior status) at the same time. Members of an age set might come together on further occasions of ritual or celebration to affirm the bond between them. Although there are fewer formal *rites de passage* in modern society (christening, twenty-first birthday and marriage ceremonies being important exceptions, along with the imported American custom of graduation balls for schoolchildren), events such as class reunions of school or university students who graduated in the same year can be seen as a version of these tribal rites; and in Japan it is customary for employees who join a firm in the same year to meet as a group for drinking parties and other social events.

Age groups in modern societies are less formally marked than the age grades of tribal societies. But age stratification theorists distinguish groups on the basis of the different cultural definitions and social expectations, roles and identities associated with them. Age stratification theory developed in America and was especially concerned with youth. For example, Parsons (1954) described the evolution of a distinctive teenage culture. He saw this as a transitional stage between childhood and adulthood, marked by distinct values which focused on 'having a good time', dating and sporting prowess: 'swell guys' and 'glamour girls' were the heroes and heroines of this culture; youth culture has 'important positive functions in easing the transition from the security of childhood in the family of orientation to that of full adult' (1954, p. 101).

Youth and adolescence are still commonly understood in terms of 'transitional status'. John Davis suggests that, since the end of the nineteenth century, youth has emerged as 'a transitional but nevertheless distinct age grade between childhood and adulthood' (1990, p. 821): the period immediately after the Second World War was crucial in consolidating this process, with the lengthening of the period young people spent at school and therefore in financial dependency on their parents; at the same time post-war affluence and full employment saw the emergence of a commercialized youth consumer culture.

Parsons also considered old age as an age grade, characterized by social isolation from kinship, occupational and community ties. Like others, he linked decline in old people's status to retirement: 'retirement leaves the older man in a peculiarly functionless position, cut off from participation in the most important interests and activities of the society' (1954, p. 103). He noted the emergence in America of segregated retirement communities, such as those of Florida and South California, where older people (of the more privileged classes) huddled together as a group. Similarly, in Britain there are 'colonies' of retired people in south-coast seaside resorts such as Bournemouth and Hastings (Phillipson 1982).

Parsons characterized age grades in terms of particular structural problems (transition and insecurity, social isolation and lack of function). There is a similarity here to the psychological framework developed by Erik Erikson (1965). Erikson distinguished eight stages of human development, each of which is marked by specific psychic dilemmas or crises which confront individuals; for example, for adolescents it is the search for a stable adult identity, while for elderly people it is the need for 'ego integrity'. This involves making sense of life histories, shaping them into some satisfactory pattern which resolves the difficulties and failures of the past. A quotation from a retired farrier taken from Blythe's study of old people (1979) nicely illustrates this latter process:

> My wife, she died four year agoo [sic]...I did properly miss my wife, and no mistake, but I had my daughters and that took it off. When you've spent your whol' life a-usin' of your hands, like I have, you don't know what to do when you can't...I have two nice daughters and grandsons that are gittin' on well, an a granddaughter that is at the teachers' college at Canterbury. I balance things up when I can. I've got no work and no wife, but I've got what I've done, haven't I? (p. 76)

Such views of age groups as characterized by distinct structural or individual dilemmas are interesting but insufficient in sociological terms. Parsons's functionalist account presented age as a source of social differentiation, but failed to conceptualize this in relation to power and inequality. Ann Foner (1975) advanced on this by presenting age stratification in terms of inequality and potential conflict: age was part of a 'family of social stratification systems' (p. 14) which involved inequalities of wealth and power. She explicitly compared age and class as parallel forms of stratification. Thus, age-related inequalities generate conflicts of interests leading to the emergence of age consciousness and solidarity, as displayed by student demonstrations or pensioners' lobbies, or, on an everyday level, the characteristic clashes between parents and teenagers.

Foner's account illustrates the potential of a systematic theory of age stratification and shows a sensitive awareness of the way age interlocks with other aspects of stratification. However, the age stratification approach did not find favour in Britain, perhaps because of its association with functionalism, which glossed over the divisive aspects of stratification and legitimated social inequality as serving positive functions. This is exemplified in S. N. Eisenstadt's functionalist account of age groups. He stated that 'the function of differential age definitions is to enable the individual to learn and acquire new roles…and in this way to maintain social continuity' (1956, p. 28). While Eisenstadt recognized the asymmetry of power between age groups, he argued that this is necessary to ensure acceptance of and respect for authority.

The major criticism of age stratification theory, however, has been that it assumes a homogeneity of experience across the strata, neglecting differences of class, gender and ethnicity. Parsons's accounts of youth cultures and of the segregated old-age communities, for example, are based on the experience of middle-class Americans and assume that such behavioural patterns are typical of the populace as a whole: elderly African Americans and Chicanos are not likely to be found in the retirement blocks of Florida. The dominance of class theory in British sociology in the 1960s and 1970s meant that age differences were viewed as an aspect of broader capitalist relations. The political economy perspective on older people and the radical approach to youth subcultures, which will be discussed later in the chapter, both drew substantially on Marxist theory. Thus, a separate theory of age stratification has been little developed in Britain.

Generations and Generation Units

Another criticism of some versions of age grade theory is that they are essentialist, presenting age differences and conflicts as universal constants. A different conceptualization that avoids this is the notion of generation. The best-known version of this is provided by Karl Mannheim in a famous paper, 'The problem of generations' (1952), offering an analysis of generation as a distinct type of 'social location' in a direct analogy with class. Mannheim is concerned to link the notion of generation to processes of social change and of intellectual and cultural development: his view of age groups is informed by the role of history: 'Individuals who belong to the same generation, who share the same year of birth, are endowed, to that extent, with a common location in the historical dimension of the social process' (Mannheim 1952, p. 290).

A 'generation' is a group of people who are born at around the same time; the term 'cohort' is often used by empirical researchers in a similar way. Each generation grows up in a specific historical context, entailing exposure to different experiences and intellectual influences, which will inform its members' feelings, behaviour and beliefs. In this way, new cultural formations come into being as each generation achieves a position of social dominance.

Mannheim recognized that a generation does not necessarily act as a unified social collectivity (any more than classes do). There might be divisions and opposing currents within a generation. When a generation (or a large part of it) did develop some sense of itself as sharing interests and experiences, Mannheim defined it as constituting a 'generation in actuality' (the analogy to Marx's 'class in itself' is clear here). Mannheim also distinguished a 'generation unit': a group within a generation that develops sufficient awareness to act coherently for itself, to 'work up the material of their common experience' (p. 304). The distinctions Mannheim is making here correspond to what I have previously defined as passive, active and politicized identities.

The virtue of the notion of generation is that it links age divisions firmly to changing historical circumstances and to cultural transformations (Abrams 1970). However, there are definitional problems in terms of how to distinguish one generation from another. Does it make any real sense to define a generation strictly as all those born in a single year? Used more generally to describe, for example, all those born in the immediate post-war years, the term becomes rather vague and this vagueness is heightened by the fact that, at some (unspecified) moment, the younger generation inevitably becomes the older generation. Moreover, the idea of generational change and conflict is often used in a fashion that overlooks divisions of class, gender, ethnicity to suggest that a whole 'younger generation' share common cultures and values.

The concept of generation was an influence on the work of Abrams, who combined concepts from Mannheim and from age grade theory in his analysis of generational conflict and the political rebellions of young people. He solved the problem of definition (to some extent) by distinguishing between a biological generation (chronologically defined) and a sociological generation (which may be made up of many biological generations but, crucially, is involved in the redefinition of culture). Thus, we hear talk of the 'sixties generation' which we could see as a generation unit, standard-bearers of new cultural, political and sexual values, 'sex and drugs and rock and roll', alongside rebellion and the hippie-based 'summer of love'.

The concept of 'generation' has slipped into popular consciousness in relation to young people, in the use of terms like the 'generation gap' or 'generation X' or 'Y' (used to describe rebellious and disaffected youth in both the 1960s and 1990s!). In the 2000s, there was talk of a 'crunch generation' or 'lost generation' suffering as a result of their elders' consumerist excesses and piling-up of unmanageable debt. More sociologically, David Woodman and Johanna Wyn (2015) employ the term to explore the situation of youth in the context of neoliberal globalization, arguing that young people now face a different world from their parents, marked by the dominance of digital media, mass uptake of higher education and an increasingly precarious labour market. They suggest this has generated a new 'generational habitus'. All this demands new strategies from youths who want to attain the ideals of 'the good life'.

The Life Course

Indeed, sociologists are increasingly alert to the importance of age as a basis for differentiated experience. Age is viewed as a significant variable in social research. Cohort analysis has been an important technique for tracing processes of social change, for example in the study of social mobility or of changing patterns of family formation. The postmodernists' stress on diversity in experience has provided an additional impetus to the study of age difference. They suggest an important role for younger people in the transition to a postmodern culture. Crook et al. (1992) see them as pioneers of the cultural changes associated with postmodernism, especially those related to the mass media and information technology. Young people are disproportionately involved in the 'new social movements'. In the Global South, younger generations have taken the lead in demanding reform in countries such as Egypt, Tunisia and Turkey. The postmodern approach also emphasizes the blurring of boundaries between age groups, as longstanding conventions are challenged and prevailing views of old age deconstructed (Featherstone and Hepworth 1989; Hazan 1994). Old rock-and-rollers, like the Rolling Stones and the

Who, in their sixties and seventies, are playing to crowded stadiums of fans, old and new.

The importance of age as a topic of empirical investigation has encouraged a pulling together of work carried out in the various sub-specialisms under the rubric of the sociology of the life course (Allatt et al. 1987; Bryman et al. 1987). This provides an umbrella for those concerned with study of the various stages in the life course to trace out connections and continuities. Featherstone and Hepworth (1989) suggest the term 'life course' can be used to challenge the stage models of age development (such as Erikson's) which present individuals as proceeding through an ordered (and unchanging) sequence of life stages. Using a postmodernist framework, they point out that the life course is historically variable and that its phases may shift. Although much work on the life course is concerned only with one particular age group, there is a basis here for developing an integrated theory of age, drawing on insights developed within areas such as gerontology or the sociology of youth. It is to these that we now turn.

Explaining the Experience of Old Age

> Ever-stricter stratification by age has emerged since industrialization. The process has accelerated in the twentieth century and...reached its peak in the decades following the Second World War. It entailed the increasing segregation of biological from socially defined old age. In the post-war period, more universally than before, old age, and the socially accepted rules associated with it, was accepted as beginning at a fixed chronological age: the state pensionable age of sixty/ sixty-five.
>
> (Harper and Thane 1989, p. 43)

This quotation described the position of the elderly in the UK in the post-war epoch. The experience of old age in the twentieth century was shaped by the institution of retirement. Social research has uncovered the disadvantaged position of elderly people as a group, although it should be stressed that the experience of individuals varies. Townsend's pioneering study of poverty in Britain (1979) distinguished old people as a major group among the poor. In 2007, 2.5 million old people were living at a level below 60% of median income (defined as the poverty line). In 2014, 0.9 million (7%) were living in severe poverty (below the 50% median line). The charity Age UK estimates that 8% of pensioners over sixty-five (about 900,000) in the UK are materially deprived, meaning that they do not have certain goods, services or experiences because of financial, health-related or social isolation barriers. According to the latest Department of Work and Pensions (DWP) statistics, nearly a million pensioners (9%) would not be able to replace a cooker if it broke down. Elder poverty increases with age; in 2013, one-fifth of those over seventy-five and a quarter of those over eighty-five suffered poverty (Age Concern 2008; Age UK 2014).

The problem of poverty is more acute among women and ethnic minority members (Ginn et al. 2001). Jay Ginn's research into pensions revealed that women were much more likely than men to rely on the state pension for the bulk of their income; 67% of men, but only 35% of women, had private pensions, and 71% of men had occupational pensions, as compared to 57% of women (Ginn 2003). This relates to women's lower earnings power, discussed in chapter 5, and to the fact that domestic responsibilities break up their working careers. Ethnic minority pensioners are also much more vulnerable: 29% of Black British and Indians are in poverty, and 43% of Pakistanis and Bangladeshis, compared to an average of 19% (Age Concern 2008).

Financial problems may be heightened by ill-health and isolation. A growing proportion of older people live on their own: 36% in 2014 as opposed to 22% in 1962 (Gilbert et al. 1989; Age UK 2014). This amounts to 3.8 million people, 70 per cent of whom are women. Again, this increases with age: 21 per cent of men and 31 per cent of women aged sixty-five to seventy-four lived alone in 2006, compared to 32 per cent of men and 61 per cent of women aged seventy-five and over (increased from 50 per cent of women in 1987) (Ford and Sinclair 1987; Age Concern 2008). Because of women's greater longevity they are more likely to be on their own, especially as they enter their seventies and eighties. Women and ethnic minority members have been shown by surveys to be more likely to suffer from chronic health problems and from restricted mobility (Fenton 1987; Arber and Ginn 1991a).

Although the British government has encouraged people without occupational pensions to supplement state pensions with private ones, the problem of poverty or low income among elderly people is likely to heighten in the future because of the increasing commonness of redundancy and early retirement. Britain in the twenty-first century faces an acute pension crisis. Many pension schemes are under-funded and hit by falling interest rates on their investments, while many younger people with insecure work histories lack the wherewithal to invest in private pensions and have no entitlement to occupational pensions. There is pressure on the state pension because of the ageing of society. Major changes are underway, with an end to many schemes in which pension levels are linked to final salaries.

The twentieth century saw striking decline in male economic activity rates. Between 1971 and 1991 the rate for economically active men aged sixty to sixty-four fell by 32 per cent to 51 per cent. In 1971, 31 per cent of men aged sixty-five to sixty-nine were in employment; by 1991, only 6 per cent of all men over sixty-five and women over sixty were economically active (Phillipson 1990; Harris 1991). In the 2000s, linked to the pensions crisis mentioned above, there was some return to economic activity, with 11 per cent of men over sixty-five and 12 per cent of women in employment (Age Concern 2008). The percentage for the whole age group had fallen to 9 per cent in 2014, perhaps because of the recession. As mentioned before, because of the perceived burden placed on the state by the ageing of the population, the British government decided formally to abolish the idea of mandatory retirement, allowing people to apply to their employers to stay working after they reach pensionable age. Nonetheless, retirement has been the context for most people's experience of old age, and the idea of retiring remains strong, despite the change in the legal framework. It is not surprising that it figures so largely in the various explanatory frameworks.

Functionalism, Modernization and Disengagement Theory

The position of the elderly in contemporary society has frequently been explained by reference to economic development. Modernization approaches, closely linked to functionalism, suggested that industrialization affected the elderly in various ways (Cowgill and Holmes 1972). Whereas, in pre-industrial society, older people continued working until prevented from doing so by bodily incapacity, under the industrial system their labour became redundant as employers preferred to utilize younger and fitter employees. Thus, industrialization inexorably led to the formalization of 'retirement' as a status for older people, and the evolution of welfare and security schemes to fund it. The previous role of older people as informal repositories of knowledge within the community was jeopardized by the development of formal mass education systems and by processes of rapid technological change which appeared to make that knowledge outdated. Older people were seen by employers as resistant to changing technology. At the same time, improvements in public health and declining mortality meant that far greater proportions of people lived into their sixties and beyond. All these developments both heightened the visibility of older people and helped to devalue their social status. Blythe (1979) suggested that old age was venerated in the past largely because it was rare!

Such a scenario lies behind the theory of 'disengagement'. The situation of the old poses something of a problem for the functionalist theory of age groups, since it is hard to see how the segregation and relative poverty of the elderly could serve as a mechanism of social integration. Indeed, in his account of the functions of age groups Eisenstadt (1956) more or less completely ignored the elderly, concentrating on youth groups. However, Cumming and Henry (1961) offered a partial (if not very convincing) explanation in suggesting that the institution of retirement offered a benign way for older people gradually to disengage themselves from active participation in society, making way for younger people to take over their places and thus maintaining social equilibrium. Another strand of functionalist thinking emphasized how older people developed their own distinctive segregated subcultures, preferring to socialize with members of their own generation who shared their values and concerns (Rose 1965).

Disengagement theory has been substantially criticized. It ignores the negative effects of such a process for older people themselves and implies that disengagement and segregation are voluntary. Moreover, it can easily be established as empirically inaccurate. Even when older people are not engaged in paid employment, very many of them remain active participants in other spheres of social life, such as voluntary and community work, politics and leisure activities. Critics such as Fennell et al. (1988) see retirement rather differently, linking it explicitly to the capitalist organization of production. This has become the dominant approach to old age and inequality in Britain.

Dependency Theory and the Political Economy of Age

The 'political economy' perspective was developed in Britain by Townsend (1981), Walker (1981) and Phillipson (1982), and in America by Minkler and Estes (1984). Critical of the functionalist presentation of older people as a homogeneous group, these authors emphasized social divisions among older people and located their position firmly within the broader structure of inequalities of wealth and power. These were seen as deriving from capitalist relations and the disadvantages of age were linked to class. Within the field of gerontology, the political economy approach opposed itself to biological and psychological understandings of ageing, arguing that the problems of old age were socially constructed rather than 'natural' (Phillipson 1982; Fennell et al. 1988). Alan Walker summarized the key concerns of the political economy approach as 'the social creation of dependent status, the structural relationship between the elderly and younger adults and between different groups of the elderly, and the socially constructed relationship between age, the division of labour and the labour market' (1981, p. 75).

The position of working-class older people who have formerly been dependent on wage labour for subsistence and who will rely heavily on the state security system after retirement is clearly very different from that of middle-class people or the capitalist elite. For middle-class people with good occupational pensions, backed by substantial savings, who own good-quality housing, retirement may indeed be viewed as 'a successfully perpetuated holiday' (Blythe 1979, p. 48). Indeed, in the twentieth century, the cruise industry has been booming, due to its appeal to affluent retired workers who may take three or four cruises a year; the young old have become addicted travellers, spending their final decades exploring the world. However, working-class elders are more likely to be forced into early retirement, because of either redundancy or ill-health (often related to their work). They are also more likely to express negative views of retirement: as Phillipson states, 'while middle- and upper-class people have resources of health and income to support a positive view of retirement, the working class has approached this period with considerable pessimism' (1982, p. 111).

A crucial part of the political economy approach to old age is the notion of structured dependency, which was elaborated by Townsend (1981). The institution of retirement forces people into dependency on the state for their subsistence needs. Since pension rates (especially in Britain) are characteristically set so low, at 'safety net' levels, low income becomes legitimated and seen as an inevitable concomitant of old age. Low incomes also mean that many older people who experience problems of health and mobility must turn to the state for further help. Institutional care for older people is organized in such a way as to deny them rights to self-determination, and agencies treat them as passive recipients of services. Older people become trapped in a cycle of helplessness and economic and psychological dependence. This dynamic has been increased since the 2008 recession by cuts to public services for the elderly.

The theory of dependency has been attacked by Paul Johnson, who presents a more positive image of retirement. He argues that the political economy approach distorts the experience of retirement by equating work with independence and ignoring consumption. The important issue is whether older people have sufficient income to be active consumers. Johnson emphasizes that some early retirement is of a voluntary nature (encouraged by employers' schemes when they wish to cut their labour costs). He considers that overall the financial situation of retired people has improved since the early twentieth century; they have greater command over resources and are less dependent on the goodwill of kin. He concludes: 'improved economic status now gives more elderly people the option of a fairly comfortable retirement which they may prefer to continued employment in unattractive work' (1989, p. 71). However, Johnson was writing before the economic crises of the twenty-first century, at a time of boom and affluence. While what he says remains true for many middle- and upper-class people, working-class elders are hardly in this position, and, as we have seen, poverty is a threat for many older women and ethnic minority members. But similar arguments have been made recently by Willetts (2011) and Howker and Malik (2013), both of whom state that greedy retired 'baby boomers' (the post-war generation of which I am a member) are living lives of affluence at the expense of a younger 'jilted generation'.

These arguments, however, focusing specifically on economic issues, do not address the issues of ageism and status; these in turn are influenced by the capitalist ethos which frames the experience of retirement. Under capitalism, status is strongly linked to participation in the production process and its economic rewards. Dependency has a social aspect as well as an economic one.

Some of the criticisms of other perspectives made by those adopting the political economy approach are overstated. For example, it is not true that functionalists viewed age groups as totally homogeneous; Parsons dealt with gender differences in his account of age groups, and Eisenstadt acknowledged that class background influenced the development of different types of youth groups. But the major achievements of the proponents of the political economy approach are to have established age divisions firmly as a form of inequality; to have highlighted the problems associated with retirement; and to have linked the precise form of contemporary age inequality to capitalist production organization, which either excludes or exploits the labour of younger and older workers. In the 21st-century context, it seems that the young and the old are set against each other as rivals, while they might more accurately be seen as caught in the web of increasing inequalities of class.

Postmodernist Approaches to Age

In contrast to the political economists, postmodernists reject the view of older people as victims and emphasize the variability of people's individual responses to ageing. Mike Featherstone and Mike Hepworth in their account of the 'postmodern life course'

(1989) suggest that a more positive approach to old age is developing among the generation who grew up in post-war affluence, overturning prevailing definitions of age-appropriate behaviour. They argue that postmodern societies are characterized by processes of de-differentiation and de-institutionalization, which potentially free people from the compulsion to 'act their age'. Successful older people (they mention Ronald Reagan and Margaret Thatcher) may provide positive images of active, socially influential old age to offset negative stereotypes. Joan Collins, Helen Mirren and Tina Turner are examples of women who have managed to transcend the decline associated with the ageing female body, maintaining their glamour and sex appeal. But it should be pointed out that it is mainly members of elite and wealthy groups who are in a position to transgress age-specific norms and afford the lavish expenditure on what Featherstone and Hepworth call 'body maintenance' (p. 146), necessary for those who want to avoid being described as 'mutton dressed as lamb'.

Post-structuralism also opens up study of discourses on age; deconstruction of existing categories follows logically from the radical contention that old age is socially constructed. One such account was offered by Haim Hazan (1994). Hazan argued that academic discourses on age themselves contributed to setting apart old people from the rest of society as something less than human, though bureaucratic discourses were perhaps most influential in this process of segregation and dehumanization. Hazan believed that the real problem for old people is the search for meaning and identity. While academic and bureaucratic discourses present old age in terms of physical deterioration, and the elderly as 'a mass of material exigencies' (p. 15), old people themselves may view their lives quite differently. Hazan suggested that they respond to stigmatized meanings in a range of ways: internalizing and accepting them, becoming 'difficult' and cantankerous, or withdrawal into silence are three of them. Resisting stigma by vigorous participation in public activities is increasingly a chosen option. Also, elders have an important social role as grandparents: according to agency Grandparents Plus, one-third of families with young children and 47 per cent of lone mothers depend on grandparents for childcare help. Across Europe, 40 per cent of grandparents provide childcare help while parents work (Grandparents Plus 2013).

However, postmodernist approaches appear one-sided as they neglect to offer any substantial account of the material deprivation which afflicts many older people. The postmodernist stress on identities as fluid, multiple and chosen appears less apt when we consider the stigmatized and non-negotiable social identities of the poor and frail elderly.

Explaining the Experience of Youth

While contemporary old age appears as a terminal stage marked by superannuation and redundancy, youth has been primarily studied as a transitional phase. The influential account of adolescence offered by G. Stanley Hall (1904) portrayed it as a time of stress and emotional turmoil as young people struggled towards discovery of their adult identities. Erikson (1965) subsequently reaffirmed this in his account of adolescence as a period of role confusion and identity crisis, a time for experimenting with possible future roles. Stage theories of this kind can be criticized for presenting an undifferentiated and universalistic view of youth as a time of crisis, ignoring the way in which youth is differently experienced and handled in different historical periods as well as variations of class, gender and ethnicity. Yet this psychological slant on youth has informed much subsequent research within social science and social policy. The predominant view of young people has emphasized deviance, rebellion and problems of adjustment, despite repeated reminders from sociologists that the majority of young people are conformist, conservative and generally share their parents' values and get on well with them (Jenkins 1983; Roberts 1983; Coffield et al. 1986; Davis 1990).

Sociologists nonetheless share the psychologists' emphasis on youth as transition. If retirement has been the key feature of the lived relations of old age, the lengthened transition from childhood and dependency to adult status and independence marks out the experience of modern youth. Until recently, such a transition was typically viewed as lasting from the onset of puberty through into the early twenties. However, the insecurities caused by neoliberal market conditions have meant that the passage to independent adulthood has been further lengthened, perhaps into people's thirties. This has been described as 'prolonged adolescence' or 'emerging adulthood' (Arnett 2004) and is characterized by failure to achieve a stable career, prolonged semi-dependence on parents and periodic returns to the parental home.

The handling of this transition in other cultures and epochs has been highly variable, as Eisenstadt's work suggests (1956). In pre-industrial and early industrializing European societies, the process was often abrupt (though there were marked differences of class and gender). Aries (1962) argued that children in pre-industrial Europe were treated simply as small adults. In the nineteenth century most working-class children were sent out to work in their early teens or younger (some as young as seven or eight). While they did not achieve full independence from their parents until they married and established their own family, they gained some status from their contributions to the family budget, while having little time or resources to develop their own distinctive cultures. Although, as Pearson (1983) has shown, there is a long history of concern about younger people being out of control, this tendency has been heightened by twentieth-century circumstances. Now all young people spend a longer time in education before they are formally allowed to enter employment, extending the period of economic dependency on parents. This was pioneered among the bourgeois class in the nineteenth century, with the rise of the ironically named independent 'public schools', to which many middle-class boys were sent. The development of mass schooling, and its consolidation after the war with a raised school-leaving age, meant that boys and girls of all classes spent much of their teenage stage out of the work-force. Since then, the school-leaving age in the UK has been raised several times, with a forthcoming requirement that all young people should stay in some form of education or training until eighteen.

In the post-war period, increased social affluence meant that dependent youth gained larger spending allowances from their parents. Also the development of the economy opened up unprecedented opportunities for young people to get reasonably well-paid jobs: thus, the 'teenage consumer' was born.

The period of teenage affluence of the 1950s and 1960s was a crucial one for establishing the contemporary view of youth and saw the birth of youth subcultures and distinct youth styles. The booming economy meant that school leavers were able to pick jobs and move around till they found one that suited them. Mark Abrams's surveys of young people as consumers revealed that in the late 1950s they had an estimated £850 million in spending power, 5 per cent of national consumer spending. Since the necessities of life were provided for them by parents, most of this money was available for leisure consumer items: for example, records, clothes, magazines, cosmetics (Abrams 1959). A rapidly expanding youth market fed off spontaneously developed youth styles, publicized them and ensured their further growth.

Davis (1990) argues that these decades witnessed the peaking of a 'cult of youth' which evolved through the century. Young people became the object of adult envy and of fear. Publicity given to youth in this period reflected the academic view of generational change suggested by Mannheim: youth were seen as pioneers of a coming culture with new values and concerns, which transcended existing social division; erroneously, perhaps, youth cultures were seen as shared by all, regardless of class: 'they're going to be classless. Their clothes already are. So are the things and places they like most – Wimpy Bars, bowling alleys, the M1' (quoted in Davis 1990, p. 185). The young pop stars who formed the aristocracy of the teenage culture might come from the back streets of London and Liverpool, or from privileged backgrounds, public schools and art colleges.

This period, however, can be seen as exceptional. In the longer run, young people have been vulnerable within the capitalist labour market. In the nineteenth century, young children were used as captive labour in factories and sweat shops. Apprenticeships were often a disguised form of cheap labour. Young people's relative lack of experience and skills expose them to exploitation. Around the world, millions of children work in dreadful conditions for a pittance, while others fall victims to sexual abuse and trafficking. Young people seeking good careers in the professions are often compelled to take up unpaid internships.

During the recessions of recent decades, the experience of youth has hinged not around affluence but around unemployment and restricted opportunities. While the 'classlessness' of 1960s youth culture was more apparent than real, it can be argued that class divergences in the experience of young people have become more marked (Roberts et al. 1990; Bates and Riseborough 1993). Young working-class people have had to contend with mass unemployment. Available jobs are often low-paid and temporary; such jobs are characteristically in the lower echelons of the service industry (in bars, call centres, hotels and retail). Woodman and Wyn (2015) report that around 40 per cent of those aged 15–24 in the OECD are in temporary work.

Such developments have seen a further lengthening of the transition period. Many working-class younger people are denied the chance to become independent, trapped in parental homes through unemployment or casualized work. More young people are spending longer in further and higher education, hoping to gain skills and qualifications which will help them to escape from the trap of unemployment and limited opportunities. New Labour governments of the 2000s encouraged this trend, setting a target for 50 per cent of youths to attend university. Research in Bristol among undergraduates from varying class backgrounds found that the students saw a degree as necessary to obtain not only well-paid professional work, but any kind of secure employment. As one student stated, this has become 'a degree generation' (Bradley et al. 2014).

At the bottom of the class hierarchy, youth homelessness has been a growing problem for some time in Britain and other countries. Research for the London charity Centrepoint stated that, in 2006/7, 75,000 young people experienced homelessness. It is particularly a problem in Scotland and Wales (Quilgars et al. 2008). But even well-qualified young people from wealthier backgrounds have difficulty getting their own homes because of the over-inflated housing market; most young people do not earn enough to get started on the mortgage ladder.

Heightened youth dependency on parents is thus a feature of most post-industrial capitalist societies. *Social Trends* (2009) reported that, in the second quarter of 2008, 29 per cent of 20- to 34-year-old men and 18 per cent of women of the same age lived with their parents. More than half (52 per cent) of men aged 20 to 24, and more than a third (37 per cent) of women in that age group lived with their parents. In 2012 it was reported that the number of people aged 20–34 living with their parents had increased by 28 per cent since 1971. Around 3.2 million young Britons were in this position, the number having risen by 6 per cent during the previous year alone. Thus Britain has come to resemble the poorer Mediterranean countries, where this has long been the case. This trend, which can result in increased tension for parents and children alike, results from youth unemployment, the rise of low-wage work and, most particularly, the spiralling costs of accommodation, discussed in earlier chapters.

Functionalism and Subculture Theory

Recent research on youth has, rightly, focused on these issues; but the major theme in the post-war sociology of youth has been the study of the distinctive subcultures which have evolved since the 1950s. The notion of youth culture or subculture has been central to most functionalist accounts of youth. Parsons's account, discussed above, pointed to subculture as a means of bridging the transition as young people develop their own behavioural patterns, which detach them from their parents and move them towards adult independence

This is the basis for Eisenstadt's extended account of youth stratification. Pointing to the ubiquity of youth-specific groupings in all types of society, he argued they act in various ways to bind young people into the social whole. In modern societies, the institutionalized forms of age distinction (for example, the high degree of age segregation in schools) serve both to socialize young people into the universalistic values needed for integration into a complex social organization

and to develop feelings of community and solidarity through identification with one's peer group. Homogeneous age groups are
also seen as an outlet for the tensions that arise between the generations in the family (for example, over young people's sexual matura-
tion) and allow them to be resolved in a relatively harmless way
(Eisenstadt 1956).

Although Eisenstadt analysed age groups primarily in terms of
social integration, he also acknowledged the existence of deviant
youth groups, such as gangs, which are disruptive and disintegrative.
He imputed their existence to the discrepancy between family aspirations and the opportunities for advancement realistically available in
society for poorer youths. In this he followed Merton (1938), whose
work has been the major influence in the American sociology of
youth. Merton offered an explanation of deviancy in terms of anomie
and the discrepancy between social goals (success, material prosperity) and the means available to gain them; where legitimate means
are not available, illegitimate means such as crime and delinquency
may be employed instead.

Most functionalist work on youth was focused on the explanation
of deviancy and delinquency, and employed the notion of subculture.
These theories and the critical responses to them from other perspectives have been thoroughly surveyed by Brake (1980, 1985). While
there are many different strands, all emphasize the development
of youth subcultures, with their own distinctive value systems.
Sometimes these are said to mirror or exaggerate the 'focal concerns'
of parent cultures (including criminal ones), sometimes to overturn
them. Deviant behaviour is said to arise from limited economic
opportunities or the social disorganization associated with urban
decline. Predominantly middle-class youth subcultural groups, such
as beatniks and hippies, can be seen as examples of Merton's retrea-
tist or innovatory mode of adaptation, whereby social goals themselves are challenged.

Functionalist approaches are standardly criticized for their neglect
of class and inequality, but, with the exception of Parsons, these
accounts of youth culture do take heed of class differences. While
Merton's original theory of anomie and deviance was couched in
terms of individual adaptations, the subcultural theorists of youth
and deviance focus on collective responses to inequality and frustrated expectations. There are marked resemblances between these
approaches and those influenced by Marxism. However, it can be
argued that functionalists put more stress on shared values, while
Marxists accentuate structured inequalities. Moreover, the functionalist stress on youth as transition implies that most deviant behaviour

is only a transient phase, associated with the problems of achieving adult identity. While both age and class are involved in subcultural formation, arguably more weight is given to age.

Radical Theories – Youth and Resistance

The radical theory of deviancy, strongly influenced by Marxism, developed in the 1960s and 1970s and became the dominant approach to the study of youth in Britain. Radical theorists ranged themselves against the psychological view of adolescence as a universal phase of emotional turmoil and criticized the notion of a 'classless' youth culture. Their concern was to show how youth and deviancy arose from the general structure of social inequality. Youth subcultures were linked to the development of capitalism and were seen as class-specific. Skinhead culture, for example, was analysed by Hebdige (1979) as a cultural style which derived from an exaggerated version of rough working-class masculinity, with its stress on sport and 'aggro' (violence and fighting) and its adoption of a parodic version of work clothing ('bovver' boots, rolled-up jeans and braces).

Mike Brake (1980) described youth cultures as 'magical' cultural solutions to the economic and social problems of class and ethnicity. They presented working-class youth with a free space, a 'moratorium', albeit brief, from the realities of their class-bound futures, analogous to the space for freedom and experimentation allowed to middle-class young people by their spell as university students: 'working-class cultures in particular infuse into the bleak world of the working-class adolescent a period of intense emotion, colour and excitement' (1980, p. 23). Middle-class forms of youth rebellion can also be interpreted in this way, as a (temporary) reaction against a future of conformism within the corporate cultures of capitalist bureaucracies.

A key feature of the radical approach was its view of deviancy and rebellion among young people as a form of 'resistance' to the capitalist system and to dominant social values (Hall and Jefferson 1976). Rather than being understood as a social problem or the result of inadequate socialization, delinquency was considered a creative response to material inequality, a manifestation of incipient class awareness. In particular, the rioting among young people which has occurred sporadically in inner-city areas or deprived estates throughout the past decades can be seen as a reaction to crises of capitalism leading to unemployment and urban decline, and to racist oppression resulting from the history of capitalist imperialism. The riots in London and other cities in 2011, although triggered as in other cases by police shooting a young Black man, saw extensive looting by young people of consumer goods, such as trainers, mobile phones and flat-screen televisions. We can interpret this as an outbreak of rage at being denied access to the luxurious lifestyle ostentatiously displayed by the rich and glamourized in the media.

Radical approaches, like the political economy perspective in ger-ontology, were important in highlighting age as an aspect of social inequality and showing how the experience of age takes specific forms in capitalist societies. They can be criticized for an over-romantic view of youth culture and of deviancy in particular, underplaying the harm done to the victims of youth crime and the deterioration of environments associated with it. Several people were killed in the 2011 riots, and properties and shops in deprived areas were damaged. As Lea and Young (1984) argue, often the major victims of crime and delinquency are the working class themselves. This problematizes the notion of youth cultures as a form of class resistance.

The overriding concern with youth cultures and deviancy and their neglect of 'ordinary kids' has been criticized. Davis suggests that the sensationalized presentation of young people in the media has been paralleled by an academic approach which presents 'over-theorized, over-generalized and generally exaggerated images of youth' (1990, p. 18). A more thorough account of youth inequality would need to study the experiences of the majority of youth who are broadly conformist. More recent accounts of youth employment and unemployment offer a more balanced view of young people (for example, Roberts 1995; Macdonald and Marsh 2005; Furlong and Cartmel 2007).

New Approaches: Feminism, Postmodernism and Post-structuralism

Another criticism of radical theories was that they ignored gender. McRobbie (1991) points to the near invisibility of young women in subcultural theories. This was put right in the late 1970s and 1980s by a series of studies dealing with young women (for example, McRobbie 1978, 1991; McRobbie and Nava 1984; Griffin 1985). These studies showed that the experience of youth is gendered. Friendship groups and leisure activities are segregated by sex. Early youth subcultures enshrined sexist values and hinged around facets of masculine behaviour (fighting, motor bikes, football). Young women were relegated to the fringe (featuring as girlfriends, groupies and earth mothers). While more recent cultural styles (goth, rave and dance cultures) are more sexually egalitarian, young women have tended to develop their own distinct forms of behaviour and 'focal concerns'. The post-structuralist influence warns us against presenting young women as passive victims of gendered conditioning. Rather, it is emphasized that they creatively use and interpret the cultural forms available to them from both spontaneous youth cultures and commercial sources (McRobbie and Nava 1984; Wolpe 1988).

More generally, postmodern and post-structural approaches to the study of youth have emphasized young people's agency. Willis et al. (1990) develop this in their account of young people as consumers of commercial culture, emphasizing the breakdown of hard and fast distinctions between 'high' and 'popular' cultural forms. Young consumers are able to subvert commercial cultural forms, imposing their own meanings on them and using tactics of bricolage to assemble their own versions of style. While Willis et al. emphasize the impact of unemployment, they suggest that consumption roles are more significant than productive ones in young people's lives: they utilize their cultural creativity to get by and develop individualized lifestyles even in the face of material constraints. Urban youth's use of graffiti and involvement in the DJ, rap and breakdancing scenes can be cited as evidence of this creative energy.

Nonetheless, evidence continues to show that the experience of youth is highly shaped by social definitions of masculinity and femininity. A preoccupation with celebrity and appearance steers young women towards conventional adult versions of femininity. There is evidence that teachers, careers advisers and social workers have tended to steer young women towards traditional feminine roles. Sharp gender distinctions pressure many working class young women inexorably towards traditional 'women's work' with its lower rewards (Griffin 1985; Pilcher 1999). For example, the take-up of apprenticeships is highly gendered, with young women going into care and hairdressing, young men pursuing car mechanics and electrical work. Walkerdine et al. (2001) show how young middle-class women face great pressure from ambitious parents pushing them towards school and career success. In the 2000s, however, the greatest pressures on young women have come from a celebrity-obsessed media culture which puts massive emphasis on beauty, sexiness and the ideal female body (McRobbie 2008). Surveys have recently suggested that the levels of psychological distress among children and adolescents have been soaring in the past decades. Eating disorders are rife.

A different input from post-structuralism is apparent in two books which investigate youth in terms of prevailing social and academic discourses. John Davis (1990) traces the way youth as a social category has been presented in the media, by policy-makers and within academic theory, and argues that common to all is an exaggerated stress on youth as a problem stage and a preoccupation with spectacular subcultures. This reflects two contradictory tendencies: both the adulation of young people as innovators (the cult of youth) and the longstanding history of fears and anxieties about moral decline and delinquency. Taken together, Davis argues, youth is used as a symbol of 'the state of the nation'. Similarly, Christine Griffin (1993) seeks to deconstruct key elements within discourses on youth to show how ideas about disaffection, deviance, adolescent disturbance and so on provide the framework for the analysis of youth in a way which may distort many young people's experience.

A key theme which unites postmodern and structural approaches is a focus on the impact of individualism, encouraged by the Thatcher era; young people are taught that they are responsible for their own fates, with success coming from hard work and skill acquisition. Roberts, discussing individualization and change (1995), argues that young people's lives have become more differentiated as old class-based forms of transition break down: 'Young people themselves will be less likely than formerly to recognize the advantages and disadvantages that they share with most others of the same gender, from the same kind of school, who live in the same localities, and so on' (Roberts 1995:116). He uses the metaphor of train journeys and car journeys to describe the changing process of transition: the train takes a regulated journey along a fixed track, while car drivers can construct their own routes and 'rat-runs' even if they arrive at similar destinations. Thus, transitional patterns are more varied and can indeed be described as fractured or fragmented. Studying young people in Holland, Du Bois-Reymond and Blasco (2003) spoke of 'yo-yo' transitions, as the youth moved frequently between different economic statuses: education, full-time work, training, unemployment and part-time work, sometimes with breaks for travelling or 'gap years'. Furlong and Cartmel (2007) suggest that young people's lives are consequently more risky and insecure.

However, research in Bristol among young adults revealed that many had adapted to these new labour market conditions and even welcomed the change and flexibility it offered them (Bradley and Devadason 2008). Similarly Woodman and Wyn (2015) suggest that young people interviewed in Australia do not aspire to the lifelong careers typical of their parents, and have learned to accept the need to take responsibility. These and similar studies show that many young people, especially those with university degrees (Bradley et al. 2014), declare themselves happy with their lives and show optimism about the future, although this may prove to be 'cruel optimism' (Berlant 2011) if their hopes and aspirations can never be fulfilled.

Age and Identity

As individuals, we are apt to be very aware of our age. Children and adolescents face legal and social constraints on their actions and are often told they are 'too young' to do certain things. As people enter their forties they experience effects of physiological ageing which make them conscious that they are beginning to 'grow old'. In societies, like Britain and America, marked by the cult of youth and beauty, ageing is looked on with fear, especially by women who attack wrinkles with botox and face-lifting surgery. Older people face the negative stereotypes of ageism and must adjust to the loss of friends and loved ones and the reality of their own approaching deaths.

But age as a basis of collective social identity is more problematic. Historically, political activity based around age differences has been rare, although pressure groups have been formed in America and Britain to lobby for pensioners' rights (Phillipson 1982). In general, political parties have not served as a vehicle for age-related interests and issues. Nor have age-based pressure groups attained the prominence of feminism or anti-racist struggles. Age as an issue has been low on the political agenda. However, books such as *Jilted Generation* (Howker and Malik 2013) and *The Pinch* (Willetts 2011) raise age inequalities as a political concern, seeking to create a sense of collective injustice among the young generation. As I have argued, we can identify an age elite seeking, like any dominant group, to maintain their privileges.

Against this, there are factors inhibiting age solidarity. First, the movement of individuals through the various age groups prevents lasting age identification. It has frequently been remarked that today's young rebels may become tomorrow's respectable citizens. Second, in contrast to other forms of social hierarchy, the powerful groups are the ones in the middle. In the UK today, middle-aged people can be seen as an age elite who hold the powerful decision-making positions in society, enjoy good lifestyles, occupy expensive homes bought before the property boom and monopolize the best-paid jobs. The powerless groups, the old and the young, who might make common cause against the age elite, are so differentiated in terms of experience and attitudes that they often feel suspicion and hostility towards each other.

The existence of youth subcultures could be read as evidence of identification among young people, indicative of a propensity to share values and activities with others of the age group. Some aspects of youth cultures express an active hostility to adult society and culture.

Such views were displayed, for example, in The Who's classic song 'My Generation'.

In other songs, the group lamented the powerlessness and lack of opportunities facing young people and the problem of 'teenage wastage': 'a young man ain't worth nothing in the world today'. In America, the young people characterized as 'generation X' and the initiators of 'grunge' culture voiced feelings of being denied opportunities and access to a good standard of living. Industrial decline had a particularly severe impact on minority ethnic and working-class young males, lying behind the riots discussed earlier.

However, such topics are the exception rather than the rule in cultural expressions of youth cultures, exemplified especially through popular music. More common themes are freedom, love and sexuality, pleasure and fun (including drinking and drug use) and a generalized rebellion against the rules and repressions of society, which is not necessarily age-specific. The more political aspects of youth cultures, as emphasized in the radical perspective, are often linked to issues of class, gender or 'race', as in the denunciations of 'Babylon' (white society and power) in Black popular music (Gilroy 1987).

Where young people have become prominent in political movements,, it has often been as an aspect of class-based or anti-racist politics. For example, young Asian men have played an active role in Britain in street demonstrations against racism or on behalf of Islamic movements. Youth wings within established parties, such as the Young Conservatives and Young Socialists, may work to promote new ideas and policies which in part are related to the broader concerns of their own age groups, although they also reflect their own commitment to the different political ideologies, so that it is difficult to disentangle class and age interests. This tendency is best illustrated by the student movement of the 1960s in America, Britain and Europe. Many of its political objectives concerned class and ethnic issues: attacks on the capitalist system and on Western imperialism, support for socialism and the colonially dominated people of Vietnam. At the same time it reflected many values which were specifically those of younger people: the attack on the materialist culture they identified with their parents, the demand for sexual liberation, calls for educational reform and student self-determination, hostility towards technology and bureaucracy with its rules and regulations ('who needs them?' sang Crosby, Stills, Nash and Young, one of the rock groups identified with student protest). It is a value many of us from the 1960s generation adhere to still!

In Britain, the late twentieth century was marked by a relative absence of new youth subcultures; young people appeared to be conformist and materialistic, interested only in acquiring designer clothing and pursuing a consumerist 'yuppie' lifestyle. It was argued that class-based subcultures were a thing of the past, because of the rise of individualism discussed above. Maffesoli (1996) coined the term 'time of the tribes' suggesting that groups of young people came together for specific consumer reasons, such as supporting sports teams or attending concerts or music festivals, which remain massively popular. Such tribal allegiances were seen as transient and changeable. However, from the 1990s a more rebellious spirit among young people has arisen, with a coalition of various youth interests (New Age travellers, ravers, environmental groups and 'tribes') forming in opposition, for example, to the Poll Tax and imposition of student fees. Demonstrations against capitalism have taken place on May Day in the UK, and young people across Europe have picketed meetings of the G8 leaders. UK Uncut, which stages raids on tax-avoiding outfits, consists largely of young people, as did the Occupy movement (Williams et al. 2013). This can be related to young people's negative experiences of neoliberalism and its politics, which expose them to unemployment and poverty. But there is also a strong concern for the welfare of the planet, which has led young people to stage environmental protests, over issues such as the extension of airports, destruction of forests and the threats of climate change.

As we have seen, older people, too, have been victims of the recession, and there have been some signs in Britain of increasing militancy among pensioners' groups. Phillipson (1982) lists the various groups which have formed since the Second World War to work for the interests of the elderly, ranging from the philanthropic Age Concern to the radical British Pensioners' Trade Union Action Association, established in 1973 to organize demonstrations and petitions. However, only a tiny minority of older people are involved in such political activities.

One thing that may impede the development of an alliance against the 'age elite' is the stigmatization that arises from ageist attitudes. Young people may keep at a distance from the 'elderly' because of the connotations of ill-health, dependency and uselessness. On the other hand, elderly people, especially in poor areas, can display fear and distrust of the young. Mark Hudson's account of a deprived working-class community in the north-east portrays a state of mutual hostility and incomprehension between young and old:

It sometimes seemed, talking to the older people...as though the younger generation had declared war on the old. They were said to be bent only on violence and destruction. They were the ones who were ruining everything with their vandalism, joy-riding and ram raiding. It was difficult to find anyone among the older generation with a good word to say about the young...They spoke of them as though they were of a species fundamentally different from themselves. (1994, p. 95)

However, generational change can shift the nature of age identities and conflicts. Many commentators have speculated that greater militancy may develop among older people, partly because of the greater numbers of early retired 'young old', partly because the newer cohorts of the elderly will contain many ex-activists from the 1960s or from the feminist movement who are experienced in political campaigning. The potential of such a movement is hinted at by the American Gray Panthers, a radical group with a broader perspective on age inequality than those associated with the single-issue pensioners' groups. The Panthers' manifestos addresssed the need to attack ageism and suggested that all disadvantaged age groups should work together:

The Philadelphia Gray Panthers shall be a coalition of old and young people working together. We shall work for the liberation of older and younger people urging re-integration into the life of the community and enhancing and revitalizing the resources of both. We shall work also for the elimination of age discrimination that has isolated both the young and the old. (quoted in Cain 1975, p. 39)

The continued ageing of the population brings a potential clash of interests between the working sections of the populace and the retired elderly whose pensions must be funded from their tax payments. As the 'burden of dependency' of non-employed pensioners rises, it is argued, intergenerational conflict may break out along these lines (Johnson et al. 1989). This position has been endorsed by government policy-makers (Phillipson 1982); and the American pressure group AGE (Americans for Generational Equity) explicitly blames the elderly for poverty among younger groupings. Sara Arber and Jay Ginn (1991b) refer to this scapegoating of the elderly as 'conflictual ageism' and point out that its main effect is to strengthen the hand of governments who want to squeeze back on pensions. Indeed, there is little evidence that such attitudes are widespread. Survey data from Europe and Britain have indicated considerable sympathy for the plight of pensioners (Walker 1993). What Arber and Ginn call 'compassionate ageism' (the view of old people as pitiable and in need of care) is probably a great deal more common.

While age divisions hold the potential for intergenerational conflict, the relative rarity of political activities organized around age reflects the way in which age disadvantages are affected by other dynamics of stratification.

Intersecting Dynamics: Age, Ethnicity, Gender and Class

American researchers coined the term 'double jeopardy' (or sometimes 'triple jeopardy') to describe the way in which disadvantages of age are compounded by ethnicity and/or gender or class. We might more aptly speak of quadruple jeopardy, for it is clear that these four factors combine to create the worst cases of poverty and misfortune.

Ethnicity

Markides and Mindel (1987) review debates about double jeopardy arising from racial discrimination. They state that the evidence is inconclusive: while ethnic minority members are more liable to poverty in old age because of the past experience of discrimination, they may be better integrated into community and neighbourhood networks and thus more psychologically braced to face old age. Moreover, ageist attitudes are less pronounced than among the majority population and respect for elders may be a core value – among Chinese and Indians, for example.

Blakemore and Boneham (1994) draw somewhat similar conclusions on the basis of their research among Asians and African-Caribbeans; they challenge the view of all minority old people as poverty-stricken victims and cite the material success of some Asians in the East Midlands cities. They emphasize the variability of response to old age among different ethnic groups, commending the self-sufficiency of the pioneer immigrant groups who came to Britain after the war. Among Asians in particular, family and community support for the elderly is strong. Asians and Caribbeans are often shocked that white people are prepared to put their elderly parents into care homes, rather than looking after them themselves. However, there are hints that this may change as the groups become absorbed into the prevailing British culture of individualism

An earlier study by Steve Fenton (1987) of African-Caribbeans in Bristol offered a more sombre view: many of his respondents suffered ill-health and poverty and were deeply unhappy with their lives in Britain. The more optimistic accounts ignore the effect of racist stereotyping and prejudice which affect those who come into contact with the agencies catering for old age. In Fenton's words: 'They face the *common* hardships of old age which, for many, are characterized by dependency, and the *specific* indignities which are a consequence of racially defined ideas and practices, and are frequently concretized in transactions with public services and officials in dependency relations' (1987, p. 2).

Young people from racialized minorities face racism and discrimination. As we have seen in previous chapters, they are more vulnerable to unemployment; they experience racism at school from both teachers and fellow pupils and have more difficulty in gaining employment in line with their qualifications. Although they may join in with white subcultural movements, the tendency among African-Caribbean and some working-class Asian youths has been to form their own gangs and groups. While Black music and fashions are extremely popular among white young people, racial tension can lead to violence between gangs where ethnic and territorial loyalties are strong. African-Caribbean culture, with its emphasis on street life and on music, has been rich in spawning youth styles and cultural forms. Unfortunately, such vibrant Black cultures tend to become ghettoized and many frustrated young men slide into drug-taking and criminal activities. The rise of knife crime and killings among Black teenagers in the UK and USA is a sad effect of such a criminal subculture.

Gender

There is little doubt that women suffer a double jeopardy of age and gender, although this is connected to one advantage they have over men: their greater longevity. As a result, they are over-represented among the 'old old' who are more vulnerable to illness – especially Alzheimer's disease – loss of mobility and the need for residential or hospital care. They are twice as likely to be housebound. Living longer, women are more vulnerable to bereavement, widowhood and isolation (Arber and Ginn 1991b).

There is a consensus that women are the greatest sufferers from poverty in old age (Fennell et al. 1988; Walker 1990). This arises from the interrelated factors of women's responsibility for domestic labour and their inferior labour market situation. Time spent looking after children means they have lower entitlement to pensions; women's earnings are generally lower so that they have less money for savings. These factors mean that women are more likely to depend on inadequate state pensions for their income. Arber and Ginn argue that the relative disadvantage of women persists across all classes, although single women from higher occupational groupings can achieve a better standard of living. There is no doubt that motherhood is a cause of disadvantage for women in later life. As Arber and Ginn put it, for women, 'personal poverty is the price of fertility' (1991b, p. 100).

In addition, women are likely to suffer more from stigmatization and ageist attitudes. There is a double standard in ageing. While it is allowed that some men age with dignity and even gain in attractiveness to women (certainly elderly millionaires seem to have no difficulty in finding a succession of young women to be their brides!), the bodies of ageing women have long been viewed with disgust. The loss of sexual attractiveness is significant as it is so crucially bound up with social definitions of femininity. Arber and Ginn (1991b) state that women suffer a double social exclusion in old age; they share with men the loss of their role in the capitalist production system, but also lose their reproductive capacities. Since women are valued for their feminine bodily attractions, many older women suffer feelings of low esteem.

Younger women's position, too, is affected by prevailing definitions of femininity and the association with domesticity and motherhood. While boys' leisure lives revolve around sport and drinking and take place to a large degree outside, in the street, girls' leisure has been more constrained, partly because of parental anxiety about young women's sexuality and personal safety. McRobbie (1978) described what she called the 'bedroom culture' of working-class teenage girls, which revolved around make-up, fashion, pop stars and gossip about boys. This preoccupation with romance and appearance channels girls towards marriage and motherhood, while their male compeers' culture involves 'learning to labour' (Willis 1977) and negotiating public space. Cann's work (2014) shows the pressure on young men to avoid cultural forms which are identified as female and focus on 'boys' things' such as sport, action films and internet wargames.

However, in academic terms young women have caught up. Their educational achievements at each level from SATS to university degrees are surpassing those of young men in most countries of the Global North. Girls are said to be breaking free of traditional restraints and engaging in forms of activity similar to boys', including delinquent behaviour such as membership of 'girl gangs'. The 2000s have witnessed a growing concern with the involvement of groups of girls in binge-drinking and street disorder. Although there is dispute as to how new these forms of female behaviour are, and whether they merely reflect a general rise in levels of drunkenness and violence in society, it can be argued that feminism has encouraged a loosening of the internal controls which used to inhibit women's behaviour (Heidensohn 1985) and has raised aspirations among young women (Bradley 1999b). However, for working-class girls, prospects remain restricted. Here the effect of class is strongly registered.

Class

> From birth until death...the influence of class continues to exert a disproportionate effect both on the quality of life and on the quantity of resources which people receive.
>
> (Phillipson 1982, p. 159)

Working-class people experience the greatest risks of poverty, isolation and ill-health in old age, and are most dependent on the state. A study of 300,000 people carried out by the London School of Hygiene showed that poorer people are much more likely to die before the age of seventy (Sloggett and Joshi 1994). By contrast, middle-class people enjoy many advantages in facing up to old age, as we have already remarked.

Class differences are equally sharp among young people, with working-class youth encountering limited opportunities and risks of unemployment. Involvement in deviant cultures purveying anti-school values only heightens the chance of entering dead-end jobs (Willis 1977; Mac an Ghaill 1988). Education is a crucial factor. Research has persistently shown how the education system processes young people through class-specific channels. Upper- and middle-class parents can afford to send children to private schools which offer a more academically orientated and disciplined environment, or manipulate access to state schools with better academic records. Working-class children habitually attend less successful state schools. There is evidence that the educational system has become more class-segregated; grammar schools used to provide a route for academically orientated working-class children to enter a middle-class world. The introduction of student loans, incurring debt levels of £27,000 upwards, may deter working-class recruits from entering universities. Despite widening participation policies, few working-class students attend the elite universities which are the gateways to top jobs (Milburn 2013).

The current economic climate might serve to unite young people through their experience of diminishing opportunities. Even middle-class young people are finding it more difficult to find jobs for which they consider themselves qualified. There was a considerable degree of graduate unemployment in Britain throughout the 1980s and

1990s. The recession of the late 2000s has again put them at risk. While it has been emphasized that youth cultures are class-specific, researchers have found that young people register little sense of class identification (Willis et al. 1990; McRobbie 1991). A shared interest in music, dancing and other youth-related cultural forms might serve to strengthen young people's sense that they are common victims of ageism.

Conclusions

'A life form in which chronological age was much less relevant was replaced by an increasingly age-relevant one' (Featherstone and Hepworth 1989, pp. 143–4). Almost all the perspectives discussed in this chapter share this view that the development of industrial capitalism increased awareness of age and greater segregation of age groups. While most societies have elements of age stratification, capitalism has promoted a distinct form of age inequality which rests upon the socially dependent status of the young and the old.

Economic rewards and status are linked to participation in the productive system. The institution of retirement promoted the withdrawal of many older people from paid work at an increasingly early age; financial hardship linked to dependency on inadequate state pensions is augmented by ageist attitudes, although middle-class affluence acts as a cushion against some of the more damaging aspects of ageing. Younger people, especially those of the working class or from ethnic minority communities, are also experiencing increasingly longer periods of dependency on their parents or on the state because of youth unemployment.

While it is acknowledged that age is a key aspect of stratification in post-industrial capitalist societies, theories of age are relatively underdeveloped. The theory of age stratification, developing from the functionalist framework, and Mannheim's analysis of generations and generation units, were a promising start, but their potential has not been fully explored. Rather, the investigation of inequalities of age has evolved within sociological subspecialisms, although there have been recent attempts to integrate those through a sociology of the life course.

Within the sociology of youth and age, radical perspectives have become dominant in the past decades. In fact, the political economy approach with its emphasis on the social construction of old age seems to have led logically into a postmodernist concern with deconstructing prevailing attitudes to age. In the study of youth, a new interest in studying discourses of age has not necessarily been at odds with radical accounts of youth subcultures and inequality.

The radical perspectives stressed that the experience of age was differentiated by class, and more recent research has highlighted the intersection of disadvantages of age with gender and ethnicity. Such divisions impede the development of coherent or long-lasting political movements based on age divisions. Nonetheless, age is an important aspect both of individual identity and of more transient but recurrent generational conflicts. With the development of neoliberal policies and global capitalism, younger and older people have suffered disproportionately from the effects of unemployment and recession. The next few decades may witness an outbreak of 'age warfare' as the disadvantaged groups take a more militant stance against ageism and the age elite.

Further Reading

Stephen Hunt, *The Life Course* (Palgrave, 2005), is a useful introduction to the sociology of age. Good textbooks on older people are Graham Fennell, Chris Phillipson and Helen Evers, *The Sociology of Old Age* (Open University Press, 1988), and Chris Phillipson, *Ageing* (Polity, 2013). Influential texts on youth are Andy Furlong and Fred Cartmel, *Young People and Social Change* (Open University Press, 2007), and Kenneth Roberts, *Youth and Employment in Modern Britain* (Oxford University Press, 1995). Mike Brake, *Sociology of Youth Culture and Youth Subcultures* (Routledge & Kegan Paul, 1980), provides a classic introduction to subcultural theories, while Ed Howker and Shiv Malik, *Jilted Generation* (Icon Books, 2013), and Robert McDonald and Jane Marsh, *Disconnected Youth* (Palgrave, 2005), explore the economic problems facing young people.

Thinking Points

- Do older people and youths share anything in common?
- Is a distinctive new generation of young people emerging as a result of neoliberalism?

8

Emergent Identities and Inequalities: Disability, Sexual Orientation and Religious Affiliation

Despite the emergence of disability politics, social scientists generally demonstrated little interest in critically examining the living conditions of disabled people, and concentrated instead on chronic illness and disability as a health issue. This silence is not new. There has been a notable absence of discussion of disability across classical sociological theories, but the general thrust is inescapable: the absence of people with impairments from the industrial labour market dictates their wider social exclusion.

(Barnes and Mercer 2002, p. 532)

The quotation from Barnes and Mercer illustrates nicely a major theme of this chapter. The constructionist position taken in this book suggests that social identities are multiple, varied and historically changing. While some sources of inequality and social identification are well-recognized and longstanding, such as the trio of class, gender and ethnicity discussed in the earlier chapters, other forms of social cleavage that generate social identities are latent, less recognized or even suppressed. In certain circumstances, these cleavages may produce active and politicized identities which force public recognition of such overlooked sources of disadvantage and discrimination. Repression sometimes leads to silence, but at other times may trigger resistance and lead to the emergence of new social movements. In this chapter I will briefly discuss three of these 'emergent' forms of social division: disability; lesbian, gay, bisexual and transgender (LGBT) identities; and religious affiliation.

There are, of course, others that could be mentioned, such as geographical region or body shape, but I have chosen to discuss three which are listed as protected diversity characteristics within the Equality Act of 2010. These three have also achieved an expanding focus within sociology. In the former two cases, academic study followed from the success of a militant and effective rights movement which sprang from the experience of stigma, oppression and exclusion. Religious affiliation is, of course, in no way a new basis of identity, politicized or otherwise, but it has not historically been primarily treated as a source of inequality. However, the notion of Islamophobia brought the issue of religious affiliation into the fore in the sociological explorations of ethnicity and inequalities (Allen 2010).

The other reason for discussing these three protected equality characteristics is that they are all the focus of major concerns and conflicts in the political configuration of the 2010s. Disabled people were particularly affected by the austerity politics of the Coalition government in the UK, especially by the infamous 'bedroom tax' which requires council house tenants with apparently an extra bedroom to move to a smaller property or pay a tax. Disabled people are particularly affected because they may have additional space requirements which the able-bodied do not and are less able to move about. LGBT people around the world have been the subject of increasingly hardline legal repression and persecution, an issue highlighted at the 2014 Commonwealth Games. Finally, the explosive religious cleavage between Muslim jihadists and the non-Muslim states and the religious schisms within Muslim states are threatening peace and stability around the world, augmented by the accusation that Israel is practising 'ethnic cleansing' against the Palestinian occupants of the Gaza Strip.

This chapter differs from the first three in that I do not systematically explore intersections, partly from lack of space and partly because research in these areas is still evolving. There is, however, a very useful chapter on intersectionality in Richardson and Monro's *Sexuality, Equality and Diversity* (2012) to which readers are commended. These are newer topics within sociology and that is reflected in this chapter, which can merely sketch out briefly the inequalities associated with disability, sexual orientation and religious affiliation, point to some of the conceptual frameworks for understanding them and discuss the implications for identity in each case.

Disability

The rise of a politicized force representing the interests of disabled groups was one of the features of political change in Britain in the twentieth century, and a key example of a 'new social movement'.

Various types of disabled people (the blind, the Deaf, people confined to wheelchairs) had, as Barnes and Mercer (2002) note, suffered severe discrimination in the labour market, where they were confined to undemanding jobs or considered unsuitable for any kind of employment. Public ignorance and stigma often led to patronizing behaviour towards them. They were frequently treated as if they were children or subhuman beings. The title of a leading BBC programme on disabilities, *Does He Take Sugar?*, was designed to expose such common public attitudes. Because of their disabilities, the blind and wheelchair users were often excluded from participation in public activities (from education to travel) because appropriate facilities were not provided. As a result of such experiences, a strong disabled movement developed from the 1970s, which held protests and demonstrations and lobbied for policy change. The militancy of the movement led to the passing of the Disability Discrimination Act (DDA) in 1995 and the establishment of the Disability Rights Commission (DRC) in 1999, headed by the charismatic Bert Massie, which was charged with monitoring the DDA. Disability is now one of the protected characteristics covered by the Equality Act which defines it as 'having a physical or mental impairment that has a "substantial" and "long-term" negative effect on the ability to do normal daily activities'. It therefore covers disabling conditions such as arthritis, chronic fatigue syndrome and mental illness, as well as the more visible impairments such as blindness or paraplegia (paralysis of the lower half of the body).

Explaining Disability

The definition of disability has in fact been a bone of contention within the disabled rights movement. In 1976, a group of activists known as the Union of Physically Impaired Against Segregation (UPIAS) introduced a set of terms intended to counter medicalized definitions of disability. While these definitions, which previously dominated thinking about disabled people, were ultimately reducible to individual pathology, the UPIAS definitions locate the 'causes' of disability within society and social organization. The UPIAS defined disability in this way:

> Disability is something imposed on top of our impairments by the way we are unnecessarily isolated and excluded from full participation in society...To understand this it is necessary to grasp the distinction between the physical impairment and the social situation, called 'disability,' of people with such impairment. Thus, we define impairment as lacking part of or all of a limb, or having a defective limb, organ

or mechanism of the body; and disability as the disadvantage or restriction of activity caused by a contemporary social organization which takes no or little account of people who have physical impairments and thus excludes them from participation in the mainstream of social activities. Physical disability is therefore a particular form of social oppression. (UPIAS 1976, p. 14)

This separation of the physiological *impairment* from the social *disablement* was an absolutely central premise of the disability rights movement and of the study of disability by academics, such as Mike Oliver, Colin Barnes and Tom Shakespeare, who were themselves disabled. It became known as the 'social model' and it was the base of the claim that disability was a source of inequality and discrimination, as indicated in the UPIAS quotation. It followed that the exclusion and disadvantage were not inherent results of being 'differently abled' but arose from society's failure to arrange things in ways that could accommodate those with impairments. As leading scholar Mike Oliver argued, it was not the limitations of individuals which should be seen as the 'problem' (Oliver 1990), but the failure of society to provide facilities and services to accommodate the specific needs of people with impairments; crucially Oliver pointed out that the consequences of this social failure did not just fall on unfortunate individuals, as in the medical model, but was experienced as a collective problem by the disabled as a group who saw it as embedded within institutions throughout society (1990). Indeed, many Deaf people who communicated by signing actively rejected the label of being disabled; they saw themselves as part of a different but highly valuable language community and refused physical treatment such as cochlear implants which might lead them to join the hearing majority.

The activities of the disability rights movement utilizing the social model led to the current requirement under the Equality Act that public organizations should make 'reasonable adjustments' to allow the disabled to take part in activities and to seek employment on a par with those not suffering impairments. Some of these 'adjustments' are now very familiar to us, such as the use of lifts and ramps for wheelchair users, the employment of interpreters using sign language for Deaf people, and the bleeping of traffic lights to alert blind or partially sighted people. A problem, though, is that the issue of what is a reasonable adjustment is a matter for debate. Physical adjustments to buildings, and the provision of specialized staff such as interpreters and of specialized computers developed for various disabilities are expensive, though some are funded through the government's Access to Work programme. But organizations and managers may be resistant to adjustments they see as 'unreasonable', so that the Act may fail to defend people adequately from discrimination.

While the social model has been crucial to disability campaigning, there has been some recent tendency to criticize it for underplaying the real limitations which impairments of certain types may place upon individuals. Tom Shakespeare, previously a strong proponent of the social model, now argues for an approach which looks in a more balanced way at the role of impairments and social disabling. In a lecture for the British Sociological Society, he criticized what he called 'the strong social model of disability, the idea that people are disabled by society, not by their bodies...It's very simple, it's not complicated: people are disabled by society *and* their bodies' (Shakespeare 2014, p. 31, my italics). Against this strong version of the social model, he argues that, because of the limitations imposed by some impairments and chronic illnesses, some people may need to be treated differently, with extra help and additional investment; a level-playing-field approach is not sufficient. For example, it is possible that some people with severe forms of mental illness may not be able to fulfil the demands of certain jobs; but this is not an excuse for denying them some form of subsistence and reasonable livelihood.

Disability and Disadvantage

We should stress that this does not mean that society is let off the hook. As noted above, despite the Equality Act, disabled people are struggling to receive equal treatment, especially in terms of employment. Disabled people are twice as likely to be unemployed as the non-disabled, a figure Shakespeare describes as 'stubborn, it just doesn't shift'. In 1995 the Labour Force Survey revealed that 20 per cent of disabled people were unemployed and 62 per cent were economically inactive, compared to figures of 8 per cent and 17 per cent of the non-disabled population (Hyde 2000). If disabled people do find jobs, they are more likely to be working part-time and to be confined to low-status unskilled jobs.

This is despite the fact that Britain has a history of legislation designed to prevent exclusion of people with impairments from the labour market. The 1944 Disabled Persons (Employment) Act set a quota for employers to hire 3 per cent of disabled workers, but it was widely disregarded and little enforced. Following stronger action on disablement in the United States, the UK passed the Disability Discrimination Act in 1996, which made it illegal to discriminate on the grounds of disability and initiated the idea of reasonable adjustments. This legislation also applies to education services, including higher education.

Despite the legislation, disabled people continue to face really major barriers in the workplace. Once in employment, they commonly encounter prejudice and further discrimination. Because of the legislation, they can apply for special devices and resources to help them do their jobs, but even with these adaptations they may appear to managers and colleagues as under-performing. Deaf and blind people, for example, inevitably find communication with hearing and sighted people more difficult, tiring and time-consuming. I have tutored Deaf students and know that they are able to achieve as much as hearing students, but they need patient one-to-one assistance which is not easily forthcoming in our speed-mad, increasingly monitored workplaces. For example, Deaf staff at one university were told their research outputs were not numerous enough and not of sufficient quality to merit the retention of their department, by people with inadequate understanding of the fact that Sign language, like Chinese, has a completely different structure and grammar from English, so that intellectually able and fluent Signers may not be able to write fluently in English. In 2008, a survey on fair treatment at work found that 27 per cent of disabled, as opposed to 17 per cent of non-disabled, had suffered bullying, harassment or unfairness in their workplace (Shakespeare 2014).

The disadvantages continue outside of employment. Although equality legislation requires public service institutions like universities to make reasonable adjustments for disabled people, many public buildings are unfriendly to wheelchair users, lacking lifts or ramps and thus restricting free movement and access. When the disabled venture into public, they may be deterred by people's responses; they report being pointed at and stared at, even being subject to verbal abuse and physical violence. In 2009, 1,211 disability hate crimes were recorded (Shakespeare 2014). Children with disabilities are more likely to be bullied in the playground and are often categorized as having Special Educational Needs (SEN) and educated in separate classes, which further leads to stigmatization and isolation from their peers.

Though people are probably increasingly aware of certain types of disability that involve physical impairments and understand that disability does not imply incapacity – because of the success, for example, of the Paralympic Games – other forms of disablement are less recognized. Not everyone is aware that chronic physical and mental conditions are covered by the legislation. Perhaps the least understood is mental illness, which remains a highly stigmatized and neglected condition. According to Simon Wessely, President of the Royal College of Psychiatrists, only about 30 per cent of people with common mental health problems get any treatment for them (Boseley 2014); Wessely asks us to consider the outrage if only 30 per cent of cancer patients were treated. Mental health services, along with geriatric care (of the elderly), are generally the Cinderella sectors of the National Health Service. Allan (2014) reports local mental health teams cannot cope with their caseloads, and that some regions within the NHS spend less than 7 per cent of their budget on mental health, even though it accounts for around 23 per cent of cases of disease. There is also an increasing occurrence of mental illness among children: 10 per cent aged five to sixteen had a clinically diagnosed mental disorder (Health and Social Care Information Centre). Services within schools and the NHS are inadequate and underfunded: according to the charity Young Minds, young people's mental health receives only 6 per cent of the NHS mental health budget.

As a result of all these factors, it is no surprise that a government survey carried out in 1985 estimated that 45 per cent of disabled adults were living in poverty and only 13 per cent could be classified as prosperous (Hyde 2000). In the twenty-first century, while policies might have improved chances for some disabled people, the problem of poverty is likely to have increased because of the welfare cuts imposed by the Coalition. Observers agree that these cuts have had the harshest impacts on the most vulnerable, and that includes disabled people. People receiving Disability Living Allowance have been targeted for investigation and some have had the allowance terminated on the grounds that they are fit to work, when subsequent investigations have overturned the verdicts. In the meantime, they have been subjected to stress and loss of income. The bedroom tax has disproportionately affected them. The Independent Living Fund and Access to Work have both received cuts.

Hyde sums up the disadvantages faced by disabled people in a strong statement:

Disabled people – nearly 4 million of the working age population – are largely excluded from satisfactory employment opportunities, experience considerably higher levels of poverty and are often dependent on state social services and benefits...Disabled people are disadvantaged because they belong to a social group that is the object of pervasive institutionalized discrimination. Thus disability engenders distinct forms of social inequality and, like gender, age and social class, should be regarded as an organizing principle of social inequality in its own right. (Hyde 2000, p. 185)

Disability and Identity

Given what we have seen of the discrimination faced by disabled people, it is not surprising if they experience their identities as stigmatized and marginalized, as conveyed in the following account of the onset of an impairment: 'I took the line of least resistance and ceased to have human contact. It is too embarrassing for other people. The street becomes unnegotiable. Because you can't see you bump into things and people think you're drunk or nutty. So you are a magnet for people's fear of the sick' (quoted in the *Guardian*, 31 August 2009).

This is how Scottish writer Candia McWilliam described to the *Guardian* newspaper her experience of blindness caused by a rare condition, blepharospasm, which means that the eyelids cannot be opened. McWilliam's reaction is typical of people who suddenly experience the onset of an impairment, according to Oliver and Barnes (1998). Feelings of helplessness and stigmatization may force people into voluntary isolation and often into despair. Those born with an impairment also experience negative social reactions, discrimination and stigma, although they may at first be sheltered by being brought up among people with similar attributes, or segregated from the non-impaired through being sent to special schools. The shock may then be postponed until they seek to enter the world of employment and find an array of barriers facing them.

The 'fear of the sick' referred to by McWilliam is reinforced by the media, which in the past have often presented negative images of disabled people. They tended to be portrayed as pathetic and in need of charity, sometimes even as threatening and dangerous. There was a lack of presentation of disabled people doing everyday social things as workers, students or family members. Oliver and Barnes argued that disabled people were in danger of internalizing these negative images, leading to low self-esteem and depression. However, recently this has been challenged by positive portrayals, especially of disabled sportswomen and men. The remarkable achievements of Paralympian athletes challenged the idea that impairments prevent people from achieving, even in the most demanding areas of life. In 2014 Prince Harry sponsored the Invictus Games for ex-soldiers who had received dreadful injuries in action, again leading to positive coverage in the media

Before his killing of his girlfriend, Oscar Pistorius, the 'blade runner', had become an international folk hero and star. This example also shows how modern technology has the potential for aiding the disabled to participate in every kind of activity. Stephen Hawking, though completely paralysed and confined to a wheelchair, used a computer voice system to aid his work as one of Britain's greatest intellectual thinkers. Another inspiring example is Hilary Lister, who became the first quadriplegic woman to sail around Britain in 2009, following the first man to do it, in 2007: Geoff Holt. Lister suffers from paralysis caused by a rare neurological disorder which means she can only move her eyes, head and mouth. Apart from demonstrating how people can use determination and courage to transcend impairment, she provides another good example of how adaptations can be made to overcome social disablement, allowing people to participate in activities using new technologies. Lister's yacht is powered by 'sip and puff': she activates its controls by blowing or sucking on a number of straws (Davies 2009). Although these cases are perhaps the exceptions rather than the rule, they may provide positive role models and hope for the future to young disabled people.

We must note, however, the potential for divisions and competition within the various categories of disablement. For instance, the disability rights movement has on the whole been led by people with visible disabilities, such as wheelchair users or blind people. The less obvious forms of disability have been less represented in these activities, and people with such types of impairment may not feel very much identified with the activist movement. There is also a tendency for some groups, such as the Deaf Sign-language users, to develop their own self-support groups and communities and stay isolated within them. Nevertheless, there are forces, such as local disability forums or trade union disabled members' committees, which seek to overcome such fracturing tendencies and build solidarity. The common difficulties and exclusions which are faced may also serve to maintain disablement as a notably vital source of politicized identities.

Sexual Orientation

There are some similarities between the situation of disabled people and that of those whose sexual orientation is not 'straight' heterosexual. Both groups have experienced stigmatization and isolation, and both as a result have developed politicized identities and vigorous and visible rights movements. However, it can be stated that, on a global basis at least, LGBT people have experienced the most violent forms of oppression.

Persecution of people who do not identify as heterosexual has been fostered by many religions, including Christianity. In Britain, consensual homosexual relations between men over twenty-one were against the law until legalized in 1967 by the Sexual Offences Act, although it only applied to England and Wales. This followed the Wolfenden Report which revealed the prevalence of homosexuality in Britain, often expressed as 'one in ten', and made a distinction between the need to preserve sexual decency in public and allowing freedom in private between consenting adults. The strict religious traditions in Northern Ireland and Scotland meant that it took longer for homosexuality to be decriminalized – until 1982 and 1980 respectively. However, even after decriminalization, the stigma attached to homosexuality meant that many gay men kept their orientation secret. Coming 'out' as gay is still a problem for many, as LGBT youths fear negative responses from their friends and families. Curiously, lesbianism was never illegal in Britain, partly, it is argued, because the Victorian view of female sexuality was that it was passive and could only be 'awakened' in response to male approaches. Thus, sexual desire between women appeared unthinkable.

Over the last 100 years, LGBT rights have slowly been attained in Europe, Australasia and North America. However, in many countries homosexuality remains illegal and LGBT people are vilified, persecuted, imprisoned and murdered. It was revealed in 2014 at the Commonwealth Games that homosexuality is illegal in forty-two out of the fifty-three member countries. In these countries LGBT people are imprisoned, attacked and sometimes murdered.

The experience of oppression and violence led to the emergence of the gay rights movement in the 1960s, which started in the USA. New York and San Francisco had large communities of gay men who decided to revolt against secrecy and suppression and declare their sexual orientation openly and in public arenas. In particular, homosexuals were denied access to bars, and therefore set up their own drinking establishments; this led to raids and brutal action by the police in both cities. Events in one New York bar, the Stonewall Inn, attained a legendary status when police raids led to several nights of rioting in Greenwich Village. The Stonewall riots are commemorated by Gay Pride marches which take place annually in many cities around the world.

The importance of the Stonewall riots is also commemorated in the name of the major charity protecting LGBT rights in the UK. Stonewall was founded in 1989 by a group of women and men who had been active in the struggle against Section 28 of the Local Government Act, a controversial piece of legislation which sought to outlaw the 'promoting' of homosexuality in schools. The Act was seen as a deliberate attack on the gay rights movement and the progress it had made since the 1960s; ironically it proved counter-productive as it fired up LGBT citizens into activism, and the campaign against Section 28 was joined by other radical groups and champions of diversity. Stonewall was one of the outcomes: it was formed as a professional lobbying group to champion gay rights. Subsequently it gained support from within all the main political parties and now has offices in England, Scotland and Wales. It is particularly concerned with fighting homophobia in the workplace.

Because of the work of Stonewall and other activist bodies around the world, the last few decades have seen considerable improvements in gay rights in some countries. Gays and lesbians have gained the right to adopt children. In 2009, lesbians who have children via fertility treatment gained the right for both partners to be treated as parents by having their names registered on the birth certificate. Marriage rights have been gained by lesbians and gay men in a handful of countries. Same-sex marriages were pioneered by the liberal Nordic countries, and in 2014 were legal in sixteen countries. In Britain, gays and lesbians first gained the right to what were known as 'civil partnerships'. These were introduced in 2004 and gave same-sex couples similar legal rights to married couples. However, they could not be carried out in places of worship, such as churches, and the use of religious symbols or readings was forbidden.

Because of this, they were seen as inferior by many gays and lesbians who demanded full marriage rights. This goal was achieved in 2013 under the Coalition government, championed by the Liberal Democrats and by Prime Minister David Cameron, although the bill aroused considerable anger among many Conservative MPs and supporters. Northern Ireland, dominated by strong religious beliefs, is excluded from the Bill, though it allows civil partnerships. The anti-immigrant party UKIP is also opposed to gay rights. Significantly, the major religious authorities in the UK, apart from the Quakers, oppose same-sex marriage. While it is now legal for same-sex couples to be married in places of worship, churches retain the right to refuse to marry them. In the three months after they were made legal, 1,400 same-sex marriages took place, showing how important this was to gay and lesbian couples

However, the opposition of religious bodies shows how fragile the broad popular acceptance of LGBT people's rights to equality is, even within socially liberal regimes. In the USA, where the gay liberation movement first emerged, same-sex marriage is only legal in certain states. However, on the positive side, polls taken by various bodies, including YouGov which conducts research for the government, found that the majority of people in the United Kingdom were in favour of same-sex marriage, with percentages in the range of 55 to

65 per cent. Support is higher among women, younger people, Scottish people and Liberal Democrat supporters, and lower among older people, Conservative voters and working-class people.

Explaining Sexual Orientation

There is a massive literature on sexualities, which cannot be fully discussed here. Readers are recommended to useful introductory texts by Weeks (1986), Bhattacharyya (2002), Jackson and Scott (2010) and Richardson and Monro (2012). Here I discuss those who have written more specifically on LGBT issues

A major theorist who has explored the history of non-heterosexuality is Michel Foucault, who focused particularly on homosexuality in his three-volume work *History of Sexuality* (1978–84). Foucault argued that the notion of 'a homosexual person' was a product of Victorian scientific and medical thinking, and a passion for classification. Before that epoch, people were simply seen as possessing a range of sexual instincts and performing various sexual acts, which might be seen as immoral and unacceptable by various religions, or made illegal in various states; but this related to the act, not the whole person. Experts in sexology developed the idea of 'the pervert', who had to be treated and cured of his vice. Foucault, himself of openly homosexual orientation, viewed human sexuality as socially constructed and malleable, rejecting the idea that people are born with a fixed sexual identity. Like other historians and sociologists (for example Kenneth Dover (1978) and Jeffrey Weeks (1981)), he pointed out that homosexual practices were perfectly acceptable in some early societies, notably Ancient Greece. Anthropologists have also documented the variability of sexual practices in different societies, including homosexuality.

In general, sociologists of sexuality such as Weeks (1981, 1986) and Plummer (1995) have taken a constructionist view of how sexual orientations are formed. They argue against the work of Freud and others who attempt to develop universal accounts of human sexual development and of deviations from the 'norm' of heterosexuality. As Weeks puts it, the early theorists of sex – even Freud, whom he describes as the most radical – 'constructed a unitary model of sexuality from which it has been difficult to escape':

> On the one hand we are offered a norm of behavior which is heterosexual, procreative and largely male, in which female sexuality has almost invariably been defined as secondary or responsive. On the

other hand, there is an ever-growing catalogue of perversions, deviations...which inevitably marginalizes and in the last resort patholo-
gizes other sexualities. The language of perversion divides the sexual
world into the normal and the abnormal, the elect and the damned.
(Weeks 1986, p. 74)

In contrast, Weeks and Plummer argue that sexual practices and
sexual desires are formed by context: they are not innate but learned,
and they are highly variable, and indeed fluid, over a person's lifetime.
Particularly influential has been the idea of 'sexual scripts' (Gagnon
and Simon 1973) which we absorb through socialization and practice
as we move into sexual encounters. Neither sexuality, then, nor actual
sexual practices are seen as 'natural' or 'instinctive', but something
we learn through interaction.

Feminist writers, such as Stevi Jackson (1993), Lynn Segal (1994)
and Adrienne Rich (1980), have also written about sexuality from a
constructionist position. They, too, highlight the way in which heterosexuality continues to be presented in modern cultures as 'normal'
and 'natural'; deviations from it are thus categorized as 'abnormal' ,
or in popular parlance 'queer'. Rich (1980), who coined the term
'compulsory heterosexuality', argued that this not only stigmatizes
those who depart from heterosexuality but stifles the range of physical expressions and instincts possessed by those who consider themselves to be 'straight'. Rich argued for the existence of a 'lesbian
continuum' of feelings between women, ranging from the desire to
be physically close to female friends to full lesbian sexual relations.
The institution of heteronormativity, thus, causes us to suppress and
regulate our desires and emotions and is also the root of homophobia
and stigmatization of those espousing an LGBT orientation. The idea
of heteronormativity is therefore key to feminist understandings of
human sexuality.

Perhaps, currently, the most popular approach to the understanding of sexual diversity is queer theory, which aimed to reappropriate
the stigmatizing term and turn it into a celebratory one. Queer theory
aims to invert the idea of heterosexuality as normal, viewing the
world through a non-heterosexual lens. It is linked to post-structuralism and postmodernism in its interests in discourses and in re-
reading texts through a queer perspective, such as Eve Sedgwick
Kosofsky's re-reading of Jane Austen's novels (1991). It also builds
on the previous tradition of gay and lesbian studies in their critique
of heteronormativity, and on the work of Judith Butler which was
discussed in chapter 5, attacking the notion of genders and sexualities
as stable identities and emphasizing the range of possibilities for

sexual expression. As Scott and Jackson (2000) point out, by doing this it attacks the notion of the hetero/homo binary divide as natural, and portrays it as merely a 'cultural artifice' (p. 181). In line with this, queer theory has taken a particular interest in transsexual and transgender identities, as they illustrate Butler's concepts of transgression as a means to subvert orthodox views on sexualities and the idea of the normal. Performativity and playing around with one's sexual identity become means of resisting heterosexual oppression. As Bhattacharyya rather neatly puts it, 'queer theory seeks to celebrate the uncertainty that causes so much anxiety to others' (2002, p. 97).

It should be briefly mentioned that certain scientists have posited that there might be a genetic cause of homosexuality, the so-called 'gay gene' (Hamer and Copeland 1995). Some gay men actually welcomed this theory as it would make it appear that their orientation had a biological basis and so could not be 'cured' by treatment, whether psychological or medical. This was rather naïve, in view of the potential of genetic engineering and testing of embryos in the uterus. However, nobody has ever managed to isolate the 'gay gene', even within the human genome project which has been codifying all our genetic material. It would seem that the constructionist approach of sociology has been vindicated.

Sexual Orientation and Disadvantage

Despite the positive moves outlined above, homophobic practice is commonly experienced in Britain by lesbian, gay, bisexual and trans people. This is particularly true in schools, where name-calling and bullying are common. LGBT also report harassment and bullying at work as their main problem. A study of gay and lesbian schoolchildren by Hunt and Jensen (2007) revealed that six out of ten had experienced bullying. There is a difficulty, however, in assessing the extent of bias and discrimination as we do not have any reliable estimate of the size of the total LGBT population (Aspinall 2009). Estimates vary widely from 0.3 to 10 per cent, with the Department of Trade and Industry (DTI) figure of 5 to 7 per cent being seen as the most reliable, according to Aspinall. This obviously relates to the fear that people have of coming out, especially older people, who may be reluctant to answer sexual identity questions where they appear in surveys. Aspinall also reports that non-response on sexual identity questions is higher among ethnic minority citizens and people from lower socio-economic groups, among whom prejudices may be stronger.

Nonetheless, a successful survey was carried out in 2013, by the European Union Fundamental Rights Agency (FRA), of LGBT experience, and it can be accessed on the FRA website. It was answered by 93,000 people identifying as LGBT across the EU member states and Croatia. The survey shows that discrimination tends to be highest in the former Soviet-bloc societies, which can be linked to the current difficulties faced by LGBT people in Russia. Among the four groups, reported experience of discrimination is highest among trans people: across Europe, 59 per cent of trans respondents said they had experienced discrimination in the past year, with the UK having one of the highest levels reported at 68 per cent. Averages across Europe for gays, lesbians and bisexuals were 41 per cent, 33 per cent and 21 per cent respectively, with the UK coming in at slightly below the average, at 36 per cent, 29 per cent and 20 per cent. For longer periods the reporting of incidents was predictably higher; in the UK nearly a third (31 per cent) of respondents reported being physically attacked or threatened with violence in the past six years, while over half (55 per cent) had experienced harassment in the past five years. Looking back at their schooldays, a quarter reported being discriminated against (the lowest proportion in Europe), and over the past year 12 per cent reported discrimination in looking for a job and 19 per cent reported it at work. Respondents also spoke of their fear of being open in public. For example, a young lesbian from Romania stated 'I never went to a [gay pride] parade, as I was scared of being assaulted in the street, as it usually happens at those events.' The use of terms like 'gay' as perjorative was also commonly reported: as a young bisexual from Spain reported: 'In Spain, it's very common to call someone gay (or similar) as an insult.'

Small-scale or qualitative studies are also able to reveal discrimination against LGBT people in specific sites. Research by Nick Drydakis (2014) demonstrated that openly gay job applicants in Cyprus were 40 per cent less likely than those who did not reveal their sexual orientation to gain interviews. Using a well-known research technique, Drydakis sent applications for advertised jobs, with CVs that were virtually the same, except that the fake gay applicants included information about their volunteer work for a (fictional) gay organization.

Scott and Jackson (2000) state that young gay men are regularly raped in prison by heterosexual men; in an environment where there is no meeting of the sexes, they are seen as a kind of stand-in for women, and also as 'fair game' because of the stigma attached to homosexuality and the belief that gays have compromised their masculinity. In general, gay men are vulnerable to assault and attack as the ultimate expression of homophobic fear and hostility. Although lesbians are not perhaps quite so endangered, they may be treated with anger by men who see their sexuality as a breach of the 'natural order' in which women are expected to be both subservient to and sexual servicers of men. Lesbianism is thus seen as a threat to masculinity, and women who reject men's advances are often abused as being 'dykes' or 'lezzers'.

As indicated in the FRA survey, trans people are particularly likely to face discrimination, as people are made uneasy by the notion of switching gender. This group has only recently been brought under the LGBT campaigning umbrella; indeed, they were only admitted as part of Stonewall in 2015. Trans campaigners are a small but militant group, as noted by a trans activist interviewed for Richardson and Monro's research, who commented: 'People complain that the T in LGBT is the tail on the dog. I said yes it is, but it's a big dog with teeth...On our own we're a tiny little animal, but if we're part of that grouping it's much harder to ignore us' (Richardson and Monro 2012, p. 44). The physical process of changing one's gender and/or sexuality is a hard, lengthy and draining process and can often provoke hostility and incomprehension among friends and family. Thus, trans people are still on the receiving end of severe discrimination, as revealed in the research of Whittle (2002) and others. A particular problem they face is that they may not be fully accepted by the gender they have chosen to join. There has even been opposition to them by some feminists, who have argued that female trans people should not be allowed to join women-only groups. They stand in particular danger of marginalization.

Obviously the situation is much worse for all these groups in the many countries where homosexuality is still illegal: sixty-eight in 2013, according to the TUC. The majority are in Africa, followed by the Middle East. It is also illegal in most Caribbean islands: Black gay men in particular face very strong hostility as homosexuality is seen as contradictory to the assertive heterosexual identity fostered in African cultures. In China and other countries, attempts to 'cure' gay men still persist, by the enforced use of electric shock treatment: homosexuality is viewed as a type of mental illness.

Sexual Orientation and Identity

Heterosexuality, because it has been naturalized and normalized, has become, in Kitzinger and Wilkinson's term (1993), a default identity: that is, it is taken for granted, so that most people do not spend much time questioning it. By contrast, since LGBT identities are socially stigmatized, the process of acknowledging oneself as gay, lesbian, bisexual or trans – whether to oneself, to others or publicly – is a more demanding and self-conscious activity. As a result, LGBT identities are much more likely to be active and to be central in an individual's view of themselves.

As we have seen, such active processes of identification led to the emergence of highly politicized identities within the gay rights movement. An important part of the movement's agenda was encouraging people to come out openly with their sexual orientation. 'Glad to be gay' was the slogan, which sought to challenge the negative views of homosexuality and proclaim the individual's right to define their own sexuality. This strand in the movement led to the controversial practice of 'outing' whereby prominent people who were concealing their homosexuality were publicly named. This related particularly to people like politicians, or religious or community leaders, who appeared through their silence to be colluding with homophobia and repression of non-heterosexuals.

Although this policy was denounced by some, it does highlight the importance of the public assertion of LGBT identity by those who can serve as positive role models to younger people and challenge negative public perceptions. Thus, people like musicians Elton John and George Michael, Sir Ian Mckellan (Gandalf in the *Lord of the Rings* films) and tennis player Martina Navratilova have played an important part in making non-heterosexual orientations acceptable. Of course, some environments (the bohemian worlds of rock and roll and of acting) are more easy to come out in than others. Football is an area where it has been very difficult for gay players to be open about their sexuality. It was something of a sensation when tough and successful Welsh rugby player Gareth Thomas announced himself publicly to be homosexual in 2009. He was subsequently voted top of the Pink List of the 101 most influential gay people in the UK and he received Stonewall's Hero of the Year award in October 2010.

The yearly Pink List is another means of encouraging celebrities in a range of spheres to declare themselves LGBT. In 2013 the list was topped by Paris Lees, a trans journalist. Other well-known people in the top ten were broadcaster Clare Balding, gold-medal boxer Nicola Adams, and Owen Jones, whose writings have been referred to in this book. Paris Lees outlined the importance of the award on the Pink News website, and stressed its centrality for the transgender/transsexual community:

> Obviously this is hugely invigorating to me personally, but I think it's even more valuable in terms of what it means for the trans community

and raising awareness. I hope that this recognition will help to open doors for All About Trans, and the work that I'm doing there which I am really passionate about, but although I'm really pleased to be named and recognized for leading a full and meaningful life, it makes me very sad that many trans people are not able to fulfil their potential...So I hope that going forward all trans people will be able to flourish and prosper and reach their full potential.

Lees has pointed out elsewhere (2014) that trans people are increasingly feeling able to live openly. This is partly due to the fact that the medical procedures which can be involved in gender reassignment are now better known and more easily accessible, but also may reflect the influence of celebrity 'outers'. Lees points to the fact that people changing their gender are much more numerous than is generally supposed and highlights how distressing and disruptive the process of transitioning can be.

The yearly Pride marches, which commemorate the Stonewall riots, have also been an important way in which the 'right to be gay' has been proclaimed and are an occasion for LGBT folk to express their identities in public. Pride marches have taken on a carnivalesque and colourful character which affirms the joyfulness of sexuality and difference. They are also an important way in which the LGBT rights movement has maintained its political presence. Another important factor here is the way in which the movement has created its own spaces for social interaction: places like Manchester's Canal Street with its gay bars and clubs provide safe places where people can meet without fear of persecution. This is important given that, for many LGBT folk, there are still locations, such as their places of work, where fear of victimization and exclusion will compel them to concealment. It is a matter of concern for many that a number of such bars have been forced out of business in the lean years of the recession, though it is also argued that younger LGBT people may feel less need for segregated 'safe' spaces.

Although the Gay Pride movement has both allowed out and confident LGBT people to express their individuality in an exuberant way and offered a space for the more timid to feel part of a collective movement, there is still a remaining problem of splits within the movement. One of Richardson and Monro's respondents described the movement as a 'hodge podge mish mash', as opposed to 'one happy family under a rainbow umbrella' (2012, p. 19). In the early days of the gay rights movement, lesbians complained that gays were marginalizing them, reproducing the pattern of patriarchal dominance in public activities. Rather shockingly, survey research by

Stonewall revealed bisexual people reporting ignorance and prejudice from gays and lesbians as well as 'straight' work colleagues (TUC 2013). Prejudice against bisexuals may relate to people's uneasiness with uncertainty, as reflected in the earlier quotation from Bhattacharyya: people may find it difficult to cope with ambiguity in assessing their own sexual positioning in relation to bisexual people. A lot of homophobic prejudice is said to stem from fears about people's own sexual uncertainties.

Here, as in the case of disability, the role of organizations like Stonewall or the LGBT self-organized groups within trade unions, is important. These can provide umbrellas for the different groups to meet, share and understand one another's positions. The term 'rainbow alliance' is often used in relation to this kind of unifying tactic or strategy, and, symbolically, the LGBT movement signifies itself with a rainbow-coloured ribbon.

Religious Affiliation

It may seem strange to include religious affiliation in a chapter on 'emergent identities', as religions and religious adherence are as old as human society. However, it is discussed here because it has recently been added as a protected characteristic under the Equality Act, and also because, though religion has always been a central concern in sociology, it has not normally been treated as an aspect of social inequality. Instead, discussion of religious identity and discrimination has tended to be merged into the study of ethnicity. Although the two are often connected, it will be argued in this chapter that they are not coterminous and should be dealt with separately.

Religion was a major theme in the works of classic sociology. Weber's famous text *The Protestant Ethic and the Spirit of Capitalism* (1930) linked Protestantism to the early emergence of industrialism in Britain, Holland and Switzerland. He argued that there was an 'elective affinity' between the two, because of the doctrine of predestination, which encouraged people to demonstrate that they were among the 'saved' by hard work in a calling (occupation). This in turn led to the accumulation and reinvestment of profits which lie at the heart of the capitalist dynamic. Other kinds of religion, in contrast, promoted conspicuous consumption, or spirituality and otherworldliness.

Durkheim's study *The Elementary Forms of Religious Life* (1915) also meditated on the contribution of religion to society. He believed that all societies needed to distinguish some kind of realm of the 'sacred' which was separate from and of higher value than everyday life. In this way individuals could transcend their own needs and values, through awareness of a higher power or authority. Although this higher authority might be conceptualized as a totem, the ancestors or a god or set of divinities, Durkheim, as a secular scientific thinker, argued that the thing that transcends individual experience is actually society itself. Effectively, the religious observer is worshipping society. Thus, religion acted to bind people into society.

Both Weber and Durkheim assumed that secularization was a growing tendency in modern life; Weber referred to it as the 'disenchantment of the world', caused by the growth of scientific rationalism. Secularization thus became a major theme of the sociology of religion. But, in fact, religions have proved remarkably robust, and we might even posit a counter 'de-secularization' process in the second half of the twentieth century, leading to a reaffirmation of certain religious faiths, for example Orthodox Christianity in Russia, Judaism in various parts of the world and, notably, Islam within communities in the Muslim diaspora.

Certainly, religion – along with territorial claims – is currently, and often has been, a major cause of wars and disputes around the world. Notable among these are the conflicts between Israel and the surrounding Arab countries, focusing on the disputed area of Palestine; the war in Syria which is informed by the division between Shi'ite and Sunni sects within Islam; and the hostilities between Muslim Pakistan and Hindu-dominated India. Religious hatreds lead to terrible crimes against individuals and communities, so that religious affiliation needs to be seen as a powerful source of identity, even in countries which are quite highly secularized, such as England or France.

Explaining Religious Discrimination

As indicated above, within the sociological classics religion was seen as an integrating force. This was Marx's position: he described religion as 'the opium of the people'. He saw it as one of the factors that prevented the working class from rising up in revolution, because of its promise of a reward in the afterlife which would compensate for the pains of life on earth: 'pie in the sky when you die', as the saying goes. Certainly, in the nineteenth century, the Methodist religion gained great popularity among working folk and was concerned to offer consolation for the deprivation and hardships of working-class life.

In these classic works, there was little exploration of religion as a source of division and discrimination. This has largely been left to historians who have explored the causes and origins of particular religious conflicts. Geo-political factors clearly play a part, as in the history of ethnic divisions. The long history of Christian and Muslim conflicts is symbolized by the Crusades, in which the two sides fought over territories in the Middle East, notably Jerusalem. This was followed by a long history of struggle between Christians and Muslim Moors in Spain, which is still commemorated in street festivals today. Since the Second World War, Jerusalem has continued to be the source of religious division, with the city partitioned between Jewish and Arab Muslim residents. While these territorial disputes and claims are similar to those by which nations and ethnicities are formed, there is an additional element when the conflict is pronounced to be a 'Holy War'. Participants are turned into Crusaders or jihadists, which remain potent and dangerous politicized identities to this day. Where, after the wars, Christians, Jews and Muslims continued to live within the same territorial boundaries, the prevailing religious groups exercised dominance over the minorities, often confining them to certain residential areas and lower-status occupations. Thus, Jews across Europe were confined to ghettos; curiously, they were also often occupied as money lenders – then seen as a discreditable job, as exemplified in the character of Shylock in Shakespeare's *Merchant of Venice* – which led to their future dominant role in banking and finance. Jealousy of the financial success and prosperity of a portion of the Jewish population was one of the factors in the rise of Nazism and anti-semitism in Hitler's Germany, leading to the horrific genocidal events of the Holocaust.

Division and discrimination arise not only between religions but also within religions, due to the formation of sects: groups which develop their own distinctive versions of the larger faith, with different beliefs and practices. The rise of sects has been linked to the process of secularization within the sociology of religion (Wilson 1966; Bruce 2011) because it signifies the diminishing power of the central authorities over church members and the growth of critical attitudes within the faith community. The big split in the Christian faith was between Catholicism and Protestantism. This was the cause of the long-running 'Troubles' in Northern Ireland between the two communities, which has also been seen as closely linked to class divides. The Catholic community in Belfast consisted primarily of poor working-class people, while the wealth of the community was held by the Protestants. Employment in profitable areas, for example the shipyards, was in their gift, while the Catholics were marginalized and at greater risk of unemployment, as is still the case today.

Catholics were also historically persecuted in England following the turbulent reign of Henry VIII and his decision to establish the separate Church of England in order to escape from the power of the Pope and facilitate the annulment of his first marriage. Struggles between Catholicism and the Church of England continued through the Tudor and Stuart eras, with different monarchs espousing different faiths, but the Church of England remained ascendant and many Catholics were savagely executed or forced to flee. However, in other countries such as France and Spain, it was Protestant minorities who were victims of persecution and compelled to emigrate to ensure their lives and livelihoods.

Christian minorities in countries like India and Egypt are still subject by Hindu or Muslim majorities to discrimination, and sometimes there has been wholesale murder of Christian communities. However, today, the two predominant forms of religious discrimination are anti-Semitism, which lingers on in Russia and Europe, and Islamophobia, which has emerged as a major phenomenon since the mid twentieth century. It has been exacerbated by the existence of Muslim terrorist groups such as Al Qaeda and Islamic State (ISIS) and the atrocities they have committed, but it predates those groups. This racist perspective is generalized to the great mass of ordinary peaceful Muslims, most of whom would themselves vigorously repudiate terrorist activities.

In 1996, the Runnymede Trust, a charitable body which acts as a watchdog against racism, established the Commission on British Muslims and Islamophobia. The Commission's report *Islamophobia: A Challenge for Us All* was published in November 1997 and is taken to be the moment when this formally emerged as a policy issue (Meer 2014). Islamophobia was defined as 'an outlook or world-view involving an unfounded dread and dislike of Muslims, which results in practices of exclusion and discrimination'. This appears as a violent form of Othering, as discussed in chapter 6. The report went on to describe Islamophobia as the fear and hatred of Islam and consequently fear and dislike of all Muslims. This then facilitates discriminations against Muslims and their exclusion from full participation in economic, social and public life. According to the report, holders of Islamophobic attitudes, from which the British popular press are not immune, tend to believe that the cultural values of Islam are too different to have anything in common with other cultures, and that it is inferior to Western culture. Islam may also be seen to be as much a political ideology as a religion, and one seen as inevitably leading to political extremism and violence.

In this perspective, 'Muslim' has become a master status in which differences of class, education, ethnicity, nationality and politics are erased and followers of Islam are all seen as a homogeneous bloc and a threat to world peace. In fact, although Muslims themselves see themselves as part of the worldwide 'ummah', the community of faith, there are great differences between the culture and practice of Islam in, for example, Turkey, Egypt, Saudi Arabia, Malaysia and Pakistan. Moreover, there is a major split within Islam between Sunni and Shi'a branches. This is a complicated dynastic schism relating to the nomination of the successor to the prophet Mohammad after his death; the Sunni majority selected Abu Bakr to be the religious leader or Caliph, but the Shi'a minority favoured Ali, a member of Mohammad's family. There are some differences between the two sects in interpretation of the Q'ran and in the requirements for prayer, but basically the rift, like so many religious divides, relates in origin to issues of politics, dynasty and territory. This sectarian division has persisted through history, with Sunni forming the majority in most countries apart from Iran and Iraq. Though most people of both sides live peacefully together and intermarry, at times rivalry and warfare break out between them, as has happened in the 2010s in Iraq and Syria. Terrorist groups Al Qaeda and ISIS are Sunni militants who reject liberal Muslims and Shi'ites as apostates.

Religious divisions continue to be a major source of instability in the world. However, the counter movement is of interfaith and multi-faith initiatives and dialogue societies, which seek to bring mutual understanding between religious communities, to build bridges between them – often by involvement in common projects – and to develop social harmony. There is a sizeable network of such groups across the UK and they are important adjuncts to multiculturalism, which was discussed in chapter 6.

Religion and Disadvantage

Although Islamophobia predates it, the destruction of the twin towers in New York on 11 September 2001 had profound effects on attitudes towards Muslims in America and Europe, as did the bomb attacks on British transport on 7 July 2005. Gallup polls showed high degrees of prejudice against and fear of Muslims among American citizens. The British Social Attitudes Survey of 2010 revealed that the British public had much more negative views of Muslims than of any other religious group. Only 25 per cent of people surveyed took a positive stance towards them, and the majority stated that it would be a matter of concern to them if a mosque was built in their neighbourhood.

Islamophobia is not just displayed in attitudes but in aggressive and violent behaviour towards individual Muslims. Chris Allen and Jorgen Neilsen published a report in 2002 for the European Monitoring Centre on Racism and Xenophobia, based on incidents in a number of EU member states. The report documented a range of incidents such as verbal abuse, spitting on Muslims in the street, tearing off women's headscarfs (hijabs), and varied physical assaults – some requiring hospital treatment. The report also highlighted negative portrayals of Muslims in the media. Certainly, TV thrillers such as the popular *Spooks* consistently present young Muslim men as terrorists and suicide bombers, while coverage of incidents in the British popular press helps to whip up public alarm and distrust of women wearing Islamic dress and men with beards and prayer caps.

It is a sad fact that religious passions have, through the ages, led to wars, killings, torture and rape, and that such hatred still persists in too many contexts today. Hate crimes are still mainly related to religious difference, though they also spring from racism, homophobia and sexism.

Apart from hostility and hate crimes, religious minorities may face discrimination in housing, education and, especially, employment, which is often closely linked to ethnicity (in the case of British Muslims who are largely non-white) or to class (in the case already mentioned, for example, of the sectarian splits in Northern Ireland).

It is not only Catholics in Northern Ireland who are poor. However, a study by Knox (Borooah and Knox 2014) of neighbourhood renewal areas (which have been identified by the government as deprived and in need of substantial investment) revealed that Catholics were over-represented among them. Knox found that sixteen of the twenty poorest neighbourhoods were Catholic. People living in these areas are more likely to be unemployed, or living on disability benefits, and live less long, compared to their more affluent neighbours. Their children do less well at school and crime rates are twice as high (2014). Any visitor to Belfast will sense the hostility between the faith communities, symbolized by the existence of a fence which, unlike the Berlin Wall, has not been demolished.

Britain's largest Muslim groups are Pakistanis and Bangladeshis, with smaller groups of Somalis and North Africans, although these latter are not sizeable enough to figure in surveys. In countries like Norway, who also have Somali migrants, these are very disadvantaged, and North Africans are placed at the bottom of the hierarchy in France and other Mediterranean countries; it is not likely that these

Muslim groups fare significantly better in the UK. However, we have plenty of evidence about the disadvantaged position of Pakistanis and Bangladeshis. They have among the highest unemployment rates for men, along with some Black groups (16 per cent for Pakistanis and 21 per cent for Bangladeshis in 2000), and a shocking 30 per cent for women; and they are particularly likely to be found in low-paid manual work, despite the fact that young Pakistanis and Bangladeshis stay on in education longer than other ethnic groups (Mason 2003; Modood 2003). Consequently, they have much lower incomes than the other main ethnic groups (Nazroo 2003). As wives are less likely to work, this means considerable danger of family poverty affecting the children. Moreover, they are likely to live in deprived areas in overcrowded rented accommodation.

It might be objected that all this is an effect of ethnicity and class origin, rather than religious discrimination, and certainly we should take an intersectional approach to understanding the position of these groups. But I would argue that there is a strong element of Islamophobia here which compounds the disadvantages of ethnicity and class. Here the point may be the visibility of affiliation to Islam, displayed in Islamic dress, particularly the wearing of hijab by women. This alerts interviewers to the faith identity of job applicants and brings into play the Islamophobic judgements of Muslims as incompatible with English culture. As part of a project on Black and Minority Ethnic women carried out for the Equal Opportunities Commission (EOC) in 2006–7, we spoke to two young women who had been to apply for jobs together. One wore very Westernized clothes, the other Islamic dress, including the hijab. They told us how the one in Western dress gained interviews, while the other was constantly rejected. Other women we spoke to for this project told us how difficult they found it to integrate into the social life of British workplaces. Social life often surrounds drinking alcohol, forbidden by Islam. Foodstuffs on offer often breached Islamic dietary rules (the prohibition on pork products). The requirement for a quiet place to pray caused difficulties and they were pestered with questions about fasting in Ramadan (Bradley et al. 2007). Yet the equality legislation requires employers in the public sector to consider these needs, and even private-sector firms often have comprehensive equality and diversity policies (as did the companies studied for this project). The Muslim women were particularly shocked by the ignorance about Islam displayed by their workmates – a common finding, as demonstrated in the comment by Muslim Labour peer Baroness Uddin: 'There is not a day that we do not have to face comments so ignorant that even Enoch Powell would not have made them' (quoted Meer 2014, p. 70).

Religious Affiliation and Identity

It is this kind of everyday experience of being different – indeed, of being made to feel the alien and unwelcome 'Other' – that lies behind the processes of identification discussed throughout this chapter. Minority religious affiliation, then, is, like disability and non-hetero-sexual orientation, likely to promote strong and active identities. These are strengthened not only by discrimination and repression but by the fact that a sense of belonging is developed through the common practices of a faith community, especially attendance at places of worship. Religious affiliation is also often marked out by symbolic features of dress and appearance: the Sikh turban, the Jewish ringlets and yarmulke (prayer cap) or the Muslim hijab or niqab (full veil).

This sense of identity may also be strengthened by living in close proximity with other members of the community. The notion of the religious ghetto carries a nasty resonance from the Holocaust and anybody who has visited the rather grim original ghetto in Venice may feel that being penned off in an enclave away from the rest of a city is not a good idea. Equally shocking to me was a visit to the fence in Belfast which still segregates the Catholic estates from Protestant areas of the city. Yet this residential separateness may be chosen as well as forced upon people, and can act as support against the ignorance and prejudice of the majority. Thus, Jews in London tend to cluster around Golders Green, Bangladeshi Muslims in Tower Hamlets. This gives them easy access to synagogues and mosques, to shops and restaurants with approved halal food, and to clubs and social spaces where they can meet with fellow religionists. Even if these areas may often appear deprived to outsiders, they offer to minorities a sense of safety from persecution, along with a sense of fellowship.

An interesting feature of religious identities is that in some cases they appear to have strengthened over the last century, rather than weakened, despite the notion of secularization; or it may be that, like LGBT citizens, believers have gained more confidence to assert their difference. Certainly, in the post-war decades, when I grew up, it was most unusual to see Muslim women wearing the headscarf or Hindu and Muslim men wearing robes, and many Jewish and Muslim people appeared to have accepted the ideas of the integrationist position – discussed in chapter 6 – that they should adopt mainstream British values and practices. Most Jewish people I knew at the time were secular, or at least liberal, and rejected the rules of Jewish orthodoxy concerning food preparation, diet and dress, and particularly the injunction about not working on the Sabbath (Saturday).

However, many of the succeeding generation of younger people have chosen to return to more orthodox modes of expressing their religious identities and to affirm these as central to their lives. This has been particularly the case with young Muslim men and women. We should emphasize that this is not primarily a matter of nationalism or ethnic identity; this generation identifies with the Islamic ummah, not – as their parents tended to do – as Pakistani or Bangladeshi. To criticisms by British feminists who see Islam as marked by patriarchal domination, young Muslim women will reply that Islam promotes equality of respect between the sexes and any patriarchalism is a hangover from feudalism and traditionalism within their countries of origin (Bullock 2002).

This has been a thorny issue within the feminist movement. Very many young Muslim women, unlike some of their mothers – and, indeed, in some cases against family resistance – have voluntarily adopted the Islamic dress code of covering hair and body when in public. They vigorously resist the idea that this has been forced upon them by men; it is not a result of male dominance but a willing display of their commitment to their faith. The problem, of course, is that in marking themselves out in this way they lay themselves open to Islamophobia and the resultant discrimination, as discussed above.

Of course, there are other young Muslim women who choose to wear Western clothing. This is important to grasp, as it highlights the diversity of ideas and practices within the Muslim communities, against the homogenizing rhetoric of Islamophobia. Indeed, there are certainly some who find the idea of hijab oppressive. There is an interesting account by an Iraqi university student from Mosul in Iraq, where ISIS is forcing people to adopt Islamic dress, including the full veil. Describing her distress at having to wear what she calls the 'ghastly black cloth', she writes:

> As women we must now also cover our faces – something I could never have imagined being imposed on me. We are no longer allowed to leave the house without a male guardian. Never in the history of Iraq have we had such draconian laws. I have stopped worrying about the air strikes against Isis ... All I am fixated on is this facecovering that haunts me even in my sleep (Ahmed 2014)

The situation for young men is rather different. They seem less set on displaying their faith through Islamic dress (men should wear loose clothing and always be covered from the navel to the knee), though a few of them do. But they are now particularly under scrutiny as potential terrorists, whereby fairly arbitrary signs, such as long beards, prayer caps or rucksacks, may trigger off nervous responses, causing them to be stopped and searched by the police. This also makes it difficult for them to find employment outside the ethnic economy. As a result, a small minority of young British Muslim men appear to have adopted the jihadi (holy warrior) identity, denouncing Western practices as decadent and immoral, and allying themselves to the mission of building a universal Islamic state under sharia law. A trickle of these young men have ended up in training camps in Pakistan or joined ISIS in Syria and Iraq. One such recruit to ISIS, Hamzah Parvez, posted a video calling young British Muslims to come to Iraq and join what he called 'the golden age of jihad'. He is quoted as saying that the UK was not a land for Muslims, that it killed Muslims every day and that others should give up 'eating Nandos every week' and come and work for Allah and the new state (*Guardian* 29 August 2014).

Parvez's statements are disturbing but they are indicative of the way in which angry Muslim youth may feel 'not at home' in British society and reject its consumerist materialism. The International Centre for the Study of Radicalization at King's College, London, which has been studying British and European fighters in Syria and Iraq, puts this down to exuberance of youth combined with misinformation and the influence of charismatic 'radical' leaders. Melanie Smith of the Centre has also been studying the online comments of twenty-one women who have gone to Syria to be 'jihadi brides'. Like their male counterparts, these young women seem alienated by the stress of living with negative attitudes to Muslims in Britain and to relish the adventure of living in an Islamic state (Khaleeli 2014).

Steve Fenton (2010) provides an interesting discussion of the spread of Islamic identification, which – as I do – he separates from purely ethnic identifications: 'the difference... is that, as a component of local ethnic identities, Islam also connects people to a global identification' (p. 223). He describes Islamic identification as a contestatory challenge to 'the West' and Westernization (see chapter 6), and as providing a clustering of like-minded states as an alternative to the 'West' or the former Soviet-bloc countries; and also as a resistance by some of the poor of the world to their economic and cultural exclusion and disenfranchisement. He gives as an example of the latter the strong Islamic identification of the rural poor in Malaysia, 'whose sense of not being incorporated in the modern wealthy Malaysia is expressed more by Islamic enthusiasm than by Malay ethnicity, although both are involved' (p. 223).

A crucial part of this movement, which has also been called Political Islam, is a counter-ideology opposed to Islamophobia, which posits

Islam and its believers as more moral and more civilized than the Global North (Modood 2007). This is exemplified by this statement about the dress code on a Muslim website

> Islam teaches that the consequences of immodesty fall not only on the individual but also upon the society that permits women and men to mingle freely, display themselves, and compete or allure one another through sexual attraction. These consequences are significant and cannot be ignored. To make women into sex objects for the pleasure of men is not liberation. In fact, it is a dehumanizing form of oppression rejected by Islam. The liberation of the Muslim woman is that she is recognized by the content of her character rather than by the display of her physical attributes. From the Islamic point of view, 'liberated' Western women – who must often worry about their looks, figure, and youth for the pleasure of others – are trapped in a form of slavery. (Masjid al-Muslimiin website, Columbia USA)

Conclusions

In this chapter I have argued that disability, LGBT sexualities and membership of religious minorities tend to promote active and politicized identities. This relates in part to the experiences of prejudice, marginalization and repression which make people extremely aware of these identities. People with physical and mental impairments are among the most vulnerable in society and often highly dependent on state or family welfare support for their subsistence. Cuts in welfare, such as were imposed after the 2008 recession, affect them disproportionately. LGBT and religious minorities are often negatively viewed and are subject to hate crimes, including assault, rape and murder.

Because of persecution, these social groups have tended to develop their own supportive and defensive organizations and communities. This is particularly the case with LGBT identifiers: as their numbers include many people from highly paid professional backgrounds, they have been able to use the 'pink pound' to develop distinctive processes of consumption in urban environments, although those in isolated areas of the country may be unable to participate. People with impairments are helped by various self-support groups and charities, while attendance at churches, mosques, temples and synagogues binds people into their faith communities.

In processes of identification, these stigmatized but active sources of identity interact with the other, possibly less active, dynamics of class, gender, ethnicity and age. A few examples are offered here. In relation to class: members of religious minorities are frequently excluded from opportunities offered to the majority and pushed into the lower strata of the occupational hierarchy, so that disadvantages springing from religious affiilation are compounded by class. Yvette Taylor's study of working-class lesbians in Scotland (2007) showed that they lacked the resources – economic, social and cultural – to participate in LGBT spaces, leading Taylor to assert that they were effectively excluded from assertive 'queerness' and that only moneyed people could access the 'gay scenes' mentioned above in the big cities. LGBT people in rural areas are particularly isolated.

In relation to gender: Islamophobia acts differently upon male and female Muslims, who are also separated by rules of sex segregation in many Muslim nations. Lesbians have commonly complained about the dominance of men in the leadership of the rights movement. In relation to ethnicity: LGBT people of African descent are particularly vilified by their societies, and in some places are in great danger of being imprisoned and murdered. Richardson and Monro suggest that the cultural expressions of gayness and lesbianism developed in the Global North may not map across easily to the Global South. In relation to age: young gays and lesbians face particular problems of bullying and exclusion by classmates, and may find it particularly difficult to face coming out. A heartening development, however, is that in 2014 Stonewall gave top marks to six universities in an assessment of 'gay friendliness', up from only two the preceding year. Most religions have youth groups and educational facilities, such as Sunday schools, which instruct young people into beliefs and practices which heighten their identification.

Like many other trade unions, my own union, the University and College Union (UCU), has four standing committees for equality groups (gender, 'race', disability and LGBT) which hold their own meetings and conferences. Some UCU members claim identification with all four groups. An intersectional perspective is thus highly relevant to the analysis of these dynamics of disadvantage.

The forms of disadvantage discussed in this chapter can in no way be reduced to economic differentiation – although they may have economic implications – but arise from processes of social and cultural interaction. While I have argued that, in the twenty-first century, disability, non-heterosexual orientation and minority religious membership are the basis for particularly extreme cases of prejudice and discrimination, the chapter also offers a positive message: vigorous, determined and visible political action can serve greatly to enhance the position of socially disadvantaged groups.

Further Reading

There is a useful chapter in *Social Divisions* (ed. Geoff Payne, Macmillan, 2000), on disability. There are a number of introductory texts by leading experts in the field: Colin Barnes and Geoff Mercer, *Disability* (Polity, 2002); Tom Shakespeare, *Disability Rights and Wrongs* (Routledge, 2013), and Colin Barnes, *Exploring Disability* (Polity, 2010). Although written some time ago, Jeff Weeks, *Sexuality* (Tavistock, 1986), remains an excellent guide to the topic. Newer texts are Stevi Jackson and Sue Scott, *Theorizing Sexuality* (Open University Press, 2010); Nikki Sullivan, *A Critical Introduction to Queer Theory* (Edinburgh University Press, 2003); and Diane Richardson and Surya Monro, *Sexuality, Equality and Diversity* (Palgrave Macmillan, 2012). Tariq Modood's *Multiculturalism* includes useful discussion of the debates between Islam and the West (Polity, 2007). Rodney Stark and Katie Corcoran, *Religious Hostility* (ISR Books, 2014), provides a picture of religious conflicts in the contemporary world.

Thinking Points

- What factors promote the emergence of politicized identities?
- Why are religious minorities and LGBT identifiers so subject to hate crimes?

9

Conclusion
Fractured Identities: Processes of Fragmentation and Polarization in Globalizing Capitalist Societies

Everything fleeting, and nothing stable, everything shifting and changing and nothing substantial.
(George Lippard, *The Quaker City*, 1845)

It was impossible, situated as we were, not to imbibe the idea
that everything in nature and human existence was fluid,
or fastly becoming so.
(Nathaniel Hawthorne, *The Blithedale Romance*, 1852)

These fragments I have shored against my ruins.
(T. S. Eliot, *The Waste Land*, 1992)

In this book I have considered class, gender, ethnicity, age, disability, sexual orientation and religious affiliation both as social categories – constructs we employ to think about processes of social differentiation – and as lived relations to which they refer. Such lived relations are real sociological phenomena in the Durkheimian sense: they exist outside of us as individuals, they put constraints upon us, they affect our life-chances. Each can be viewed as a different type of social location (Mannheim 1952) or different set of social arrangements. Although they are all involved with each other, I have suggested that we can identify for each a distinct 'existential location'. All these lived relations involve differential access to power and resources and are therefore aspects not only of social differentiation but also of social inequality. They merge together to form the complex hierarchies which are characteristic of contemporary societies.

In the first edition of this book, the focus was very strongly on the notions of fragmentation and fracturing, which reflected the mood of the time (the 1990s). The postmodern and post-structural critique of modernism, which has been reviewed throughout the book, was rather fashionable and dominant within sociology and the other social science disciplines. To reprise the debate, modernist approaches, deriving from the classical sociological theories of industrial and capitalist development, or from modified versions or adaptations of them, presented class, gender, 'race' and age as persisting materially based structures of inequality which are integral features of the construction of society. Post-structuralists viewed them as discursive constructs, contingent upon the particular sets of discourses in which they are embedded, and upon specific cultural and historical events which form their context. Consequently, they are fluid and variable. Postmodernist work also highlighted the way processes of cultural change have eroded and destabilized long-standing relationships to create a more fragmented and individualized society. These approaches stress difference and diversity.

However two decades later, the situation appears somewhat different. While in this book I have highlighted differences and divisions within the categories of inequality, the major focus of social criticism in the twenty-first century appears to lie on increasing inequalities, the polarization between the rich and poor, the advantaged and disadvantaged. Class has re-emerged as a major topic of study in sociology. In the context of the widespread adoption of neoliberal principles (the primacy of the market, deregulation of capital, removal of protections for employees, privatization of public institutions, the erosion of welfarism) and of the austerity policies adopted in response to the world recession of 2008, it is polarization rather than fragmentation that draws our attention. However, as I argued in the previous edition, such polarization can be documented and yet be seen to be coexisting with fragmentation.

In this final chapter, I start by setting out three different possible strategies for understanding social inequalities, all of which have their adherents. I then consider the frameworks which may explain why social fragmentation remains a key feature of modern societies. I follow this with discussion of current processes of polarization and a plea that our sociological preoccupation with difference and diversity does not lead us to neglect what remains arguably the most crucial structuring principle in our society: the inequalities deriving from divisions of class.

Understanding Inequalities

I suggest we can distinguish three possible approaches to thinking about inequalities and social divisions, which have evolved as a result of the dialogue between modernists and their post-structural critics:

1 Acceptance of Lyotard's dictum that local narratives must replace grand narratives. Totalizing theories of inequality are rejected as essentialist and distortive. This leads to study of particular manifestations of inequality in very specific contexts, to the tracing of the history of such manifestations in these contexts, or to the study of particular discourses or language games which are implicated in inequalities.

2 While accepting local variations and internal divisions, an affirmation that these exist within the framework of powerful and controlling unitary tendencies, notably that of the globalization of capital. This strategy was adopted by some people espousing a postmodern stance such as Harvey and Jameson, who emphasized the structuring power of globalization. Arif Dirlik argued that a focus on difference serves to disguise 'the power relations that shape a seemingly shapeless world' and the way in which 'totalizing structures persist in the midst of apparent disintegration and fluidity' (1994, pp. 355–6). This approach counters post-structuralism with a renewed metanarrative, that of a capitalist globalization, and – we should add from a 21st-century perspective – of neoliberalism in ascendance.

3 A suggestion that previous modernist theories were largely flawed because of the failure to appreciate the way that different dynamics of inequality intersect. Thus, rather than abandoning modernist theories, the aim should be to provide better versions of them (Holmwood 1994; Marshall 1994). As Walby argued, most existing accounts have been able to accommodate only two, at the most, of the dimensions of 'race', class and gender. The now popular notion of intersectionality, influenced by the thinking of Crenshaw, is seen as a way to address this problem, and has been increasingly utilized by sociologists of gender and ethnicity. It is not necessarily easy to develop general theories using intersectionality because of the multi-dimensional nature of inequalities which has been discussed in this book. Thus, an intersectional approach tends to focus on specific contexts in which intersections can be explored, and to favour empirical explorations to generate local narratives.

Which of these three options offers the best understanding of social inequalities? My argument has been that fragmentation coexists with polarization, the local with the global. As Maynard argues, 'it is not necessary to abandon categories such as woman...in order to recognize that they are internally differentiated' (Maynard 1994, p. 22). The first strategy, then, will not do on its own. It needs to be supplemented by some account of general and unifying tendencies as in the second strategic option. The problem is that such accounts often slip back towards the traditional 'one-sided story' (Marshall 1994, p. 6) of social development, in which the power of global capital seems so formidable that other aspects of inequality become subordinated to it. In this sense, the third position can offer a corrective. As Giddens states: 'It has become commonplace to claim that modernity fragments, dissociates...Yet the unifying features of modern institutions are just as central to modernity...as the disaggregating ones' (1991, p. 27).

Fragmentation and Intersectionality

'If the seventies were dominated by the exhilaration of discovering and naming ourselves as women, bound together in sisterhood, the eighties have been dominated by the discovery and definition of our differences as women' (Musil, quoted in Yuval-Davis 1993, p. 4). Musil's comment epitomizes the shift in feminist analysis that occurred in the 1980s, and the general tendency in sociology to emphasize diversity and fragmentation. The notion of fragmentation is not new. Indeed, the quotations at the top of this chapter suggest it has been a continual theme ever since humans conceived the idea of 'modern society'. But at the end of the twentieth century it became something of an obsession within stratification theory and it also had a major impact on social policy; the terminology of 'Equal Opportunities' was replaced by 'Equality and Diversity'. Yet the fusion of the separate Commissions dealing with gender, race relations and disability to form the Equality and Human Rights Commission is also symbolic of the tension that exists between differentiation and unity identified in the quotation from Giddens.

It is worth exploring in a little more detail the processes that lie behind our experiences of fragmentation. Here I distinguish four different forces which are at play.

1 *Internal fragmentation,* or fragmentation occurring within a collectivity as a result of tendencies inherent within it. For example,

if classes are seen to be groups sharing a common relationship to processes of production, consumption and distribution, such as occupational groups, it is possible to subdivide these internally on the basis of more minutely specified shared characteristics: the working class can be split into unskilled, semi-skilled and skilled sections, and so on.

Many examples of internal fragmentation have been touched on in preceding chapters. Weberian class analysis has always made the issue of fragmentation central, as opposed to the Marxist stress on unifying tendencies (see p. 77). As discussed in chapter 3, in contemporary class analysis both the working- and middle-class groupings can be seen as fragmenting. Racial and ethnic categories, too, are subject to splitting. We have seen how the original formulation of 'Black' as a way of characterizing race relations has given way to a recognition of the different social locations of different ethnic groups. Newer categories such as 'African-Caribbean' are themselves liable to fragmentation, where the primary identification is made to a specific island of origin. The former Soviet Union provides another prime example of ethnic fragmentation. The arbitrary nature of age-group boundaries means that new internal boundaries could easily be drawn. For example, we have noted the division between the 'old old' and 'young old' which is made by gerontologists, and also by elderly people themselves. Other broad age groups could be divided in a similar fashion. Finally, the logic of relations of sexuality and reproduction, crucial aspects of gender differentiation, allows for fragmentation of genders on the basis of heterosexual, homosexual, bisexual and transgender orientation and also by reproduction status: whether people are married, single, have children or not. These distinctions bring divergences of preoccupations and interests.

2 *Fragmentation as a result of general processes of social change*
Classes can be said to be fragmenting when a particular class formation goes through processes of decomposition as a result of economic change. For example, Esping-Andersen (1993) is implicitly employing such a framework in his account of how old classes are collapsing and new ones coming to replace them with the shift to a post-industrial economy. This form of fragmentation should be a temporary one, as decomposition will eventually be followed by recomposition: new classes are formed. But since processes of social change are habitually slow, piecemeal and uneven, the period of fragmentation may be prolonged.

The notions of decomposition and recomposition have been less explicitly employed in relation to ethnicity, gender and age. However, the upheavals in Europe in the 1980s and 1990s (caused partly by the break-up of the Soviet Union, partly by the formation of the EC and partly by the influx of refugees because of famine and warfare around the globe) could be seen as an example of the decomposition and recomposition of established racial and ethnic hierarchies. New migrant groups may form the basis of new settler communities, while older groups face expulsion. Global interchange may also lead to shifts in the nature of gendered roles as traditional practices are challenged – while medical advances may lead to changes such as the phenomenon of the ageing population, which we have seen to impact on the fortunes of older people.

3 *Intersectionality,* which arises from the interaction of the various dynamics. Thus, classes are divided by gender, age, ethnicity, region and so forth. Processes of intersectionality have been highlighted constantly through this study and have been presented as of crucial importance. My strategy in the book has been to show how two of the dynamics under discussion interact with each other. Of course, in any given concrete situation numerous dynamics are at play. For example, Wilson's account of the ghetto underclass shows not only how forces of class and 'race' combine to push African Americans into unemployment and social disorganization, but also how age and gender come into play as young Black men demonstrate their virility through sexual predation and street violence.

It is still an issue whether we should seek to uncover systematic ways in which dynamics of stratification interact, to search for a 'unified' system, or whether we should follow Brah's prescription that relations between them are best viewed as 'historically contingent and context-specific' (1993, p. 14). Knowles and Mercer (1992) contend there is no general relationship between 'race' and gender and that we should approach particular instances through case studies. In this book, while arguing that each dynamic has a logic derived from its existential base, I have presented intersections within particular contexts. My own view is that the search for a unified system is not fruitful; but I believe we can uncover *characteristic* patterns in the way the elements inter-relate, sufficient to merit the formulation of sociological generalizations. Indeed, I consider this a central task for stratification theorists in the future.

4 *Fragmentation as a synonym for individuation* In this scenario, collective and communal ties and identities in society are seen to be dissolving with the rise of individualism and consumer culture.

'There is no such thing as society', declared Margaret Thatcher, famously. Of course no sociologist could accept such a statement! But there are many different ways of conceptualizing society, one of which is that it is made up of self-interested, atomized individuals. The view that the progress of industrial development fosters greater individualization and breaks up social collectivities is a longstanding one. It lay behind many modernist theories, such as Tonnies's account of the switch from *Gemeinschaft* to *Gesellschaft*, or Durkheim's characterization of industrial societies as based on organic rather than mechanical solidarity. The theme was taken up by postmodernists, who emphasized the importance of consumer choices and the cult of individualized lifestyles. However, such views rest on extrapolation from individual definitions of personal identity. As Marshall et al. (1988) suggested in reference to class consciousness, individualistic and collectivistic meanings and impulses coexist.

Polarization and Power

Since the 1960s, class analysis has been preoccupied with issues of fragmentation when considering both the working and middle classes. But when the capitalist class is brought into consideration, a contrary theme, that of polarization, emerges. Polarization is a term used by Marxists to indicate a concentration of individuals at both ends (poles) of the class spectrum, accompanied by widening differences in the fate of those at the top and bottom. Such 'immiseration' implies increased inequality between the dominant and subordinate classes. Here I argue that, in the 2010s, social polarization has emerged as a major trend. Neoliberal policies have created a world in which the wealthy enjoy ever more luxurious lifestyles, from which a large section of the population are excluded, and social power becomes ever more concentrated in the hands of the few. Polarization in the twenty-first century, however, is not just a matter of class disparity as in the Marxist version: disadvantages caused by gender, age, ethnicity, disability and religion are all implicated in the polarizing tendencies.

'Give a man a gun and he can rob a bank. Give a man a bank and he can rob us all.' This slogan, which I saw on the back of a van I was following, is a pithy contemporary and very topical version of the old saying, 'there's one law for the rich and one for the poor' (as well as reflecting the popular dislike of bankers whose actions triggered the 2008 recession). In the contemporary context, poor people, especially aggrieved young men from disadvantaged class and ethnic backgrounds, may take to crime, including gun crime, to supplement meagre family incomes and buy the consumer goods they need or want. Mothers in poverty may shoplift to feed their children, and a few welfare claimants may earn money 'off the books'.

By contrast, it can be argued that the capitalist system, which is currently pushing down wages in what has been termed 'a race to the bottom', and taking massive profits which are passed on as huge incomes and bonuses to elite managers and to investors, is a kind of legalized robbery. Members of the ruling class and huge corporations like Amazon and Google can use their money and power to indulge in tax avoidance, aided by skilled lawyers and accountants. Financial scandals have been rife in the twenty-first century. Formula One racing supremo Bernie Ecclestone, threatened with a jail sentence for corruption and bribery, paid the German state £60 million to avoid prosecution: it could be argued that he in effect bribed his way to avoid conviction for bribery! Even Christine Lagarde, head of the International Monetary Fund, has been investigated for financial malpractice.

Likewise, while bailiffs come round to impound furniture and electrical appliances from the homes of the poor who fall behind with their bills, when the Royal Bank of Scotland faced financial crisis in 2008, the UK government used taxpayers' money to bail it out. But the public gained nothing from this, and the bankers continued to pay bonuses to themselves and their favoured employees on top of big salaries (the bonuses received by women, interestingly, are smaller). A young economics graduate fresh from the University of Bristol, interviewed for a project on graduate employment, reported being paid £90,000 per annum by a merchant bank one year out of his degree, over twice as much as most of those who tutored him, and more than I have ever earned as a professor with two degrees and a Ph.D.! Meanwhile, benefit claimants who fail to turn up for an appointment at the Job Centre have their benefits stopped, leaving them to starve and freeze. In such circumstances, suicides among the unemployed are rising.

Contemporary critic Owen Jones sums up this situation very nicely, using the idea of the 'establishment' to explain how the elite class run Britain and apparently manipulate the rest of us into accepting this status quo:

The establishment includes politicians who make laws; media barons who set the terms of the debate; businesses and financiers who run the economy; police forces that enforce a law that is rigged in favour of the powerful... It is unified by a common mentality, which holds that those at the top deserve their power and their ever-growing fortunes, and which might be summed up by the advertising slogan 'because I'm worth it'. This is the mentality that has driven politicians to pilfer expenses, businesses to avoid tax, and City bankers to demand ever bigger bonuses while plunging the world into economic disaster. All these things are facilitated by laws that are geared to cracking down on the smallest misdemeanours committed by those at the bottom of the pecking order, for example benefit fraud. 'One rule for us, one rule for everybody else' might be another way to sum up establishment thinking. (Jones 2014a)

These different sets of rules and resources – that is, differentials in power and status – lie behind the patterns of inequality we have explored in this book. As Jones argues, these are justified by the ideology of neoliberalism, with its cult of the 'free' market, its advocacy of privatization accompanied by reduced taxation, and its hostility to collective bodies such as trade unions that oppose the status quo. This ideology, which works against the real interests of the majority of people in society, is sold to you and me under the guise of freedom and the rights of the individual. Polarization is justified by those on top by appeal to the fourth variant of fragmentation, individualism: we all have a chance to win, but some of us are not clever or hard-working enough to do so! I have argued in the preceding chapters that, in the twenty-first century, governments committed to neoliberal economic ideas have pursued austerity policies which have created a widening of the already massive gap between the privileged and the disadvantaged classes in the societies of the Global North. In this era, women, ethnic minorities, the young, the old, the disabled have been the losers, and the international super-rich and national elite classes have been the winners, and the beneficiaries of other people's suffering.

This polarization is not confined to the more developed nations, but is a worldwide trend. According to Naomi Klein (2014), worldwide, the top 3 per cent of the population controls 55 per cent of all wealth, up from 45 per cent in 1989, the result of a quarter of a century of deregulated capital. For example, Burke (2014) reports on India's super-rich class: a survey sponsored by the Kotak Mahindra Bank, which was based on interviews with 150 individuals of high net worth stated that the rich class would quadruple their wealth in the next four years, with a massive increase in the number of people worth £2.2 million. This group already holds assets of $1 trillion, about one-fifth of the country's total wealth. The report described the luxurious lifestyle of these people, with their fabulous mansions, spectacular parties and appetite for expensive foreign cars, such as

Mercedes and Lamborghinis. A wedding of a member of the Mittal family, whose wealth comes from internationally based steel production, cost some £47 million, with hundreds of guests flown to Barcelona to take part in the three-day celebration. Yet in the Mittals' country, the rural poor live in basic mud houses with dirt floors amid streets strewn with rubbish.

Former communist countries have also taken the path of mushrooming inequalities. The penchant of multi-millionaire Russians for taking over football clubs is well known. Where once the Bolsheviks overthrew the aristocracy, a new class of plutocrats has arisen in Vladimir Putin's Russia, taking advantage of globalization and the introduction of market principles. Danny Dorling, author of many studies of inequality, reveals that there are over 2,000 Russian millionaires living in London, attracted by the UK's low levels of tax (Dorling 2014). In China, too, research has revealed increasing inequality: the poorest quarter of the population control only 1 per cent of the wealth, despite the growing affluence of their society. The Gini coefficent, which represents the range from absolute equality at 0 to absolute inequality at 1, rose in China over two decades from 0.45 to 0.73 (Kaiman 2014). This is an interesting argument against the commonly cited 'trickle-down' theory used to justify tax cuts and other concessions to the wealthy, on the grounds that if they thrive, everyone else will too. The trickle-down myth is also refuted by the ONS statistics for the UK for 2014, which revealed that, while bonuses rose by 5 per cent, wages fell by 0.2 per cent and the cost of living increased by 1.9 per cent. Net result: the average family, especially those on benefits, in self-employment, on zero-hours contracts or in public-sector employment, saw their living standards fall, while the rich rejoiced at the 'recovery' from the recession.

Another major form of economic polarization has historically been that between the Global North and the Global South, the growing gap between the rich and poor nations, which continues to be a striking feature of the contemporary world order. The less-developed societies of Africa, and to a lesser extent those of South America and some parts of Asia, have struggled to keep going in the face of famine, natural disasters, internal conflicts and debt. The UNICEF Annual Report for 1994 estimated that the poorest forty or fifty countries had experienced a substantial decline in their share of world income: one-fifth of the world's people shared less than 1.5 per cent of world income (Brittain 1994). Some 1 billion people were surviving on less than a dollar a day. At the same time, there is a dramatic discrepancy within those countries between the relative affluence of the economic and political elites who share in the lifestyle of the West and the condition of the peasantry and the industrial poor, as in the cases of China and India mentioned above.

These tendencies must be seen in the context of a feature which has been emphasized throughout this book: the ever-increasing power and reach of globalizing capital. The economic as well as the cultural dimensions of this power are encapsulated in an evocative comment from Japanese writer Harumi Murakami, when he describes 'the massive capital web' in his novel *Dance, Dance, Dance*:

> Everything before is nothing compared to the exacting detail and sheer power and invulnerability of today's web of capitalism. And it is mega-computers that have made it all possible, with their inhuman capacity to pull together every last factor and condition on the face of the earth into their net calculations. Advanced capitalism has transcended itself. Not to overstate things, financial dealings have practically become a religious activity...People worship capital, adore its aura, genuflect before Porsches and Tokyo land values. It's the only stuff of myth that's left in the world. (1994, p. 55)

It is easy to become hypnotized by this phenomenon and overlook the contribution of other aspects of inequality to deepening social divisions. While the term 'polarization' comes from class analysis, it can also be applied to ethnicity, age and gender. At the same time, the interaction of the four dynamics is displayed in concomitant tendencies for class polarization, arising from capital globalization, to display itself within ethnic and age groups and among women.

Two forms of ethnic polarization can be discerned. We have seen that ethnic divisions often coincide with the class divisions charac-teristic of post-industrial change, so that members of the groups at the bottom of each national ethnic hierarchy are over-represented among the poor and the labour surplus class. This has a specifically racial dimension, as people of African, Asian and Arabic origin, racialized on the basis of colour, are particularly affected in this way. A more broadly ethnic form of polarization can be seen emerging with the renaissance of nationalist and neo-fascist movements which set a mythologized 'native' population against all 'aliens' in the society.

Age polarization also seems to be an emergent trend. We have noted the potential for increased suspicion between young and old as age groups are more explicitly drawn into competition for scarce national resources, especially as globalization and economic restruc-turing are curbing economic opportunities for both young and old. After the rejection of independence for Scotland in the referendum of September 2014, young supporters of the 'yes' campaign blamed their defeat on the conservatism and timidity of the older generation who feared to take the risk of an uncertain economic future. A growing polarization among the elderly can also be discerned, as the experience of those affluent pensioners experiencing a 'golden age' of retirement diverges from that of the aged poor. Blakemore and Boneham comment: 'Social divisions among older people as a whole are widening...The uneven spread of occupational pension schemes and other changes are leading to increasing fragmentation and inequality. The frontiers of old age faced by black and Asian people involve possibilities of widening gaps between winners and losers' (1994, p. 141).

It may seem strange to talk about polarization between the sexes, as some progress towards equality was achieved in the second half of the twentieth century in many countries. However, the very gains made by women have provoked confrontation. It may not be too much of an exaggeration to speak of a 'sex war' (especially in America) as women prepare to defend their new privileges and men fight back to restore waning patriarchal dominance. Issues such as the increase in trafficking and grooming of children and young women as prostitutes, legal and definitional struggles around sexual harassment and 'date rape', the diminishing funding from the government for the facilities to support victims of domestic violence, the men's 'backlash' in the workplace against equal opportunities programmes which they see as bias towards women, are signs of conflicts around gender interests. The conditions of intensive modern motherhood, with the requirement for women to ferry children to after-school clubs, meet them at school gates and attend endless school activities, are hardly compatible with the long hours' culture typical of professional work, driving women into less prestigious jobs, part-time work or running micro-businesses – while managers, forever mindful of the 'bottom line', are reluctant to employ younger women because of having to pay them during maternity leave. A survey of managers carried out by a law firm, Slater and Gordon, revealed that 40 per cent were wary of employing women of childbearing age or who had children, or of appointing a mother to a senior post (*Guardian* 12 August 2014). At the same time, there is evidence of growing inequalities among women, as equal opportunities have helped some professional women to smash the 'glass ceiling', but do little to improve the prospects of low-paid women workers from working-class backgrounds. A report from Europe suggested that 'the price to be paid for a minority of women to achieve equality with men could be greater inequalities for those at the bottom of the ladder' (Commission of the European Communities (CEC) 1992a, p. 52).

I have suggested that the economic changes that spring from the global restructuring of the economy have effects on all four dynamics of stratification. These combine to produce growing disparities between privileged and underprivileged groups.

Contradictory Tendencies

At the beginning of this book, I suggested that a 'both/and' approach would be more fruitful than an 'either/or' one. I re-emphasize this now. The discussion above confirms the view that contemporary societies are both fragmented *and* subject to polarizing and unifying tendencies. This is reflected in the insight of Musil, who characterized the 1970s as a period where unity among women was identified, and the 1980s as marked by the recognition of diversity and differences of interest. But, she concluded, 'the challenge of the nineties is to hold on simultaneously to these two contradictory truths: as women, we are the same and we are different' (quoted in Yuval-Davis 1993, p. 4).

We should not underestimate the impact of postmodernism and post-structuralism. They certainly made a significant contribution to the major shift in the sociological analysis of social inequalities – discerned, for example, by Griffin in her account of youth studies: 'by the end of the 1980s many radical analyses were considering the intersections of "race", sex/gender, age, class and (less fully) dis/ability rather than the overwhelming focus on class relations which had characterized the radical texts of the 1970s' (1993, p. 55). But now we need to move beyond the critical deconstruction of classic stratification theories offered by postmodernism, returning to some of the key issues and themes of structural and materialist approaches. In this way, we may reach a better understanding of the *double and contradictory* nature of the dynamics of inequality, at once unifying and dividing.

I have suggested that an analysis of the polarizing tendencies of globalizing capitalism is needed. Rather than seeing this as 'disorganized', as do Lash and Urry, I see this as 'reorganized' through the implementation of neoliberal principles by governments in thrall to the interests of transnational corporations (Williams et al. 2013). Marx famously described the state as 'a committee for managing the affairs of the bourgeoisie'. Despite the prevalent parliamentary arrangements in contemporary states which are supposed to result in a balance of power and checks to despotism, in many countries the tendency has been for decision-making to be concentrated into the hands of government 'inner cabinets'. In Britain, this can be exemplified by the Conservative government, often described as a rule by millionaires (Cameron, Osborne and co.) for millionaires. The campaign for a yes vote in the Scottish referendum was fired by a rejection of an over-centralized government at Westminster. But even in countries with social democratic regimes, such as France or Sweden, the pressure of global capital has been hard to resist and similar policies have been introduced. For example, the Transatlantic Trade and Investment Partnership (TTIP) under negotiation between the EU and the United States will allow corporations to sue governments if they take actions seen to be detrimental to their business. Increasingly, transnational corporations (TNCs) are able to evade the legal controls of individual nation-states. The power of capital, as Murakami suggests, is formidable and growing.

Fractured Identities

As individuals, we stand at the points of intersection between all these processes of fragmentation and polarization. We are all exposed to the dynamics of class, gender, ethnicity and age, all of which are potential elements in our individual identities. But it has been argued in this book that there is no necessary relation between social location and identification; only in certain circumstances will passive identities become active or politicized. While some people may be galvanized into action by their experience of the injustices of 'race', gender or disability, many will struggle to understand their own feelings of confusion and displacement, falling back on the fragmenting rhetoric of individualism: 'We are all different.'

Postmodernists rightly emphasized that we function as active agents in the construction of our identities, rather than responding automatically to the dynamics that act upon us. But this is not exactly a matter of choice, as is sometimes implied. Few of us can, as yet, *choose* to be English, male and middle class if we were born Nigerian, female and working class, even though technologies of the future may make some of these changes possible. Identities are *not* free-floating. The lived relations in which each of us is located put constraints and limits upon the possible range of identifications, though within those limits we can work creatively with the potentialities at hand. Above all, as has been emphasized in preceding chapters, the construction of identity is a *political* process. It is framed by changing political movements, practices and discourses which promote awareness.

I would like to offer an example which illustrates the complexities of inequality and identity in the contemporary world, and the problems that result. While I was working on this book, the Jay Report was published, revealing that in Rotherham over several decades 14,000 children, many of them in the care system, had been subject to sexual abuse, while the responsible authorities had apparently turned a blind eye to what was happening. In the media there was a major debate as to whether this was largely a matter of class (as the young girls who were abused were vulnerable children from deprived backgrounds and the perpetrators of the crimes were largely poor working-class men) or of 'race' relations (as the girls were predominantly, though not exclusively, white, the men were mainly Pakistani, and the authorities were accused of ignoring what was going on because of racial sensitivities). But, of course, the answer is that it was about class *and* ethnicity, and also, markedly, about age and gender; to understand the situation, we need to employ an intersectional analysis.

As young feminists have pointed out, trafficking of young women and girls and abuse of girl children is a widespread global phenomenon, which is based on men's beliefs that they have a right to control women and to have access to their bodies. In 2014, a study by UNICEF revealed the massive extent of child sexual abuse. It found that 120 million girls under twenty had endured forced sexual acts; in about 60 per cent of the cases, they had been physically punished in addition. In the Rotherham case, there was clearly a class element; these girls from poor backgrounds were seduced by presents and money which it was difficult for them to resist, while combined disadvantages of class and ethnicity affected the Pakistani men, who are one of the most disadvantaged groups in the labour market. They are highly concentrated in two areas of employment: taxi driving and restaurant work. These jobs in turn drew them into the 'night-time economy' with its semi-legal activities and atmosphere of over-indulgence. Moreover, religion played a part: the Muslim men looked on these young women with contempt. Because of their dress, exposure of flesh, lifestyle and behaviour, they considered them immoral and contaminated already, so that the abuse was seen as deserved. Indeed, Western young women are often viewed in this way in more traditional countries where women are strictly controlled by their families; liberated young tourists are thus seen as 'easy game'. The sexual mores of the secularized Global North and of the Muslim world here come into conflict. Age is clearly a crucial factor, as well: because of their youth, when the children did try to complain about what was happening, they were disbelieved or ignored, and their powerlessness forced them to accept the ongoing abuse. This is common for victims of abuse: the UNICEF study found that half of the girls aged fifteen to nineteen had never told anybody about it. Thus, gender, class, ethnicity, age and religion came together to ruin the lives of the abused children.

As Ray Davies put it in his hit song *Lola*, it's a mixed-up, muddled-up, shook-up world that we all have to confront and negotiate. There is no going back to the homogeneity and simplicity of primitive tribal life. Haraway (1990) has used the image of the 'cyborg' – half-organism, half-machine – as a metaphor to point to the impossibility of separating what is 'natural' and what is 'social' in our make-up. The cyborg is the latest in a line of mythological hybrids, from mermaids and gorgons to Frankenstein's monster, which express society's concern with categorization and anxiety about phenomena that do not fit neatly into the existing sets of categories. Nationalist claims about the need for ethnic purity are a recent manifestation of this prevalent way of thinking. Haraway is right to challenge this kind of thinking, with its tendency to reduce identity to one single element rather than recognize its inevitable complexity. As the new theorists of ethnicity have stressed (Bhabha 1990a; Gilroy 1993), we are all hybrids and monsters now.

But how new *is* this? Can we speak of a new postmodern phase which has caused this fracturing of identities? Or is it the way we comprehend social reality that has changed? Are we dealing, in Bauman's terms, with a sociology of postmodernism or a postmodern sociology?

The answers must be tentative. People have always been subject to processes of economic differentiation, together with differences of ethnicity, gender and age. The potential for fracturing of identities has long existed. There is, however, a sense that fragmentation has increased in the past decades. Certainly, we are living in a period of rapid change. On the other hand, as has been argued in this book, there are clear continuities with the past. Capitalist industrialism has always been a dynamic and fluid system. As Davis points out, each generation of sociologists is inclined to consider itself as 'astride some major historical watershed': 'Sociological theory has indeed tended to conceptualize social change in terms of more or less clear-cut breaks of a fundamental nature...whereas the trend of change, whilst extensive and rapid enough in many senses, has nonetheless been essentially uneven, embodying leads, lags and continuities' (1990, p. 217).

The change, then, may be partly in our perceptions of society. Giddens (1991) has found one way to explain this in his assertion that a period he describes as 'late modernity' is characterized by a much higher degree of 'reflexivity' about ourselves and our place in society. This is superficially persuasive. It is eloquently exemplified in the anthem '1st Transmission' by British African-Caribbean band Earthling, in which the singer claims that while London is his city, Jamaica is his country and Africa is his history; he isn't who the audience thinks he is, and he is both Marcus Garvey and Harvey Keitel. The lyric playfully and with irony celebrates the elasticity of identity, proclaiming the singer's right to multiple self-definitions while resisting others' attempts to label him. However, the problem with Giddens's approach is that it makes some unsubstantiated assumptions about the behaviour of people in the past. Study of history will cast doubt on the view that our forebears were less sophisticated than ourselves. Study of the Victorians reveals their awareness of complexities and ambiguities (Houghton 1957). And if you want sophisticated understandings of psychological anxieties about identity or of the interactions and play between the sexes, look no further than the works of Shakespeare.

Nonetheless, the processes of globalization have, I believe, brought increasingly complex and sometimes confusing encounters between people of different genders, ethnicities and cultures and challenged existing practices of gender, age and class. One of the yes voters in the Scottish referendum was an Indian woman born in Britain, living in a civil partnership with a Scottish woman; she described her mixed-race son as 'Scottish, English, Indian and British, a rich and sometimes overpowering brew of an identity that so far no box has been big enough to contain' (Ramaswamy 2014). In some ways, such complexities enrich our lives; in other ways they present us with disturbing dilemmas and doubts about who we are.

What Is To Be Done? Final Thoughts

In a speech to the annual conference of the British Sociological Association, Steve Fuller argued that a key role for sociology was to help guide our society towards a better future. This, he argued, had been the objective of the early contributors to the discipline, such as Comte, Marx and Durkheim. I could not agree more, but it can be a daunting prospect. This final chapter has presented a sometimes bleak picture of the world we inhabit, dominated by the awesome power of global capital, widening gaps between the rich and the poor, and the apparently irresistible, if hardly uncontested, grip of neoliberal policies, which foster the power of wealthy elites who believe themselves entitled to their position of privilege. Terrible wars are destroying people's lives and livelihoods in Ukraine, Gaza, Iraq, Syria and parts of Africa, wars in which disadvantages of nationality/ethnicity, religion, class, gender and age are highly implicated and displayed. While hierarchies of class, ethnicity, gender, age, disability, sexuality and religion may be shifting and transforming, the polarization discussed in this chapter currently appears dominant. Above all, the economic divisions of class have been sharpened by globalism and neoliberalism. As many have pointed out, it is children in particular who suffer from the resultant poverty. A sad fact is that unhappiness among children in Britain appears to be on the increase. A report by the Children's Society rated Britain thirtieth out of thirty-nine Western countries on children's wellbeing. In particular, girls were unhappy about their appearance.

But it is not all gloom. Against the injustices explored in this book, many counter movements and counter ideologies have arisen and are still arising. Feminism is resurgent in the UK, energizing a new cohort of young women. The brave activists of feminist direct action group Pussy Riot have confronted the dictatorial power of President Putin in Russia. In China, a wave of strikes is manifesting the discontent of working people with the rising inequality mentioned above. In Spain and Greece, among other countries, young people have manifested their discontent with the way society and economy are being managed. In India, there have been massive demonstrations after a series of horrific rapes and murders of young women. Sporadic bursts of anti-capitalist activism have characterized the last two decades, such as the worldwide Occupy movement. Another important trend has been the use of social media and the internet to communicate and to campaign. Organizations like 38 degrees and Change.org use the potential of digital technology to remedy the democratic deficit. Where trade unions have remained strong, as in Sweden and Denmark, they are able to stand against the race to the bottom. For example, Chakraborty (2014) reports that in New York hotel cleaners are paid at the equivalent of £17.66 an hour, almost three times what a cleaner in London hotels could expect: the difference is that in New York 70 per cent of hotel workers are unionized as opposed to about 4 per cent in London

Indeed, as Dorling (2014) points out, growing inequality is in no way inevitable. He cites evidence that it is currently decreasing in several countries, such as Brazil, the Netherlands and Sweden. Indeed, all the Nordic countries show us that there are different ways of doing things. If you visit Norway or Finland, you, like me, will be struck by the lack of obvious display of wealth and conspicuous consumption; Nordic people still find this distasteful. In Latin America, too, countries experiment with alternatives. Costa Rica has no army, high taxes which go to support education and health, and some of the most progressive policies on rainforest conservation. It is also, along with its neighbor Panama, one of the countries that score highest on the happiness index (Britain does not do well on this index). In Uruguay, President Jose Mujica refuses to live in the presidential palace, preferring a modest smallholding, drives a 25-year-old Volkswagen Beetle and gives away 90 per cent of his salary, much of it to single mothers, according to Tremlett (2014). As sociologists, part of our duty must be to present these alternatives and argue for them.

To me, the referendum on Scottish independence has been one of the most fascinating events of 2014. On the face of it, it appeared to be a movement of fragmentation, the break-up of Britain; if Scotland broke away, Wales seemed likely to follow, and the disadvantaged parts of England, the North East, North West and Cornwall, might start to consider their futures. Nationalism has usually been considered a regressive force by sociologists, based as it often is on narrow ideas of ethnic belonging and exclusion, and having links to the kind of jingoism and imperialism associated with parties of the far right and Nazism. But the Scottish yes campaign was not simply of this kind; it appeared, rather, as a protest against polarization, the polarization of rich and poor, the privileged and the disadvantaged. The campaigners wanted to end the 'bedroom tax', to stop spending on nuclear weaponry and divert it to education and welfare, and to rescue the NHS from the onslaughts of privatization. Although the motives of people on both sides of the debate might have been differentiated, mixed and confused, what was at issue here was the thirst for a fairer, more just and equal society, the same impulse that has led the Trade Union Congress to campaign under the slogans 'Jobs, Growth and Fair Pay' and 'Britain Needs a Pay Rise'.

We live in a diverse and fractured world, but at the heart of complexity lies the longstanding struggle between capital and labour. As Zoe Williams (2014) recently argued, it was a mistake to think it was vanishing, and now it is back with a vengeance. It is not just left-wing politicians and radical sociologists who are disturbed about rising inequalities; concern has been displayed by the Organisation for Economic Cooperation and Development (OECD), the Pope and the Archbishop of Canterbury, and even the governor of the Bank of England. While everybody seems to feel rather powerless to change things, as the campaigning group 38 degrees emphasizes, people in unity *can* assert power. For those of us who care about social justice and inequality, the struggle continues. Williams describes it as being as 'elemental and timeless as a love story'. There is still a world to win.

Bibliography and Sources

Abercrombie, N. and Urry, J. 1983: *Capital, Labour and the Middle Classes*. London: Allen & Unwin.

Abercrombie, N. and Warde, A. 2000: *Contemporary British Society*. Cambridge: Polity.

Abrams, M. 1959: *The Teenage Consumer*. London: London Press Exchange.

Abrams, P. 1970: Rites de passage: the conflict of generations in industrial society. *Journal of Contemporary History*, 5(1), 175–90.

Abu Odeh, L. 1993: Post-colonial feminism and the veil: thinking the difference. *Feminist Review*, 43, 26–37.

Ackroyd, S. 2012: Economy, class, ideology and the transformation of the organizational field in Britain and the USA: a neo-Marxian view [keynote address presented to BSA Annual Conference, Leeds University, April].

Afshar, H. 1994: Muslim women in West Yorkshire. In H. Afshar and M. Maynard (eds.), *The Dynamics of 'Race' and Gender*. London: Taylor & Francis, 127–47.

Afshar, H. and Maynard, M. (eds.) 1994: *The Dynamics of 'Race' and Gender*. London: Taylor & Francis.

Age Concern 2008: *Older People in the United Kingdom: Facts and Statistics*. London: Age Concern.

Age UK 2014: *Later Life in the UK*. London: Age UK.

Ahmed, L. 2014: What terror feels like. *The Guardian* 30 August.

Allan, C. 2014: Focus on historical sexual abuse ignores today's harsh mental health cuts. *The Guardian* 6 August.

Allatt, P., Keil, T., Bryman, A. and Bytheway, B. (eds.) 1987: *Women and the Life Cycle*. London: Macmillan.

Allen, C. 2010: *Islamophobia*. Farnham: Ashgate.

Allen, C. and Neilsen, J. 2002. *Summary Report on Islamophobia in the EU15 after 11 September 2001*. Vienna: European Monitoring Centre on Racism and Xenophobia.

Allen, S. 1994: Race, ethnicity and nationality: some questions of identity. In H. Afshar and M. Maynard (eds.), *The Dynamics of 'Race' and Gender*. London: Taylor & Francis, 85–105.

Allen, S. and Macey, M. 1990: Race and ethnicity in the European context. *British Journal of Sociology*, 41(3), 375–93.

Allen, S. and Wolkowitz, C. 1987: *Homeworking: Myths and Realities*. London: Macmillan.

Amos, V. and Parmar, P. 1984: Challenging imperial feminism. *Feminist Review*, 17, 3–18.

Anderson, B. 1991: *Imagined Communities* (2nd edn). London: Verso.

Anderson, B. 1994: Exodus. *Critical Enquiry*, 20, 314–27.

Anderson, E. 2009: *Inclusive Masculinity*. London: Routledge.

Anderson, E. and McCormack, M. 2014: Theorizing masculinities in contemporary Britain. In S. Roberts (ed.), *Debating Modern Masculinities: Change, Continuity, Crisis*. Basingstoke: Palgrave, 125–56.

Anderson, P. 1964: Origins of the present crisis. *New Left Review*, 23, 26–53.

Anthias, F. and Yuval-Davis, N. 1983: Contextualizing feminism: gender, ethnic and class divisions. *Feminist Review*, 15, 62–75.

Anthias, F. and Yuval-Davis, N. 1993: *Racialized Boundaries*. London: Routledge.

Arber, S. 1994: Wrinkles in the fabric of society. *Times Higher*, 18 November.

Arber, S. and Ginn, J. 1991a: The invisibility of age: gender and class in later life. *Sociological Review*, 39(2), 260–90.

Arber, S. and Ginn, J. 1991b: *Gender and Later Life*. London: Sage.

Aries, P. 1962: *Centuries of Childhood*. Harmondsworth: Penguin.

Arnett, J. 2004: *Emerging Adulthood: The Winding Road from Late Teens Through the Twenties*. Oxford: Oxford University Press.

Aspinall, P. 2009: *Estimating the Size and Composition of the Lesbian, Gay and Bisexual Population in Britain*. Research Report 37. Manchester: EHRC.

Atkinson, W. 2010: *Class, Individualization and Late Modernity*. Basingstoke: Palgrave.

Atkinson, W. 2012: Economic crisis and classed everyday life: hysteresis, positional suffering and symbolic violence. In W. Atkinson, S. Roberts and M. Savage (eds.) *Class Inequality in Austerity Britain: Power, Difference and Suffering*. London: Palgrave, 13–32.

Atkinson, W. and Bradley, H. 2013: Ordinary lives in contemporary Britain. SPAIS Working Paper. Bristol: University of Bristol.

Atkinson, W., Roberts, S. and Savage, M. (eds.) 2012: *Class Inequality in Austerity Britain: Power, Difference and Suffering*. London: Palgrave.

Bagguley, P. and Mann, K. 1992: Idle thieving bastards? Scholarly representations of the underclass. *Work Employment and Society*, 6(1), 113–26.

Banks, O. 1981: *Faces of Feminism*. Oxford: Martin Robertson.

Banyard, K. 2010: *The Equality Illusion*. London: Routledge.

Barker, M. 1981: *The New Racism*. London: Junction Books.

Barnes, C. and Mercer, G. 2002: *Disability*. Cambridge: Polity.

Barrett, M. 1980: *Women's Oppression Today: Problems in Marxist Feminist Analysis*. London: Verso.

Barrett, M. 1992: Words and things: materialism and method in contemporary feminist analysis. In M. Barrett and A. Phillips (eds.), *Destabilizing Theory*. Cambridge: Polity, 201–19.

Barrett, M. and Phillips, A. 1992: *Destabilizing Theory*. Cambridge: Polity.

Barth, F. (ed.) 1969: *Ethnic Groups and Boundaries*. Bergen: Universitets forlarget.

Bartky, S. 1990: *Femininity and Domination*. New York: Routledge.

Bates, I. 1993: 'A job which is right for me'? Social class, gender and individualization. In I. Bates and G. Riseborough (eds.), *Youth and Inequality*. Milton Keynes: Open University Press, 14–41.

Bates, I. and Riseborough, G. (eds.) 1993: *Youth and Inequality*. Milton Keynes: Open University Press.

Bates, L. 2014: *Everyday Sexism*. London: Simon and Schuster.

Bauman, Z. 1988: Sociology and postmodernity. *Sociological Review*, 36(4), 790–813.

Bauman, Z. 1992: *Intimations of Postmodernity*. London: Routledge.

Bauman, Z. 2000: *Liquid Modernity*. Cambridge: Polity.

Beauvoir, S. de 1949: *Le Deuxième Sexe [The Second Sex]*. Paris: Gallimard.

Beck, U. 1992: *Risk Society*. London: Sage.

Beck, U. 1998: *World Risk Society*. Cambridge: Polity.

Beck, U., Giddens, A. and Lash, S. 1994: *Reflexive Modernization: Politics, Tradition and Aesthetics in the Modern Social Order*. Cambridge: Polity.

Beechey, V. 1977: Some notes on female wage labour in capitalist production. *Capital and Class*, 3, 45–66.

Belger, T., Bax, T. and Bawden, A. 2014: 'No one wants to strike. But we are left with no option. *The Guardian* 9 July.

Bell, D. 1973: *The Coming of Post-industrial Society*. New York: Basic Books.

Berlant, L. 2011: *Cruel Optimism*. Durham, N.C.: Duke University Press.

Berman, M. 1983: *All That is Solid Melts into Air: The Experience of Modernity*. London: Verso.

Bernard, J. 1976: *The Future of Marriage*. Harmondsworth: Penguin.

Berthoud, R. and Gershuny, J. 2000: *Seven Years in the Lives of British Families*. Bristol: The Policy Press.

Bhabha, H. 1990a: The third space. In J. Rutherford (ed.), *Identity*. London: Lawrence & Wishart, 207–21.

Bhabha, H. (ed.) 1990b: *Nation and Narration*. London: Routledge.

Bhattacharyya, G. 2002: *Sexuality and Society*. London: Routledge.

Blackwell, L. and Guinea-Martin, D. 2005: Occupational segregation by sex and ethnicity in England and Wales, 1991 to 2001. In *Labour Market Trends*. London: ONS, 501–16.

Blackwell, T. and Seabrook, J. 1985: *A World Still to Win*. London: Faber and Faber.

Blakemore, K. and Boneham, M. 1994: *Age, Race and Ethnicity*. Milton Keynes: Open University Press.

Blau, P. and Duncan, O. 1967: *The American Occupational Structure*. New York: Wiley.

Blauner, R. 1969: Internal colonialism and ghetto revolt. *Social Problems*, 16(4), 393–408.

Blythe, R. 1979: *The View in Winter*. London: Allen Lane.

Bocock, R. 1992: Consumption and lifestyles. In R. Bocock and K. Thompson (eds.), *Social and Cultural Forms of Modernity*. Cambridge: Polity, 119–68.

Bocock, R. 1993: *Consumption*. London: Routledge.

Bodily, C. 1994: Ageism and the deployment of 'age': a constructionist view. In T. Sarbin and J. Kitsuse (eds.), *Constructing the Social*. London: Sage, 174–94.

Borooah, V. and Knox, C. 2014: Access and performance inequalities: post primary education in Northern Ireland. *Journal of Poverty and Social Justice*, 22(2), 111–35.

Boseley, S. 2014: Only a third of depression cases treated. *The Guardian* 14 August.

Bottomore, T. and Brym, R. (eds.) 1989: *The Capitalist Class*. Hemel Hempstead: Harvester Wheatsheaf.

Bourdieu, P. 1986: *Distinction*. London: Routledge.

Bourdieu, P. 1998: *Acts of Resistance*. Cambridge: Polity.

Bourdieu, P. and Wacquant, L. (1989): Towards a reflexive sociology: a workshop with Pierre Bourdieu. *Sociological Theory*, 7(1), 26–63.

Bradley, H. 1989: *Men's Work, Women's Work*. Cambridge: Polity.

Bradley, H. 1992: Changing social divisions: class, gender and race. In R. Bocock and K. Thompson (eds.), *Social and Cultural Forms of Modernity*. Cambridge: Polity, 11–56.

Bradley, H. 1994: Class and class consciousness in a northern conurbation. In R. Blackburn (ed.), *Social Inequality in a Changing World* [papers presented to Cambridge Social Stratification Seminar, September 1993], 151–68.

Bradley, H. 1999a: Inequalities: coming to terms with complexity. In G. Browning, A. Halcli and F. Webster (eds.), *Theory and Society: Understanding the Present*. London: Sage, 476–88.

Bradley, H. 1999b: *Gender and Power in the Workplace*. London: Macmillan.

Bradley, H. 2012: *Gender*. Cambridge: Polity.

Bradley, H. 2014: Class descriptors or class relations? Thoughts towards a critique of Savage et al. *Sociology*, 48(3), 429–36.

Bradley, H., Abrahams, J., Bathmaker, A.-M., et al. 2014: *A Degree Generation: The Paired Peers Project Year 3 Report*. Bristol: Leverhulme Trust / University of Bristol.

Bradley, H. and Devadason, R. 2008: Fractured transitions: young adults' pathways into contemporary labour markets. *Sociology*, 42(1), 119–36.

Bradley, H. and Healy, G. 2007: *Ethnicity and Gender at Work*. London: Palgrave.

Bradley, H., Healy, G., Forson, C. and Kaul, P. 2007: *Ethnic Minority Women and Workplace Cultures: What Works and What Doesn't*. Manchester: Equal Opportunities Commission.

Brah, A. 1986: Unemployment and racism: Asian youth on the dole. In S. Allen, A. Waton, K. Purcell and S. Wood (eds.), *The Experience of Unemployment*. London: Macmillan, 61–78.

Brah, A. 1992: Difference, diversity and differentiation. In J. Donald and A. Rattansi (eds.), *'Race', Culture and Difference*. Milton Keynes: Open University Press, 126–45.

Brah, A. 1993: Re-framing Europe: engendered racisms, ethnicities and nationalisms in contemporary western Europe. *Feminist Review*, 45, 9–28.

Brah, A. 1994: 'Race' and 'culture' in the gendering of labour markets. In H. Afshar and M. Maynard (eds.), *The Dynamics of 'Race' and Gender*. London: Taylor & Francis, 151–71.

Brake, M. 1980: *Sociology of Youth Culture and Youth Subcultures*. London: Routledge & Kegan Paul.

Brake, M. 1985: *Comparative Youth Culture*. London: Routledge & Kegan Paul.

Brannen, J. and Moss, P. 1991: *Managing Mothers*. London: Unwin Hyman.

Braverman, H. 1974: *Labor and Monopoly Capital*. New York: Basic Books.

Brewer, M., Muriel, A., Phillips, D. and Sibieta, L. 2008: *Poverty and Inequality in the UK: 2008*. London: Institute for Fiscal Studies.

Briggs, A. 1974: The language of 'class' in early nineteenth-century England. In M. Flinn and T. Smout (eds.), *Essays in Social History*. Oxford: Oxford University Press, 154–78.

Briskin, L. and McDermott, P. (eds.) 1993: *Women Challenging Unions*. Toronto: University of Toronto Press.

Brittain, V. 1994: Millions of children 'traumatised by war'. *The Guardian* 16 December.

Brodie, H. 1986: *Maps and Dreams*. London: Faber and Faber.

Brown, C. 1984: *Black and White Britain*. London: Heinemann.

Brownmiller, S. 1976: *Against Our Will: Men, Women and Rape*. Harmondsworth: Penguin.

Bruce, S. 2011: *Secularization: In Defence of an Unfashionable Theory*. Oxford: Oxford University Press.

Bruegel, I. 1989: Sex and race in the labour market. *Feminist Review*, 32, 49–68.

Bryan, B., Dadzie, S. and Scafe, S. 1985: *The Heart of the Race*. London: Virago.

Bryman, A., Bytheway, B., Allatt, P. and Keil, T. (eds.) 1987: *Rethinking the Life Cycle*. London: Macmillan.

Bullock, K. 2002. *Rethinking Muslim Women and the Veil*. London: Insitute for Islamic Thought.

Burd-Sharps, S., Lewis, K. and Borges Martins, E. 2008: *The Measure of America*. New York: Columbia University Press.

Burke, J. 2014: As India's super-rich list explodes, the shopping has only just begun. *The Guardian* 25 July.

Butler, J. 1990: *Gender Trouble*. New York: Routledge.

Cain, L. 1975: The young and the old: coalition or conflict ahead? In A. Foner (ed.) *Age in Society*. London: Sage, 35–45.

Calvert, P. 1982: *The Concept of Class*. London: Hutchinson.

Campbell, B. 1993: *Goliath*. London: Methuen.
Campbell, B. 2013: The end of the equality paradigm – The Kilburn Manifesto. Our Kingdom website, November 2013: Opendemocracy.net.
Campbell, B. 2014: *End of Equality*. London: Seagull Books.
Cann, V. 2014: The limits of masculinity: boys, taste and cultural consumption. In S. Roberts (ed.), *Debating Modern Masculinities: Change, Continuity, Crisis*. Basingstoke: Palgrave, 17–34.
Carby, H. 1982: White woman listen! Black feminism and the boundaries of sisterhood. In Centre for Contemporary Cultural Studies (ed.), *The Empire Strikes Back*. London: Hutchinson, 212–36.
Carchedi, G. 1977: *On the Economic Identification of Social Classes*. London: Routledge.
Carrell, S. 2009: Prize winning novelist has sight restored. *The Guardian* 31 August.
Cashmore, E. and Troyna, B. (eds.) 1982: *Black Youth in Crisis*. London: George Allen & Unwin.
Cashmore, E. and Troyna, B. 1983: *Introduction to Race Relations*. London: Routledge & Kegan Paul.
Castles, S. 1984: *Here for Good*. London: Pluto.
Castles, S. and Kosack, G. 1973: *Immigrant Workers and Class Structure in Western Europe*. Oxford: Oxford University Press.
Cavendish, R. 1982: *Women on the Line*. London: Routledge.
Centre for Contemporary Cultural Studies (eds.) 1982: *The Empire Strikes Back*. London: Hutchinson.
Chahal, K. 1999: *Minority Ethnic Homelessness in London: Findings from a Rapid Review*. London: National Health Service.
Chakraborty, A. 2014: Poverty pay is not inevitable. *The Guardian* 9 September.
Charvet, J. 1982: *Feminism*. London: Dent.
Chaudhuri, A. 1994: *Afternoon Raag*. London: Minerva.
Child Poverty Action Group 2014: *Fighting the Injustice of Poverty*. London: CPAG.
Chodorow, N. 1978: *The Reproduction of Mothering: Psychoanalysis and the Sociology of Gender*. Berkeley: University of California Press.
Clark, A. 1982: *Working Life of Women in the Seventeenth Century* (1st edn 1919). London: Routledge.
Clarke, J. and Critcher, C. 1985: *The Devil Makes Work*. London: Macmillan.
Coates, D. 1989: Britain. In T. Bottomore and R. Brym (eds.), *The Capitalist Class*. Hemel Hempstead: Harvester Wheatsheaf, 19–45.
Cockburn, C. 1983: *Brothers*. London: Pluto.
Cockburn, C. 1985: *Machinery of Dominance*. London: Pluto.
Cockburn, C. 1991: *In the Way of Women*. London: Macmillan.
Coffield, F., Borrill, C. and Marshall, S. 1986: *Growing up at the Margins*. Milton Keynes: Open University Press.
Cohen, P. 1988: The perversions of inheritance: studies in the making of multi-racist Britain. In P. Cohen and H. Bains (eds.), *Multi-racist Britain*. London: Macmillan, 9–118.

Cohen, S. 1972: *Folk Devils and Moral Panics*. London: MacGibbon & Kee.

Collins, P. H. 1990: *Black Feminist Thought*. London: HarperCollins.

Commission of the European Communities (CEC) 1987: *Men and Women of Europe in 1987* (Supplement to *Women of Europe* 26). Brussels: CEC.

Commission of the European Communities 1988: *Women of Europe: Ten Years* (*Women of Europe* 27). Brussels: CEC.

Commission of the European Communities 1989: *Employment in Europe*. Brussels: CEC.

Commission of the European Communities 1992a: *Women of Europe, 70*. Brussels: CEC.

Commission of the European Communities 1992b: *Legal Instruments to Combat Racism and Xenophobia*. Brussels: CEC.

Connell, R. 1987: *Gender and Power*. Cambridge: Polity.

Connell, R. 2005: *Masculinities*. Cambridge: Polity.

Connell, R. 2007: *Southern Theory: The Global Dynamics of Knowledge in Social Science*. Cambridge: Polity.

Cowgill, D. and Holmes, L. 1972: *Aging and Modernization*. New York: Appleton-Century-Crofts.

Cox, O. 1970: *Caste, Class and Race*. New York: Monthly Review Books.

Crenshaw, K. 1991: Mapping the margins: intersectionality, identity politics, and violence against women of color. *Stanford Law Review*, 43: 1241–99.

Crompton, R. 1993: *Class and Stratification* (3rd edn 2008). Cambridge: Polity.

Crompton, R. and Gubbay, J. 1977: *Economy and Class Structure*. London: Macmillan.

Crompton, R. and Jones, G. 1984: *White-Collar Proletariat*. London: Macmillan.

Crompton, R. and Mann, M. (eds.) 1986: *Gender and Stratification*. Cambridge: Polity.

Crompton, R. and Sanderson, K. 1990: *Gendered Jobs and Social Change*. London: Unwin Hyman.

Crook, S., Pakulski, J. and Waters, M. 1992: *Postmodernization*. London: Sage.

Crowley, H. 1992: Women and the domestic sphere. In R. Bocock and K. Thompson (eds.), *Social and Cultural Forms of Modernity*. Cambridge: Polity, 69–118.

Cumming, E. and Henry, W. 1961: *Growing Old: The Process of Disengagement*. New York: Basic Books.

Curran, J., Stanworth, J. and Watkins, D. (eds.) 1986: *The Survival of the Small Firm*. Aldershot: Gower.

Curthoys, A. 1993: Feminism, citizenship and national identity. *Feminist Review*, 44, 19–38.

Dahrendorf, R. 1959: *Class and Class Conflict in Industrial Society*. London: Routledge.

Dahrendorf, R. 1987: The erosion of citizenship and its consequences for us all. *New Statesman* (12 June), 12–15.

Dale, A. 1986: Social class and the self-employed. *Sociology*, 20(3), 430–4.

Daniel, W. W. 1968: *Racial Discrimination in Britain*. Harmondsworth: Penguin.

Davies, B. 1989: *Frogs and Snails and Feminist Tales*. Sydney: Allen and Unwin.

Davies, C. 2009: Finishing line: disabled sailor defies the odds. *The Guardian* 1 September.

Davis, J. 1990: *Youth and the Condition of Britain: Images of Adolescent Conflict*. London: Athlone Press.

Davis, K., Leijenaar, M. and Oldersma, J. 1991: *The Gender of Power*. London: Sage.

Davis, K. and Moore, W. 1945: Some principles of stratification. *American Sociological Review*, 10, 242–9.

Dawe, A. 1970: The two sociologies. *British Journal of Sociology*, 21(2), 207–18.

Dean, H. 1991: In search of the underclass. In P. Brown and R. Scase (eds.), *Poor Work*. Milton Keynes: Open University Press, 23–39.

Delphy, C. 1977: *The Main Enemy*. London: Women's Research and Resources Centre.

Dennis, N., Henriques, F. and Slaughter, C. 1956: *Coal Is Our Life*. London: Eyre & Spottiswoode.

Devadason, R. 2012: Humanitarians without Borders: work, mobility and wellbeing. UNHCR Policy & Evaluation Paper Series 237: www.unhcr. org/4fbf50549.html.

Devine, F. 1992: *Affluent Workers Revisited*. Edinburgh: Edinburgh University Press.

Devine, F. 2004: *Class Practices: How Parents Help Their Children Get Good Jobs*. Cambridge: Cambridge University Press.

Dirlik, A. 1994: The postcolonial aura: third world criticism in the age of global capitalism. *Critical Inquiry*, 20, 328–56.

Donald, J. and Rattansi, A. (eds.) 1992: *'Race', Culture and Difference*. Milton Keynes: Open University Press.

Dorling, D. 2014: *Inequality and the 1%*. London: Verso.

Dover, K. 1978: *Greek Homosexuality*. Cambridge, Mass.: Harvard University Press.

Drydakis, N. 2014: Sexual orientation discrimination in the Cypriot labour market. Distastes or uncertainty? *International Journal of Manpower*, 35(5), 720–44.

Du Bois-Reymond, M. and Blasco, A. L. 2003: Yoyo transitions and misleading trajectories: from linear to risk biographies of young people. In A. Walther, A. L. Blasco and W. McNeish (eds.), *Young People and Contradictions of Inclusion*. Bristol: The Policy Press, 19–41.

Duchen, C. 1987: *French Connections*. London: Hutchinson.

Durkheim, E. 1915: *The Elementary Forms of Religious Life*. London: George Allen and Unwin.

Durkheim, E. 1952: *Suicide*. London: Routledge.

Durkheim, E. 1964: *The Division of Labour in Society*. New York: Free Press.

Dworkin, A. 1981: *Pornography: Men Possessing Women*. London: Women's Press.

Edgell, S. 1993: *Class*. London: Routledge.

Ehrenreich, B. and English, D. 1979: *For Her Own Good*. London: Pluto.

Eisenstadt, S. 1956: *From Generation to Generation: Age Groups and Social Structure*. New York: Free Press.

Elshtain, J. B. 1987: Feminist political rhetoric and women's studies. In J. Nelson, A. Megill and D. McCloskey (eds.), *The Rhetoric of the Human Sciences*. Madison: Wisconsin University Press, 319–40.

Equality and Human Rights Commission (EHRC) 2008: *Fairness: A New Contract with the Public*. Manchester: EHRC.

Erikson, E. 1965: *Childhood and Society*. Harmondsworth: Penguin.

Erikson, R. and Goldthorpe, J. 1992: *The Constant Flux: A Study of Class Mobility in Industrial Societies*. Oxford: Clarendon Press.

Esping-Andersen, G. (ed.) 1993: *Changing Classes*. London: Sage.

Faludi, S. 1992: *Backlash*. London: Chatto & Windus.

Featherstone, M. 1991: *Consumer Culture and Postmodernism*. London: Sage.

Featherstone, M. and Hepworth, M. 1989: Ageing and old age: reflections on the post-modern life course. In B. Bytheway, T. Keil, P. Allatt and A. Bryman (eds.), *Becoming and Being Old*. London: Sage, 143–57.

Featherstone, M. and Hepworth, M. 1990: Images of ageing. In J. Bond and P. Coleman (eds.), *Ageing in Society: An Introduction to Social Gerontology*. London: Sage, 250–76.

Fennell, G., Phillipson, C. and Evers, H. 1988: *The Sociology of Old Age*. Milton Keynes: Open University Press.

Fenton, S. 1987: Black elderly people in Britain. Working Paper. Department of Sociology, University of Bristol.

Fenton, S. 2010: *Ethnicity: Racism, Class and Culture*. Cambridge: Polity.

Feuer, L. 1969: *The Conflict of Generations: The Character and Significance of Student Movements*. New York: Basic Books.

Field, F. 1989: *Losing Out: The Emergence of Britain's Underclass*. Oxford: Blackwell.

Finch, J. and Bowers, S. 2007: Directors' Earnings Break Through the £1bn Barrier. *The Guardian* 29 August.

Firestone, S. 1971: *The Dialectic of Sex*. London: Jonathan Cape.

Fleming, S. 1991: Sport, schooling and Asian male youth culture. In G. Jarvie (ed.), *Sport, Racism and Ethnicity*. London: Falmer, 30–57.

Foner, A. 1975: Age in society: structure and change. In A. Foner (ed.), *Age in Society*. London: Sage, 13–34.

Ford, J. and Sinclair, R. 1987: *Sixty Years On: Women Talk about Old Age*. London: Women's Press.

Foucault, M. 1972: *The Archaeology of Knowledge*. London: Tavistock.

Foucault, M. 1978–84: *The History of Sexuality* (Vols. I–III). London: Allen Lane.

Frankenberg, R. 1993: Growing up white: feminism, racism and the social geography of childhood. *Feminist Review*, 45, 51–84.

Fraser, N. and Nicholson, L. 1988: Social criticism without philosophy: an encounter between feminism and postmodernism. *Theory Culture and Society*, 5, 373–94.

Friedan, B. 1965: *The Feminine Mystique*. Harmondsworth: Penguin.

Friedmann, G. 1955: *Industrial Society*. New York: Free Press.

Frisby, D. 1985: *Fragments of Modernity*. Cambridge: Polity.

Fukuyama, F. 1989: The end of history? *The National Interest*, 16(Summer), 3–18.

Fuller, M. 1982: Young, female and black. In E. Cashmore and B. Troyna (eds.), *Black Youth in Crisis*. London: Allen and Unwin, 87–99.

Fundamental Rights Agency 2013: *Lesbian, Gay, Bisexual and Transgender Survey. Results at a Glance*. Vienna: FRA.

Furlong, A. and Cartmel, F. 2007: *Young People and Social Change*. Milton Keynes: Open University Press.

Gabriel, J. and Ben-Tovim, G. 1979: The conceptualization of race relations in sociological theory. *Ethnic and Racial Studies*, 2(2), 190–212.

Gagnon, J. and Simon, H. 1973: *Sexual Conduct*. London: Hutchinson.

Gelb, J. and Palley, M. L. 1982: *Women and Public Policies*. Princeton: Princeton University Press.

Gellner, E. 1983: *Nations and Nationalism*. Oxford: Basil Blackwell.

Gerth, H. and Mills, C. 1970: *From Max Weber*. London: Routledge.

Ghosh, A. 1994: *In an Antique Land*. London: Granta Books / Penguin.

Giddens, A. 1973: *The Class Structure of the Advanced Societies*. London: Hutchinson.

Giddens, A. 1976: *New Rules of Sociological Method*. London: Hutchinson.

Giddens, A. 1984: *The Constitution of Society: Outline of a Theory of Structuration*. Cambridge: Polity.

Giddens, A. 1990: *The Consequences of Modernity*. Cambridge: Polity.

Giddens, A. 1991: *Modernity and Self Identity*. Cambridge: Polity.

Gifford Inquiry 1989: *Loosen the Shackles*. Liverpool: Liverpool 8 Law Centre.

Gilbert, N., Dale, A., Arber, S., Evandrou, M. and Laczko, F. 1989: Resources in old age: ageing and the life course. In M. Jefferys (ed.), *Growing Old in the Twentieth Century*. London: Routledge, 93–114.

Gill, R. 2007: *Technobohemians or the New Cybertariat? New Media Work in Amsterdam a Decade After the Web*. Amsterdam: Institute of Network Cultures.

Gillan, A. 2008: 'Proud to be Welsh and a Sikh': schoolgirl wins court battle to wear religious bangle. *The Guardian* 30 July.

Gillborn, D. 1998: Race and ethnicity in compulsory schooling. In T. Modood and T. Acland (eds.) *Race and Higher Education*. London: Policy Studies Institute, 11–23.

Gillborn, D. and Youdell, D. 2000: *Rationing Education: Policy, Practice, Reform and Equity*. Milton Keynes: Open University Press.

Gilroy, P. 1987: *There Ain't no Black in the Union Jack*. London: Routledge.

Gilroy, P. 1993: *The Black Atlantic*. London: Verso.

Ginn, J. 2003: *Women, Pensions and the Lifecourse*. Bristol: The Policy Press.

Ginn, J., Street, D. and Arber, S. 2001: *Women, Work and Pensions*. Milton Keynes: Open University Press.

Girma, M., Radice, S., Tsangarides, N. and Walter, N. 2014: *Detained: Women Asylum Seekers Locked Up in the UK*. London: Women for Refugee Women.

Glasgow, D. 1981: *The Black Underclass*. New York: Vintage Books.

Glass, D. (ed.) 1954: *Social Mobility in Britain*. London: Routledge.

Glendinning, C. and Millar, J. (eds.) 1992: *Women and Poverty in Britain: The 1990s*. London: Harvester Wheatsheaf.

Glucksmann, M. 1990: *Women Assemble*. London: Routledge.

Goldthorpe, J. 1980: *Social Mobility and Class Structure in Modern Britain*. Oxford: Clarendon Press.

Goldthorpe, J. 2000: *On Sociology: Numbers, Narratives and the Integration of Research and Theory*. Oxford: Oxford University Press.

Goldthorpe, J. and Heath, A. 1992: Revised class schema. Working Paper 13. Joint Unit for the Study of Social Trends.

Goldthorpe, J., Lockwood, D., Bechhofer, F. and Platt, J. 1969: *The Affluent Worker in the Class Structure*. Cambridge: Cambridge University Press.

Goodman, A. and Webb, S. 1994: *For Richer For Poorer*. London: Institute of Fiscal Studies.

Gorz, A. 1982: *Farewell to the Working Class*. London: Pluto.

Gorz, A. 1989: *Critique of Economic Reason*. London: Verso.

Government Equalities Office 2008: *Framework for the Future – the Equality Bill*. London: HMSO.

Grandparents Plus 2013: *Grandparenting in Europe*. London: Grandparents Plus.

Greer, G. 1971: *The Female Eunuch*. London: Paladin.

Griffin, C. 1985: *Typical Girls*. London: Routledge.

Griffin, C. 1993: *Representations of Youth*. Cambridge: Polity.

Griffin, S. 1981: *Pornography and Silence*. New York: Harper & Row.

Groves, D. 1992: Occupational pension provision and women's poverty in old age. In C. Glendinning and J. Millar (eds.), *Women and Poverty in Britain: The 1990s*. London: Harvester Wheatsheaf, 193–206.

Hall, G. S. 1904: *Adolescence*. New York: D. Appleton & Co.

Hall, S. 1980: Race, articulation and societies structured in dominance. In UNESCO, *Sociological Theories: Race and Colonialism*. Paris: UNESCO, 305–46.

Hall, S. 1990: Cultural identity and diaspora. In J. Rutherford (ed.), *Identity*. London: Lawrence & Wishart, 222–37.

Hall, S. 1992a: The west and the rest: discourse and power. In S. Hall and B. Gieben (eds.), *Formations of Modernity*. Cambridge: Polity, 177–228.

Hall, S. 1992b: The question of cultural identity. In S. Hall, D. Held and A. McGrew (eds.), *Modernity and its Futures*. Cambridge: Polity, 277–326.

Hall, S. 1992c: New ethnicities. In J. Donald and A. Rattansi (eds.), *'Race', Culture and Difference*. London: Sage, 252–99.

Hall, S., Critcher, C., Jefferson, T., Clarke, J. and Roberts, B. 1978: *Policing the Crisis*. London: Macmillan.

Hall, S. and Jefferson, J. (eds.) 1976: *Resistance through Rituals: Youth Subculture in Postwar Britain*. London: Hutchinson.

Halsey, A., Heath, A. and Ridge, J. 1980: *Origins and Destinations*. Oxford: Clarendon Press.

Halson, J. 1991: Young women, sexual harassment and heterosexuality: violence, power relations and mixed-sex schooling. In P. Abbott and C. Wallace (eds.), *Gender, Power and Sexuality*. London: Macmillan, 97–114.

Hamer, D. and Copeland, R. 1995: *The Science of Desire: Search for the Gay Gene and the Biology of Behaviour*. New York: Simon and Schuster.

Haraway, D. 1990: A manifesto for cyborgs: science technology and socialist feminism in the 1980s. In L. Nicholson (ed.), *Feminism/Postmodernism*. London: Routledge, 190–233.

Harding, S. 1986: *The Science Question in Feminism*. Ithaca, NY: Cornell University Press.

Harding, S. (ed.) 1987: *Feminism and Methodology*. Milton Keynes: Open University Press.

Harper, S. and Thane, P. 1989: The consolidation of 'old age' as a phase of life, 1945–65. In M. Jefferys (ed.), *Growing Old in the Twentieth Century*. London: Routledge, 43–61.

Harris, C. 1987: The individual and society: a processual approach. In A. Bryman, B. Bytheway, P. Allatt and T. Keil (eds.), *Rethinking the Life Cycle*. London: Macmillan, 17–29.

Harris, C. 1991: Recession, redundancy and old age. In P. Brown and R. Scase (eds.), *Poor Work*. Milton Keynes: Open University Press, 103–15.

Harris, I. 1995: *Messages Men Hear*. London: Taylor and Francis.

Hartmann, H. 1976: Patriarchy, capitalism and job segregation by sex. *Signs*, 1(3), 137–68.

Hartmann, H. 1981: The unhappy marriage of Marxism and feminism: towards a more progressive union. In L. Sargent (ed.), *Women and Revolution: The Unhappy Marriage of Feminism and Marxism*. London: Pluto, 1–41.

Hartsock, N. 1987: The feminist standpoint: developing the ground for a specifically feminist historical materialism. In S. Harding (ed.), *Feminism and Methodology*. Milton Keynes: Open University Press, 157–80.

Harvey, D. 1989: *The Condition of Postmodernity*. Oxford: Blackwell.

Harvey, D. 2005: *A Brief History of Neoliberalism*. Oxford: Oxford University Press.

Hazan, H. 1994: *Old Age: Constructions and Deconstructions*. Cambridge: Cambridge University Press.

Hearn, J. and Parkin, W. 1993: Organizations, multiple oppressions and postmodernism. In J. Hassard and M. Parker (eds.), *Postmodernism and Organizations*. London: Sage, 148–61.

Hebdige, D. 1979: *Subcultures: The Meaning of Style*. London: Methuen.

Heidensohn, H. 1985: *Women and Crime*. London: Macmillan.

Herrnstein, R. and Murray, C. 1994: *The Bell Curve: Intelligence and Class Structure in American Life*. New York: Free Press.

Hobsbawm, E. 1968: *Industry and Empire*. Harmondsworth: Penguin.

Hochschild, A. 1989: *The Second Shift*. New York: Viking.

Holmwood, J. 1994: Postmodernity, citizenship and inequality. In R. Blackburn (ed.), Social Inequality in a Changing World [papers presented to Cambridge Social Stratification Seminar, September 1993], 7–27.

hooks, b. 1982: *Ain't I a Woman? Black Women and Feminism*. London: Pluto.

Houghton, W. 1957: *The Victorian Frame of Mind*. New Haven: Yale University Press.

Howker, E. and Malik, S. 2013: *Jilted Generation: How Britain has Bankrupted its Youth*. London: Icon Books.

Hudson, M. 1994: *Coming Back Brockens*. London: Jonathan Cape.

Humphries, J. 1983: The emancipation of women in the 1970s and 1980s. *Capital and Class*, 20, 6–27.

Hunt, P. 1980: *Gender and Class Consciousness*. London: Macmillan.

Hunt, R. and Jensen, J. 2007: *The School Report: The Experiences of Young Gay People in Britain's Schools*. London: Stonewall.

Hunt, S. 2005: *The Life Course: A Sociological Introduction*. London: Palgrave.

Huws, U. 2003: *The Making of a Cybertariat: Virtual Work in a Real World*. New York: Monthly Review Press.

Hyde, M. 2000: Disability. In G Payne (ed.) *Social Divisions*. Basingstoke: Macmillan, 185–202.

Iganski, P. and Mason, D. (2002): *Ethnicity, Equality and the British National Health Service*. Aldershot: Ashgate.

Jackson, S. 1993: Love and romance as objects of feminist knowledge. In M. Kennedy, C. Lubelska and V. Walsh (eds.), *Making Connections*. London: Taylor & Francis, 39–50.

Jackson, S. and Scott, S. 2010: *Theorizing Sexuality*. Milton Keynes: Open University Press.

Jacobs, J. 1993: Careers in the US service economy. In G. Esping-Andersen (ed.), *Changing Classes*. London: Sage, 195–224.

Jameson, F. 1991: *Postmodernism or, the Cultural Logic of Late Capitalism*. London: Verso.

Jefferys, M. (ed.) 1989: *Growing Old in the Twentieth Century*. London: Routledge.

Jenkins, R. 1983: *Lads, Citizens and Ordinary Kids*. London: Routledge.

Jenkins, R. 1986: *Racism and Recruitment*. Cambridge: Cambridge University Press.

Jenkins, R. 1992: *Pierre Bourdieu*. London: Routledge.

Jenson, J., Hagen, E. and Reddy, C. (eds.) 1988: *Feminization of the Labour Force*. Cambridge: Polity.

Johnson, P. 1989: The structured dependency of the elderly: a critical note. In M. Jefferys (ed.), *Growing Old in the Twentieth Century*. London: Routledge, 62–71.

Johnson, P., Conrad, C. and Thomson, D. (eds.) 1989: *Workers Versus Pensioners: Intergenerational Justice in an Ageing World*. Manchester: Manchester University Press.

Jones, O. 2011: *Chavs: The Demonization of the Working Class*. London: Verso.

Jones, O. 2014a: *The Guardian* 26 August.

Jones, O. 2014b: *The Establishment – and How They Got Away With It*. London: Allen Lane.

Jones, T. and McEvoy, D. 1986: Asian enterprise, the popular image. In J. Curran, J. Stanworth and D. Watkins (eds.), *The Survival of the Small Firm*. Aldershot: Gower.

Joppke, C. 2004: The retreat of multiculturalism in the liberal state: theory and policy. *British Journal of Sociology*, 55(2), 237–57.

JRF (Joseph Rowntree Foundation) 2014: *Monitoring Poverty and Social Exclusion 2014*. York: JRF.

Kaiman, J. 2014: China gets richer but more unequal. *The Guardian* 28 July.

Kalra, V. 2003: Police lore and community order: diversity in the criminal justice system. In D. Mason (ed.), *Explaining Ethnic Differences*. Bristol: The Policy Press, 139–52.

Kemp, T. 1978: *Historical Patterns of Industrialization*. London: Longman.

Kerr, C., Dunlop, J., Harbison, F. and Myers, C. 1962: *Industrialism and Industrial Man*. London: Heinemann.

Khaleeli, H. 2014: Married to jihad. *The Guardian* 6 September.

Kimmel, M. 1987: The contemporary crisis of masculinity in historical perspective. In H. Brod (ed.), *The Making of Masculinities*. London: Allen & Unwin, 121–53.

Kitzinger, C. and Wilkinson, S. 1993: The precariousness of heterosexual feminist identities. In M. Kennedy, C. Lubelska and V. Walsh (eds.), *Making Connections*. London: Taylor & Francis, 24–36.

Klein, N. 2014: *This Changes Everything*. New York: Simon and Schuster.

Klingender, F. 1935: *The Condition of Clerical Labour in Britain*. London: Martin Lawrence.

Knowles, C. and Mercer, S. 1992: Feminism and antiracism: an exploration of the political possibilities. In J. Donald and A. Rattansi (eds.), *'Race', Culture and Difference*. London: Sage, 104–25.

Kosofsky, E. S. 1991: *Epistemology of the Closet*. Hemel Hempstead: Harvester Wheatsheaf.

Kumar, K. 1978: *Prophecy and Progress*. Harmondsworth: Penguin.

Kymlicka, W. 1995: *Multicultural Citizenship: A Liberal Theory of Minority Rights*. Oxford: Oxford University Press.

Labour Force Survey, 1994–5. London: HMSO.

Lareau, A. 2003: *Unequal Childhoods: Class, Race and Family Life*. Berkeley: University of California Press.

Lasch, C. 1977: *Haven in a Heartless World*. New York: Basic Books.

Lash, S. 1984: *The Militant Worker: Class and Radicalism in France and America*. London: Heinemann.

Lash, S. 1990: *The Sociology of Postmodernism*. London: Routledge.
Lash, S. and Urry, J. 1987: *The End of Organized Capitalism*. Cambridge: Polity.
Laslett, P. 1977: *Family Life and Illicit Love in Earlier Generations*. Cambridge: Cambridge University Press.
Lawler, S. 2008: *Identity*. Cambridge: Polity.
Lea, J. and Young, J. 1984: *What Is to Be Done about Law and Order?* Harmondsworth: Penguin.
Lees, P. 2014: Celebrity transitioning. *The Guardian* 12 August.
Lees, S. 1993: *Sugar and Spice: Sexuality and Adolescent Girls*. Harmondsworth: Penguin.
Lewycka, M. 2012: *Two Caravans*. Harmondsworth: Penguin.
Liddiard, M. and Hutson, S. 1990: Youth homelessness in Wales. In C. Wallace and M. Cross (eds.), *Youth in Transition*. London: Falmer, 164–80.
Lockwood, D. 1958: *The Black-Coated Worker*. London: Allen & Unwin.
Lockwood, D. 1975: Sources of variation in working-class images of society. In M. Bulmer (ed.), *Working-class Images of Society*. London: RKP, 16–31.
Lockwood, D. 1988: The weakest link in the chain? In D. Rose (ed.), *Social Stratification and Economic Change*, London: Unwin Hyman, 57–97.
Lovenduski, J. 1986: *Women and European Politics*. Brighton: Harvester.
Luckmann, B. 1970: The small lifeworlds of modern man. *Social Research*, 37(4), 580–96.
Lyon, D. 1994: *Postmodernity*. Milton Keynes: Open University Press.
Lyotard, J.-F. 1984: *The Postmodern Condition*. Manchester: Manchester University Press.
Mac an Ghaill, M. 1988: *Young, Gifted and Black*. Milton Keynes: Open University Press.
Macdonald, R. and Coffield, F. 1991: *Risky Business*. London: Falmer.
Macdonald, R. and Marsh, J. 2005: *Disconnected Youth: Growing Up in Britain's Poor Places*. Basingstoke: Palgrave.
Mackay, F. 2011: A movement of their own: voices of young feminist activists in the London Feminist Network. *Interface*, 3, 152–79.
Maffesoli, M. 1996: *The Time of the Tribes*. London: Sage.
Mallet, S. 1975: *The New Working Class*. Nottingham: Spokesman.
Mandel, E. 1975: *Late Capitalism*. London: New Left Books.
Mann, M. 1986: A crisis in stratification theory? In R. Crompton and M. Mann (eds.), *Gender and Stratification*. Cambridge: Polity, 40–56.
Mannheim, K. 1952: *Essays in the Sociology of Knowledge*. London: Routledge.
Markides, K. and Mindel, C. 1987: *Aging and Ethnicity*. Beverly Hills: Sage.
Marshall, B. 1994: *Engendering Modernity*. Cambridge, Polity.
Marshall, G. 1990: *In Praise of Sociology*. London: Unwin Hyman.
Marshall, G., Rose, D., Newby, H. and Vogler, C. 1988: *Social Class in Modern Britain*. London: Unwin Hyman.
Marx, K. 1976: *Capital (Vol. I)*. Harmondsworth: Penguin.

Marx, K. and Engels, F. 1934: *Manifesto of the Communist Party*. London: Lawrence & Wishart.

Mason, D. 1992: Some problems with the concepts of race and racism. Discussion Papers in Sociology S92/5. University of Leicester.

Mason, D. 2000: Ethnicity. In G. Payne (ed.), *Social Divisions*. Basingstoke: Macmillan, 91–114.

Mason, D. (ed.) 2003: *Explaining Ethnic Differences: Changing Patterns of Disadvantage in Britain*. Bristol: The Policy Press.

Maynard, M. 1994: 'Race', gender and the concept of difference in feminist thought. In H. Afshar and M. Maynard (eds.), *The Dynamics of 'Race' and Gender*. London: Taylor & Francis, 9–25.

McDowell, L. 1996: *Capital Culture*. Oxford: Blackwell.

McDowell, L. 2000: Learning to serve? Employment aspirations and attitudes of young working-class men in an era of labour market restructuring. *Gender, Place and Culture*, 74, 389–416.

McGrew, A. 1992: A global society? In S. Hall, D. Held and A. McGrew (eds.), *Modernity and its Futures*. Cambridge: Polity, 61–116.

McIntosh, M. 1979: The welfare state and the needs of the dependent family. In S. Burman (ed.), *Fit Work for Women*. London: Croom Helm, 153–72.

McKenzie, L. 2012: The stigmatised and de-valued working class: the state of a council estate. In W. Atkinson, S. Woods and M. Savage (eds.), *Class Inequality in Austerity Britain: Power, Difference and Suffering*. London: Palgrave, 128–44.

McKenzie, L. 2015: *Getting By: Class, Culture and Estates in Austerity Britain*. Bristol: The Policy Press.

McNay, L. 1992: *Foucault and Feminism*. Cambridge: Polity.

McRobbie, A. 1978: Working-class girls and the culture of femininity. In Women's Studies Group (ed.), *Women Take Issue*. London: Hutchinson, 96–108.

McRobbie, A. 1991: *Feminism and Youth Culture*. London: Macmillan.

McRobbie, A. 2008: *The Aftermath of Feminism*. London: Sage.

McRobbie, A. and Nava, M. (eds.) 1984: *Gender and Generation*. London: Macmillan.

Meacham, S. 1977: *A Life Apart*. London: Thames & Hudson.

Meer, N. 2014: *Key Concepts in Race and Ethnicity*. London: Sage.

Mercer, K. 1990: Welcome to the jungle: identity and diversity in postmodern politics. In J. Rutherford (ed.), *Identity*. London: Lawrence & Wishart, 43–71.

Merton, R. 1938: Social structure and anomie. *American Sociological Review*, 3, 672–82.

Milburn, A. 2012: *University Challenge: How Higher Education Can Advance Social Mobility*. London: Social Mobility Commission.

Milburn, A. 2013: *State of the Nation 2013: Social Mobility and Child Poverty in Britain Today*. London: Social Mobility and Child Poverty Commission.

Miles, R. 1982: *Racism and Migrant Labour*. London: Routledge.

Miles, R. 1989: *Racism*. Milton Keynes: Open University Press.

Miles, R. 1993: Europe 1993: the significance of changing patterns of migration. *Ethnic and Racial Studies*, 16(3), 459–66.

Millett, K. 1971: *Sexual Politics*. London: Sphere.

Milne, S. 2007: You can't say it's a problem and then do nothing about it. *The Guardian* 16 August.

Minkler, M. and Estes, C. (eds.) 1984: *Readings in the Political Economy of Old Age*. New York: Baywood Publishing.

Mirza, H. 1992: *Young, Female and Black*. London: Routledge.

Mitchell, J. 1975: *Psychoanalysis and Feminism*. Harmondsworth: Penguin.

Modood, T. 1992: *Not Easy Being British*. Stoke-on-Trent: Trentham Books.

Modood, T. 2003: Ethnic differentials in educational performance. In D. Mason (ed.), *Explaining Ethnic Differences: Changing Patterns of Disadvantage in Britain*. Bristol: The Policy Press, 53–68.

Modood, T. 2007: *Multiculturalism: A Civic Idea*. Cambridge: Polity.

Modood, T., Berthoud, R., Lakey, J., et al. (eds.) 1997: *Ethnic Minorities in Britain: Diversity and Disadvantage*. London: PSI.

Mohanty, C. 1992: Feminist encounters: locating the politics of experience. In M. Barrett and A. Phillips (eds.), *Destabilizing Theory*. Cambridge: Polity, 74–92.

Moore, S. 1988: Getting a bit of the other: the pimps of postmodernism. In R. Chapman and J. Rutherford (eds.), *Male Order*. London: Lawrence & Wishart, 165–87.

Morris, L. 1990: *The Workings of the Household*. Cambridge: Polity.

Morris, L. 1994: *Dangerous Classes*. London: Routledge.

Murakami, H. 1994: *Dance, Dance, Dance*. London: Hamish Hamilton.

Murray, C. 1984: *Losing Ground*. New York: Basic Books.

Murray, C. 1990: *The Emerging British Underclass*. London: Institute of Economic Affairs.

Myles, J., Picott, G. and Wannell, T. 1993: Does post-industrialism matter? The Canadian experience. In G. Esping-Andersen (ed.), *Changing Classes*. London: Sage, 171–94.

Naipaul, V. S. 1994: *A Way in the World*. London: Heinemann.

National Union of Students (NUS) 2013: *That's What She Said*. London: NUS.

Nayak, A. and Kehily, M. J. 2008: *Gender, Youth and Culture: Young Masculinities and Femininities*. Basingstoke: Palgrave.

Nazroo, J. 2003: Patterns of and explanations for ethnic inequalities in health. In D. Mason (ed.), *Explaining Ethnic Differences: Changing Patterns of Disadvantage in Britain*. Bristol: The Policy Press, 87–104.

Nicholson, L. (ed.) 1990: *Feminism/Postmodernism*. London: Routledge.

Nicolaus, M. 1967: Proletariat and middle class in Marx: Hegelian choreography and the capitalist dialectics. *Studies on the Left*, 11.

Oakley, A. 1974: *The Sociology of Housework*. Oxford: Martin Robertson.

Oakley, A. 1981: *Subject Woman*. Harmondsworth: Penguin

O'Donnell, M. 1985: *Age and Generation*. London: Tavistock.

Offe, C. 1985: *Disorganized Capitalism*. Cambridge: Polity.

Office of National Statistics (ONS) 2012: *Statistical Bulletin: Households and Families*. London: ONS.

Office of National Statistics 2013: *Self-employed Workers in the UK – February 2013*. London: ONS.

Oliver, M. 1990: *The Politics of Disablement*. London: Macmillan.

Oliver, M. and Barnes, C. 1998: *Disabled People and Social Policy: From Exclusion to Inclusion*. Harlow: Longmans.

O'Hara, M. 2014: *Austerity Bites*. Bristol: The Policy Press.

O'Neill, J. 1995: *The Poverty of Postmodernism*. London: Routledge.

Ortner, S. 1974: Is female to male as nature is to culture? In M. Rosaldo and L. Lamphere (eds.), *Woman, Culture and Society*. Stanford: Stanford University Press, 67–88.

Pahl, R. 1984: *Divisions of Labour*. Oxford: Blackwell.

Pakulski, J. and Waters, M. 1996: *The Death of Class*. London: Sage.

Parekh, B. 2002: *Rethinking Multiculturalism: Cultural Diversity and Political Theory*. Cambridge, Mass.: Harvard University Press.

Parkin, F. 1972: *Class Inequality and Political Order*. London: Paladin.

Parkin, F. 1979: *Marxism and Class Theory: A Bourgeois Critique*. London: Tavistock.

Parmar, P. 1990: Black feminism: the politics of articulation. In J. Rutherford (ed.), *Identity*. London: Lawrence & Wishart, 101–26.

Parsons, T. 1954: *Essays in Sociological Theory*. Glencoe, Ill.: Free Press.

Pearson, G. 1983: *Hooligan: A History of Respectable Fears*. London: Macmillan.

Perfect, D. 2012: *Gender Pay Gaps 2012*. London: EHRC.

Phillips, A. 1987: *Divided Loyalties*. London: Virago.

Phillips, A. 1992: Universal pretensions in political thought. In M. Barrett and A. Phillips (eds.), *Destabilizing Theory*. Cambridge: Polity, 10–30.

Phillipson, C. 1982: *Capitalism and the Construction of Old Age*. London: Macmillan.

Phillipson, C. 1990: The sociology of retirement. In J. Bond and P. Coleman (eds.), *Ageing in Society: An Introduction to Social Gerontology*. London: Sage, 144–60.

Phillipson, C. 1993: Understanding old age: social and policy issues. In P. Kaim-Caudle, J. Keithley and A. Mullender (eds.), *Aspects of Ageing*. London: Whiting & Birch, 42–58.

Phizacklea, A. 1990: *Unpacking the Fashion Industry: Gender, Racism and Class in Production*. London: Routledge.

Phizacklea, A. and Miles, R. 1980: *Labour and Racism*. London: Routledge.

Pickett, K. and Wilkinson, R. 2010: *The Spirit Level*. Harmondsworth: Penguin.

Pilcher, J. 1999: *Women in Contemporary Britain*. London: Routledge.

Pilkington, A. 1984: *Race Relations in Britain*. Slough: University Tutorial Press.

Pilkington, A. 1992: The underclass thesis and 'race' [paper presented to British Sociological Association Annual Conference, University of Kent, April].

Pilkington, A. 2003: *Racial Disadvantage and Ethnic Diversity in Britain.* London: Palgrave.

Pilkington, H. and Johnson, R. 2003: Peripheral youth: relations of identity and power in local/global context. *European Journal of Youth Studies,* 6(3), 259–83.

Platt, L. 2009: *Ethnicity and Family.* London: EHRC.

Plummer, K. 1995: *Telling Sexual Stories.* London: Routledge.

Pollert, A. 1981: *Girls, Wives, Factory Lives.* London: Macmillan.

Pollert, A. 1988: Dismantling flexibility. *Capital and Class,* 3(4), 42–75.

Porter, M. 1983: *Home and Work Consciousness.* Manchester: Manchester University Press.

Pringle, R. 1989: *Secretaries Talk.* London: Verso.

Pringle, R. and Watson, S. 1992: 'Women's interests' and the post-structuralist state. In M. Barrett and A. Phillips (eds.), *Destabilizing Theory.* Cambridge: Polity, 53–73.

Putnam, R. 2007: E pluribus unum: diversity and community in the twenty-first century – the 2006 Johan Skytte Prize, *Scandinavian Political Studies,* 30(2).

Quilgars, D., Johnsen, S. and Pleace, N. 2008: *Youth Homelessness in the UK.* York: Joseph Rowntree Foundation.

Race for Opportunity 2009: *Race to the Top.* London: RfO.

Ramaswamy, C. 2014: I'm Indian, English and my heart belongs to Glasgow. Will my son's identity be as borderless in a post-indyref world? *The Guardian* 9 September.

Randall, V. 1982: *Women and Politics.* London: Macmillan.

Rapoport, R. and Rapoport, R. 1975: *Leisure and the Family Life Cycle.* London: Routledge.

Rattansi, A. 1992: Changing the subject? Racism, culture and education. In J. Donald and A. Rattansi (eds.), *'Race', Culture and Difference.* Milton Keynes: Open University Press, 11–48.

Reay, D., Crozier, G. and Clayton, J. 2009: 'Strangers in Paradise': working-class students in elite universities. *Sociology,* 43(6), 1103–21.

Reay, D., Crozier, G. and Clayton, J. 2010: 'Fitting in' or 'standing out': working-class students in UK higher education. *British Educational Research Journal,* 32(1), 1–19.

Rex, J. 1970: *Race Relations in Sociological Theory.* London: Weidenfeld and Nicolson.

Rex, J. 1982: West Indian and Asian youth. In E. Cashmore and B. Troyna (eds.), *Black Youth in Crisis.* London: Routledge & Kegan Paul.

Rex, J. 1986a. The role of class analysis in the study of race relations – a Weberian perspective. In J. Rex and D. Mason (eds.), *Theories of Race and Ethnic Relations.* Cambridge: Cambridge University Press, 64–83.

Rex, J. 1986b: *Race and Ethnicity.* Milton Keynes: Open University Press.

Rex, J. 1992: Race and ethnicity in Europe. In J. Bailey (ed.), *Social Europe.* London: Longman, 106–20.

Rex, J. and Moore, R. 1967: *Race, Community and Conflict.* London: Oxford University Press.

Rex, J. and Tomlinson, S. 1979: *Colonial Immigrants in a British City: A Class Analysis.* London: Routledge & Kegan Paul.

Rich, A. 1980: Compulsory heterosexuality and lesbian existence. *Signs,* 5(4), 631–90.

Richards, W. 1994: Are you too old at forty? *AUT Woman,* 33.

Richardson, D. and Monro, S. 2012: *Sexuality, Equality and Diversity.* Basingstoke: Palgrave Macmillan.

Richardson, J. and Lambert, J. 1985: *The Sociology of Race.* Ormskirk: Causeway Books.

Riches, G. 2014: Brothers of metal! Heavy metal masculinities, moshpit practices, and homosociality. In S. Roberts (ed.), *Debating Modern Masculinities: Change, Continuity, Crisis.* Basingstoke: Palgrave, 88–105.

Riley, D. 1988: *Am I That Name?* London: Macmillan.

Riseborough, G. 1993: GBH – the gobbo barmy harmy: one day in the life of the YTS boys. In I. Bates and G. Riseborough (eds.), *Youth and Inequality.* Milton Keynes: Open University Press, 160–228.

Roberts, K. 1983: *Youth and Leisure.* London: Allen & Unwin.

Roberts, K. 1995: *Youth and Employment in Modern Britain.* Oxford: Oxford University Press.

Roberts, K., Campbell, R. and Furlong, A. 1990: Class and gender divisions among young adults at leisure. In C. Wallace and M. Cross (eds.), *Youth in Transition.* London: Falmer, 129–45.

Roberts, K., Cook, F., Clark, S. and Semeonoff, E. 1977: *The Fragmentary Class Structure.* London: Heinemann.

Roberts, S. 2014: Introduction: masculinities in crisis? Opening the debate. In S. Roberts (ed.), *Debating Modern Masculinities: Change, Continuity, Crisis.* Basingstoke: Palgrave, 1–16.

Rohrlich-Leavitt, R. (ed.) 1975: *Women Cross-Culturally: Continuity and Change.* The Hague: Mouton.

Rosaldo, M. and Lamphere, L. (eds.) 1974: *Women, Culture and Society.* Stanford: Stanford University Press.

Rose, A. 1965: The subculture of aging: a framework in social gerontology. In A. Rose and W. Peterson (eds.), *Older People in Their Social World.* Philadelphia: Davis, 3–16.

Rowbotham, S. 1981: The trouble with 'patriarchy'. In Feminist Anthology Collective (eds.), *No Turning Back.* London: Women's Press, 72–8.

Runnymede Trust 1997: *Islamophobia: A Challenge for Us All.* London: Runnymede Trust / Home Office.

Rutherford, J. (ed.) 1990: *Identity.* London: Lawrence & Wishart.

Said, E. 1985: *Orientalism.* Harmondsworth: Penguin.

Sarre, P. 1989: Race and the class structure. In C. Hamnett, L. McDowell and P. Sarre (eds.), *The Changing Social Structure.* London: Sage, 124–57.

Saunders, P. 1984: Beyond housing classes: the sociological significance of private property rights in means of consumption. *International Journal of Urban and Regional Research,* 8(2), 202–27.

Saunders, P. 1990: *Social Class and Stratification.* London: Routledge.

Saunders, P. 1994: Is Britain a meritocracy? In R. Blackburn (ed.), *Social Inequality in a Changing World* [papers presented to Cambridge Social Stratification Seminar, September 1993], 85–111.

Savage, M. 2000: *Class Analysis and Social Transformation*. Milton Keynes: Open University Press.

Savage, M., Barlow, J., Dickens, A. and Fielding, T. 1992: *Property, Bureaucracy and Culture: Middle-class Formation in Contemporary Britain*. London: Routledge.

Savage, M., Devine, F., Cunningham, N., et al. 2013: A new model of social class? Findings from the BBC's great British Class Survey experiment. *Sociology*, 47(2), 219–50.

Scase, R. 1992: *Class*. Buckingham: Open University Press.

Schreiner, O. 1911: *Women and Labour*. New York: Frederick A. Stoles.

Scott, J. 1979: *Corporations, Classes and Capitalism*. London: Hutchinson.

Scott, J. 1982: *The Upper Classes*. London: Macmillan.

Scott, J. 1991: *Who Rules Britain?* Cambridge: Polity.

Scott, J. 2000: Class and stratification. In G. Payne (ed.), *Social Divisions*. Basingstoke: Macmillan.

Scott, J. W. 1988: *Gender and the Politics of History*. New York: Columbia University Press.

Scott, S. and Jackson, S. 2000: Sexuality. In G. Payne (ed.), *Social Divisions*. Basingstoke: Macmillan, 168–84.

Seabrook, J. 1988: *The Leisure Society*. Oxford: Blackwell.

Seager, A. 2007a: Pub firm widens gap. *The Guardian* 30 August.

Seager, A. 2007b: City bonuses hit record high with £14bn payout. *The Guardian* 28 August.

Segal, L. 1994: *Straight Sex*. London: Virago.

Sennett, R. and Cobb, J. 1977: *The Hidden Injuries of Class*. Cambridge: Cambridge University Press.

Shakespeare, T. 2014: People are disabled by society and their bodies. *Network* (British Sociological Association) (Summer).

Sharpe, S. 1976: *Just Like a Girl*. Harmondsworth: Penguin.

Shepherd, J. 2009: 'Lost generation' fear as young jobless rate soars. *The Guardian* 19 August.

Showalter, E. 1987: *A Female Malady*. London: Virago.

Simons, J. 1992: Europe's ageing poulation – demographic trends. In J. Bailey (ed.), *Social Europe*. London: Longman, 50–69.

Sivanandan, A. 1982: *A Different Hunger*. London: Pluto.

Sivanandan, A. 1990: All that melts into air is solid: the hokum of New Times. *Race and Class*, 31, 1–31.

Sloggett, A. and Joshi, H. 1994: Higher mortality in deprived areas: community or personal disadvantage. *British Medical Journal*, 309, 1470–4.

Smart, B. 1990: Modernity, postmodernity and the present. In B. Turner (ed.), *Theories of Modernity and Postmodernity*. London: Sage, 14–30.

Smith, D. 1977: *Racial Disadvantage in Britain*. Harmondsworth: Penguin.

Social Trends. 1995: London: HMSO.

Social Trends. 2008: London: HMSO.

Social Trends. 2009: London: HMSO.

Solomos, J. 2003: *Race and Racism in Britain*. Basingstoke: Palgrave.

Solomos, J. and Back, L. 1996: *Racism in Society*. Basingstoke: Macmillan.

Spencer, A. and Podmore, D. 1987: *In a Man's World*. London: Tavistock.

Stacey, J. 1993: Untangling feminist theory. In D. Richardson and V. Robinson (eds.), *Introducing Women's Studies*. London: Macmillan, 49–73.

Standing, G. 2011: *The Precariat: The New Dangerous Class*. London: Bloomsbury.

Stanfield, J. (ed.) 1993: *A History of Race Relations Research*. London: Sage.

Stanley, L. and Wise, S. 1983: *Breaking Out*. London: Routledge.

Steedman, C., Urwin, C. and Walkerdine, V. (eds.) 1985: *Language, Gender and Childhood*. London: Routledge & Kegan Paul.

Steger, M. 2003: *Globalization: A Very Short Introduction*. Oxford, New York: Oxford University Press.

Stiglitz, J. 2002: *Globalization and its Discontents*. New York: W.W. Norton.

Still, J. 1994: 'What Foucault fails to acknowledge …': feminists and *The History of Sexuality*. *History of the Human Sciences*, 7(2), 150–7.

Strathern, M. 1993: *After Nature: English Kinship in the Late Twentieth Century*. Cambridge: Cambridge University Press.

Stuart, A. 1990: Feminism: dead or alive? In J. Rutherford (ed.), *Identity*. London: Lawrence & Wishart, 28–42.

Sullivan, O. 2000: The division of domestic labour: twenty years of change? *Sociology*, 34(3), 437–56.

Sydie, R. 1987: *Natural Women, Cultured Men*. Milton Keynes: Open University Press.

Tackey, N.D., Barnes, H. and Khambhaita, P. 2011: *Poverty, Ethnicity and Education*. York: Joseph Rowntree Foundation.

Tahlin, M. 1993: Class inequality and post-industrial employment in Sweden. In G. Esping-Andersen (ed.), *Changing Classes*. London: Sage, 80–108.

Tang Nain, G. 1991: Black women, sexism and racism: black or anti-racist. *Feminist Review*, 37, 1–22.

Taylor, B. 1983: *Eve and the New Jerusalem*. London: Virago.

Taylor, Y. 2007: *Working-Class Lesbians: Classed Outsiders*. Basingstoke: Palgrave Macmillan.

Tester, K. 1993: *The Life and Times of Post-modernity*. London: Routledge.

Theroux, P. 1992: *The Happy Isles of Oceania*. Harmondsworth: Penguin.

Thomas, K. 1976: Age and authority in early modern England. *Proceedings of the British Academy*, 62(2), 205–48.

Thompson, K. 1976: *Auguste Comte: The Founder of Sociology*. London: Nelson.

Thompson, K. 1992: Social pluralism and postmodernity. In S. Hall, D. Held and A. McGrew (eds.), *Modernity and its Futures*. Cambridge: Polity, 221–72.

Thompson, P. 1993: Postmodernism: fatal distraction. In J. Hassard and M. Parker (eds.), *Postmodernism and Organizations*. London: Sage, 183–203.

Tong, R. 1989: *Feminist Thought*. London: Unwin Hyman.

Touraine, A. 1971: *The Post-industrial Society*. New York: Random House.

Townsend, P. 1979: *Poverty in the United Kingdom*. Harmondsworth: Penguin.

Townsend, P. 1981: The structured dependency of the elderly: a creation of social policy in the twentieth century. *Ageing and Society*, 1(1), 5–28.

Toynbee, P. and Walker, D. 2008: *Unjust Rewards*. London: Granta.

Tremlett, G. 2014: The avuncular anarchist: Uruguay's guerilla president. *The Guardian* 18 September.

TUC 1994: *Ethnic Minorities in the Labour Market: Preliminary Report*. London: TUC.

TUC 2013: *LGBT Equality at Work* (3rd edn). London: TUC.

Turner, B. 1989: *Status*. Milton Keynes: Open University Press.

UNICEF 2012: *Report Card*. New York: UNICEF.

UNICEF 2014: *Hidden in Plain Sight*. New York: UNICEF.

UPIAS 1976: *Fundamental Principles of Disability*. London: Union of the Physically Impaired Against Segregation.

Useem, M. 1984: *The Inner Circle*. New York: Oxford University Press.

Van den Berghe, P. 1978: *Race and Racism: A Comparative Perspective*. New York: Wiley.

Vincent, C. and Ball, S. 2006: *Childcare, Choice and Class Practices: Middle-class Parents and Their Children*. London: Routledge.

Walby, S. 1986: *Patriarchy at Work*. Cambridge: Polity.

Walby, S. 1990: *Theorizing Patriarchy*. Oxford: Blackwell.

Walby, S. 1992: Post-post-modernism? Theorizing social complexity. In M. Barrett and A. Phillips (eds.), *Destabilizing Theory*. Cambridge: Polity, 31–52.

Walby, S. 1993: 'Backlash' in historical context. In M. Kennedy, C. Lubelska and V. Walsh (eds.), *Making Connections*. London: Taylor & Francis, 79–89.

Walker, A. 1981: Towards a political economy of old age. *Ageing and Society*, 1(1), 73–94.

Walker, A. 1989: The social division of early retirement. In M. Jefferys (ed.), *Growing Old in the Twentieth Century*. London: Routledge, 73–94.

Walker, A. 1990: Poverty and inequality in old age. In J. Bond and P. Coleman (eds.), *Ageing in Society: An Introduction to Social Gerontology*. London: Sage, 229–49.

Walker, A. 1992: The poor relation: poverty among older women. In C. Glendinning and J. Millar (eds.), *Women and Poverty in Britain in the 1990s*. London: Harvester Wheatsheaf, 176–92.

Walker, A. 1993: Older people in Europe: perceptions and realities. In P. Kaim-Caudle, J. Keithley and A. Mullender (eds.), *Aspects of Ageing*. London: Whiting & Birch, 8–24.

Walker, M. 1995: All the King's forces. *The Guardian* 16 January.

Walkerdine, V., Lucey, H. and Melody, J. 2001: *Growing Up Girl*. London: Palgrave.

Wallace, C. and Cross, M. (eds.) 1990: *Youth in Transition*. London: Falmer.

Wallace, C. and Pahl, R. 1986: Polarization, unemployment and all forms of work. In S. Allen, A. Waton, K. Purcell and S. Wood (eds.), *The Experience of Unemployment*. London: Macmillan, 116–35.

Wallace, M. 1990: *Black Macho and the Myth of the Superwoman*. London: Verso.

Wallerstein, I. 1974: *The Modern World System*. New York: Academic Press.

Walter, N. 2010: *Living Dolls: The Return of Sexism*. London: Virago.

Ward, M. 2014: 'We're different from everyone else': contradictory working-class masculinities in contemporary Britain. In S. Roberts (ed.), *Debating Modern Masculinities: Change, Continuity, Crisis*. Basingstoke: Palgrave, 52–69.

Weber, M. 1923: *General Economic History*. London: Allen & Unwin.

Weber, M. 1930: *The Protestant Ethic and the Spirit of Capitalism*. London: Allen and Unwin.

Weber, M. 1949: *The Methodology of the Social Sciences*. Glencoe, Ill.: Free Press.

Weber, M. 1964: *The Theory of Social and Economic Organization*. London: Macmillan.

Weber, M. 1968: *Economy and Society*. New York: Bedminster Press.

Weeks, J. 1981: *Sex, Politics and Society*. London: Longmans.

Weeks, J. 1986: *Sexuality*. London: Tavistock.

Weeks, J. 1990: The value of difference. In J. Rutherford (ed.), *Identity*. London: Lawrence & Wishart, 88–100.

Westergaard, J. 1994: Amnesia over the upper class [paper presented to Conference in celebration of Richard Brown's contribution to British Sociology. Durham, September].

Westergaard, J. and Resler, H. 1975: *Class in a Capitalist Society*. London: Heinemann.

Westwood, S. 1984: *All Day, Every Day*. London: Pluto.

Westwood, S. 1990: Racism, black masculinity and the politics of space. In J. Hearn and D. Morgan (eds.), *Men, Masculinities and Social Theory*. London: Unwin Hyman, 55–71.

Wetherell, M., Stiven, H. and Potter, J. 1987: Unequal egalitarianism: a preliminary study of discourses concerning gender and employment opportunities, *British Journal of Social Psychology*, 26, 59–71.

Wheelock, J. 1990: *Husbands at Home*. London: Routledge.

Whittle, S. 2002: *Respect and Equality: Transsexual and Transgender Rights*. London: Cavendish Publishing.

Willetts, D. 2011: *The Pinch: How the Baby Boomers Took Their Children's Future and Why They Should Give it Back*. London: Atlantic Books.

Williams, S., Bradley, H., Erickson, M. and Devadason, R. 2013: *Globalization and Work*. Cambridge: Polity.

Williams, Z. 2014: This story is as timeless as love, and filmmakers know it. *The Guardian* 22 September.

Willis, P. 1977: *Learning to Labour*. Aldershot: Gower.

Willis, P., Jones, S., Canaan, J. and Hurd, G. 1990: *Common Culture*. Milton Keynes: Open University Press.

Wilson, B. 1966: *Religion in Secular Society*. London: C. W. Watts.

Wilson, E. 1977: *Women and the Welfare State*. London: Tavistock.

Wilson, W. J. 1987: *The Truly Disadvantaged*. Chicago: University of Chicago Press.

Wilson, W. J. (ed.) 1993: *The Ghetto Underclass*. London: Sage.

Wilton, T. 1993: Queer subjects: lesbians, heterosexual women and the academy. In M. Kennedy, C. Lubelska and V. Walsh (eds.), *Making Connections*. London: Taylor & Francis, 167–79.

Witz, A. 1992: *Professions and Patriarchy*. London: Routledge.

Wolf, N. 1990: *The Beauty Myth*. London: Chatto and Windus.

Wolpe, A. 1988: *Within School Walls*. London: Routledge.

Wollstonecraft, M. 1982: *A Vindication of the Rights of Woman* (1st edn 1792). Harmondsworth: Penguin.

Wood, J. 1984: Groping towards sexism: boys' sex talk. In A. McRobbie and M. Nava (eds.), *Gender and Generation*. London: Macmillan, 54–84.

Woodman, D. and Wyn, J. 2015: *Youth and Generation*. London: Sage.

Woodward, K., Murji, K., Neal, S. and Watson, S. 2014: Class debate. *Sociology*, 48(3), 427–8.

Wrench, J. and Lee, G. 1978: A subtle hammering – young black people in the labour market. In B. Troyna and D. Smith (eds.), *Racism, School and the Labour Market*. Leicester: National Youth Bureau, 29–45.

Wright, E. O. 1976: Class boundaries in advanced capitalist societies. *New Left Review*, 98, 3–41.

Wright, E. O. 1985: *Classes*. London: Verso.

Young, I. 1981: Beyond the happy marriage: a critique of the dual systems theory. In L. Sargent (ed.), *Women and Revolution: The Unhappy Marriage of Marxism and Feminism*. London: Pluto, 43–69.

Yuval-Davis, N. 1993: Beyond difference: women and coalition politics. In M. Kennedy, C. Lubelska and V. Walsh (eds.), *Making Connections*. London: Taylor & Francis, 1–10.

Zaretsky, E. 1976: *Capitalism, the Family and Personal Life*. London: Pluto.

Index